Practical Object-Oriented Development with UML and Java™

Practical Object-Oriented Development with UML and Java™

RICHARD C. LEE
WILLIAM M. TEPFENHART

An Alan R. Apt Book

Pearson Education International
Upper Saddle River, NJ 07458

Cataloging in Publication Data

CIP data on file

Vice President and Editorial Director, ECS: *Marcia J. Horton*
Publisher: *Alan R. Apt*
Associate Editor: *Toni D. Holm*
Editorial Assistant: *Patrick Lindner*
Vice President and Director of Production and Manufacturing, ESM: *David W. Riccardi*
Executive Managing Editor: *Vince O'Brien*
Assistant Managing Editor: *Camille Trentacoste*
Production Editor: *Joan Wolk*
Director of Creative Services: *Paul Belfanti*
Creative Director: *Carole Anson*
Art Director: *John Christiana*
Cover Art and Design: *John Christiana*
Art Editor: *Greg Dulles*
Manufacturing Manager: *Trudy Pisciotti*
Manufacturing Buyer: *Lynda Castillo*
Marketing Manager: *Pamela Shaffer*

If you purchased this book within the United States or Canada, you should be aware that it has been wrongfully imported without the approval of the Publisher or Author.

© 2002 Pearson Education Inc.
Pearson Education International

Printed in the United States of America

10 9 8 7 6 5 4 3 2 1

ISBN 0-13-122559-6

Pearson Education Ltd., *London*
Pearson Education Australia Pty. Ltd., *Sydney*
Pearson Education Singapore, Pte. Ltd.
Pearson Education North Asia Ltd., *Hong Kong*
Pearson Education Canada, Inc., *Toronto*
Pearson Educacíon de Mexico, S.A. de C.V.
Pearson Education—Japan, *Tokyo*
Pearson Education Malaysia, Pte. Ltd.
Pearson Education, Inc., *Upper Saddle River, New Jersey.*

Contents

Preface

Practical Object-Oriented Development with UML and Java is for busy professional software analysts and developers who work on large systems. If you do not have time to take a class and need to get up-to-speed on object-oriented technology using unified modeling language (UML) and Java, then this book is a self-teaching guide for you. It will help you understand the differences between object-oriented analysis, object-oriented design, and object-oriented programming. Our goals are to

- Teach you to build an object-oriented application using Java and make the right trade-off decisions to meet your business needs
- Clarify the basic concepts associated with object-oriented technology
- Supply sufficient depth in coverage for students and practitioners entering the field to get them up-to-speed
- Expose some of the myths surrounding object-oriented technology while focusing on its practicality as a software engineering tool
- Provide a practical approach to analysis, design, and programming in object-oriented technology
- Show how to implement object-oriented technology using Java
- Balance theory with application practices in the existing literature

You do not have to know computer science or advanced mathematics to understand the important object-oriented concepts and issues in depth. Even the programming chapters do not require a background in Java; they illustrate how working code in Java is produced.

OBJECT-ORIENTED TECHNOLOGY

We are software developers of large systems. We have delivered code written in several dozen programming languages representing a half-dozen software technologies. There have been few software revolutions that we have not experienced over the last 30 years. So it is from some nontrivial perspective that we say that it is our belief that object-oriented technology is the most important software technology with which we have worked.

Why do we say this? Well, object-orientation has changed the way we build software and the way applications intercommunicate over worldwide networks and across multi-vendor computers. Moreover, the object model is changing the way we design business processes and the way we think about an enterprise.

Most enterprises are in the process of redesigning themselves to meet current business challenges introduced by the Internet. Object-orientation is playing a major role in this effort by providing a model that captures the business processes, procedures, policies, and rules that facilitate design. The use of tools that translate the model into an operational system speeds implementation of the redesign. As market or business conditions change, these systems should be regenerated to reflect these changes by updating the model and using these tools. Solid software engineering practices have taken us farther and faster than any other approach in previous decades.

It is a common belief that object-oriented technology has put a dent in the software crisis, meaning that the mechanisms of object-oriented technology are becoming for software what the bolts and beams are for construction design and what the chip is for computer hardware design. This belief stems from the following:

- The proficiency of a higher-level object-oriented model provides the software designer with real-world, programmable components, thereby reducing software development costs.
- Its capability to share and reuse code with object-oriented techniques reduce time to develop an application.
- Its capability to localize and minimize the effects of modifications through programming abstraction mechanisms allows for faster enhancement development and provides more reliable and more robust software.
- Its capability to manage complexity allows developers to address more difficult applications.

The collection of object-oriented concepts is a tool set for modeling reality. This object-oriented tool set gives developers the best means of managing the complexity. Certain object-oriented concepts help developers produce flexible and maintainable software.

WHY UNIFIED MODELING LANGUAGE?

As practitioners of object-oriented technology, we know that all the methods, if practiced properly, result in the same or a similar model. Different modeling language notations, however, can be impediments to progress. The unified modeling language (UML) has become an industrial standard that has integrated different modeling notations into a single modeling language notation. This is reason enough to have chosen the UML.

UML is a language for documenting our analysis and design models. It gives us all the drawing icons necessary to capture most of the concepts or *mechanisms* that we find valuable in solving real business problems. Also, it provides all the necessary diagrams that are vital for documenting our models. Finally, it is a living language that gives us the ability to extend the notation for mechanisms not yet defined by the distinguished group of Grady Booch, James Rumbaugh, and Ivor Jacobson at Rational Software Corporation.

UML is not the central subject of this book. It is presented as a means of documenting the analysis and design models that are developed as a result of the methods that are the central subject of this book. All of the figures of UML are presented and discussed in terms of what information is captured within them and how that information is captured.

WHY JAVA?

It is true that Java is exclusively an object-oriented programming language and that this exclusivity tends to limit its use compared to the multi-paradigm programming language C++. Yet Java has one benefit that far outweighs any general limitations. In particular, Java runs on the Java Virtual Machine (Java VM). This allows a Java program to run on any machine that has an implementation of the Java VM running on it. This frees developers from having to design and implement the same functionality for several different combinations of hardware and operating systems.

There are positive consequences to the use of the virtual machine that may not be apparent at first glance. For one, vendors can now focus on development of tools and products knowing that they have to invest development dollars on only one implementation and not five or six. This means that they can emphasize the realization of greater functionality (read that as greater business value). This impacts reuse efforts as well. One can develop libraries on any hardware running any operating system and reuse the code without modification for platform differences. Programming errors will not appear in one version of the code for a given platform and not in another. The broader base of reuse of the same code means that greater reliability of components can be achieved in less time and cost. Analysis can focus on business value; design can focus on greater flexibility and maintainability; and implementation and testing can now focus on quality, reliability, and performance. The net result of this change in focus is better code for less money.

These benefits are seen when one looks at the large number of Java libraries (frameworks) that are now available from Sun. There is now a good set of general utility libraries, a high-performance graphical user interface library (e.g., SWING), and libraries of special-purpose business classes available to developers. Compared to the C++ versions of these libraries, they are far more sophisticated, provide much greater functionality, and are more easily incorporated into a final product. Because these libraries are available across all projects and are well documented in other books, they are widely used. Hence, expertise in their use is readily available.

This is to be compared to the C++ versions that have entirely different application programming interfaces (APIs). In the C++ world, a developer may be an expert for one product on one platform and know nothing about other products for other platforms. Few programmers have actually written code for the PC, Mac, and Unix platforms.

The direct incorporation of the Java VM in modern web browsers makes it possible for Java programs to be downloaded from the Internet and run from within the browser. This has helped provide greater functionality within the browser environment and has spawned a new class of applications. It is safe to say that it would have been impossible for us to have achieved the recent gains in functionality being delivered to users via the Internet without Java. Java programs now appear as both client and server applications. The widespread use of Java in the modern World Wide Web is unlikely to diminish until a new (as yet unrecognized) technology provides a greater set of abstractions and the same broad platform support.

OUR APPROACH TO OBJECT-ORIENTED TECHNOLOGY

We are not object-oriented purists, and neither are we theorists. We are developers willing to use any good idea that will help us achieve two very critical business goals: lower development cost and reduced time-to-market for enhancements. We believe that these technical objectives—reliability, maintainability, and flexibility—are critical to meeting these business goals.

Our approach to using object-oriented technology is to mange the complexity of developing software so it is reliable, maintainable, and flexible. Managing complexity is the key to achieving these objectives and, thus, our business goals. To manage complexity in complex problem domains, we find that the developers are required to know how objects, classes, relationships, and rules fit into the object paradigm. When we model most complex problem domains, we find objects, classes, and many relationships among objects. In addition, we need to capture the rules (policies) within that domain. Thus, we have to use very rich static modeling techniques to capture the data (object) relationships.

Many object-oriented experts consider relationships as "bad" because they violate the encapsulation principle. From our perspective, it helps us manage the complexity of the problem domain and helps us to achieve our business goals. We gladly use it, and we look for more mechanisms and language support in this area. In Chapter 9 on declarative semantics we write that rules and policies should be captured as an integral part of our model and not in special subsystem extensions.

Using mechanisms to help us model complex problem domains is consistent with our choice of UML as our modeling language and Java as our programming language. Both UML and Java allow us to define any needed mechanism that helps us to build more manageable software.

We discuss behaviors (dynamic and static) and polymorphism for capturing the procedural aspects of the model. The use of finite state machine or some other state model helps us manage procedural complexity while addressing timing, synchronization, and interrupts. We also present exceptions for managing error recovery (an important topic because error recovery can comprise half of a programs logic). These areas are generally ignored or overlooked by most object-oriented books.

We believe the key to success in building large object-oriented systems requires that developers and programmers know more than what is taught in most object-oriented books. Building large systems requires using mechanisms promoted by some object-oriented experts but not accepted by all. Professional developers need to at least understand how these aspects of the problem domain can be handled before they can be productive team members. This book will not make you an expert. You still need experts or consultants to develop the system. By applying the 80/20 rule, this book provides the 80 percent that can make you productive and understand how the experts solve the difficult 20 percent.

In this book we do not cover the latest trends or fads in object-oriented technology, including object design patterns, the standard template library, and distributed object computing. Although they are interesting, we are not convinced that they contribute significantly to our goal of providing a practical framework for enabling developers new to object-oriented programming to get up-to-speed as soon as possible.

Finally, we do not agree with most experts that object-oriented technology is a mature technology. We believe it is maturing. Object-oriented technology has the enormous potential to help us manage complexity that did not exist with the earlier technologies (procedural, functional, rule-based, etc.). We see in object-oriented technology and Java many different abstraction mechanisms merging (integrating) into a truly powerful technology. This merging is not yet complete, but it is far more complete in Java than in any other endeavor in object-oriented technology.

ORGANIZATION OF THE BOOK

We take the reader through our rational in applying object-oriented techniques and methods. These are not a set of absolute laws. Our goal is to make you think about good object-oriented concepts and good design principles when developing software and programming in Java.

We have written and designed this book to be a self-teaching guide that should be read in sequential order. We have adopted a method that Richard has used for years teaching object-oriented concepts and basic skills; however, we do not advocate this as a method for building object-oriented systems. Each chapter discusses a major step of our approach to object-oriented technology. Most chapters conclude with a step-by-step guide or recipe. We hope the reader will use these steps only as a guide; always rely on common sense rather than following prescribed steps blindly.

Chapter 1 introduces abstraction as a mechanism for controlling complexity and establishes object-orientation as the modern inheritor of the long line of abstraction mechanisms.

Chapter 2 presents the basic principles of object-orientation.

Chapter 3 begins the process of development by using the use-case approach to develop a specification model.

Chapter 4 begins the process of developing an analysis model by identifying objects/classes/interfaces.

Chapter 5 describes how to differentiate between "real" objects and "false" objects by identifying attributes (data) and services associated with the object.

Chapter 6 demonstrates how to capture objects' behavior.

Chapter 7 describes how to identify and describe dynamic behavior.

Chapter 8 describes the various relationships (generalization/specialization, link, object aggregation, etc.) that are available for organizing all the objects in the system.

Chapter 9 describes how to incorporate declarative facts into the object-oriented model about object knowledge and a rule-based mechanism for their implementation.

Chapter 10 reviews the analysis model and restructures it to take into account helper classes.

Chapter 11 addresses some elements of developing the design model.[1]

Chapter 12 presents programming in the Java language.

Chapter 13 introduces how classes and interfaces are implemented using Java.

Chapter 14 describes how static behavior can be implemented.

Chapter 15 describes how dynamic behavior can be implemented.

Chapter 16 describes how generalization/specialization can be implemented.

Chapter 17 describes how additional relations can be implemented.

Appendix A presents a summary guide of the unified modeling language.

Appendix B presents a summary of Java.

Appendix C presents a comparison of Java and C++.

USING THIS BOOK

This book is primarily targeted at experienced software developers and upper-level college students. It is based on the material taught in industrial courses attended by

---

[1] Design is very complex and, from a system perspective, is a separate topic from object-oriented technology. However, Chapters 14 through 22 present design material from the perspective of how the analysis concepts can be implemented. Idioms and design patterns are presented in all of the implementation chapters.

competent programmers. The material of this book is presented in two courses of one-week duration. The first week covers the first 11 chapters while the second week covers the remainder of the book. This course has always been taught utilizing a project in which the students develop a computer game rather than a homework-based approach. At the end of the first course, students have a design for a game. At the end of the second course, students have a fully functional implementation of their design.

We have chosen the project-based approach for several reasons. First, we have found that homework problems either are too trivial to effectively communicate the significance of the concepts or are too complex to be performed in a reasonable period of time. Second, the value of this paradigm is best learned from the consistent application of the concepts that can only be achieved via a project. Third, a substantial project gives a sense of real accomplishment as the projects are not simple little programs that can be finished in a single day of programming. Fourth, the project is developed in a team context with the periods of discussion, decision making, and reversals of decisions that actually occur when developing a program. Fifth, for most university students this will be the first program of substantial size that they will have to specify, analyze, and design. Finally, the selection of a project of suitable scale enables the student to master all of the key concepts.

The typical project that is employed in a university environment is a large adventure game in which characters explore some virtual world picking up treasures, fighting monsters or villains, and achieving some final objective. These games typically incorporate a hundred classes and just as many relationships. These games include many different kinds of terrain, weapons, monsters, treasures, and characters. With the widespread use of networked games, many project teams have chosen to develop multiplayer games. In most cases, the games developed by project teams have the same levels of complexity as many commercially developed products.

A reasonable project team consists of three or four students. A larger team spends too much time coming to agreement and a smaller team tends to become overwhelmed. The team works on the project during class time so that the instructor can review progress and answer questions concerning the application of the concepts, so class size is kept to a manageable size. The students have to work on the project weekly so as to complete the project on time, and activities are scheduled to correspond with lectures.

Following is a suggested schedule of course activities. It assumes a standard 15-week schedule with the final exam given in week 15. A key feature of this schedule is that it allows generous time early in the semester to define the game and develop the use cases. Lectures occasionally precede the activities performed by the team by as much as three weeks. This has been found to be advantageous because it prevents students from making common mistakes, such as confusing attributes and associations or object state with object attributes.

Acknowledgments

We owe so much to many people. The impetus of this book came from requests from people who wanted a book that presented more of an engineering approach to the development of Java programs. We appreciates their persistence and their encouragement, ignoring the perils to our personal lives.

Because we are basically developers (not researchers, academics, or writers), we have leveraged off the work of object-oriented researchers (who originated all the ideas) and object-oriented writers (who presented these ideas to us in earlier writings). We simply apply these ideas to building real applications in a useful way. To all the originators of the ideas, concepts, mechanisms, and techniques and to the greater object-oriented writers before us, we acknowledge them; without them, this book would not have been possible.

Theories and ideas are wonderful; however, to practitioners, experience is the best teacher. We could not produced this book without our experiences in applying object-oriented technology and the methods to real projects. We thank our many bosses, present and past, who had the courage to let us do leading-edge (and many times bleeding-edge) software development. Without their support, we would not have been able to test what we have written. We also thank reviewers William McQuain of Virginia Tech University and Michael Huhns of the University of South Carolina.

Richard Lee thanks the multitude of people who have worked for him and who were the pioneers in applying the ideas written in this book on real projects. They shared with him both the excitement and the misery of being "first" to apply Java technology to large projects in their respective companies. To all of you, Richard owes his thanks.

William Tepfenhart thanks his colleagues at Monmouth University for their support while putting together this book. Most importantly, he appreciates the patience of his family and their willingness to accept that there were times when deadlines took priority.

RICHARD C. LEE
WILLIAM M. TEPFENHART

A Practical Guide
to Object-Oriented Development
Using UML and Java™

1

Managing Complexity
with Abstraction

In the early 1960s, developers used no method other than their own creativity to create programs. Performance and using less core (memory) were the major constraints. In fact, the average desktop computer of today would put the largest machines of the 1960s to shame in every way. They were limited in processor speed, memory, and storage capacity. Virtual memory had not been invented, and, as a result, the core had to hold both the operating system and the programs running on it.

Most programs were neither large nor complex by today's standards. However, even then developers had difficulty remembering all the information they needed to know to develop, debug, and maintain their software. There are three basic reasons why this was the case:

1. It is intrinsically difficult to understand a problem to the degree necessary to express a logically complete solution that can be coded.
2. The programming languages developers were using supported a relatively primitive set of abstractions.

3. Most developers used spaghetti code and the infamous GOTO as accepted ways to increase performance and use less core.

For example, when one of the authors first started in this field in the early 1960s, he wrote some mission-critical software for his employer. This code is still in use today. About 10 years ago, his former employer called him and asked him to help them make modifications to this code. The employer's programmers had studied the code but could not figure out how the software worked. As his former employer succinctly put it, "We know that the program works as we have been using it for 20 years, but when we study the code we cannot figure out how you made it work." His former employer sent the author the code for him to study. After a couple of weeks, he concluded that he could not help his former employer design the modification as he also did not know how he got it to work 20 years ago. Thus, his former employer had no choice but to leave the code untouched and make the modifications at a different level with code that was comprehensible.

In the late 1950s and early 1960s, higher-level languages (COBOL, FORTRAN, ALGOL) were introduced to help solve some of these problems. These languages certainly helped automate the management of local variables and did implicit matching of arguments to parameters.

In conjunction with these new languages, developers used a more structured method to design and develop software. This gave rise to structured analysis and design and modular programming. These techniques raised the expectations of what a computer could do in our user community. As developers attempted to satisfy their user community by trying to solve more complex problems using the computer, the tasks became so large and complex that even the best programmers could not comprehend them. So programming changed from being a creative individual activity to a structured team activity.

When this happened, we observed that a program we expected one programmer to write in three years could not be written by *three* programmers working for *one* year. It is this phenomenon that led to Fred Brooks's memorable phrase: "The bearing of a child takes nine months, no matter how many women are assigned." Of course, software complexity was the main reason behind the nonlinear behavior of the development effort.

In imperative programming, the interconnections between software components are very complicated, and a large amount of information must be communicated among the various team members to get it correct. The key question is what brings about this complexity? Sheer size alone cannot bring about complexity, for size itself is not a hindrance to the concept of partitioning the software into many pieces. In fact, the method of structured analysis and design assumed that large programs differ from small programs only in size. If size were the issue, structured analysis and design would have solved the difficulty.

Unfortunately, the aspect of software development using the imperative-programming model that makes it among the most complex tasks for humans is its high degree of *coupling*. Coupling refers to the dependence of one portion of code on either another section of code and/or some data storage. A high degree of coupling is an inherent aspect of imperative programming. It was commonplace for programmers to fix a problem in one part of a program only to have another part of the program break.

In designing imperative programs, we partition our program into subroutines (essential tasks). However, if these subroutines are useful to other parts of the program, there must be some communication of information either into or out of these subroutines. Remember that data are not managed; thus, a complete understanding of what is going on usually requires knowledge of the subroutine and all the routines that use it. This is poor *cohesion*. Cohesion refers to how well a set of code and its associated data fit together. This is especially true when you consider the data that may be needed. In most imperative-programming languages, variable names (means of accessing data) could be shared only if they are in a common pool.

In brief, much of the complexity of imperative programming came from the high degree of coupling and poor cohesion in the way we built the software.[1] It is now apparent to us that using classic methods in software development almost always results in systems being built with poor cohesion and high coupling; this makes the system inflexible and unmaintainable.

There needed to be a better method to develop software. It needed to be one that gave developers a chance to meet their customers' needs in a natural and understandable fashion. To be able to accomplish this, developers could not use the same building blocks (functions, entities, or rules) as used in classic methods. They needed to use a new abstract mechanism as the building block for software. The result has been the development of the object-oriented paradigm.

COMPLEX SYSTEMS

Before we can determine if a paradigm helps manage complexity better than other paradigms, we must first understand the characteristics (attributes) of complex applications or systems. Studies have identified five key attributes of complex applications/systems. They are as follows:

1. Complex systems take the form of a hierarchy. A complex system is composed of interrelated subsystems that have their own subsystems and so on until some lowest level of elementary components is reached.
2. The choice of which components in a system are primitive is relatively arbitrary and is largely up to the discretion of the observer of the system.
3. Intracomponent linkages are generally stronger than intercomponent linkages.

---

[1] Data modeling is still imperative programming because most of the functions and/or transactions are still written using a procedural language. Moreover, rule-based systems (i.e., artificial intelligent systems) also had coupling and cohesion issues.

4. Hierarchical systems are usually composed of only a few different kinds of subsystems in various combinations and arrangements.

5. A complex system that works is invariably found to have evolved from a simple system that worked.

A good example of a complex system is a human being. Let us compare the mechanisms available in the object-oriented paradigm to the mechanisms that a biologist uses to analyze a human being. In biology, the building block (primitive component) is the cell, which comprises a membrane, cytoplasm, and nucleus. Similarly, in the object-oriented paradigm, the primitive component is an object that has two subcomponents, data and function. Cells are joined together to form organs; similarly, objects are joined together via relationships to form subsystems. Organs are organized in some hierarchical manner to form biological systems; subsystems are joined via various relationships to form systems/applications.

In a human being, the "cell" and the "organ" behave in both a static (same every time) and a dynamic (not necessarily the same) manner. Object-oriented technology includes techniques to capture the dynamic behavior of both an object and a subsystem. Furthermore, a human being may actually change his or her behavior completely by providing different services. Similarly, in object-oriented technology, there are techniques and mechanisms to migrate an object of one type to another type. Moreover, additional techniques and mechanisms are still being developed to support other concepts necessary to model our perception of reality.

System Development Is Modeling

The development of a large system is a modeling activity. In fact, software development can best be understood as the development of a series of models, each of which provides greater detail and increased logical correctness about the system than the model before it. These models can be loosely classified as

- Specification model—a black box model of the system that describes it in terms of the business value provided by it
- Analysis model—a model of the problem that demonstrates how the specification model will be realized
- Design model—a description of how the analysis model will be coded
- Code model—an implementation of the design model, which on compilation and execution provides the solution to the business problem

The code model, which is the ultimate product of software development, requires complete detail and logical correctness. Despite half a century of hope to the contrary, computers just cannot fill in gaps in logic on the programmer's behalf.

There are many different software development processes that control the activities and level of detail while constructing the four models when developing complex systems. The conventional waterfall process model develops each system model sequentially and describes the later activities associated with testing, delivery, and maintenance. It starts with a process phase in which the developer focuses time and energy on constructing a specification model. The specification model is developed to completion before the next phase of activities in which the emphasis is on performing an analysis of the specification. Each phase is complete before any work is done on the next phase. Iterative models, such as rapid prototyping, iteratively develop all of the models cycling through the phases. This book presents numerous methods for constructing all four models without specifying any specific process for organizing and controlling the act of developing them within a project.[2] Any good book on software engineering will describe a half dozen major software development processes with guidelines on when each is most appropriate.

A Strategy for Modeling

While a software development process tells developers what needs to be done and the order in which things are done, it does not tell them how to actually perform the work. The one universal strategy by which developers perform their work and which holds across all programming paradigms is the divide-and-conquer approach. This approach takes a big problem and breaks it into a number of smaller problems. One then works on the smaller problems, perhaps breaking them into even smaller problems. The solutions to the smaller problems are combined to solve the bigger problem.

The various programming paradigms employ the divide-and-conquer approach differently. These different paradigms vary in terms of the abstractions in which they express the parts. In a functional paradigm, this approach is known as functional decomposition. A complex function is divided into simpler functions, each of which provides a simpler mapping of input to output. In procedural paradigms, the strategy is to break complex procedures into smaller procedures and subroutines.

The object-oriented approach breaks a complex system into component parts in the form of objects and the relationships among them. Complex objects are broken into component parts, which are again expressed as objects. The developer can focus on the individual objects one at a time. The individual objects are joined by relationships to form the system. The system is then understood in terms of the objects that constitute it and the interactions among them.

---

[2] This book is structured along the lines of the conventional waterfall model. This means that techniques for developing one model are completely described before moving to techniques for developing the next model. It would be virtually impossible to construct a book that provided clear guidelines that skip from one model level to the next.

ABSTRACTION MECHANISMS

The introduction of object orientation has given developers a set of abstraction mechanisms that better serve their needs. As a result, modern developers have many different abstraction mechanisms available to them that were not available in the early days of programming. We can partition these abstraction mechanisms into several groups:

- Type abstractions
- Service activation abstractions
- Processing control abstractions
- Relationships abstractions
- Behaviors
- Rules

The following sections trace the development of these abstraction mechanisms in greater detail starting from their early beginnings to their modern forms.

To understand how the object-oriented paradigm uses the type-abstraction mechanism to manage complexity, we first review the various ways software engineers/programmers have used type abstraction before the object-oriented paradigm. From a historical perspective, object-oriented use of the abstraction mechanism is a natural progression of abstracting from functions and simple data types to modules and abstract data types and then to objects. The evolution of data abstraction mechanisms is summarized in Figure 1-1, in which two separate concepts eventually merged into one, namely, the object, that was immensely more powerful.

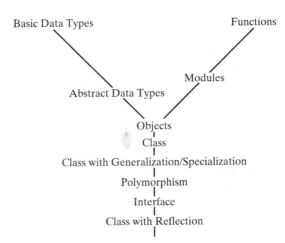

Figure 1-1   Evolution of Data Abstractions.

Basic Data Types

Early assembly language programmers had only very basic data types available to them when programming. The basic integer, floating point number, and character were the core data types. Early programming languages extended the core set to include arrays and extended precision versions of these data types. Capturing information about a person, address, and telephone number such that each could be processed independently required at least three variables that were all arrays of characters. These variables had to be managed separately and together to maintain the appropriate meaning of each variable and the composite.

Functions

With the advent of imperative-programming languages, functions and procedures became the early abstract mechanisms widely used to write programs. Functions allowed tasks that were used in many places, even in different applications, to be collected in one place and reused. Procedures allowed programmers to organize repetitive tasks in one place. Both of these abstractions prevented code from being duplicated in several places.

Functions and procedures also gave programmers the ability to implement information hiding. One programmer writes a function or a set of functions that will be used by many other programmers. Other programmers do not need to know the exact details of the implementation; they only need to know the interface. Unfortunately, abstract functions are not an effective mechanism for information hiding. They only partially solve the problem of multiple programmers making use of the same names.

To illustrate this, we will look at how we write a set of functions to implement a simple stack. First, we establish our visible interfaces: init (initialize the stack), push (place something on the stack), and pop (take an item off the top of the stack). After defining the interface, we need to select some implementation technique such as an array with top of stack pointer, a linked list, and so on. We elect to implement the stack by using an array and proceed to code the functions. It is easy to see that the data contained in the stack itself cannot be made local to any of the functions because all the functions need to use it; therefore, the variable must be shared.

In imperative-programming languages, such as COBOL, or C before the introduction of static modifier, the only choices for keeping data are local variables and global variables. As a result, the stack data must be maintained in global variables if we want the data to be shared by all the functions. Unfortunately, there is no way to limit the accessibility or visibility of global variable names.

Let us assume that we have named the array for our stack *stackarray*. All other programmers working on the project that uses our functions must know about stackarray because they must not create a variable using the same name. This is true even though the data are used only by the stack functions written by us and should not be used outside these functions. Similarly, the names init, pop, and push are now

reserved and cannot be used by other programmers on the project for other purposes, even if that portion of code has nothing to do with the stack.

In advanced imperative-programming languages such as ALGOL and Pascal,
the block scoping mechanism offered a slightly better control over name visibility
than just local and global names. However, this mechanism did not solve the information hiding problem presented above. To solve this problem, a different abstract
mechanism had to be developed.

Modules

A module is an abstract mechanism that is useful for creating and managing name
spaces. In its basic form, a module gives the programmer the ability to divide the
name space into two parts, public and private. The public part is accessible to everyone, while the private part is accessible only within the module. Variables (data),
functions, procedures, and types can all be defined in either part of the module. This
abstract mechanism was popularized by David Parnas, and he gave us the following
guidelines for using modules:

1. The designer of the module must provide the intended users with all the
    information needed to use the module correctly and nothing more.
2. The designer of the module must provide the implementer with all the
    information necessary to complete (code) the module and nothing more.

These guidelines are similar to how the military handles secret documents by
the "need to know" rule. If you do not need to know some information, you do not
have access to it. This explicit and intentional concealment of information is information hiding, which is a key principle of the object-oriented paradigm.

The module, as an abstract mechanism, solves our information hiding problem.
We can now hide the details of the stack. When a mechanism does this, it isolates
one part of the system, namely, the module, from all other parts of the system. When
this is done, we increase the maintainability of the software produced because the
isolation allows code to be modified or extended and bugs to be fixed without the
risk of introducing unnecessary or unintended side effects.

However, a module has a major shortcoming. Let us look at the stack problem
again. What if a user wants to use two or more stacks? We cannot handle this with a
module. As a mechanism, the module does not allow us to perform **instantiation**,
which is the ability to make multiple copies of the data areas. This idea of instantiation is another key principle of the object-oriented paradigm.

For a better example of why instantiation is an important and desired capability, consider the following situation: we need to develop a new type of number called
Complex. We define the arithmetic operations (addition, subtraction, multiplication,
etc.) for complex numbers and functions to convert a conventional number (integer,
float, double, etc.) to a complex number. If we were to use a module as the way to
capture our new type of number Complex, we would have a small problem—we can

manipulate only one complex number at a time. A complex number system with such a restriction would not be very useful.

Abstract Data Types

An abstract data type is a programmer-defined data type that can be manipulated in a manner similar to the programming language predefined data types. Like a predefined data type, an abstract data type corresponds to a set (perhaps an almost infinite set) of legal data values and a number of functions that can be performed on these values. Programmers can create instances of this abstract data type by assigning legal values to the variables. Furthermore, one can use the functions to manipulate the values assigned to the variables. In brief, an abstract data-type mechanism must be able to

1. Extend a programming language by adding programmer-defined type(s).
2. Make available to other code a set of programmer-defined functions that are used to manipulate the instance data of the specific programmer-defined type.
3. Protect (hide) the instance data associated with the type and limit the access to the data to only the programmer-defined functions.
4. Make (unlimited) instances of the programmer-defined type.

Modules, as defined here, can address only items 2 and 3 directly. With appropriate programming skills, some of the other capabilities may be addressed. However, packages found in languages such as Ada and CLU are a much better example of an implementation of the abstract data-type mechanism. Thus, we can solve our instantiation problem for the stack and for complex numbers by using an abstract data-type mechanism.

Objects

An object is an integration of the abstract data type with the module in the sense that an object packages (encapsulates) the data with the functions that operate over the data. This is a very powerful combination in the sense that it eliminates the limitations of modules because we can now make multiple instances of our abstract types and operate over them with the functions that are bound to the data structure. With the use of visibility constraints, name conflicts are eliminated or greatly reduced as function names can now incorporate the abstract type with which they are associated.

From a formal perspective, an object is defined by

1. Its responsibilities—Responsibility is the value that this object adds to the system in terms of the attributes and behaviors the object provides.
2. Its rule set—Rule sets may be used to infer attribute values that are not stored directly, to represent data triggers, to represent referential or

semantic integrity constraints, to represent operations in a nonprocedural manner, and to represent control regimens (e.g., resolve multiple inheritance conflicts).

3. Its type(s)—An object may implement the services of any specific type without being constrained in its implementation of the services.

4. Its relationships with other objects—These relationships may be either peer-to-peer or hierarchical.

It is important to recognize that objects can exist without a class mechanism (discussed next) for their creation, although the creation and management of objects created through direct programmer effort is very difficult.

Objects can exhibit both static and dynamic behavior based on values assigned to attributes. Hence, many objects that have the same attributes and functions, but possessing different values for those attributes, can exhibit very different behaviors at any given time. This is one of the strengths of this abstraction, namely, that a single structure can capture the variations normal for real problems.

Class

Class is a mechanism by which knowledge about objects can be captured. A class defines an abstract data type and binds with it the methods (functions) that operate over the data fields. From a modeling perspective, a class is a template for a *category* (we will use the term **category** during analysis as it is more natural and **class** for design and implementation). A class defines

1. *Characteristics* (*attributes*)—data variables
2. *Services* (*behavior*)—operations (functions)
3. *Rules and policies*—constraints that are applied
4. *Relationships*—a class defines relationships with other objects that can be either peer-to-peer or hierarchical

Classes are used to define and create objects. The definition identifies the data variables and functions along with the visibility restrictions. One can think of class in much the same way as a cookie cutter for making holiday cookies. Each cookie produced using the cookie cutter is identically shaped, but each cookie can be individually decorated. Variations in frosting and any added sprinkles can make thousands of distinct cookies. In the same fashion, a class produces objects that have identical structure, but the data values associated with each object can vary significantly.

Generalization/Specialization

Object-oriented programming added an additional mechanism to class: generalization/specialization. Generalization/specialization is a relationship between classes that allows them to share the same code. This reduces the code size and provides far more maintainable software. In addition, it helps us by giving us good cohesion and a lower degree of coupling in our implementation.

The value of generalization/specialization is evidenced by its long history of use (from the time of Aristotle) in many areas of study. The biological taxonomy is the most widely known, but other areas of study have equivalent taxonomies. As discussed earlier, the development of a program is a modeling activity, and it makes sense to employ such a well-known modeling concept to programming.

The structure that results from organizing classes according to the generalization/specialization relationship can form a hierarchy or a lattice. Java constrains the classes to a hierarchical structure for generalization/specialization on classes, while C++ allows a lattice structure. Generalization/specialization is implemented by using inheritance in many object-oriented languages, including C++. For many people it helps initial understanding to consider the two terms synonymous; however, it is important to distinguish between two concepts. Generalization/specialization refers to an organization of information, while inheritance is the propagation of information from one definition to another.

Polymorphism

Polymorphism extends generalization/specialization to allow the shared code to be tailored to fit the specific circumstances of each of the individual classes. Generalization/specialization and polymorphism work together to support the independence (low degree of coupling) of individual components (objects) that support an incremental development process (good cohesion).

As useful as generalization/specialization and polymorphism are in helping us organize (or structure) our classes and objects, these mechanisms only help us manage relationships that are heritable. In reality, we certainly have heritable relationships with our children, parents, and grandparents, but we also have other types of relationships that need to be managed. For instance, married people have spouses who cannot be modeled by using generalization/specialization and/or polymorphism (even though many married people may wish that they could polymorph their other half). Moreover, in most organizations people work in teams to get a job done, and there is a hierarchical structure of people who make up the organization. Again, these structures cannot be modeled by using the few mechanisms that we have discussed. Therefore, the need exists for more mechanisms to enable the object-oriented paradigm to accurately model our perception of reality.

Interface

From a modeling perspective, the category (class) was the building block of any object-oriented design. Java formally added another building block construct to the object-oriented model—Interface.[3] This concept is fundamental to building

---

[3] An interface is a pure abstract class in C++; in analysis we will call this an object type.

frameworks that promise to improve productivity and lower maintenance costs. An interface is a collection of services[4] (i.e., service name, its arguments, its return type, and the exceptions that can be thrown). There is no implementation (code) associated with the definition. Thus, two unrelated (by classification) objects may implement different code for the same interface.

From a modeling perspective, we view an interface as an *object-type*[5] classification. With a type there is no implicit hierarchical classification among types. Thus, from a modeling perspective, a category (class) has hierarchical structure and is the primary path of classification of an object while its type(s) (interfaces) are a secondary way of classifying the object. Note that there is a very subtle, but important, difference between the class (category) and the interface (type) concept. Two objects that are in a subcategory are by definition related in a hierarchical classification. By definition, these objects are also instances of the category. However, object a can implement all the services of interface i and another object b can also implement all the services of interface i. They are both instances of the interface i; that is, they are both of the same type, but they do not have to be related in any hierarchical classification (category).

Reflection

Java also added another runtime capability to the object-oriented paradigm that can affect the way we choose to model the application—reflection.[6] Reflection is the ability for an application to get detailed information about an object pertaining to its "classes" and "interfaces." With reflection, an application at runtime can

1. Determine the class of an object.
2. Get information about a class's modifiers, member variables, methods, constructors, and superclasses.
3. Find out what constants and method declarations belong to an interface.
4. Create an instance of a class whose name is not known until runtime.
5. Get and set the value of an object's field, even if the field name is not known to your program until runtime.
6. Invoke a method on an object, even if the method is not known until runtime.
7. Create a new array, whose size and component type are not known until runtime, and then modify the array's components.

The reflection Application Programming Interface (API) is not intended to be used as a replacement for other mechanisms more natural to the Java programming

---

[4] Service is the function prototype or function declaration.

[5] We will use type as the name of the concept in analysis and use interface as a means of implementing the type concept in design and coding.

[6] This is the technique that the JavaBeans "introspection" mechanism uses to determine the properties, events, and services (methods) that are supported by a bean.

language. For example, if you are in the habit of using function pointers in another language, you might be tempted to use the Method objects of the reflection API in the same way. Resist the temptation! Your program will be easier to debug and maintain if you do not use Method objects. Instead, you should define an interface and then implement it in the classes that perform the needed action.

SERVICE ACTIVATION ABSTRACTIONS

Closely related to data-type abstraction mechanisms are service activation abstractions. These are abstractions that identify the mechanisms by which data processing is activated to achieve business value. Again, object orientation is the heir to a logical progression from the function call to event processing, message passing, and subscription.

Function Call

Historically, access to program services was achieved by making a function call. This meant that the programmer identified the specific function by name, passed required arguments, and bound the result of the computation to an appropriate variable.

Event Processing (Asynchronous Communication)

Event processing separated the circumstances in which the need for a service arose from the invocation of the service. This was accomplished by the introduction of an intermediate construct, the event, between the two. The event would identify the circumstances in which it was generated (usually by values assigned to attributes of the event). When specific service needs were identified in the program, one would then generate the event, which would be placed on an event queue. When it was the event's turn to be processed, the event handler would select the appropriate service to invoke and pass that event to the service as an argument.

Breaking the recognition for the need for a service from the invocation of the service has several important consequences. First, this allows the handling of an event, regardless of where it was generated, to be localized to one region of the program. This is high cohesion. The separation via the event construct directly supports low coupling; neither the generator nor processor of the event depends on each other.

Message Passing (Synchronous Communication)

Object-oriented programming added several new ideas to the concept of function call. First is the idea of *message passing*. In object-oriented programming, an action is initiated by a service request (message) sent to a specific object, not as in imperative programming by a function call using specific data. On the surface, this may appear to be just a change of emphasis. The imperative-programming style places a primary importance on the functions, while the object-oriented style places primary importance on the object (value). For example, do you call the push function with a stack and a data value, or do you ask a stack to push a value onto itself?

If this is all there is to message passing, it would not be a very powerful mechanism. However, message passing gives us the ability to overload names and reuse software; this is not possible using the imperative-programming functional call style. Implicit in message passing is the idea that the interpretation of a message can vary with objects in different classes; that is, the behavior (response that a message will elicit) depends on the class of the object that receives the message.

In object-oriented programming, names of functions are unique only within a class.[7] We can use simple, direct, and meaningful names for our functions across classes, leading to more readable and more understandable code. This also provides for better cohesion at the implementation level than does a conventional imperative-programming language.

The message passing mechanism has additional implications. In particular, the act of passing a message from one object to another can be accomplished utilizing very sophisticated mechanisms that allow the objects to exist in different programs running on different machines. This is very different from a function call that basically assumes that the function is implemented at the place where the call is performed.

Subscription (Asynchronous Communication)

Although event generation has been around for a long time, object orientation has added a few new wrinkles to the use of this means of communication. In subscription, an object registers with an event handler that it is interested in receiving events handled by it. When the event handler receives an event, it sends a message to the object that the event has occurred and includes the event (or a copy of it) in the message. The object is then allowed to process the event as dictated by its needs. The event handler itself does not have to know how the event is handled. This has the effect of increasing the decoupling between the generator of the event and the object that processes the event.

Java has made event generation an integral part of its framework communication system. It has also provided the infrastructure (multithreading, listeners, multicasting, broadcasting, etc.) for the application programmer to use this form of communication between objects.

PROCESSING CONTROL ABSTRACTIONS

Not all abstraction mechanisms are purely object-oriented. There are processing control abstraction mechanisms that have been incorporated into object-oriented approaches.

---

[7] Class is an implementation concept; in analysis, we will define categories, which implies a hierarchical relationship between categories.

Single Program Execution

In the early days of programming, one program at a time was executed on the computer. Each program was a stand-alone application that ran from start to finish without any interruptions except the pauses associated with getting input from the user. The consequence of this was that a solution to a business program had to be implemented in one very large program. The sheer size of the program made it difficult to develop.

When a program became too large to run on the machine, it was necessary to break it into two programs. One would then run the first program to completion, which included writing the state of the computation to persistent storage. To complete the processing of the data, one would have to run the second program. It would read the saved state of the computation and then complete the processing. If one were lucky, there was a good place to break the program in half.

Artifacts of this single program execution approach continue to propagate themselves to this day. An example is seen in the compiler and linker division of functionality for taking source code and producing executables. The compiler reads in a set of files sequentially and processes each (sequentially) to a point where an object file is generated. The object files are then combined by the linker to produce executables. This was one area in which dividing the problem into two parts made sense and continues to be of value, although the need to do so may no longer exist.

Multitasking

Multitasking was introduced as a mechanism by which more than one program could execute on the same machine at virtually the same time through time-sharing. Multitasking required the introduction of the concept of a **process**. A process is a representation of the execution of a program. In time-sharing, each process is given individual time slices during which it can execute. With the introduction of processes, it was now possible for the same program to execute as more than one process.

Multitasking also allowed very large programs to be broken into several smaller programs that all ran at the same time. The overall functionality of the large program could be achieved by the smaller programs through interprocess communications. The advantage of this was that a large problem could now be divided into smaller parts. This allowed developers to manage the complexity of a large system with much greater ease. They could now solve each part of the problem and implement the solution as an individual program.

Sequential Execution

All programmers are familiar with writing sequential programs. You probably have written a program that displays "Hello, World!" or sorts a list of names or computes a list of prime numbers. These are sequential programs: each has a beginning, an execution sequence, and an end. At any given time during the runtime of the program, there is a single point of execution.

Multithreading

Multithreading incorporated the concurrency concept of multitasking into the execution of a process. A *thread* is similar to the sequential execution described previously. A single thread also has a beginning, a sequence, and an end, and at any given time during the runtime of the thread, there is a single point of execution. However, a thread itself is not a process; it cannot run on its own. Rather, it runs within a process.

There is nothing new in the concept of a single thread as this is just the concept of sequential execution. The real hoopla surrounding threads is not about a single sequential thread. Rather, it is about the use of multiple threads[8] in a single process (as defined by the program), with the threads running at the same time and performing different tasks. Programming with threads is much easier when performed in an environment that has built-in language support.[9]

RELATIONSHIPS

Until object and class abstractions were added to the programmer's toolbox, it was extremely difficult to capture specific kinds of information within a program. In particular, we refer to relationships that can exist between data elements. Previously, we introduced the generalization/specialization relationship as a relationship between abstract data types (classes). We now introduce associations and aggregations as relationships between instances of abstract data types (objects). Even though the introduction of objects and classes simplified capturing and use of relationship information, no object-oriented language has actually provided explicit representation mechanisms for relationships.

Associations

Let us look at an instance of marriage more closely. Let us assume that Joe is married to Jane. From Joe's perspective, the marriage relationship captures the fact that

---

[8] Some texts use the name *lightweight process* instead of thread. A thread is similar to a real process in that a thread and a running program are both a single sequential flow of control. However, a thread is considered lightweight because it runs within the context of a full-blown program and takes advantage of the resources allocated for that program and the program's environment.

[9] As a sequential flow of control, a thread must carve out some of its own resources within a running program. It must have its own execution stack and program counter for example. The code running within the thread works only within that context. Some other texts use *execution context* as a synonym for thread.

Jane is his wife and provides a set of "wifely" services to Joe. Similarly, from Jane's perspective, the marriage relationship captures the fact that Joe is her husband and provides a set of "husbandly" services to Jane. Thus, it is very common to have role names (husband, wife) associated with a relationship (marriage). In some sense, the role names help us define what services are expected to be accessible via that relationship. For example, if Jane is also Joe's supervisor at work, a second relationship (supervisor–subordinate) must be established to capture the "subordinate" services of Joe. This second relationship is necessary to maintain the semantic consistency of the relationship. Joe can stop being Jane's subordinate at work and stay married to Jane. This kind or relationship, where one object knows about another object for specific services, is called a *link*.

If we define marriage as being only between two persons of different gender, then we need to categorize people into two categories (classes): male and female. Note that Joe, an object, is an instance of male and that Jane, another object, is an instance of female. Now, since all marriage links are between one object of the class male and another object of the class female, we can capture all the marriage links by using a higher-level concept called an *association*. An association describes a group of links with common structure and common semantics. All links in an association must connect objects from the same class to objects from a second class. Note that from an object-oriented perspective, the common semantics means that services provided by each object in the same class are the same. Also, remember that providing the same service does not mean that the behavior is identical. For instance, if we define "mow the lawn" as one of the services of husband, then every male object must have a "mow the lawn" service. However, the method that each male object uses to mow the lawn can be very different (polymorphism). Specifically, Joe can actually mow the lawn himself, while Jack may pay one of his kids to mow the lawn, and Jim may use a professional lawn mowing company.

With the marriage relationship, one can argue that not only is the behavior (how the service is provided) different but also the services provided by each partner are different for each marriage. This is certainly more likely to be true today than when people had fixed concepts associated with the roles of husband and wife. If this is correct, we would not be able to abstract each of the marriage links into a group; we would require a unique template for each group of links with different services. That is, each marriage would be a different association.

Associations are bidirectional; thus, it is common to give a name to an association in each direction. In our marriage example, from the female's direction it is husband and from the male's direction it is wife. By the way, it is common practice to name a relationship with the same name as the class with which it is associated. This practice is not recommended as it captures no semantic meaning (poor cohesion). This is effective only if there is only one association between the classes; if there is more than one association, a better convention should be used. For example, consider the relationship between a person and a company. It is very common for a person to be both an employee and a stockholder of a company, especially now with an increase of employee-owned companies. To model these two different relationships accurately, we would create two associations between the class person and the class company. One association would represent the employer–employee relationship and the second would represent the ownership relationship.

In theory, associations may be binary (between two classes), ternary (between three classes), or higher. In practice, however, the vast majority of associations are binary or ternary; we have only rarely used the higher forms. Higher-order associations are very difficult to draw, implement, and think about; they should be avoided if possible.

The notion of association is not a new concept; it has been widely used for years in database modeling. However, very few programming languages explicitly support the association mechanism. Nevertheless, we believe that we should model an association as a separate abstraction that contains information that depends on two or more classes rather than a single class.

Some would argue that capturing an association as a separate abstraction violates the encapsulation principle of a class. However, there is information that we need to model that naturally transcends a single class. In the marriage relationship, for example, the marriage date and the church where the ceremony is held are examples of information that naturally transcends either class of female and male.

Not capturing an association accurately will cause programs to contain hidden assumptions and dependencies that will make them hard to maintain. For instance, in our employer–employee example, a person's salary is not really information about a person. Consider the case in which you need to model a person who has two or three jobs with different employers.

Conceptually, and especially during analysis, we recommend that a link should be treated as an object. Because an object has attributes (i.e., may store information) and provides services, a link has the potential to store data and provide services. In our marriage relationship, for example, the attributes could be date of marriage and the church where the ceremony was held. Although associations (and aggregations) are not directly supported by present-day programming languages, our goal should be to demonstrate the usefulness of these mechanisms and to encourage the development of programming languages that will support these mechanisms that help us manage complexity.

Aggregation

From these examples, we can see that an association is a very weak relationship. People regularly change employers. In fact, management talks about people needing to change careers and employers many times during their working career. Furthermore, marriage in the United States is certainly not permanent as we read about subsequent marriages and divorced, single parents. Thus, an association is like a "Hollywood marriage"—it can be changed very rapidly.

There are other relationships, however, like a car with its parts or a purchase order with its line items, that do not allow changes as easily. Furthermore, these specialized forms of an association have special properties. We would like to have another relationship mechanism to capture these more specialized forms of an association because the special properties need to be enforced. The new mechanism is called *aggregation*.[10] In this mechanism, an object that represents the whole is associated with a set of objects representing its components. A good example of a relationship that is probably best modeled by an aggregation is a bill-of-material and all of its associated line items.

Aggregation contains the following properties:

> **Transitivity**—Transitivity is the property that if object A is a part of object B and object B is a part of object C, then object A is a part of object C. In our example, consider the possibility that a line item may have subline items. By transitivity, the subline items are also part of the bill-of-material.
>
> **Antisymmetricity**—Antisymmetricity is the property such that if object A is a part of object B, then object B cannot be a part of object A. Again using our example, a line item may not be part of a subline item.

Finally, some of the attributes and/or methods of the assembly usually propagate to its components as well. In our example, the bill-of-material usually has an order number that is also used by all the line-items and subline items.

There are at least two difficulties in dealing with aggregations. First, the components must all be of the same semantic domain. For example, a computer terminal is composed of a CRT, keyboard, cables, and so on. However, a terminal is also made of glass, silicon, steel, and plastic. The "made-of" decomposition of the terminal is not the same as the "composed-of" decomposition; it would be incorrect to mix components in these two decompositions. The second difficulty has to do with "optional components." For example, a car normally has door handles as part of the car. If all the door handles were removed, is the car still a car? Now, we need to be careful; it seems like a car still exists. However, it is true that car handles are optional, but what about tires? The logic can then be extended to include every part of a car. But if every part is optional, then a car may exist with no parts. We will see that we can allow only a certain amount of flexibility when we define the aggregation using conditional components.

Behavior

Relationship mechanisms give us a way to organize classes/objects in both a peer-to-peer (association) and hierarchical (generalization/specialization and aggregation) structures. This structural portion of the model is called the static model by many

---

[10] This is also called the whole-parts, assembly-parts, or the part-of relationship. In terms of a modeling mechanism, we can define an aggregation as relating an assembly class to a set of component classes. Aggregation reduces complexity by letting us treat many objects as one object and giving us a better mechanism than a link to model specific domain entities (e.g., purchase order, cars, assemblies).

object-oriented experts. We would prefer to use James Martin and James Odell's term and call it the *structure analysis*. However, a structure analysis of an application/system is not adequate; we also need to do a *behavior analysis*. Behavior analysis is the process we use to look at how each object (class) provides its services (i.e., the methods).

With the class/object mechanism, we create the conceptual building blocks of our model. The class mechanism, like a blueprint, defines the data structure and provides an index for the system functions. Services (functions and procedures) are tied to a specific class, and an object (as well as its associated data) can only be manipulated by the functions that are associated with the class of which the object is an instance. Without classes and objects, we can neither define any data nor use any methods (code).

When we specify "how a service is provided," we are defining "how a class of objects will perform that service." From an analysis perspective, there are two types of behavior, static and dynamic.

Static Behavior

In static behavior, the operation (code) within the method will not be affected by any external or internal events (actions). A good example of static behavior is the "square root" service for number. If one requests the "square root" service from the number 4, which is an instance of number, the result will always be 2. It is 2 today. No external or internal action can cause the method of number to change the result of computing the square root. If there were only static methods in reality, we would have a very nice model by just managing the structure portion of the model. In fact, writing the method (code) would be easy, as we would be using the same techniques we used in imperative programming.

Dynamic Behavior

If all behaviors in the world were static, it would not be interesting. Fortunately, we live in a dynamic world. For example, look at how a loan agent will respond to your asking, "What is the prime loan interest rate?" The answer to this question can change almost hourly. Similarly, how does the airline reservation clerk answer your question, "What is the lowest fare from New York to San Francisco for January 15?" This answer may change as you are trying to make a decision on the telephone. These are two examples of dynamic behavior. The reasons for these changes in behavior may be captured by letting an object exist in many different states. Then an object's response can be based on its state. This kind of behavior is not handled very well by using the imperative-programming technique. Such methods are better captured by using another mechanism called a finite-state machine.

To better understand the concept of states, let us look at the reservation process in an airline reservation system. When a request comes in, a reservation is created and moves to the requested state. While in the requested state, if there are seats,

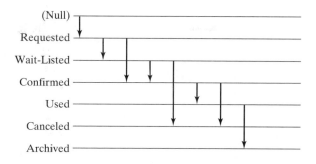

Figure 1-2   Reservation Fence Diagram.

the airline reservation system can confirm the reservation; however, if there are no seats, it puts the reservation on the wait list. When a confirmed reservation is canceled, the reservation is moved to the canceled state. If the person shows up and flies at the given time, the reservation is moved to the used state, and when the plane lands, the reservation is moved to the archived state. A similar scenario holds for a reservation on the wait list. Thus, the reservation object could have the following states: requested, wait-listed, confirmed, canceled, used, and archived. A change of state may occur when a service of the object is requested. When a method associated with a service changes the state of the object, the state is recorded in the data portion of the object. Usually, there is a finite set of sequences of state changes that is allowed with an object. The complete set of sequences is called the life cycle of the object. Because all possible sequences of state changes are usually programmed using a finite-state machine mechanism, we need a way of capturing this information in a graphical form. One such mechanism is the fence diagram. Figure 1-2 is a fence diagram that shows the life cycle of the reservation object.

RULES

With the addition of relationships (inheritance, aggregation, and association), object-oriented technology added some powerful mechanisms for specifying the data semantics of any application domain. The use of classic techniques for specifying static behavior and the use of finite state machines for specifying dynamic behaviors are powerful mechanisms for capturing the procedural semantic. However, one of the weaknesses of current object-oriented methods is the lack of mechanisms to support declarative semantics. In most object-oriented methods, declarative semantics (i.e., rules) are left to the inventiveness of the analyst/developer. If we assume that the purpose of the new method is to help us manage complexity by giving us mechanisms that model the full semantics of the problem domain, then we need to add mechanisms that handle rules (or declarative semantics) to our repertory.

For the novice, declarative semantics addresses the issues of global control description and business rules. Because most declarative semantics are explicitly specified in rules, we focus on the issue of rules. The types of rules we are interested in capturing are (1) control rules, (2) business rules, (3) exception handling rules, (4) contention rules, and (5) triggers.

SUMMARY

In this chapter, we have introduced some of the basic characteristics of complex systems. In particular, a complex system is characterized by five key attributes:

1. Complex systems take the form of a hierarchy. A complex system is composed of interrelated subsystems that have their own subsystems and so on, until some lowest level of elementary components is reached.
2. The choice of which components in a system are primitive is relatively arbitrary and is largely up to the discretion of the observer of the system.
3. Intracomponent linkages are generally stronger than intercomponent linkages.
4. Hierarchical systems are usually composed of only a few different kinds of subsystems in various combinations and arrangements.
5. A complex system that works is invariably found to have evolved from a simple system that worked.

In terms of developing complex systems, we have presented this as a modeling activity with four major models being developed:

1. Specification model
2. Analysis model
3. Design model
4. Code model

Supporting the development of these models is the strategy of divide and conquer.

The history of software development is marked by a successive introduction of abstraction mechanisms that have given developers a greater ability to manage complexity. These abstraction mechanisms (supported by languages and methods) have allowed us to tackle more difficult problems. These abstraction mechanisms are

- Type abstractions

  - Basic data types
  - Abstract data types
  - Functions
  - Modules

- Objects
- Class
- Class with generalization/specialization
- Polymorphism
- Interface
- Reflection

- Service activation abstractions

  - Function call
  - Event processing
  - Message passing
  - Subscription

- Processing control abstractions

  - Single program execution
  - Multitasking
  - Sequential execution
  - Multithreading

- Relationships

  - Associations
  - Aggregations

- Behaviors

  - Static behavior
  - Dynamic behavior

- Rules

2

The Object-Oriented Paradigm

Maintainable, flexible, and reliable software is difficult to produce. Software systems are complex and, as suggested by Brooks, complexity is a part of the essence of the system. No process of abstraction can eliminate complexity in its entirety; however, we believe that we can create mechanisms that help us manage these complexities. Furthermore, we believe some difficulties are not "accidents"; they arise as a consequence of the way software is constructed. It is our belief that changing the way we construct software will ameliorate these so-called "accidental" difficulties.

In this chapter, we introduce the object-oriented paradigm. We then establish 13 basic principles that characterize object-orientation. This is followed by an example illustrating the basic principles and how they are applied.

THE OBJECT-ORIENTED PARADIGM

Paradigm is defined as "a set of theories, standards, and methods that together represent a way of organizing knowledge." This is the expanded definition of the word given in Thomas Kuhn's book *The Structure of Scientific Revolution.* Developers have been using other paradigms such as imperative programming (C, Pascal, Cobol, Ada), logic programming (Prolog, C5), and functional programming (FP, ML).

The programming language we use directly influences the way we view (model) reality. In the 1970s, when we were using programming languages such as C, Pascal, and PL/1, we used an imperative-programming paradigm for modeling reality—the structured method. In the 1980s, when we were using SQL and 4GL with relational databases, we used a data-modeling paradigm for modeling reality—entity-relationship diagrams. In the 1990s, we were programming using C++, Smalltalk, and Objective C. We have used the object-oriented paradigm to model reality; however, we have found many limitations[1] with this paradigm. Java now provides us with a refined paradigm that addresses some of the limitations of the object-oriented paradigm, including extending the paradigm to accommodate network computing. Java programming is a refinement of the object-oriented programming paradigm.

From a language perspective, the difference between an imperative language such as C and an object-oriented language such as Java is only the addition of a few new keywords and data types plus some additional features. However, making effective use of these new facilities requires the developer to shift his or her perception to an entirely different approach for modeling and problem solving. Object-oriented programming is a new way of thinking about what it means to compute, how we organize our information inside a computer system, and how we describe our view (model) of reality. In a similar vein, Java programming constructs give us an opportunity to add modeling mechanisms to our object-oriented model that were previously not used.

What Is an Object?

The most fundamental concept/mechanism of object-oriented programming is the *object*. There are three different perspectives from which one can view an object. The first perspective is from application modeling. The second perspective is from design modeling. The third perspective is from a formal viewpoint.

From an application modeling perspective, an object has the following components:

1. *Characteristics (attributes)*
    An attribute is internal information that describes the object.[2] Attributes are made of two subcomponents[3]:

    a. Attribute Name, which is the name of the attribute. For example, for a "Person" object, an attribute name could be: name of the person.
    b. Attribute Value, which is the value that is assigned to the attribute name. For example, if Bill Tepfenhart were the "Person" object, the "height" attribute value would be 6 feet 2 inches.

---

[1] This is not a negative statement. All paradigms have limitations.

[2] A "Person" object may have the name, height, weight, color of hair, color of eyes as attributes.

[3] For we programmers, this is the data variable and its value.

2. *Services* (*Behaviors*)
A collection of services that have some semantic meaning is sometimes called a *protocol*. Each service has two subcomponents:

a. *Interface*, which is the *prototype*[4] for accessing object's service (and its internal information).
b. *Implementation*, which is the internal procedural (*method*[5]) for providing the service.

3. *Unique Identifier*
Each object gets a unique identifier at creation, which cannot be changed.[6]

4. *Rules and Policies*
Rules and policies establish constraints that are applied to the object.

5. *Relationships*
Objects stand in relationships with other objects. These relationships can be either peer-to-peer or hierarchical.

From a design modeling perspective, an object

1. Is an example (*instance*) of a *category*[7] (*class*). Like biological classification, an object is a thing that fits into the category. Categories in Java form a hierarchy of generalizations/specializations. A subcategory inherits attributes, services, relationships, and rules of the category.

2. May be an example of a *type*[8] (*interface*). A *type* is a collection of service declarations (i.e., service name, arguments, return type, and exceptions thrown) with no implementation. For example, each one of us who are citizens of the United States has a duty (service) to vote. Certainly each one of us implements this service very differently; yet, we are all still citizens. Very few modelers will try to capture the "citizenship" concept as a category. This concept is better modeled by using the type construct.

---

[4] Because *interface* has many definitions, we use the term *prototype* when it is not clear that this specific meaning of *interface* is being used.

[5] We will use *method* to mean implementation in this book. Caution: Java specification uses *method* to mean services (operations or functions). They address implementation as a concept in a very limited manner.

[6] This means a relational database key is not sufficient. You may still have such a key for the user, but you must also have an object identifier, which is usually the machine identification number plus the time in milliseconds when the object was created.

[7] In this book, we use two analysis concepts: category and type. In design for Java programming, the category will usually be implemented by using the Java "class" construct and the type will be implemented by the Java "interface" construct.

[8] Note that type and interface have many different definitions. We hope that you will recognize the usage of these terms from the context of the sentence or paragraph.

3. Can be a category or a type. These are objects of the class "metaclass." They may have attributes, services, object relationships, and rules; however, they may not be in a generalization/specialization relationship.
4. Created (*instantiated*) by a category (*class*) object[9]; this is how we make objects.
5. Can communicate via either synchronous (*service invocation*) or asynchronous (*event generation*) with other objects.
6. Can be "persistently"[10] associated with another object(s) in either a peer-to-peer or hierarchical relationship.

From a formal perspective, an object is defined by

1. Its Responsibilities. The value that this object adds to the system.
2. Its Rule Set

   a. Attribute Assertions: Range, Enumeration, and Type constraints.
   b. Operational Assertions: Pre-, Post-, and Invariance conditions.
   c. Class Invariance: A logical statement(s) about subsets of properties of the object that must be true at all times.
   d. Inference Engine: Inference logic may be: first-order predicate calculus, temporal, fuzzy, deontic, epistemic, or non-monotonic logics.
      Rule Sets may be used to infer attribute values that are not stored directly, represent data triggers, represent referential or semantic integrity constraints, represent operations in a non-procedural manner, and represent control regimens (e.g., resolve multiple inheritance conflicts).

3. Its Classification. An object must be in some category (class) even if it is a category of one object. However, usually an object is in a category that is part of a hierarchical structure where the object inherits attributes, service interfaces, and service implementations from categories higher up in the classification.
4. Its Type(s). An object may implement the services of any specific type without being constrained in its implementation of the services.
5. Its Relationships with other Objects, which can be either a peer-to-peer or hierarchical.

What Is a Class?

Class can be viewed from four basic perspectives: modeling, design, implementation, and compilation.

---

[9] The class itself is an object. Consider the analogy: Each tract home is an object, but the plan for these tract homes is also an object; you can touch it.

[10] In this context, persistence means information kept beyond the life of a transaction or session.

From a modeling perspective, a class is a template for a *category*; it defines:

1. *Characteristics* (*Attributes*) as data variables—Java data members.
2. *Services* (*Behavior*) as operations—Java member functions.

    a. *Interface* is the protocol for accessing object's services and its internal information.
    b. *Implementation* is the internal procedural for providing services.

3.   *Rules and Policies* as constraints that are applied.
4. *Relationships* with other objects that can be either peer-to-peer or hierarchical. A class can also have relationship with other classes via generalization/specialization.

From a design perspective, a class is a special kind of object. It is a collection of all the objects that it created (instantiated). It is used to create and destroy objects that belong to its collection. It can also be used to hold data and provide for the group services such as find an instance, keep averages, and keep shared information.

From an implementation perspective, a class is a "global" object with class data members and class services. An application can access its services[11] using the class name. An application can create objects by using its constructor[12] to "instantiate" an object. Finally, a class is used to implement the category concept in the Java programming language.

From a compiler's perspective, the class is a programmer's defined data type. It is a mechanism for defining and creating runtime objects.

PRINCIPLES OF OBJECT-ORIENTATION

Because this is a book for developers, we will treat an object as a software package consisting of the attributes (data) and the methods (code) that act on those data. We can understand object-orientation better when examined in light of 13 basic principles that apply to objects. These principles are derived from the abstractions introduced in the previous chapter.

Principle 1. Encapsulation

The concept that an object is a software package consisting of the attributes and the methods that act on those data leads us to the concept of encapsulation.

> **Encapsulation.** The object contains both the data and the methods (code) that manipulate or change that data.

---

[11] The static member functions of a class plus the constructor(s) are the class services.

[12] It is not good practice to use the constructor directly; an application normally uses a factory to create objects. However, the factory mechanism for object instantiation is beyond the scope of this book.

For many people, encapsulation is a subtle concept whose value is not immediately apparent; however, it is extremely important in the realization of quality software. It allows similar sets of data (based on data types) that have been bound to different kinds of objects to be modified by separate and distinct methods (code) that are appropriate for that kind of object. This eliminates the need to check that data are being manipulated by the appropriate sets of functions. This need is eliminated because the functions for manipulating the data of an object have been bound to the object.

Principle 2. Information Hiding

Encapsulation alone does not prevent the data of an object from being manipulated by functions other than the methods bound to the object. Protecting data from manipulation by entities outside the object can be achieved by requiring that access to data can only be provided by the services of the object that contains the data. The services of an object define how other objects gain access to its methods. Each object advertises the public services it is willing to provide to all objects.[13] The idea of providing services leads us to the concept of information hiding.

Information Hiding. The object that contains the attributes (data) defines what services (functions) are available to the other objects and prevents other objects from access or knowledge of the data (attributes) and how a service (method/code) is provided.

Information hiding is important because it allows an object complete control over the integrity of the data contained within it. This gives us high cohesion and low coupling concerning the manipulation of data.

Principle 3. Message Passing

Let us define an agent as an object that provides services and a client as an object that uses one or more of these services.[14] Before a client may use an agent's services, an interface must be defined. This interface definition is called the prototype of the service. The prototype is made from four parts: (1) the name of the service (called the selector by some experts), (2) the arguments for the service (called the signature by some experts), the data type[15] of the value the service call returns, and (4) the exceptions that may be thrown by the service call. Every object must define its prototype

---

[13] An object can also provide other services (protected and private) that are restricted only to specific other objects. We discuss this in depth later.

[14] An agent may also be called a server. Another way of referring to the agent–client relationship is that of requestor–provider. In this terminology, the client is the requestor of a service and the agent is the provider of the service. An agent may be a better term to use during analysis, as the word server may then be reserved to mean the actual object that does the work.

[15] Remember that all categories (classes) and types (interfaces) are just programmer-defined data types from a language perspective.

for each service it plans to provide. The set of defined prototypes is the protocol of the object (or alternatively it is the object's interface where interface is used in a lay-person's context and not in the Java language context). The protocol defines how a client may invoke (or request) the services of this object.

A good example of an object and its protocol is the icon system that we all use in a windowing system. A very common action in this system is to select an icon and then use a pull-down menu to get all of the services that we can choose for that icon. Thus, in an object-oriented system, the icon is really an object and the menu defines the object protocol.

One object can use the public service of another object by using the message-passing mechanism (paradigm) to send a message that conforms to the prototype of the service. If object 1 (the client) wants to use a service of object 2 (the agent), the client sends a message to the agent requesting the specific service of the agent. Note that the message must be directed to a specific object and contain the name of the requested service. Furthermore, the message may contain additional information (arguments) needed by the agent to perform the requested service.

For example, in the programmer's parlance, object 1 makes a function call to the service (function) that belongs to object 2 and passes all the appropriate parame-ter values needed by the function call. Because we stated that message passing is implemented by a function call in Java, it is fair to ask in what sense a message-passing mechanism is different from a function call mechanism. Certainly, in both cases there is an implicit request for action and there is a set of well-defined operations that will be performed to fulfill the request. There are, however, two important distinctions.

First, in a message-passing mechanism, each message is sent to a designated receiver (agent). In the imperative-programming paradigm, a function call mecha-nism has no designated receiver (agent). This distinction supports encapsulation.

Second, the interpretation of the message (method or set of operations/code used to fulfill the service request) depends on the receiver and may vary with differ-ent receivers. This distinction is necessary to support information hiding and poly-morphism, which we explain later. This leads to the third principle of Java programming, message passing.

Message Passing. An object may communicate with another object only via the message-passing mechanism.

Each message must be sent to a designated receiver, and the interpretation of the message depends on the receiver. Figure 2-1 illustrates an object invoking the services of three objects.

Principle 4. Late Binding

Another way in which message passing in the object-oriented paradigm differs from a function call is that the specific receiver of any given message is not usually known until runtime, so the determination of which method to invoke cannot be made until

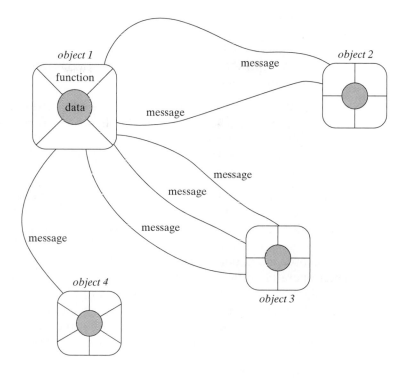

Figure 2-1   Message Passing Among Objects.

then. Thus, there is late binding between the message (service request/function call) and the method (code fragment) that will be used to fulfill the request for action. This can be contrasted to the early binding (compile or link time) of the function call to the code fragment in the imperative-programming paradigm.

The support for late binding defines the fourth principle of Java programming, late binding.

Late Binding. Support for the ability to determine the specific receiver and its corresponding method (code) to be executed for a message at runtime.

Late binding enables us to model a real behavior of the world. For example, if you are reading this book in a class at school, it is unlikely that you could have known who your classmates would be before the first day of class. You only know who your classmates are once the class has begun, and even then some individuals might register late. At the time the class was scheduled to be offered, it was not known who would attend or even how many would attend. This is an example of late binding.

Principle 5. Delegation

From a client's perspective, it is the agent that provides the service. It is possible that the agent actually delegates the work to a third object. This leads to the fifth principle of Java programming, delegation:

> **Delegation.** Work is passed, via message passing, from one object (client) to another object (agent) because from the client's perspective the agent has the services that the client needs. Work is continuously passed until it reaches the object that has both the data and the method (code) to perform the work.

Delegation is sometimes referred to as the perfect bureaucratic principle. Consider, for example, a corporation or a governmental organization. The chairperson of the board sends a service request (message) to the chief operating officer to build a new plant in Texas. From the perspective of the chairperson of the board, it is the chief operating officer's responsibility to provide the service. However, we all know that the chief operating officer has neither the skills nor the knowledge (information) to actually build a plant in Texas. So the chief operating officer has a method that delegates the work to the head of projects. The head of projects has a method that delegates the work to the chief engineer who has the staff to build a plant in Texas. In fact, the chief engineer's method delegates specific tasks to the appropriate heads of various disciplines to build the plant. It is the specific engineers who have the knowledge and the skills to design the plant to be built.

Here we see the fifth principle of Java programming applied. The work is delegated to the object that has the information (data) and the skills (method) to perform the task. The bureaucratic part comes from the fact that both the chief operating officer and the head of projects advertise the service "build a new plant," even though neither one has the information or the skills to perform the task. However, they have access to resources (objects) that can perform the task, so they can then take the responsibility for performing the task.

What got delegated is the authority to get the work done; responsibility cannot be delegated. From the chairperson of the board's perspective, it is the responsibility of the chief operating officer to fulfill the request to build a new plant in Texas. Similarly, from the chief operating officer's perspective, it is the responsibility of the head of projects to fulfill the request to build a new plant in Texas. When the head of projects accepts this request, he or she has accepted the responsibility relative to the chief operating officer to perform the work. However, neither the chief operating officer nor the chairperson knows how the work will be done. This is applying the information hiding principle.

Principle 6. Class/Instance/Object

Now let us look at some other object-oriented concepts. Categorizing helps us organize the complex world in which we live. We can make certain assumptions about an object that is in that category. In Java programming, we usually implement the concept of category by using the class construct. If an object is an instance of a class, it will fit the general pattern for that class. (Remember that an object is an example of a category. When we mapped Category to Class, we also mapped object to instance of that class.) This leads us to the sixth principle of Java programming, class/instance/object.

> **Class/Instance/Object.** All objects are instances of a class. Instances can be created (instantiated) or destroyed (deleted) at runtime. How the object provides a service is determined by the class of which the object is an instance.

Thus, all objects of the same class use the same method (code) in response to a specific service request (function call). Earlier we discussed the prototype of a service and the protocol as it relates to an object. Now with the concept of a class, we see that not only are the prototypes and the protocol defined for a class and applicable to every object that is an instance of that class but also that the implementation (method/code) for providing the service is defined by the class for these objects.

Principle 7. Generalization/Specialization without Polymorphism

Not only do we organize our objects into categories (classes) but also we arrange our categories (classes) into a hierarchy from the general to the specific. This leads us to the seventh principle of Java programming, generalization without polymorphism.

> **Generalization/Specialization without Polymorphism.** Classes can be organized by using a hierarchical inheritance structure. In the structure, the specialized class (subclass) inherits the attributes, the relationships (defined below), the prototypes and the methods from the generalized class (superclass) that is higher in the (tree) structure. An abstract superclass is a class that is used to create only subclasses; therefore, there are no direct instances of that class.

Principle 8. Generalization/Specialization with Polymorphism

There are always exceptions to the rule; to handle exceptions to the rule within our hierarchical structure, we define the eighth principle of Java programming, generalization with polymorphism, as a modification of the seventh principle.

> **Generalization/Specialization with Polymorphism.** Classes can be organized by using a hierarchical inheritance structure. In the structure, the subclass inherits the attributes, relationships, prototypes, and methods from the superclass that is higher in the tree. However, a subclass may create its own method to replace a method of any of its superclasses in providing a service that is available at the superclass level when an

instance of that subclass is the agent. For instances of the subclass, its method *overrides* the superclass method for providing the same service.

Principle 9. Relationships

Although generalization is a powerful concept, there are relationships between objects that cannot be captured using this concept. This leads us to the ninth principle of Java programming, relationships.

> **Relationships.** Collaborations between objects to provide a service to a client are usually captured by an association relationship, which is technically called a **link**.

The definition of the different kinds of relationships (i.e., association, aggregation, composition, link, generalization, specialization) are explained in depth in later chapters. Later in this book, we discuss an aggregation relationship; a link is sufficient here, as an aggregation is really a link with special properties.

Principle 10. Interface/Instance/Object

Java has added a few important constructs and mechanisms so that we can add some concepts to our analysis and design when we are using the Java language for implementation. One of these new constructs is an interface. This leads us to the tenth principle of Java programming, interface.

> **Interface/Instance/Object.** All objects that implement an interface are also instances of that interface. However, instances of an interface cannot be created (instantiated) or destroyed (deleted) as an interface instance. Each must be created or destroyed as an instance of the class to which it is a member.

Principle 11. Generalization/Specialization of Interfaces

Furthermore, although each interface is only a collection of service prototypes, one interface may have a generalization/specialization hierarchical relationship with other interfaces. This leads us to the eleventh principle of Java programming, generalization/specialization of interfaces.

> **Generalization/Specialization of Interfaces.** Interfaces can be organized by using a hierarchical inheritance structure. In the structure, the specialized interface inherits the service protocol (i.e., all the service prototypes) from the generalized interfaces that are higher in the (tree) structure.

There is no polymorphism version of interface generalization/specialization as in a technical sense; every instance of an interface can define its own implementation.

Principle 12. Reflection

Another important concept from Java is reflection. This leads us to the twelfth principle of Java programming, reflection.

> **Reflection.** Each object knows the detailed information about the class(es) and interface(s) to which it is an instance. This means that an application can, at runtime, acquire detailed information about the object from the object itself.

Principle 13. Multithreading

Finally, Java added support in the language for multithreading. This leads us to the thirteenth principle of Java programming, multithreading.

> **Multithreading.** Each object can have concurrent execution paths. This means that an object can handle multiple events (or service request) in a concurrent manner.

OBJECT-ORIENTED MODEL OF COMPUTATION

The problem-solving view of object-oriented programming (thus, Java programming) is very different from the pigeonhole model used in imperative programming. In the object-oriented paradigm, we never use any of the conventional terms such as *assignments*, *variables*, or *memory addresses*. Instead, we use terms such as *objects*, *messages*, and *services*. We have a universe of well-behaved objects that courteously ask each other to perform services for themselves. We have a community of helpers that assist us in solving problems.

The idea of creating a universe of helpers is very similar to a style of computer simulation called "discrete event-driven simulation." In this style, the user creates models of various elements of the simulation and describes how they interact with each other. Then, via some discrete event, the elements are set in motion.

This is almost identical to the way we do object-oriented modeling/programming. We define various objects in the universe that will help us solve the problem as well as how they interact with each other, and then we set them in motion. As a result, we consider object-oriented programming as using a simulation model of computation instead of a pigeonhole model of computation.

This simulation model also provides the designer or programmer with a better metaphor for problem solving. When we think in terms of services and methods (how to provide the service), we can bring a wealth of experience, understanding, ideas, and intuition from our everyday life. In contrast, most of us have very little insight into how to structure a program that thinks about problem solving in terms of pigeonholes or slots containing values.

EXAMPLE

To illustrate how the object-oriented paradigm helps us manage complexity, let us apply this modeling technique to a real-world situation. First we will describe the situation, and then we will discuss how we would use the object-oriented paradigm to capture the situation. This example will be used in the first half of the book to clarify additional concepts as they are introduced.

The Example

In this example, we have a family with a father (John), a mother (Jane), two sons (Peter and Paul), and two daughters (Elizabeth and Mary). John is an actor and Jane is a dentist. All the children are students and the family dog is Lassie. Their family physician is Alice. This family owns a house in the suburbs. Although mowing the family lawn is normally a chore for the father, it can also be a paid chore for any one of the children. However, working within the neighborhood is Jack, a professional lawn mower.

One morning, Jane notices that the lawn needs mowing, so she mentions to John that it is time to mow the lawn. John agrees and says that he will mow the lawn this evening. Later that evening, John comes home and is exhausted from a long day at the studio and decides to pay one of his children to mow the lawn. He looks for one of his children; he sees Mary first. He asks Mary to mow the lawn for five dollars. Mary agrees; however, Mary knows that Jack, a professional lawn mower, is willing to mow the lawn for four dollars. So Mary calls Jack to mow the lawn for four dollars, and Jack agrees to mow the lawn. Jane comes home later that evening and she sees the lawn mowed. Thinking that John mowed the lawn, Jane complements John on the excellent condition of the lawn.

Building the Model

Now let us do an object-oriented analysis of this situation.

Finding the Objects and Services

These are the following tangible objects in our model: John, Jane, Peter, Paul, Elizabeth, Mary, Lassie, the family lawn, Jack, and Alice. Jack, the professional lawn mower, advertises a mow lawn service. John, as the father of the house, also provides a mow lawn service that is limited to the family lawn. Each of the children also provides a mow lawn service, for a specific price.

Prototype

The prototype of the mow lawn service is not the same for each of the objects. For example, the prototype[16] for Jack's mow lawn service may have the name (selector) "mow the lawn" and the arguments (signature)—address of the lawn, whom to send bill, address where to send the bill. The four children's prototype for "mow the lawn" service may look similar to Jack's, as the children are willing to mow any lawn for cash. The children's prototype may have the name "mow the lawn," and the arguments address of the lawn and money (in form of cash). Finally, John will only mow the family lawn as his chore. John's prototype may have the name "mow the lawn" and no arguments. John had a default value for the lawn to be mowed, namely, the family's lawn, when Jane asked him to mow the lawn. He also knew that he would not get paid for mowing the family lawn.

Message Passing

Jane, the client, solves the problem of getting the lawn mowed by finding an appropriate agent, John, to whom she passes a message containing her service request for action. For John to process the message, Jane's message must follow the protocol/prototype that John has defined for the service. Because Jane sent a message that John can interpret (i.e., the message is consistent with a prototype within the protocol that John has advertised), John must have a method (some algorithm or set of operations) to perform the requested service ("mow the lawn").

Responsibility and Dynamic Behavior

In this case, John behaves in a dynamic manner. If he is not tired at the end of the day, he mows the lawn himself; if he is tired, however, he asks one of his children to mow the lawn. Alternatively, if John always mows the lawn himself, as Jane apparently assumed, then John's behavior would be considered static.

John's method was an algorithm based on whether he was tired at the end of the day. As we know, on this particular day, he delegated the work to mow the lawn to his daughter Mary. Furthermore, Mary subsequently delegated the work to Jack.

In either scenario (whether John used a dynamic or static method for his behavior), when John accepted the message, he accepted the responsibility to satisfy Jane's request. Similarly, when Mary accepted the request from John to "mow the lawn" for five dollars, Mary accepted the responsibility to satisfy John's request.

Information Hiding

Jane did not know, and probably did not want to know, the particular method that John used to provide the service "mow the lawn." She was very content that the lawn was mowed when she got home. If she had investigated, however, Jane would have found that Jack paid Mary to mow the lawn for four dollars. Similarly, John did not

---

[16] We have ignored return value and exceptions to keep the example simple.

know the particular method that Mary used to mow the lawn. The principle of information hiding is being applied to the client's view in both cases.

In the object-oriented paradigm, the agent's service is defined to the client in terms of responsibilities. Jane's request for action (i.e., service from John) must indicate only the desired outcome (mow the lawn). John is free to pursue any technique that achieves the desired results and is not hampered by interference from Jane. It is John's responsibility to define how he will provide for the requested service by defining the method to provide the service.

Delegation

From this example, we see another principle, all too human, in message passing. The first thought of every client and agent is to find someone else to perform the work. This is the application of the principle of delegation. Of course, objects cannot always respond to a message by asking another object to perform an action. If this were allowed, there would be an infinite circle of requests, like a bureaucracy of paper pushers, each passing papers to some other member of the organization. At some point, at least a few objects need to perform some work other than passing the request to some other object. These ideas are used in our mowing the lawn example. From Jane's perspective, her husband John has provided the service "mow the lawn," which is the reason she complements John for the excellent condition of the lawn. From John's perspective, it was Mary who mowed the lawn. John, then, may also thank Mary for the excellent job that she did. But in fact, if the behaviors or methods (how we provide the services) were not hidden (information hiding) from Jane, she would have known that Jack mowed the lawn.

To better understand the message-passing mechanism, let us look at a different scenario. John could have sent his message "mow the lawn" to one of his sons. Let us assume that he sent it to Peter instead of Mary. Peter's behavior or method is different from Mary's. Specifically, he needs all five dollars to pay for the gasoline to get to tomorrow's ball game. So, Peter mows the lawn himself. John and Jane had a choice of which person to request the service (or send the message). However, the client must send the message to a designated receiver, and the designated receiver must provide the service. If Jane had called Alice, the family physician, to mow the lawn, she would have been in error since Alice does not provide a mow lawn service. If Alice understands the message, she would probably send back an error message "physicians do not mow lawns." More likely, this would result in an invalid message for the recipient.

Reflection

Now with Java reflection, Mary could have asked Alice for all the services that she provides. Then Mary would have discovered that Alice does not support the "mow the lawn" service in real-time.

Category (Class)

Now let us look at some other object-oriented principles and concepts. Although Mary may have never dealt with Jack, she has some ideas about the behavior that she can expect from Jack when she requests his service. This is due to the fact that Jack is a professional lawn mower and the information that she has about lawn-mowing professionals. Because Jack is an instance of the category (class) **LawnMower,** he will fit the general pattern for lawn mowers. We can use the word *LawnMower* to represent the category of all lawn mowers. This is an application of the class/instance/object principle.

Generalization/Specialization

Mary has additional generic information about Jack that goes beyond his being an instance of the class **LawnMower**. She also has generic information about Jack because Jack is also in the class **HouseCareProfessional**. She knows that Jack will come to the house to do the mowing, just as the other housecare professionals such as the rug cleaner and the gardener. This is different from the class **HealthCareProfessional** who usually does not make house calls. Furthermore, Mary knows Jack is also in the class **SmallBusinessOwner**, and as such he will ask for money as part of the service and will give a receipt, just as would any other small business owner. Mary has organized her knowledge of Jack in terms of a hierarchy of classes.

The generalization tree that is in Mary's mind is shown in Figure 2-2. We have used the united modeling language (UML) notation. Generalization/specialization (inheritance) is shown as a solid line from subclass to superclass with a triangular head on the superclass end. Instantiation of a class is shown with a dashed line from the instance to the class with a triangular head on the class end. Classes and instances are shown as rectangles. Instances are distinguished from classes by underlining the name.

Jack is an instance of the class **LawnMower**, but the **LawnMower** is a specialized form (subclass) of the class **HouseCareProfessional**. Furthermore, **HouseCareProfessional** is a subclass of the generalized form (superclass) of **SmallBusinessOwner**, and she can continue up the hierarchy to **OrganicMatter** via **Human** and **Mammal**. Thus, there is a lot of generic information that Mary has about Jack that is not directly attributed to Jack being in the class **LawnMower**. This is due to the fact that Mary assumes that the knowledge of a more general class applies to a specialization of that class. Mary's classification of Jack is the application of the generalization with polymorphism principle.

Multithreading

Mary is a typical teenager. She is talking on the telephone, listening to the radio, and doing her homework at the same time. How does one model these concurrent tasks being done by Mary in our model? This is an opportunity to use multitasking, which allows an object to have concurrent execution paths.

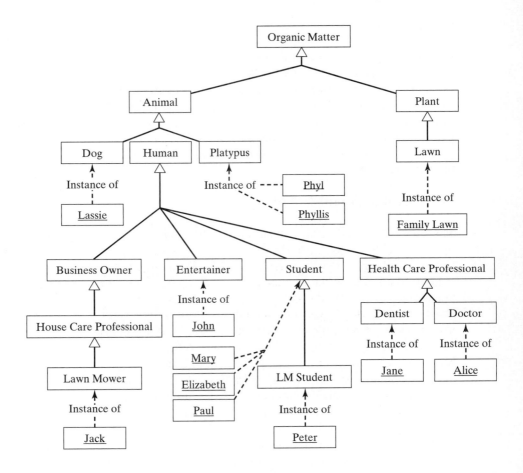

Figure 2-2   Generalization/Specialization—Hierarchy for the Lawn Mowing Example.

Type (Interface)

Now let us assume that Jack, John, Jane, and Alice are also all members of the Parent-Teacher Association (PTA). We can assume that all the service prototypes that each member provide are identical even if the methods (implementations) are very different. To capture the membership of the PTA, we can use the type (interface) concept; that is, we create a type (interface) that represents all the services of a PTA member. Then, each person implements all the services of a "PTA member." Thus, we have a very powerful way of capturing this very complex situation in which objects of different classes can have common services. By using types (interfaces), we can manage these objects as if they were in a virtual class.

Generalization/Specialization with Polymorphism

Generalization (inheritance) works in a manner that every parent wishes. The children (subclasses) inherit all the attributes (knowledge) and all the methods (behavior) of the parent (superclass). In addition, children can have additional attributes (smarter than the parent) and have additional methods (can do more than parent). This is what we call the "good child" form of specialization. Unfortunately, not all children are "good children." We need a way of modeling the "bad child." Let us look at this next.

We know that mammals reproduce by giving birth to children; certainly humans do and so does the dog Lassie. However, Phyllis, the female platypus, reproduces by laying eggs instead of giving birth. Thus, the subclass **Platypus** provides the service of reproduction in a different manner than does the rest of the mammals.

If we want to capture this fact and still use our generalization hierarchy, we must have a way of handling the exceptions to the general rule. We do this by providing a way for the subclass to provide a different method for a service that is defined in the superclass (parent class). In our example, the superclass **Mammal** has defined a service called "reproduce." The method for the service reproduce is to give birth to live children. **Platypus** is a subclass of **Mammal**. In the "good child" form of specialization, Phyllis would reproduce by giving birth to live children. However, Phyllis is a "bad child"; she has chosen to reproduce by laying eggs. In this form of specialization, called generalization with polymorphism, Phyllis provides her own method (i.e., laying eggs) for the service reproduce. Thus, Phyllis will use a different method of providing the service reproduce than Lassie. Phyllis is an example of the need to modify the generalization without polymorphism principle.

In our example, we need to use generalization with polymorphism. Mary and all the other students will respond to the "mow the lawn" message by delegating any request that pays over five dollars to Jack as he will mow the lawn for four dollars. However, Peter is an exception as he will always respond to the "mow the lawn" request by doing it himself. Thus, we must use generalization with polymorphism to capture Peter's behavior (see Figure 2.2).

Relationship: Collaboration

Let us look more closely at the method that Mary uses to "mow the lawn." For Mary to call Jack to mow the lawn, Mary has to have access to Jack. Normally, this is done when Jack sends flyers around the neighborhood advertising his service. Mary sees the flyer and puts Jack's name and telephone number into her diary. Although this action may seem innocuous, Mary has established a relationship with Jack. At the instant Mary put his name into her diary, she decided to consider using his service when the occasion arises. A connection was established between Mary and Jack. In fact, the reason Jack sends out the flyers is to establish relationships that will add to his customer base. Every person who reads the flyer and saves Jack's name, telephone number, and kind of service has established a relationship with Jack. We can name that relationship from two perspectives: (1) from Jack's perspective, all the people who keep the flyer information are customers, and (2) from these people's (and Mary's) perspective, Jack is a professional lawn mower.

This kind of relationship, where one object knows about another object for specific services, is called a *link*. Let us assume that the neighborhood is called Fun-Town and that we have a category (class) of people called **FunTowner**. Because Jack is an instance of **LawnMower** and every one of his customers is an instance of **Fun-Towner**, we can capture this link at a higher-level concept called *association*. An association describes a group of links with a common structure and common semantics. All links in an association must connect objects from one same class to objects from a second same class. Thus, if we have a second person Joan who also is an instance of **LawnMower** and every one of her customers is an instance of **Fun-Towner**, we have a second link that belongs to the same association.

Associations are bidirectional. It is common to give a name to an association in each direction. In our example, from **LawnMower**'s direction it is customer and from the **FunTowner**'s direction it is lawn mower.[17] Without the association, there would be no vehicle for Mary to access the services of Jack.

Table 2-1 summarizes the key object-oriented concepts using the "mowing the lawn" example.

Table 2-1 Key Object-Oriented Concepts

Objected-Oriented Concept	Explanation/Example
Client	Requestor of the service (i.e., sender of the message—Jane)
Agent (server)	Agent to whom the message is sent (i.e., John)
Object	Jane, John, Mary, Lassie
Prototype	mowTheLawn (String address, float payment)
Service name (selector)	"mow the lawn"
Signature	Additional information (arguments) needed to carry out the request (i.e., amount to be paid)
Services	John and Jack both provide the service "mow the lawn"
Method	This is the operation(s) of providing the service that is hidden from the client
Message sending	Jane's request to John to "mow the lawn"
Responsibility	John's responsibility to satisfy Jane's request
Dynamic behavior	John's method of mowing the lawn

[17] In actuality, a link is implemented via pointers from one object to another object(s). A *pointer* is an explicit reference to an object; thus, an association is implemented in a class as a class pointer attribute to the other class. For example, in the data portion of a class **FunTowner**, there may be a data member *lawn mower* that points to a **LawnMower** object. Conversely, the data portion of class **LawnMower** may contain a data member *customer* that points to a set of **FunTowner** objects that are the customers.

Table 2-1   Key Object-Oriented Concepts (*continued*)

Objected-Oriented Concept	Explanation/Example
Information hiding	Object's attributes and methods
Delegation	John delegates the work to Mary
Reflection	Asking Alice for her services
Category (class)	Mammal, BusinessOwner
Instance	Same as an object
Generalization/ Specialization[a]	LawnMower is a specialized form of a HouseCare Professional. HouseCare Professional is a Human, which is a specialized form of Mammal
Attribute	Name, Address, etc.
Subclass	Subclass will inherit attributes and services (both prototype and methods) from its superclass(es) (i.e., Human will inherit all the attributes and methods of Mammal)
Superclass	Dentist is a subclass of the superclass HealthCare Professional
Abstract superclass[b]	Class used to create only subclasses (i.e., Mammal)
Type (interface)	Member of PTA
Polymorphism	Phyllis laying eggs
Collaboration	Object that helps another object in performing the method (i.e., Jack helps Mary in providing the "mow the lawn" service)

[a] This is usually implemented by inheritance; however, it can also be implemented by association and delegation.

[b] An abstract class may have attributes that are inherited; however, an interface may not have any attributes.

SUMMARY

The 2 fundamental abstractions on which object-orientation is based are objects and classes. The 13 principles of object-orientation are as follows:

1. **Encapsulation**. An object contains both the data and the methods (code) that manipulate or change the data.
2. **Information Hiding**. The services of an object define how other objects have access to its methods and, therefore, its data. Each object advertises public services that it is willing to provide to other objects.
3. **Message Passing**. An object (client) may communicate with another object (agent) only via the message-passing mechanism. A client requests a service of an agent by sending a message that matches a predefined protocol that the agent defines for that service.
4. **Late Binding**. The specific receiver of any given message is not known until runtime, so the determination of which method to invoke cannot be

made until then. See Generalization/Specialization with Polymorphism, which is principle 8.

5. **Delegation**. Work is passed, via the message-passing mechanism, from one object (client) to another object (agent) because from the client's perspective the agent has the service(s) that the client needs. Work is continuously passed until it reaches the object that has both the data and the method (code) to perform the work. Delegation is sometimes called the perfect bureaucratic principle.

6. **Class and Objects.** All objects are instances of a class. How an object provides a service is determined by the class of which the object is an instance. Thus, all objects of the same class use the same method (code) in response to a specific service request.

7. **Generalization/Specialization without Polymorphism**. Classes can be organized by using a hierarchical inheritance structure. In the structure, the specialized class (subclass) inherits the attributes, the relationships (defined below), the prototypes and the methods from the generalized class (superclass) that is higher in the (tree) structure. An abstract superclass is a class that is used to create only subclasses; thus, there are no direct instances of that class.

8. **Generalization/Specialization with Polymorphism.** Classes can be organized by using a hierarchical inheritance structure. In the structure, the subclass inherits the attributes, relationships, prototypes, and methods from the superclass that is higher in the tree. However, a subclass may create its own method to replace a method of any of its superclasses in providing a service that is available at the superclass level when an instance of that subclass is the agent. For instances of the subclass, its method *overrides* the superclass method for providing the same service.

9. **Relationships.** Association and aggregation are used to capture the collaboration between objects necessary to provide a service to a client.

10. **Interface and Objects.** All objects that implement an interface are also instances of that interface. However, instances of an interface cannot be created (instantiated) or destroyed (deleted) as an interface instance. Each must be created or destroyed as an instance of the class to which it is a member.

11. **Generalization/Specialization of Interfaces.** Interfaces can be organized by using a hierarchical inheritance structure. In the structure, the specialized interface inherits the service protocol (i.e., all the service prototypes) from the generalized interfaces that are higher in the (tree) structure.

12. **Reflection**. Each object knows the detail information about the class(es) and interface(s) to which it is an instance. This means that an application can at runtime acquire detail information about the object from the object itself.

13. Multithreading. Each object can have concurrent execution paths. This means that an object can handle multiple events (or service requests) in a concurrent manner.

3

Building a Specification Model

In the previous chapter, the object-oriented way of organizing reality was introduced. Organizing all of reality for modeling is not a simple activity, even if one does it the object-oriented way. Practically speaking, one does not attempt to organize all of reality. One usually deals with modeling a specific application domain. That is, one has to select a manageable domain within which the model will be developed. This chapter identifies two methods for capturing this bounding of domain: *use cases* and *contracts*.

Use cases capture the functional requirements and the value propositions[1] of a proposed system with its associated high-level processes (i.e., those processes that are outside the system boundary) that are needed to achieve these specific value propositions.[2] Contracts articulate the services (operations) provided by the system (application software) to achieve these value propositions. One of the key values of producing use cases and contracts is that they ease discussions between stakeholders

---

[1] The value propositions are the reasons why the system is being built. They identify the value that various features provide the business.

[2] The authors have also used it to capture the performance characteristics/requirements of the system from a usage perspective. Capturing these parameters is useful for performance testing.

and analysts/developers. They are typically written using business terms natural to the majority of stakeholders.

INTRODUCTION TO USE CASES

Ivar Jacobson, in *Object-Oriented Software Engineering: A Use-Case Driven Approach*, established a scenario-based approach for establishing a boundary on the domain called the *objectory method*. This method focused on identifying the important elements of a domain in terms of how they contributed or behaved while providing a service. He called each scenario, a "use case" because it described a use of the system.[3]

Various authors define use cases differently.

- A use case specifies a sequence of actions, including variants, that a system performs and that yields an observable result of value to a particular actor (Jacobson, Booch, Rumbaugh)
- A use case is a description of all the possible sequences of interactions among the system and one or more actors in response to some initial stimulus by one of the actors. (Rumbaugh)
- A use case is a collection of possible sequences of interactions between the system under discussion and its external actors, related to a particular goal. (Cockburn)

The common threads in all of these definitions are actors and sequences of interactions. In this approach several concepts are important: the goal, the system, the actor, the use case, and the use-case bundle.

- The *goal* is the business value to the "user(s)" of the system who usually initiates the interaction with the system.
- The *system* is the application with all its associated hardware that will be used by the "users."
- An *actor* is the external entity that interacts with a system.
- A *use case* is a description of an interaction that achieves a useful goal for an actor.
- A *use-case bundle* is a collection of use cases that are highly correlated with some activity or organizing business element. A use-case bundle gives us a way to organize our use cases into collections that will help us better understand the functionality of the system that we are developing.

---

[3] The use of the system is assumed to achieve some useful goal for the user of the "system." Use cases, therefore, are trying to capture the value proposition from an external view. Namely, the goal is to capture the value proposition from the user's perspective.

System

Historically, systems have been understood utilizing three basic models: black box, white box, and transparent box. Each successive model (Figure 3-1) provides increasing detail into the internals and implementation of the system. The black box model, shown as the solid boundary, emphasizes the value the system provides and where it fits into the rest of the business computing environment. It presents the system without concern about how it provides the business value. Here the key concepts are the users of the system (including other systems) and the value the system provides to each user.

The white box model, shown as the oval, presents the system in terms of what specific business functions the system provides. This model emphasizes how objects in the system map to business processes. We can use a white box model to capture the detailed, essential use cases that are both primary and secondary. A white box model does not concern itself with the hardware or software architecture.

The transparent box model, shown as the very small circles, presents the internals of the system and how they contribute to the business functionality. Each circle represents an internal element, whether it be source code or device. In this model, technology entities employed within the system are included as well as details about how they work together to provide the business functionality.

In the design of use-case cases, we should view the system as a black box. Experience has shown us, however, that it is sometimes necessary to take at least a white box view to determine the sequence of interaction between an actor and the system. This helps us define the use case. Furthermore, when we are doing low-level concrete use cases, we probably have to take a transparent view of the system.

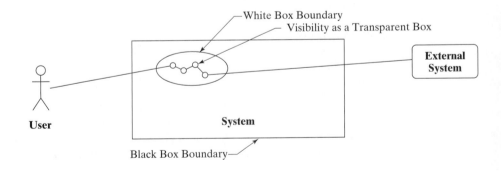

Figure 3-1   Visibility into the Internals of a System According to the Black Box, White Box, and Transparent Box Models.

Actors

The use-case model divides the world into two parts: the system and the users (the external entities that use it). Actors are a mechanism for categorizing the users (usually a physical entity) of the system who share a set of common interactions to achieve a goal or set of goals. An actor can be a user, an external system, or a device. An actor can make a service request of the system, be requested to provide a service, and interact with the system through a complex dialog of service requests between the actor and the system. It is the usage of a set of common iterations in a like manner to achieve a goal that is the key to the categorization. Thus, an actor is a representation[4] of any entity that can initiate an action on the part of the system or receive a request for an action from the system. An actor can be characterized by requests that it initiates to the system or the requests to which it can respond. In a real sense, the complete set of requests/responses for all actors establishes a boundary on the domain of which the system can be aware. That is, a system can never respond to aspects of a domain for which it has not been designed (i.e., it will not process requests [inputs] for which it has not been designed).

Occasionally, a number of actors may share common requests that they all invoke on the system. Rather than explicitly associate the same set of requests with each actor, we can introduce a generalized actor that encompasses those common requests. The other actors are treated as specializations and inherit the ability to perform those requests from the generalization.

Use Cases

A **scenario** is a little story that outlines some expected sequence of request and responses between a user(s) and the system. It is used to convey how a specific user[5] employs the system to achieve some useful goal. Writing a scenario is a simple game of "what happens next." Most scenarios are simple; there is only one logical sequence of operations from the initial state. Other scenarios are more complicated, with multiple exception cases (things going wrong) or different interaction paths (options).

A use case is closely related to a scenario.[6] Figure 3-2 illustrates a simple use-case diagram for a course registration system.[7] A use case describes a system in terms of sequences of interactions between various actors and the system (i.e., a specific

---

[4] In a standard use case, an actor's instance is the initiator. The initiator is the entity that starts a series of interactions with the system. In addition to the initiator, a use case may have participating actors that are entities that did not initiate the interaction.

[5] A specific user is an instance of an actor. For example, Joe is a user. Joe is an instance of the actor, that is, user.

[6] A use case is the generalized form of a family of scenarios; therefore a scenario is a specific instance of a use case.

[7] A detailed discussion about use case diagrams appears later in this chapter.

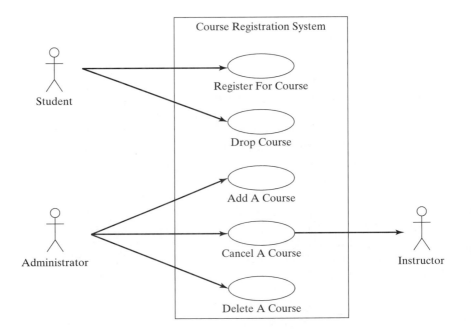

Figure 3-2   Simple Use-Case Diagram.

use case captures all the scenarios that begin with the same request to achieve the same user goal). Also, it is a formal way of describing all the interactions between the actors and the system to achieve the business goals of the system. The actor that initiates the use case is called the initiation actor. In most interactions, the dialog may result in the interaction of the system with other actors; these actors are called participating actors. The interaction assumes that the system is a "black box" and uses domain elements as actors that interact with the system in a request/response manner. A use case identifies the pre-conditions that must exist for it to be valid, the post-conditions that define the state of the system after the use case has concluded, detailed business (non–technology-dependent) that is performed, business exceptions that may arise, and business constraints that apply to the system in reacting to a specific actor request.

   In capturing the functional aspects of the system, one of the difficulties in generating a useful discussion of a system is keeping the description at a consistent level of abstraction. For use cases to be successfully developed, it is necessary to know the dimension of the functional description that one is attempting to capture. Then one can determine the level of detail in the information that should be captured.

   In one dimension, we can distinguish between **high-level** and **low-level** functional descriptions of a system. A high-level description provides general and brief descriptions of the essence of the business values provided. It is not concerned with how the business values are achieved. A low-level description provides business details showing the exact order of activities, tasks, or alternatives.[8]

In a second dimension, we can distinguish between **primary** and **secondary** functions of the system. Primary functions are the essential business functionalities of the system—the functions provided to users—and constitute the reason for which the system exists. The secondary processes deal with the rare and exceptional cases.[9] These are the functions that are necessary to deliver a robust system.

Finally, in a third dimension, we can distinguish between the **essential** and the **concrete** functions of the system. The essential use cases are business solutions that are independent of implementation (hardware and software), while the concrete use cases are design-dependent. The distinction between essential and concrete is the distinction between black box and transparent box models.

Relations Among Use Cases. A typical use case outlines some sequence of interactions between the initiator of a service request to the system and the system. It often happens that some sequences of interactions are common across multiple use cases. In this situation, we can extract these common sequences as a use case. We then include the use case[10] so formed within the use cases from which they were extracted. When this situation exists, we say that each of the "multiple" use cases includes the common use case (i.e., we can have an **include** relationship between use cases). The includes relationship allows us to localize in one use case a common sequence of activities among several use cases. This has the advantage that when changes occur in this common sequence, then it only needs to be changed in one place.

In addition, we can have the situation in which several use cases are identical with the exception of one or two specific subsequences of interactions. In this case, we can extract the common core (base use case) and treat the use cases that differ as extensions[11] of this base use case. Thus, an **extend** relationship exists between an extension and the core. This allows us to capture in an easy form those situations in which the sequences captured in several use cases may differ as the result of a simple conditional at the end of the sequence.

Finally, in the development of a high-level use case, it is often the case that it can encompass several detailed and extended use cases. The relationship that exists between the high-level use case and the detailed and the extended use case is a **generalization/specialization** relation.

---

[8] A high-level description of Shakespeare's *Romeo and Juliet* is that it is a love story. A low-level description includes the kinds of details about the story as presented in study guides. Neither level description is actually the story.

[9] It can be argued that secondary processes are not rare or occasional if one includes within this category processes such as backing up data, downloading needed data from other systems. Such processes may not be the primary reason for building the system, but are essential processes that are almost always required. We consider those cases to be primary cases.

[10] This is like a common subroutine that is used by many routines.

[11] This is like subclassing where you are only allowed to add code to the parent routine.

Subject of Description.   As stated previously, a use case can be classified in three different dimensions:

1. primary vs. secondary
2. essential vs. concrete
3. high level vs. low level

A use-case description of a system will emphasize one of each pair of factors. Several groupings are commonly used to scope the level of detail captured in use cases.

- primary, essential, high level
- primary and secondary, essential, low level
- primary, concrete, low level
- primary and secondary, concrete, low level

Generating a full detailed functional description of a system involves successively producing the various kinds of use cases starting from the top and working the way downward. These common kinds of use cases are described below.

At the most abstract level are the primary, essential, high-level use cases. They basically define how the system supports the business processes involved in attaining the business value propositions. These use cases usually define only the functions that will be performed by the system; they do not clearly define the inputs and outputs (i.e., interfaces or the services associated with the system or actors) of the "processes" or process owners, nor do they define how the process will perform its work. They are useful in getting a high-level understanding of the workflow. In addition, they give us an order of magnitude on the number of detailed use cases (primary and secondary, essential, low-level use cases) that will be produced and a framework to identify the critical success factors for the project.[12] For example, we can use these use cases to prioritize the features according to business value and estimate usage based on the value proposition. If rare and unusual use cases or reliability are critical to our system design, secondary use cases should also be developed to help size the problem.[13]

To understand a very large and complex system, we may require the development of essential and low-level use cases (both primary and secondary). When we do this, several use cases may be required to provide the details that are summarized in one primary essential high-level use case. We use these use cases to capture the interfaces needed to support the business goals. They can be used to capture the sequence of interactions (service request/events) between the system and all the actors; however, all the interfaces are described in a technology-independent

---

[12] The critical success factor in a lot of reengineering process efforts may not be the system; it is the successful deployment of the new business processes to the users!

[13] These use cases are not usually sufficient to write an interface contract for the system.

manner. Use cases written at this level are the minimum level needed to write an interface contract for the system.

However, for some contracts, more specific details (i.e., technology-dependent constraints) are needed. In these cases, primary, concrete, and low-level use cases are developed. In the primary, low-level, and concrete use cases, not only are the sequence of interactions captured but also technology-based design decisions are included.[14] Finally, when our system also has critical rare and unusual functions or has robustness as a key requirement, we will develop both primary and secondary, low-level concrete use cases. When we take use cases to this degree of detail, we deal with the initialization, recovery, and secondary use cases that are necessary for a robust system.

Information Captured.   One of the reasons for employing a use-case approach to bounding our system is the ease with which information can be identified. Use cases can capture the following set of information:[15]

- Actors
  A use case identifies all actors that participate in it. In some situations, there won't be an actor explicitly identified (a common situation with supporting use cases) and this must be noted.[16]
- Relationships with other use cases
  A use-case description identifies the relationships (generalization/specialization, include, and extend relationships) that use cases have with each other.
- Pre-conditions
  A use case may require specific conditions to hold for it to be successfully invoked. All such conditions must be identified. In some cases, systems are intended to exhibit modality in behavior. That is, they are expected to operate in different modes and exhibit different behaviors for different modes. A pre-condition identifies the mode required and any other conditions that must hold for the use case to be valid. This includes information such as the action requested, confirmation of user identity, values that must hold, and any other factor that affects successful conclusion of the use case.

---

[14] This is an encroachment upon architecture and/or design. Yes, theory is perfect, but practice is more useful.

[15] The authors have also extended this to include usage data that help them tune for performance on large systems.

[16] The purpose of use cases is to capture the interaction between actors and the system. In the situation addressed here, the actor that is participating is implicitly identified from the use case that includes it. Included use cases can be incorporated into several use cases, each of which deals with different actors. It is for this reason that we state that a use case might not explicitly identify an actor.

- Details[17]

  A use case describes the details about how a system provides some service. The details of a use case identify the details of the sequences of interactions. The details are captured as step-by-step interactions among domain objects. Each step provides sufficient detail to identify which entities are involved, what each entity does, and the result of the step. This can be accomplished using text or sequence diagrams.

- Post-conditions

  The execution of a use case is intended to bring about some desired computation or state. The post-conditions identify exactly what results are expected from execution of the use case. This includes any side effects produced such as any objects created and all objects destroyed. We recommend the following be specified:

  Instance creation or destruction
  Relations (association and aggregation) formed or broken
  Value changes in variables
  State changes (including final state)

- Exceptions

  Every action performed in a use case is susceptible to error. Desired data may not be located, computations might be aborted, and connectivity lost. It is necessary to identify all possible errors that can occur in the use case. In addition, it is useful to identify what the specific actions should be taken to recover. Hence, for each exception we wish to know the circumstance in which it can occur and the action that should be taken.

- Constraints

  It is also necessary to identify all constraints that might apply to the use case. Such constraints can be on the values being manipulated, resources allocated to it, and resource allocations to various steps. There are usually the invariant conditions (i.e., the conditions that must always be true). The invariant conditions must hold at the beginning (pre-condition) of the service (operation) and at the end (post-condition) of the service (operation). Violation of these constraints can also give rise to errors and these errors should be identified as an exception.

- Variants/Alternatives

  It is also necessary to identify all variations that might apply to the use case. These are usually the variations that are not covered by independent use cases. Usually these variations are either easily handled or they are considered as part of another use case.

Of course, the actual information that is captured in a specific use case varies according to several factors. In particular, it varies on whether it is (1) high level or

---

[17] The details section is not developed for high-level use cases.

low level and (2) essential or concrete. Table 3-1 summarizes the information that is typically developed for common kinds of use cases that are developed.

Table 3-1 Information Associated with the Different Kinds of Use Cases[a]

Use Cases	High-Level Primary Essential[b]	Low-Level Primary and Secondary Essential	Low-Level Primary Concrete	Low-Level Primary and Secondary Concrete
Actors	B	B	B,T	B,T
Relations		R		R
Pre-conditions	E	E	E	E
Details	H	H	D	D
Post-conditions	E	E	E	E
Exceptions		A		A
Constraints	A	A	A	A
Variants	A	A	A	A

[a] B, essential business information; T, essential technological information; R, essential information describing relationships between primary with secondary, extending, and included use cases; E, essential information; H, high level information about the interaction between system and actors; D, detailed concrete information that applies to use cases that are not generalizations; A, information included as appropriate for the specific use case (not all use cases have exceptions, constraints, or variations).

[b] Included or extending use cases follow the guidelines for the kind of use case to which they are related.

This table correlates information with the various kinds of use cases. It can be used to guide the development of a use case. For example, the development of high-level, primary, essential use cases requires that one identify

- the essential business information (i.e., establish the business value proposition)
- the pre-conditions that must apply for the use case to complete
- the post-conditions that are promised
- any constraints or variations that might exist

According to Table 3-1, one will not be identifying relationships among use cases, details, or exceptions as this information is not appropriate for this kind of use case.

Use-Case Bundles

Use-case bundles are collections of use cases that are highly correlated with some activity or organizing business element. They make sense only when the business value being provided by a system necessitates significant functionality such as might be found in a fly-by-wire aircraft system, computer aided design (CAD) program, or software for a telecommunications switch.[18] To facilitate understanding, a domain can be partitioned into smaller units such that we gain insight into the whole domain by studying the parts. Some basic criteria for bundling use cases into a package are described below. It is highly likely that the wording of the simple descriptions of the use cases will clearly indicate which of the criteria is best for establishing use-case bundles.

- Same actor—same state
  An extremely simple package is achieved by bundling together all use cases initiated by the same actor in the same state of the system. Because a large system can have a number of different states from which different actors make requests, such a packaging scheme often results in a balanced set of bundles that encompass a reasonable number of use cases each.
- Common entities
  Many times it makes more sense to bundle according to the use cases that deal with the same entities. In this case, multiple actors may be involved in managing different aspects of the same entity. For example, a web-based store front may have a component of the software that deals with customer orders. In this case, we may have actors (customers) that input those orders, actors that bill (credit card transaction system) against orders, actors (shipping clerks) that ship orders, and actors (managers) who wish to tailor the inventory to best support customers. The one thread that binds all of these actors together is "orders" and "order management." Bundling together all of these use cases together makes sense, particularly when there is another entity (such as "product" and "product management") that is the focus of many actors as well. Such bundling focuses on common elements.
- Specific workflow
  Alternatively, a system that supports actors in doing their jobs can be bundled using workflow. In this situation, a bundle describes a set of activities that are performed by a single actor in the course of performing some aspect of their job. The use cases describe different paths through the workflow. This approach to bundling use cases is similar to the viewpoints approach.[19]

---

[18] Systems that have extensive user interfaces occasionally fall into this category. Visual editing and multimedia programs in which one can place many business objects, establish relationships among them, edit the model, validate the model, and distribute the model amongst many individuals are complex enough that there are many sequences of events that can occur.

[19] The viewpoints approach is based on viewing a system from an ethnographic studies perspective. It emphasizes how an individual works to solve a problem.

DOCUMENTING USE CASES

An important aspects of use cases is documenting them in a fashion that provides greater understanding of the domain. Since a picture is worth a thousand words, a highly useful and informative way to document use cases is to use the UML notation.

Use-Case Diagram

A use-case diagram shows how use cases are related to each other and to actors. An example use-case diagram is illustrated in Figure 3-3. An actor is illustrated as a stick figure person, even in situations in which it is an external system. Individual use cases are represented as ovals labeled with the name of the use case. Lines connect actors with the use case they initiate or connect the use cases with the participating actors from which the system makes requests. If the interaction is unidirectional, the line is terminated by an arrow. The direction of the arrow is from the requestor to the provider of a service. In the example, the bank manager makes a request of the system that makes a request of the account database.

In some situations, the interaction is bidirectional and the link is illustrated as a double-headed arrow. In this case, the actor can generate a request of the system or it can request the actor to take some action. This might be the case in which the manager wants to monitor specific accounts for specific activities and the system generates alerts requesting manager attention when specific events occur. The system may perform periodic queries against the account database to identify when the event occurs.

Use-case and actor generalizations/specializations that were previously identified are also documented in use-case diagrams. The relationship is illustrated with a triangle at the end of a line. The lines originate at the specializations and point with the triangle towards the generalization. In the example, the actor bank employee is a generalization of the specialization actors bank teller and bank manager. The idea here is that some use cases (look up account balance, change customer address, etc.) can be performed by either a bank manager or bank teller.

UML has a mechanism for illustrating supporting use cases, that is, a notation for the extends and includes relationships. A dashed arrow is drawn between the supporting use case and the use case that it supports with the arrow labeled by the kind of relationship being represented. The direction of the arrow indicates the direction of the relationship. For use cases that extend another, the arrow points from the extending use case. The arrow points towards the included use case. This is illustrated in Figure 3-4. The Make Deposit use case includes the Get Customer Info use case. The Make Electronic Deposit extends the Make Deposit use case by adding functionality.

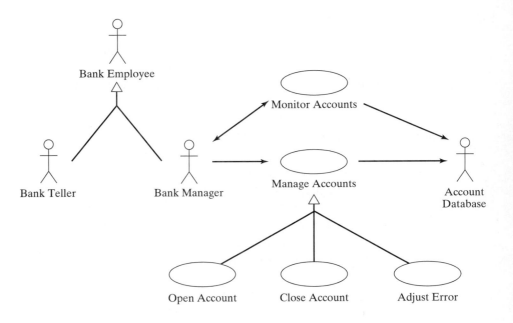

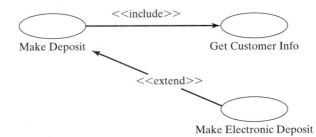

Figure 3-3   An Example Use-Case Diagram Illustrating Actor Generalization/Special-ization, Use-Case Generalization/Specialization, and Bidirectional Interaction Between a Use Case and an Actor.

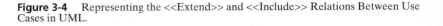

Figure 3-4   Representing the <<Extend>> and <<Include>> Relations Between Use Cases in UML.

Sequence Diagram: Documenting the Details

The details of a use case can be documented utilizing sequence diagrams.[20] A sequence diagram shows the order in which messages are exchanged between the actor(s) and the system. The sequence diagram has the participants represented by rectangular boxes. From that rectangular box, there is an extended vertical dashed

---

[20] Sequence diagrams are further discussed in Chapter 7.

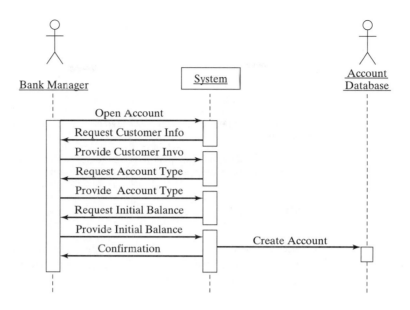

Figure 3-5   Sequence Diagram Illustrating the Detailed Interaction Between the System and Actors for the Open Account Use Case.

line. Message exchanges between participants are illustrated as directed arrows and are labeled by the message being communicated. The sequence of messages is read from the top down; thus, time elapses from top to bottom. Also when the dashed line is replaced with a rectangle, this means that the object is active and using resources during that time period.

An example of a sequence diagram capturing the open account use case is illustrated in Figure 3-5. This example shows how a bank manager requests the system to create a new account. The system asks for information about the customer, which the bank manager provides. The system then requests the bank manager to identify the type of account, which the bank manager provides. The system requests the initial balance information, which the bank manager provides. Once all of the information has been acquired, the system requests the account database to create a new account. The bank manager is then informed by the system that an account has been successfully created.

Textual Description

In addition to graphic representations of use cases, it is common practice to use textual descriptions of individual use cases. A textual description contains the information identified in the previous section. A typical template is illustrated in Figure 3-6. The key value of textual descriptions is that more information is captured than in graphical descriptions. As a result, most practitioners use a combination of use-case

Use-Case Name

Description: A one or two sentence description of the use case.
Actors: Identifies the actors participating in the use case.
Includes: Identifies the use cases included in it.
Extends: Identifies the use case that it may extend.
Pre-Conditions: Identifies the conditions that must be met to invoke this use case.
Details: Identifies the details of the use case.
Post-Conditions: Identifies the conditions that are assured to hold at the conclusion of the use case.
Exceptions: Identifies any exceptions that might arise in execution of this use case.
Constraints: Identifies any constraints that might apply.
Variants: Identifies any variations that might hold for the use case.
Comments: Provides any additional information that might be important in this use case.

Figure 3-6   Template for Documenting Use Cases.

diagrams to provide an overview of the system, sequence diagrams to capture the interactions, and textual descriptions to capture the pre-conditions, post-conditions, exceptions, invariant conditions, and variations.

GUIDELINES FOR DEVELOPING USE CASES

This section presents a set of practices the authors have found useful in developing use-case descriptions. The guidelines are presented here to help avoid analysis paralysis. Analysis paralysis occurs when the analyst is unable to write any scenarios or creates too many detailed scenarios. The purpose of use-case modeling is to understand the external behavior of the system. The later stages will be much easier if the up-front requirements are clear and unambiguous.

The following sections provides guidelines for problem areas that many people encounter when trying to develop use-case descriptions. The basic areas are

- Avoiding analysis paralysis
- Identifying actors
- Identifying use cases
- Establishing use-case bundles
- Developing use-case details
- Identifying supporting use cases
- Developing boundary use cases

Avoiding Analysis Paralysis

The following guidelines are specifically targeted to avoid analysis paralysis:

1. Write two or three of the most common simple transactions first.
2. Try to create more "abstract" scenarios when two or three scenarios look very similar.

3. Be cautious of creating more than 30 use cases to cover the fundamental system actions.

4. Additional use cases for unusual events should be chosen with care and kept to a manageable number.

5. Perform the analysis in an incremental fashion. First develop a primary, high-level, essential use-case model. Second, use that model to develop a primary and secondary, low-level, essential use-case model. Third, use the resulting model to guide development of the primary, low-level, concrete use cases. Finally, use that model to develop primary and secondary, low-level, concrete use cases.

6. Within a model, develop it iteratively. Provide very brief descriptions initially and then refine them.

Identifying Actors

It is critical to identify all external entities that will interact with the system. Each external entity is an actor. As actors are identified, they must be documented. In particular, we must identify all of the responsibilities that each has to fulfill using the system or must provide to the system. This helps identify the set of actions that the actor will take with regard to the system. Some guidelines follow.

1. Identify the actors first, then document their responsibilities. This prevents us from getting too involved in documenting one actor and forgetting others.

2. Focus efforts on actors that initiate actions on the system. These are the easiest actors to identify and if not identified here are likely to remain missed for a long time. Other actors from which requests are made will show up later in the process if missed here.

3. Identify the different roles that a single individual might take with respect to the system and introduce actors for each role. This helps identify different modes of operation that the system might have to exhibit.

It is often difficult to identify all actors that interact with a system. In this section, four high-level categories of users are discussed to help give a systematic way of identifying actors.

- Users

  Though we can think of a specific individual as a user, we want to view these individuals with respect to the role that they play with respect to the system. Thus, a person that adds data, uses the data, and generates reports is acting in three different roles that will be reflected as three different actors. It is easy to overlook individuals that employ the system. Given the large variety of roles for possible users, we can only give a short list of use subcategories that may be helpful.

- Targeted end-users
- Administrators
- Managers
- Customers[21]

Each of the above subcategories can describe different individuals and encompass multiple actors to capture the various roles of each individual.

- Applications

  All external applications (both individual processes and software systems) that interact with the system are actors.[22] For the moment, we must ignore machine boundaries because they have not been established. This means that applications that will eventually run on the same platform as our system are treated as external applications from the perspective of our system boundaries.

  Care must be taken to establish if different processes of a given external system are directly involved, as each of those will be a separate actor. Do not include processes within the hypothetical system being described (even if you think they will be there) because the purpose here is to establish the application domain. That is, we wish to draw a boundary between the application and the outside world.

- Devices

  Identify all devices that interact with the system. Normally, this does not include things like monitors, keyboards, mice, and other standard user interface types of devices.[23] Instead, we are talking about external sensors and actuators.

- External Events (e.g., Cron)

  As we are building more real-time and asynchronous interactive systems, the recognition of external events as potential actors is becoming more important. For example, it is a common situation that a system activity is initiated by the passage of time. As a result, time can be treated as though it were actor. The authors call that actor cron after the UNIX mechanism for invoking functionality at particular times.[24] While cron may be implemented as a timer within the completed system, the timer is still driven by

---

[21] The authors have worked upon systems in which the customer required (demanded) an interface that would enable them to gain insights into the system and how the users employ it. Despite the cost and effort in creating those interfaces, most of them were never used by anyone other than system testers.

[22] This does not include the services of the operating system or the framework. Instead, we are talking about business applications that the system may need to interact with it to accomplish its business goals.

[23] User interface devices are important if one is developing user interface frameworks. Generally, one can assume that an appropriate set of framework classes will handle the interaction with these devices. It is recognized that some people treat devices as interfaces to actors. This practice allows a single sensor to serve several different roles with respect to the system.

[24] Cron is named after the titan Cronus, the son of Uranus and Gaea. He was the Greek god of fate.

a clock external to the program. Cron can be used to capture periodic activities and time outs. If more than one periodic trigger is needed, then multiple cron actors can be introduced.

These categories are to be used to help identify actors in a system manner. These categories are common enough across systems that using them as a trigger will allow discovery of actors.

Identifying High-Level and Essential Use Cases

From a modeling perspective, a use case is to capture the series of interactions between an actor and the system that achieves some useful business goal for the initiator of the interaction. The identification of responsibilities of the actors is a good base from which to find reasons for the actor to interact with the system. For each actor, ask the following questions:

- What are the processes that they participate in that achieves some business goal?
- How in the process do they use the services of the system to complete their tasks in achieving the goal?
- What are the fundamentally different processes that they participate in?
- What is the initial event that starts the process?
- What is the event that starts the series of interactions with the system?

Each process that achieves a useful business goal is definitely one use case. The other fundamentally different processes in which they participate usually results in other use cases. Though the standard practice of documenting use cases is to start from the external event to the system, in certain circumstances, one may want to document the use case from the external event to the actor.

For documenting the use cases identified, one can simply construct a table[25] of (1) name of the use case, (2) initiating actor, (3) service request to event (action) that an actor initiates, (4) a short description, and (5) the business goal of that initial service request or event. This table is used to develop the use cases. There will be at least one use case for each event; but in certain circumstances, more than one use case may be needed to capture the necessary information.

While it is our goal to identify all use cases each actor can initiate, it is often the case that some uses of the system will be overlooked. As a result, this table will be updated with new entries as the use-case model is further developed in later steps. Some simple guidelines for performing this step follow:

1. When identifying the use cases, give a descriptive name and a one or two sentence description of each. Name use cases based upon the goal the

---

[25] The authors also add economic value to the customer, frequency of use, usage distribution to this table to help prioritize the use cases (corresponding to feature), and to size performance requirements.

actor is attempting to achieve and, if necessary, to distinguish variations, the circumstance in which it is invoked. Use a verb to start the name of the use case. The one or two sentence description serves to identify the approximate interaction that is to be captured in the use case. All of this information should appear as separate columns in the table.

2. Do not jump ahead and use the template described in a later step of this approach as your sole mechanism for documenting these use cases. It is necessary to get a good overview of the use cases (such as provided in a table) to accomplish the next steps.

3. Do not introduce too much detail in the basic descriptions. It is normal for a description to seem trivial by the time one completes documenting a use case. The value of keeping it simple is to give us a mental nudge when we are bogged down in details later.

4. It is important to distinguish the service request or event notification the actor is initiating from the manner (action) in which the actor invokes the request or event notification. In many cases the same service request can be invoked in multiple fashions: by keystrokes, menu items, or buttons. However, the resulting activities of the system are identical. It is this later component that we are attempting to capture in use cases.

5. Avoid technology-dependent use cases[26] (load, save, start up, and shutdown). We are still addressing business use cases. There is not enough information available to effectively identify appropriate behavior. These use cases will be the last ones to be developed because we must wait until sufficient details are known to identify what information must be initialized during startup and preserved during shutdown.

6. Identify general activities first. These general activities constitute high-level use cases that are actually defined by a set of low-level use cases.[27] The low-level use cases are where the specific activities are identified. (Example, managing accounts is a high-level use case while adding an account, updating an account, and deleting an account are low-level use cases that establish detailed activities for managing an account.)

7. Immediately document actors identified as a result of describing a use case. These actors must be documented in terms of what actions they are required to provide.

8. If multiple actors can initiate the same set of actions, introduce an abstract actor of which all the others are specializations. This simplifies development of the use cases later and provides insight into various

---

[26] According to some experts, there are various kinds of use cases. For the use-case experts, we are working on essential use cases and not on real use cases at this time.

[27] There is great controversy over which use cases need to be documented. We suggest that you use common sense instead of following some insane rules with a million exceptions. The use case is to help us bound the business domain and ease design. Do the use cases that are consistent with these goals.

degrees of access to system functionality that various individuals are provided.

Establishing Use-Case Bundles

This activity is optional and should only be performed if one is dealing with a very large-scale system that involves hundreds of use cases.[28] Getting a handle on them all can be a daunting task. The goal is to partition the use cases into meaningful packages that can be understood. Each package constitutes a context.

In this activity we must adopt a set of criteria that produces an effective organization of the use cases. The criteria identified in the section where context was introduced should be considered. Some things to keep in mind when selecting criteria by which to develop bundles are

- No use-case bundle should contain an excessive number of use cases (such as might result from describing the whole system). This defeats the purpose of partitioning the domain in the first place.
- It is also not particularly useful to have bundles that only contain one or two use cases. Again, this defeats the purpose of partitioning the use cases. We won't be able to see the forest for all of the trees.
- The bundles have to make sense from a domain perspective. It does not help to have disparate use cases bundled together without some underlying aspect of the domain unifying them all.

Developing Use-Case Details

Once we have identified the use cases and organized them into meaningful bundles, we can begin to develop detailed descriptions of each use case. Work with one bundle at a time as documented in your context diagram. Often, if these cases are well developed, some members of a development team can proceed with other analysis activities while the remaining bundles are being documented.

We suggest using the template illustrated in Figure 3-6. It captures all of the information associated with use cases, organizes that information in a fashion consistent with how details are identified, and provides a comments section where additional information can be recorded. Use of this template helps assure that all use cases are documented in exactly the same fashion. Some basic guidelines follow.

1. When filling out the template, do not leave portions of the document that you have established that do not apply blank. An appropriate notation should appear in that portion—this lets others know that it has actually been considered.

---

[28] Even with 30 use cases, it is not unusual for the context diagram to span multiple pages. The placement of use cases on the various pages can follow the same guidelines presented here.

2. Start each use case on a new page. In actual practice, use cases get rewritten many times before they've become stable. Starting a new use case on a new page allows us to print only the changed case without getting the following use cases disorganized or killing an extra tree by printing out all of the use cases.
3. Think of the use-case description from the actor's perspective.
4. Emphasize interactions (service requests) and events between the system and the actor without decomposing the internal processing of the system.
5. Discussion of internal processing or design decision may be necessary and is permissible (by our practical use of this technique) to find participating actors, but it should be done with the understanding of the consequences (i.e., early design commitment) and must be documented in the details section.
6. Variations of the use case that will not be covered with independent use cases should also be documented in the variant section.

Additional Details for Primary and Secondary, Essential, High-Level Use Cases.   As stated previously, use cases are easiest to develop in an iterative fashion. In each iteration, the goal is to provide greater detail about the use case. If one is using the template presented above, the first few passes will concentrate on the top half of the template. In particular, we focus on the following sections of the template: Actors, Includes, Extends, Pre-Conditions, and Post-Conditions. This allows us to develop details and get them in a steady state before we tackle the lower half of the template, which are closely related to the upper half. Some guidelines to following during the early iterations are

1. Start simple and slowly introduce complexity. Focus first on the simple case where everything is perfect and no problems exist. It is not a bad idea to give a very brief set of details initially for each use case, focusing only on course features. This allows one to identify supporting use cases that simplify the process by extracting common details into other use cases.
2. Worrying about screens can lead to difficulty in writing the use case. Often, one gets about halfway through the use case and then starts describing what some screen looks like. The description can go on for pages if the screen layout is complex. Instead, one should only identify the objects present on the screen. Even then, only focus on those that apply to the use case. Don't worry about the layout of the buttons and fields on the screen. It is the interaction with the screen that is important in the use case. That can be done as a figure in the comment section of the use-case description or in a separate description from the use case.
3. Including lots of ifs and jumps in the details interferes with understanding the domain. Almost everyone has heard of spaghetti code, but using ifs and jumps in use cases leads to spaghetti text. The problems are the same between spaghetti code and spaghetti text—no one can understand what is intended (not even the author).

4. It is important to label each step appearing within the details section of the template with a number. This allows us to make cross-references to that step in other sections of the use case (and across use cases). This is extremely significant when it comes to identifying exceptions and constraints.

Additional Details for Primary and Secondary, Concrete, Low-Level Use Cases. When dealing with primary and secondary, concrete, low-level use cases we are introducing details that border on design. At this point, we are looking into the structure of the system rather than the system itself. For example, some messages may be translated into service requests on domain objects that are captured within the system. For example, if we have an account object then we may include within the use-case details a statement to the effect that the account object is sent an update method. Some guidelines that apply for these use cases are given below.

1. The development of these use cases should only be attempted by individuals with significant design skills. An extremely common problem encountered is for a poor design to be specified in these use cases.
2. Frequent use of the word system in each detailed description indicates another problem. Usually, there is an element missing from the design. This missing element is often a control object that manages an interaction among many different objects. If these control objects are not introduced into the model, the result is a bloated system object that has to manage interactions among hundreds of objects.
3. For each step in the details section, identify what errors or alternatives can occur. Each error is examined in terms of what actions should be taken to keep the model consistent. The information necessary to identify what actions should be taken are often clear from the context in which the error occurs.
4. Capture exceptions in a table that includes three columns: the step in which the error occurs, a label for the error, and the actions that should be performed. As was the case with the details section, it is useful to number each step in the actions to be performed (starting at 1 for each exception).
5. If the detail section of a use case includes another use case, identify all of the exceptions that the included use case can throw for that step. This allows the including use case to identify the error condition to which it must react. Of course, these exceptions will be identified in the exceptions section of the description for the included use case.

Identifying Supporting Use Cases

Supporting use cases are use cases that are included in other use cases or extend another use case. We are concerned with three different kinds of use cases: included, extending, and generalizing. Some guidelines for identifying and using supporting use cases follow.

1. View includes as a relation that identifies a use case that acts like a sub-routine to other use cases. Typically, included use cases do not have actors that initiate them. We can consider these use cases as inheriting actors.
2. The pre-conditions section of the use-case description should identify what information is required for this use case to execute normally. If we are writing a "save" use case, one piece of information that might be required is the filename.
3. In some cases, a number of use cases all share a common structure with the exception of some minor additional steps. These cases can be simplified as an extension of a common core use case. In this case, the use case exploits the details of another use case and identifies where the additional details are incorporated.
4. The pre-condition section of a use case that extends another identifies the condition that determines if the extension should be invoked.
5. In some cases, the same general activity may take place in several use cases, but they have significantly different details depending upon the entities that participate in them. Even though generalizations should have been identified earlier than this point, it is still a good idea to examine the use cases to determine if new generalizations can be added.

Developing Boundary Use Cases[29]. The most common situation encountered among people writing use cases for the first time is that they immediately start writing use cases for starting and stopping the system. The main problem is that they don't even know what the system is to do, yet they are worried about what initialization activities have to take place. Some guidelines to establish when boundary use cases should be developed are

1. Initialization activities are highly design dependent. If one is developing essential use cases, then there will not be sufficient information to identify what actions should be performed during startup and shutdown. These events should not be developed for essential use cases.
2. If one is developing concrete use cases, the boundary use cases should only be addressed once all of the essential and secondary use cases have been developed. At this point, one has sufficient detail to identify if connections to external actors should be created during initialization or not, if specific structural details have to be constructed, and so on.

CONTRACTS

Contracts are a mechanism that was introduced by Bertrand Meyers in the development of Eiffel to develop reliable, extensible, and reusable software modules. The

---

[29] The authors use the term *boundary* to indicate an activity that occurs at the beginning and end of system activities.

idea has been adopted by others in the development of the (BON) method for object-oriented analysis and design.

The basic idea is that a contract is a formal agreement that expresses the rights and obligations between a client and a provider of a service. The contract establishes the conditions under which a service is provided. It identifies what conditions (pre-conditions) the client must satisfy for the request to be successfully completed and what the provider of a service guarantees for a result (post-condition) if the pre-condition were met. It can be summarized as follows:

> If a calling routine promises to call our service with the pre-condition satisfied, then the service (method) promises to return a final state in which the post-condition is satisfied.

The reliability concept of contracts is based on the following principles:

- A software system or software element is not correct or incorrect per se. A software system or element can only be consistent or inconsistent with its specification.
  Correctness should actually be applied to the software and its specification.
- For a program to be correct, any execution of it starting in the state where the pre-condition is true results in a state where the post-condition is true.
- The pre-condition states the properties that must hold before the service is called.
  This is the obligation of the caller.
- The post-condition states the properties that must hold after the service has executed.
  This is the obligation of the method being executed.
- Under no circumstances shall the body of the service (method) ever test for the pre-conditions.
  This prevents unnecessary defensive programming.
- Assertions are not an input checking mechanism. A pre-condition is a software routine to software routine specification. It will not handle human errors.
- Assertions are not control structures. Assertions are not used for flow control. A run-time assertion violation is a bug in the program.
- Every feature appearing in a pre-condition must be available to every client, that is, the client must be able to validate each feature of a pre-condition.
- Invariant condition must be satisfied by both the constructors and all the methods.

The use of contracts changes development from a defensive programming activity to a trusted programming activity.

A simple example for computing the square root of a number illustrates the use of contracts. The conventional approach taken in defining a subroutine for computing the square root captures two separate tasks: (1) finding and returning the square root when passed a non-negative number and (2) returning something reasonable when passed a negative number. The first task is well understood. The second task, though, is not. The key problem is that the supplier doesn't know what constitutes a reasonable result from the perspective of the requester.

In a perfect world, pre-conditions and post-conditions would be all that is necessary to establish guaranteed services. However, the real world is another matter. For example, connections between two machines can be lost, resources can be unavailable, or a signal is received from hardware. The situations in which a service provider is unable to meet its obligations is termed a failure.

The contractual approach for dealing with failures is for the service provider to raise an exception that identifies the failure. This provides a consistent error handling approach from the service providers perspective. The exception is then handled by the client in a fashion that is appropriate for the specific client. As a result, various clients can deal with the exception in their own ways.

The development of use cases identified pre-conditions and post-conditions. These are the same pre-conditions and post-conditions that are used in specifying a contract. The pre-conditions establishes the conditions that must be met by the client before requesting the service. The post-conditions establishes the result of the operation provided by the service provider assuming the pre-condition has been met. The operation identifies what transformation, function, or service is provided. The exceptions section of the use-case description identifies the failures that the service provider admits can occur while providing a service.

From the perspective of understanding the system, the use of contracts is especially useful. The contracts identify the specific services the system will provide, what the requester of a service must assure to get the service, and what exceptions will be raised when the system fails. In short, it defines the system interface.

RECOMMENDED APPROACH

This chapter has presented use cases and contracts as a means for bounding the business domain. The recommended approach is

1. Develop a primary, essential, high-level use-case model.
2. If the business domain is not well understood, use the model of step 1 to develop a primary and secondary, essential, low-level use-case model.
3. If the technology is not well understood, use the model of step 2 to develop a primary, concrete, low-level use-case model.
4. If reliability is an issue, use the models of step 2 and step 3 to help develop a secondary, concrete, low-level use-case model.

In developing any of the above use-case models, the following guidelines are recommended.

1. Write two or three of the most common simple transactions first.
2. Try to create more "abstract" scenarios when two or three scenarios look very similar.
3. Be cautious of creating more than 30 use cases to cover the fundamental system actions.
4. Additional use cases for unusual events should be chosen with care and kept to a manageable number.
5. Within a model, develop it iteratively. Provide very brief descriptions initially and then refine them.

Once use cases have been identified, use them to establish system level contracts. In the contracts, identify (1) the pre-conditions, (2) the post-conditions, (3) the operation, and (4) exceptions.

EXAMPLE

The lawn mowing example of the previous chapter was presented to demonstrate how a real-world situation could be modeled using an object-oriented way of organizing reality. Knowing or having the ability to model such a situation is not sufficient reason for building a system. It is necessary to establish a business value that justifies the initial development of this model and its transformation into a system. So what kind of business value can be established to justify a system that describes how a family deals with the situation of mowing the lawn?

In this chapter, we will generalize this situation into a home care system. The goal of this home care system is to acquire better insight into how and why a family spends its money.[30] The system may include other home care activities like painting the walls, fixing the plumbing, adding extensions, replacing appliances, and other common activities. In terms of our stated business value for the system, this allows the system to capture how the home is maintained. One practical subsystem may be to track the breakage situations that cost money to repair.

In the design and implementation of this model, we will use a simulation approach to the design of the system.[31] For a standard simulation, there is one key actor: a simulation clock. The simulation clock drives the system from a time-dependent aspects; however, we want our system to also react to asynchronous events. To

---

[30] Because this is an example that we don't have to sell to management or actually implement, we are free to establish the business domain however we wish. Neither of the authors would actually want to go to management and explain that we want to implement a lawn mower simulation.

[31] The simulation clock and the examine surroundings daemon are both examples of actors (cron) that correspond to external events, namely the passage of time. This allows us to focus on what happens as a result of time passing without worrying about how it is implemented within the system. We also won't have spontaneous events getting generated by the system without an external source creating the conditions for creation of the event. Spontaneous events are rather difficult to explain and code.

handle these asynchronous events, we will add another daemon called asynchronous event daemon.

This is how the two actors (or event generators) works:

- The simulation clock is a periodic timer that periodically sends a message to the system indicating the current simulation increment. The system responds to this event by informing all active objects in the simulation to perform the actions appropriate for the current time in the simulation.
- The asynchronous event daemon sends an event notification to the system when an event occurs. Anything can register an event with the asynchronous event daemon. The system responds by having all the system parts examine the environment to determine if some action needs to be taken.

For example, if the laundry is done every day at 9 PM; the simulation clock can be used to initiate the correct behavior. Similarly, if the washing machine breaks down (causes an event), the asynchronous event daemon can be used to notify the system. [Note that this system is very inefficient as it will still need to be observed.]

In the previous chapter the mother, Jane, noticed that the lawn needed mowing. Does this make Jane an actor with respect to our system? Actually, Jane is a part of our system in the sense that she is one of the objects that participates in the system. Does this make the lawn one of our actors because we could say that the lawn told Jane that it needed cutting? We could take this perspective, but that decision could lead to the situation in which everything around the house is an actor with the possible exception of the family members. We decided to have the lawn send an event to the asynchronous event daemon. Then we will assert that it was the receipt of an event (i.e., a message) from the asynchronous event daemon that caused Jane to look at the grass, observe that it was too tall and, hence, decide that it needed mowing. This, of course, assumes that Jane was outside at the time she received the message to examine her surroundings. [32]

These two actors together can drive the simulation in non-repetitive fashion; that is, the effects of these two actors can combine. For example, the clock simulation can schedule John to activate his conditional mow the lawn service, which is state dependent on every Saturday at 2:35 PM. But we can also use the asynchronous event handler to change John's state by sending an event on a rainy Saturday that will prevent John from mowing the lawn that day.

To make the model effective for use cases, we add two more actors[33]:

- Observer, which subscribes to and gets updates on the status of the simulation.

---

[32] If Jane had been inside the house at the time, she might have noticed that the carpet needed vacuuming.

[33] We can also argue that a good reason for separating the two roles is that it might be possible to replace the human that is fulfilling the role of director with an external program (scenario generator). Likewise, the observer might be replaced by a system that collects data from the simulation for use in statistical studies of simulation results.

- Director, which sends commands to the system to control the evolution of the simulation.

Based on these descriptions, we have four actors: (1) simulation clock, (2) asynchronous event daemon, (3) observer, and (4) director. We have also identified the basic functional response of the system to messages from these actors. Now we will define them in more details.

The functional response of the system due to messages from the simulation clock is the *tick*.

- The system responds by running the simulation forward in time one increment of simulation time.
- The system forwards simulation information requested by the observer to the observer.

The functional response of the system due to messages from the asynchronous event daemon is the *look*.

- The system responds by having all self-directed objects examine their surroundings and responds to any situation that they may identify by assigning and scheduling work.

The functional responses of the system due to messages from the observer[34] is *subscribe*.

- The system stores the subscription so that it can start forwarding state change information to the observer.

The functional responses of the system due to messages from the director is the set.

- The system sets the appropriate simulation variable. These messages are used to trigger the primary high-level essential use cases.

The use-case diagram for our use cases is given in Figure 3-7. As can be seen from the figure, we have kept the number of use cases to a minimum while capturing the key details of the system.

The use cases are documented textually as well. We use Table 3-1 to identify the information captured in the text. The use-case descriptions are given in Figures 3-8 through 3-11 The description identifies the case, provides a very high-level description of it, identifies the actors involved, the pre-conditions, the details, the

---

[34] We could add a start and stop message to be sent from the observer to the system for starting and stopping the simulation. These messages would have the effect of sending a start and stop message to the simulation clock and the observe surroundings daemon.

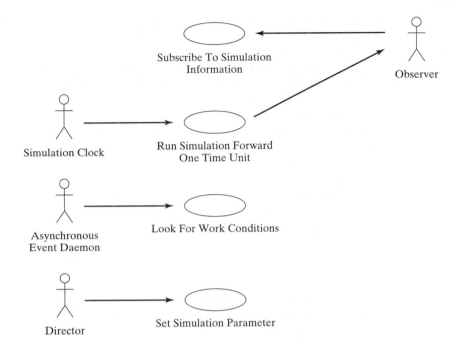

Figure 3-7   Use-Case Diagram for the Primary, High-Level, Essential Use Cases of the Lawn Mower Example.

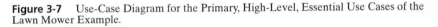

Look for Work

Description: This use case establishes what work is to be performed within the simulation as a result of simulated people observing the simulated surroundings.
Actor: Asynchronous event daemon.
Pre-Conditions: None.
Details:
   1. The asynchronous event daemon sends a look message to the system.
   2. Every person at the home looks in the immediate surroundings for something that is not in a correct state (check environment).
   3. If a work item is identified, the work item is scheduled to be performed (schedule work).
Post-Conditions: Any work items within the location of a person is scheduled to be addressed.
Comments: If we allow the observer to start and stop the simulation, then a pre-condition would be that the simulation is running.

Figure 3-8   Textual Description of the Look for Work Use Case.

post-conditions, and any comments. Those areas that do not apply (pre-conditions) are not left blank but are filled in with appropriate notations so that we know that this aspect has been considered. In this case, we do not have any pre-conditions that must hold for the message to be handled.

Run Simulation Forward One Time Unit

Description: This use case details how the simulation is kept current with the simulation time.
Actor: Simulation clock, observer.
Pre-Conditions: Sufficient real-time has passed from last update.
Details:
    1. The simulation clock sends a tick message to the system.
    2. Every object computes their current state taking into account the change in simulation time.
    3. The system forwards state change information to the observer.
Post-Conditions: The model has been updated to reflect the new simulation time.
Comments: If we allow the observer to start and stop the simulation, then a pre-condition would be that the simulation is running.

Figure 3-9   Textual Description for the Run Simulation Forward One Time Unit Use Case.

Set Simulation Parameter

Description: This use case allows the simulation to be tailored based on user settable parameters.
Actor: Director.
Pre-Conditions: None.
Details:
    1. The director sends a message to the system identifying a simulation parameter and a value.
    2. The system sets the simulation parameter to the new value.
Post-Conditions: A value of a simulation parameter is changed and the simulation continues taking into account the new value for the parameter.
Comments: Example parameters might include the real clock time between simulation clock ticks (e.g., 3 seconds must pass between ticks) and the simulated time increment for the simulation clock (e.g., each tick corresponds to one hour) or tailor what is to occur in a simulation (e.g., it is supposed to rain on Saturday).

Figure 3-10   Textual Description for the Set Simulation Parameter Use Case.

Subscribe to Simulation Information

Description: This use case describes how the system is informed about what simulation information the observer wants from the simulation.
Actor: Observer.
Pre-Conditions: None.
Details:
    1. The observer sends a subscribe message to the system.
    2. The system configures itself so that all information of the requested type is passed to the observer.
Post-Conditions: The system is configured to forward specific information to the observer.
Comments: None.

Figure 3-11   Textual description for the Subscribe to Simulation Information Use Case.

Now that we have the simulation of Time Forward use case and the Look for Work use case, how do we develop the use case associated with mowing the lawn? The use cases that deal specifically with mowing the lawn are essential low-level use cases that further define how the high-level functionality is achieved. We can model the mowing the lawn scenario described in the earlier chapter with three essential low-level use cases: (1) Check the Lawn, (2) Schedule Mowing the Lawn, and (3) Mowing the Grass.

If we consider the Check Environment step, we should recognize that there are quite a few specialized use cases for this high-level use case. In particular, there are different surroundings that can be examined and the examination requires that a person be in the appropriate location to observe the need. Thus, for example when we are at the outside of the house, we may want to "check the lawn"; however, when we are inside the house we may want to "check the carpet." Hence, we introduce a generalization use case, Check Environment, of which Check the Lawn is a specialization along with other use cases (e.g., Check the Carpet).

The Check the Lawn use case captures the situation in which Jane notices that the lawn needs cutting. This is now a specialized version[35] of Check Environment. Furthermore, the Look for Work use case includes the Check Environment use case.

In our model, the Schedule the Work is also a use case that has a specialized version for the lawn by Schedule Mow the Lawn. This is done by Jane by requesting John to mow the lawn whereby he agrees to schedule his mowing the lawn that evening.

The third use case, Mow the Lawn, captures how the lawn gets mowed. It covers the details about how the father, John, involves the children, and the professional lawn mower, Jack. This is a specialization of the Take Corrective Action use case.[There are a number of other use cases of a similar nature (for example, Vacuum the Floor).]

Of course, the pre-condition for the Take Corrective Action use case is that a work item has been identified. This generalization is included in the Look For Work use case to provide the functionality in which a work task is scheduled to be performed once it has been identified.

A portion of the use-case diagram for our system is illustrated in Figure 3-12. It shows how the Asynchronous Event Daemon triggers the Look for Work use case. This use case includes the Check Environment use case, which is a generalization for the Check the Lawn and Check the Carpet use cases. The Look for Work use case also includes the Take Corrective Action use case, which is a generalization for the Mow the Lawn and Vacuum the Carpet use cases.

These use cases must be documented so that our understanding of what the system is doing is captured. Again, we can turn to Table 3-1 to identify the information that should be captured in Primary Low-Level Essential use cases. The information

---

[35] [This use case is one of several specialized use cases that can potentially occur when we examine our surroundings in the Look for Work use case.]

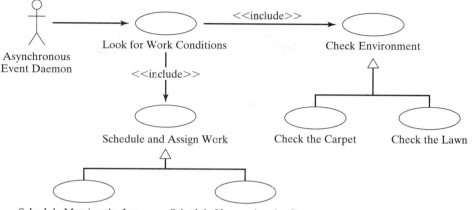

Asynchronous
Event Daemon

Look for Work Conditions

<<include>>

Check Environment

<<include>>

Schedule and Assign Work

Check the Carpet

Check the Lawn

Schedule Mowing the Lawn   Schedule Vacuuming the Carpet

Figure 3-12   Portion of the Use-Case Diagram for the Primary Low-Level Essential Use
Cases Detailing the Low-Level Use Cases Associated with the High-Level Use Look For
Work Conditions Use Case.

Check the Lawn

Description: This use case deals with the situation in which a person observes the lawn
to determine if it needs mowing.
Actor: System.
Specializes: Check environment.
Includes: None.
Extends: None.
Pre-Conditions: *Person* must be in the vicinity of the *lawn*.
Details:
    1. The system sends a message to the person to check the lawn.
    2. The person looks at the height of the lawn.
    3. If the height is greater than some value, the lawn needs mowing, otherwise
    it doesn't.
    4. The person sends a *message* identifying the need to mow the lawn.
Post-Conditions: The need to mow the lawn is established (either it does or it doesn't).
Exceptions: None.
Constraints: None.
Variants: None.
Comments: Should have threshold for the height of the grass be particular to the person.

Figure 3-13   Textual Description of the Check the Lawn Primary Low-Level Essential
Use Case.

that we have to capture includes the name of the use case, a high-level description,
any use-case relationships, the pre-conditions, the details, the post-conditions, constraints, and variants. Again, the template is employed for a textual description. An
example textual description for the Check the Lawn use case is Figure 3-13. The
other use cases discussed above are left as an exercise for the reader.

The Check the Lawn use case demonstrates a tricky point about use cases. In particular, this is a use case that is a specialization of a use case that is included within another use case. A question arises concerning the actor that triggers it. Specifically, who is the actor? Ultimately, in this specific example, this use case is triggered by a message received by the Asynchronous Event Daemon.

SUMMARY

This chapter has introduced use cases as a means of bounding a domain. The fundamental concepts associated with use cases have been defined, namely the goal, system, the actors, use cases, and use-case bundles. They can be summarized as follows:

1. The *goal* is the business value to the "user(s)" of the system who usually initiates the interaction with the system.
2. The *system* is the application with all its associated hardware that will be used by the "users." There are three standard views of the system: black box, white box, and transparent box. Use cases uses the black box view of the system in analysis.
3. An *actor* is external entity that interacts with a system. An actor can be a user, external system, or device. An actor can make a service request of the system, be requested to provide a service, and interact with the system through a complex dialog of service requests between the actor and the system.
4. A *use case* is a description of an interaction that achieves a useful goal for an actor. The actor that initiates the use case is called the initiation actor. In most interactions, the dialog may result in the interaction of the system with other actors; these actors are called participating actors. The interaction assumes that the system is a "black box" and uses domain elements as actors that interact with the system in a request/response manner. A use case identifies the pre-conditions that must exist for it to be valid, the post-conditions that define the state of the system after the use case has concluded, detailed business (non-technology-dependent) that is performed, business exceptions that may arise, and business constraints that apply to the system in reacting to a specific actor request.
5. A *use-case bundle* is a collection of use cases that are highly correlated with some activity or organizing business element. A use-case bundle gives us a way to organize our use cases into collections that will help us better understand the functionality of the system that we are developing.

The various relationships that a use case may hold with other use cases have been introduced. As will be shown in the next chapter, use cases and contracts help us identify objects that will be part of our model.

4

Finding the Objects

The previous chapter presented use cases as a means of capturing a specification model. The material of that chapter was not directly associated with object-orientation other than the fact that UML provides a graphical representation for use cases. Use cases apply to many different paradigms.

This chapter describes the first real step in our method for building an analysis model consistent with the 13 basic principles of object-orientation supported by Java. We begin at a logical starting point—finding the objects.[1] We cover many different techniques for identifying potential categories and types to classify objects in this chapter. The goal here is not to master all of them but to provide a solid background by which developers can direct their efforts. We recommend one technique, recognizing that it isn't the newest, most comprehensive, or trendy approach. Instead, we concentrate on presenting a technique that is easy for someone new to the object-oriented paradigm to apply.

---

[1] We are not really finding objects; we are actually finding categories and types (analysis concepts) that will be implemented using classes and interfaces.

OBJECT-ORIENTED ANALYSIS: MODEL OF AN APPLICATION DOMAIN

When we analyze systems, we create models of application domain of interest to our business. The model can be very specific and highly specialized (i.e., vendor ledger system) or can cover a whole enterprise. In either case, the model represents an aspect of reality and is built in a manner that helps us manage the complexity and understand the business reality. The model is always much simpler than reality, just as any toy model is simpler than the real thing. For example, a toy fire truck is much simpler than the real fire truck. Even sophisticated airplane models are still simpler than real airplanes. In our case, however, if the model is rich enough, we can manipulate the model to help us invent or redesign our businesses.

With traditional analysis methods, we model the world using functions or behaviors as our building blocks. We have seen some of the weaknesses of such a modeling paradigm. With object-oriented analysis, we model reality with objects as our building blocks, hoping to eliminate the shortcomings of a modeling paradigm based on functions. In the Java object-oriented paradigm, we describe our world using the object categories (classes) or object types (Java interface). We assign service prototypes to interfaces, and we assign both attributes (data variables) and services[2] (both the service prototypes and the service methods/implementations) to these object categories (classes). We also define relationships (generalization/specialization, association, and aggregation) between the classes, and interfaces can be organized using generalization/specialization. We capture the description of the service methods (implementations) using either structured pseudo code or UML's extended Harel state diagrams. Then, we model the behavior of the world as a sequence of messages that are sent between various objects that are instances of the various object categories or object types. By using this form of analysis, we can more easily design and program the software in an object-oriented manner to achieve the benefits of flexible and maintainable software.

BUILDING THE OBJECT-ORIENTED MODEL

In traditional textbooks, building the object-oriented model is considered the requirements phase of the project. What makes this phase very confusing to developers is that two very distinct but related activities are taking place simultaneously: problem analysis (domain analysis) and business solution description (product description).

There are at least two reasons to keep these activities non-sequential and non-mutually exclusive. First, a large number of product developments require little or no problem analysis. Usually, problem analysis is applied only to new, difficult, or yet unsolved problems. Companies usually do not waste time or resources on a

---

[2] Services are also called (1) operations (language perspective), (2) functions (imperative programming perspective plus C and C++), and (3) methods (Smalltalk perspective).

problem that is already well understood. Second, when doing problem analysis, most teams initiate the problem analysis. When some part of the problem or problem domain is well understood, the teams start to work on the business solution description to solve that part of the problem. This back-and-forth process gives the team an effective way of monitoring its own progress.

The goal of problem analysis is a relatively complete understanding of the problem and the constraints on the possible business solutions. The goals of business solution description are a correct, complete, unambiguous, verifiable, consistent, modifiable, traceable, organized, concise description of the business solution that is understandable to the customer/user/buyer. This does not mean that the goals of a business solution description are always met, but one should come close.

In problem analysis, the developers/analysts/system engineers acquire knowledge of the problem (and the problem domain) at hand and identify all the possible constraints on the problem's solution. Much of the time is spent interviewing users and business/domain experts and brainstorming ideas. During this period, there is considerable expansion of information and knowledge about the problem to be solved. The issues that need to be addressed during this activity are (1) finding a way of trading off constraints and (2) finding ways to organize the plethora of information and knowledge acquired.

In a business solution description, the developers/analysts/system engineers make some of the difficult decisions on constraint trade-offs and describe the external behavior of the product to be built. In this activity, (1) ideals are organized, (2) conflicting views are resolved, and (3) inconsistencies and ambiguities are eliminated.

The end result of problem analysis and business solution description should be a model that

- Organizes the data into objects and classes and gives the data a structure via relationships of generalization/specialization, aggregation, and association.
- Organizes the services (functions) into classes or interfaces and gives them conceptual grouping via the generalization/specialization hierarchical structure.
- Defines the external interfaces (service prototypes) for all the class and interface services.
- Specifies local functional behaviors (business logic) for the services that an instance of that class must support.
- Captures control or global behavior (event trace diagrams, i.e., sequence diagrams).
- Captures constraints (limits and rules).

In our version of object-oriented analysis for Java programming, we do not differentiate between problem analysis and business solution description; we build a model of reality that should capture both. This is consistent with the idea that a good and effective method should have seamless steps and preferably no transformation from one step to another. The first step in this method is finding the classes and interfaces.

IDENTIFICATION OF OBJECTS, CLASSES, AND INTERFACES

Identifying classes,[3] interfaces, and objects is the most important and difficult step in any method for modeling. Identifying them is important because the requirements specification, design, and code will use them as the building blocks; mistakes in properly identifying them will have an impact on the extensibility and maintainability of the software. Identifying them is difficult (at least for most beginners) as it requires in-depth knowledge and skill in the object-oriented paradigm and the ability to apply it to the applications. It typically takes three months to one year of practice for the necessary skills to mature but can take longer depending on the person's attitude (toward object orientation), aptitude, and amount of on-the-job training/experience.

In theory, identifying objects and classes should not be difficult. We deal with objects and classes every day of our lives. For example, a child's toy (a toy fire truck or a doll) is merely a model of a real world entity (a truck or a person). The toy fire truck has attributes that are either constant (i.e., height, width, color) or variable (i.e., battery level and relative state of newness or disrepair), as well as services (i.e., move forward, move backward, turn on siren). It also has exception conditions such as battery drained, broken wheel, etc.

Making mental models and using abstractions are standard human approaches for dealing with the complexity of everyday life. Therefore, if software professionals understand their application domain, identifying object classes and object types requires merely capturing the relevant models/abstractions of the application-domain needed to solve the problem. Then why is identification still so difficult?

Thinking in terms of objects in everyday life may appear to be easy and natural, but thinking about software development analogies in terms of objects takes some time. When developers first apply an object-oriented method, they are often unsure of what constitutes a software object or class or interface. Even when they know the definition, they are not always sure that something meets the definition of an object or a class or an interface. Furthermore, object-orientation requires a firmer definition of objects than common in daily life. When dealing with the table object, it is not common practice to debate what are the essential characteristics that define a table, but this is exactly what is required in object-orientation.

This difficulty has provoked a philosophical debate and much confusion. There are basically two fundamentally different views of how objects and classes came to being: empiricist and phenomenalist. The empiricist view says that they are out there just waiting to be perceived. According to Betrand Meyers, "the objects are just there for the picking." Therefore, developers must be blinded to them because they

---

[3] Technically, a class is also an object. In the next few chapters, we will treat a class like an object. For the experienced reader, we are really interested in finding classes and not instances of a class in this chapter.

are too accustomed to functional decomposition and are still trying to use functions as their building blocks.

The phenomenalist view says that objects come from both the world and our consciousness through a dialectical process. Other phenomenalists suggest that real-world objects are a reflection of social relations and human thinking processes.

We are members of the phenomenalist school as not only do we believe that objects (really classes and interfaces) come from our consciousness, but we must also now "objectify" the world to get maximum benefit from this new technology. It is this "objectifying" that makes object identification difficult even for experienced object-oriented analysts.

Over the past 10 years, object-oriented practitioners and researchers have developed many techniques (often indirect) to combat this issue. These techniques were based on the assumption that there is a mapping (hopefully, one-to-one) between things that neophytes can identify as well as objects and/or classes that neophytes have difficulty recognizing. This allows the object-oriented neophytes to do useful work while acquiring the skills and experiences to make the full paradigm shift to object-oriented.

Different methodologists have their own favorite approaches, and many of these techniques are tightly coupled to a few approaches. Most books and articles discuss only a small number of these identification techniques, and some approaches are rarely taught. Some of the techniques are well suited for object-oriented design,[4] but less useful during object-oriented domain analysis (i.e., requirements analysis). Some techniques are safe in the sense that they identify minimally false objects and are easy to use but identify only the obvious objects and classes.

Because there is not necessarily an easy one-to-one mapping between objects and classes with "other things," all these techniques have shortcomings, namely, that using these techniques may produce false-positive identification and that none of these techniques provide a complete list of "objects."[5] We believe that there neither is nor will be a technique that will help us find all the classes and interfaces and only all the classes and interfaces. This is consistent with our phenomenalist view; we believe that we will mature our perception of reality via a dialectical process because the real world of objects is a reflection of social relations and our thinking processes. As with most things, it is the responsibility of your management and yourself to manage this risk.

These techniques then give us a list of potential "objects," albeit an incomplete list and may be divided into two categories, current and traditional. Current techniques are the most effective and state-of-the-art, although they require significant training and experience to be used effectively. Traditional techniques are usually highly indirect and are easy to use and misuse, especially for beginners. Miscellaneous techniques are limited in scope, but useful given the right situation.

---

[4] In our definition of design we mean modeling the technology domain.

[5] For example, all the abstractions of concepts or ideas that need to be modeled as objects.

CURRENT TECHNIQUES

Current techniques rely on experience and knowledge of the domain to be captured in the object model. They cover the range from using the things to be modeled to extending existing models of the domain.

Using the Things to Be Modeled

This is the preferred method of experienced object-oriented software engineers. It recognizes that the application domain entities need to be identified before identifying the corresponding objects and categories (classes). This technique is advocated by such noted authors as Coad and Yourdon, Shlaer and Mellor, and so on. This technique is highly effective because it is natural, direct, and reliable. Unfortunately, it tends to help only in finding the terminators and other tangible objects that are the easiest entities to identify and classify. Abstract classes and interfaces are not readily identified using this technique. Furthermore, this technique requires that the user makes the paradigm shift to the object-oriented mindset. Although this paradigm shift should be the ultimate goal, on-the-job training may be very expensive.

The steps of this technique are to

1. Identify individual or group things, such as persons, roles, organizations, locations, logs, reports, forms, etc. in the application domain that is to be modeled.
2. Identify the corresponding objects and categories (classes).

Using the Definitions of Objects, Categories, and Types

This technique assumes that the most effective approach is a direct approach and that the software engineer has experience in identifying objects, categories (classes), and types (interfaces). The technique is very simple; the developer uses object abstraction, knowledge of the application domain, the definition of category (class), and the definition of type (interface) to intuitively identify them. This is the same way experienced developers would recognize functional and process abstractions.

This is a direct and effective approach that provides the best partitioning of the requirements into categories (classes) and types (interfaces). When used properly, this technique produces the fewest false-positive identifications. This technique has no limitations, but it requires a significant paradigm shift for the developer.

This paradigm shift requires significant training, practice, intuition, and experience, which usually takes at least six months of on-the-job training. Moreover, there are no tricks or tools to help in this technique as the tools are designed only to document the results.

Using Object Decomposition

This technique assumes that many objects (thus categories/classes) are aggregates of component objects. Furthermore, it assumes that decomposition is a good way to identify the component objects (thus categories/classes) and that you have some of these aggregate objects (or categories/classes) identified.

The steps of this technique are

1. Find the aggregate objects or categories/classes.
2. Use object decomposition to identify their component objects or categories/classes.

This technique is a natural way to deal with aggregates; unfortunately, not all objects and/or categories are aggregates or components of an aggregate. Furthermore, real world aggregates normally physically contain their components; and because of this property, novices often nest the implementation components within this aggregate when an association relationship may be a better model of the implementation components. This can lead to both subtle modeling issues and technical issues such as recompilation, reuse, and maintenance. Finally, this technique does not support the identification of types/interfaces.

Using Generalization

This technique assumes that objects are identified before their categories (classes) and types (interfaces), that every object is an instance of some category, and that the commonalities among objects can be used to generalize categories.

The steps of this technique are

1. Identify all objects.
2. Look for two or more objects that share the same attributes and services.
3. Generalize these common aspects to form a category (class).
4. To continue finding categories (classes) (see Using Subclasses).

The primary benefit of this approach is that it promotes reuse and supports the development of one or more classification hierarchies.

Using Subclasses

When using subclasses, we skip finding objects and directly start identifying categories (classes). It assumes that separate categories (classes) often contain common resources (i.e., attributes, services, methods, etc.) and that they can be changed into subcategories (subclasses) that inherit the common resources from a common superclass.

The steps of this technique are

1. Identify categories (classes) that share common resources (i.e., attributes, service prototypes, service implementations, aggregation relationships, association relationships, etc.).

   2.   Factor out the common resources to form a superclass (parent) and then
           use generalization/specialization (inheritance) for all categories (classes)
           that share these resources to form simpler subcategories (subclasses).
   3.   If the only common factors are service prototype(s), use the type (inter-
           face) to factor out these common factors.

The key benefit of this technique is reuse, but it has some serious drawbacks.
When misused, it leads to unmaintainable and opaque classes that reuse randomly
unrelated resources that do not logically belong to subcategories (subclasses) of the
same parent category (superclass). It also may produce inappropriate or excessive
generalization/specialization (inheritance) coupling.

Using Object-Oriented Domain Analysis

This technique assumes that an object-oriented domain analysis (OODA) of an
application in the same problem domain has been done previously. Given the
OODA, the steps of this technique are

   1.   Analyze the results of the given OODA (in the same domain).
   2.   Reuse (with or without modification) objects or categories (classes) or
           types (interfaces) from the OODA.

This technique supports reuse and tends to maximize cohesion in categories
(classes) and minimize message and generalization/specialization (inheritance) coupling. If one assumes that the previous OODA is solid, this technique also naturally
gives a "reality check" on the current project as the objects, classes, and interfaces
should be the similar to the ones in the OODA. Thus, considerable time and effort
could be saved if the original OODA is relevant and complete.

Unfortunately, this technique has limitations. Finding adequate and relevant
OODA is not easy. Most systems have either incomplete OODA or no OODA
model at all. For reuse to be effective, the problem domain must be well documented
and understood by the developers. Tailoring for performance and other business
constraints in a specific project may lower reuse. Finally, although it is easier to reuse
then to reinvent, the not-invented-here (NIH) syndrome of many developers must
be successfully overcome.

Reusing an Application Framework

This technique[6] assumes that at least one OODA has been done to create an application framework of reusable classes. An application framework is a reusable

---

[6] This is the technique that Sun Microsystems is trying to support by providing application developers with
the Java Platform, and IBM is trying to do the same at the analysis level with its San Francisco Project.

domain-specific template of classes (categories) and/or subassemblies and all its associated classes (categories) that implement some common capabilities. Because it is domain-specific, it usually applies specifically to applications that are in the same domain.

The steps of this technique are

1.   Identify one or more relevant application frameworks in the same application domain.
2.   Reuse the interfaces (types) and classes (categories) from previously developed frameworks. Note that some of the classes and interfaces may need to be modified to be reused in your specific application.

This technique may be considered an enhancement of the OODA technique described above; thus, it has all the advantages and limitations of the above technique. Moreover, it has additional limitations. Your current developers must be able to identify one or more relevant application frameworks that have been previously developed and stored in a repository. Most likely, not all the needed classes and interfaces will be in the application framework(s) examined. *This is the recommended approach when you are in the design stage of Java software development as the Java platform is very complete.*

Reusing Class Hierarchies

This technique assumes that a reuse repository with relevant reusable class hierarchies has been developed. To use this technique, the steps are

1.   Look for classes (categories) in the reuse repository that can be reused, either with or without modification.
2.   After identifying the classes (categories), attempt to reuse the associated class hierarchy (category generalization/specialization structure).
3.   After modifying the classes (categories), attempt to create new classes or new interfaces (i.e., abstract classes or interfaces) by grouping common attributes and services.
4.   If the classes are parameterized, supply the generic formal parameters. *Note that this is not presently supported in Java.*

This technique has the same advantages as using OODA. In addition, this technique maximizes the use of generalization/specialization (inheritance) and is a natural fit for Smalltalk (an object-oriented language). As with all techniques, it has additional limitations beyond those for OODA. The existing classification hierarchies may not be relevant to the current application. Existing classes (categories) may need to be parameterized, or new subclasses (subcategories) may need to be derived.

Reusing Individual Objects and Classes

If a reuse repository with relevant reusable objects and classes has been developed, we can reuse specific objects and classes.

The steps of this technique are

1. Look for relevant objects and classes (categories) in the reuse repository that can be applied to the application.
2. If necessary, modify the classes (categories).
3. Supply generic formal parameters to parameterized classes as necessary. *Note that this is not presently supported in Java.*

This technique has some very serious shortcomings that will be discussed later in this book.

Using Subassemblies

This technique assumes that developers are incrementally developing subassemblies using a recursive development process. This technique is similar to functional decomposition; instead of a function, take an object and decompose it into other objects (subassemblies). Continue the decomposition until there are only terminal objects (i.e., objects that do not need to send messages to other objects at a lower level) at the leaves of the decomposition.

The steps of this technique are

1. Identify all the objects (classes) at the current level that must remain temporarily incomplete because they depend on one or more as yet unidentified objects.
2. Develop a skeleton specification/design for the services of the temporarily incomplete object using either (1) structured English, (2) an object-oriented specification language such as object-oriented software design language (OOSDL), or (3) a program design language (PDL).
3. Create the appropriate child subassemblies (objects) at the next lower level to handle the messages for the incomplete objects at the higher level.
4. Do step 1 at the current level that has the new subassemblies.

This technique has several advantages. It supports incremental identification of objects (i.e., categories/classes). It also identifies all the subassemblies in an application domain. It is very similar to functional decomposition, so there is less culture shock for developers trained in the structured methodology. However, there are limitations to this technique; it identifies only assembled objects. Thus, one must have some other technique to identify fundamental components of the subassemblies. In addition, interfaces are not identified and associations have a tendency to be made an aggregation.

Using Personal Experience

This technique will eventually become more popular and maybe the most viable of all the techniques given as developers gain more experience in using the object-oriented methodology. It assumes that the developers have previously designed one or more relevant classes in the application domain. To build the new models, the developers reuse some of the objects, classes, and interfaces that have been developed on the previous projects.

The steps of this technique are to

1. Find objects, categories (classes), and object types (interfaces) that correspond to ones found in previous models that are in the same application domain.
2. Modify the classes and interfaces as necessary to support the present project.

By building on one's experience, this technique provides a reasonable "reality check" on the current project. Thus, the quality of the classes and objects may be substantially improved, as they are based on classes and interfaces that are already built and tested. It is also very natural to want to leverage off the application experience of the developer. However, there are drawbacks. This technique assumes relevant previous experience, which is not always present. This is especially dangerous when the previous experience is based on functional decomposition projects, the developers have a tendency to identify suboptimal classes. In such a situation, past experience may be of limited value and possibly even misleading. Moreover, this technique is very informal, and different developers may identify substantially different objects types and object categories given the same starting information; thus, a high subjective technique. Also, it may not minimize the message and generalization/specialization (inheritance) coupling.

TRADITIONAL TECHNIQUES

Traditional techniques focus more on discovering a domain model rather than using existing domain models. We feel that it is a good practice for an individual learning object modeling techniques to understand and apply these techniques before using current techniques.

Using Nouns

Pioneered by Russell J. Abbott and popularized by Grady Booch, this technique was widely used between 1983 and 1986 and was included in many object-oriented development methods. This technique, when coupled with use cases, is particularly easy. In many cases, objects are identified as the use cases are written.

The steps of this techniques are

1. Obtain (i.e., from a requirement document) or explicitly author narrative English text that represents an informal description of the problem to be solved. If use cases were used to scope the domain, then they can serve as the narrative text. The text should use the words of the application domain (i.e., use the terms of the domain experts).

2. Use the nouns, pronouns, and noun phrases to identify objects, categories (classes), and types (interfaces); that is, find the "real-world" objects, categories, and types. Singular proper nouns (Jim, he, she, employee number 5, my workstation, my home) and nouns of direct reference (the sixth player, the one millionth purchase) are used to identify objects. Plural nouns (people, customers, vendors, users, employees) and common nouns (everyone, a player, a customer, an employee, a workstation) are used to identify classes or interfaces.

3. Use verbs (pay, collect, read, request) and predicate phrases (are all paid, have simultaneously changed) to identify the services.

This technique has many advantages. Narrative languages (English, Chinese, French, German, Japanese, etc.) are well understood by everyone on a project and can be an effective communication medium for both technical and nontechnical project staff. Moreover, there usually is one-to-one mapping from nouns to objects or classes or interfaces.

Using nouns requires no learning curve; the technique is straightforward and well defined and does not require a complete paradigm shift for the beginner. Moreover, this technique does not require a prior OODA as you can apply it to an existing requirement specification written for structural analysis and/or any other methodology.

This technique has some shortcomings, however. For one thing, this is an indirect approach to finding objects, interfaces, and classes. Nouns are not always classes or interfaces or objects in the problem domain. Many sentences in a functional specification are in the wrong form for easy identification of the objects, classes, and interfaces. For example, "roll back the transaction" or "the software will compute the average salary." In many cases, the nouns, especially subjects of sentences, refer to (1) an entire assembly or a computer software configuration (i.e., CICS), (2) a subassembly or a software component, (3) an attribute, or (4) a service. Later, we will discuss these shortcomings and how we can address them.

Using Traditional Data Flow Diagrams

This technique is the result of many software developers and managers who had invested a large sum of money in expensive computer-aided software engineering (CASE) tools that supported data flow diagrams (DFDs). In their need to make a transition from functional decomposition requirements analysis methods (i.e., structured analysis) to object-oriented design, they wanted a "holy grail" that would protect their investment and make the transition easier.

This technique comprises the following:

- Terminators on context diagrams (CDs)
- Data stores on DFDs
- Complex data flows on DFDs

Before you use this technique, a structure analysis must be completed and all the CDs and DFDs must be written.

To use this technique, do the following

1. Map each terminator on the CDs to an object to encapsulate the interface.
2. Identify one class to encapsulate the interface of each set of similar or identical "terminator" objects.
3. Map each data store on the DFDs to an object.
4. Map data stores that contain more than one data field to an aggregate object.
5. Map all or part of the data transformation associated with the data store to the service of the object, and, thus, the class.
6. Map complex data flows (i.e., record with numerous fields) to an object.
7. Identify subtransformations associated with the parts of the data flow and then map these subtransformations to services of the object.

The major benefit of this technique is that it requires no paradigm shift by the analysts and developers. If the original DFDs are well constructed, false-positive identification of objects and classes are rare. Finally, there are a lot of projects that already have the CDs and DFDs.

Unfortunately, the shortcoming is also directly related to not making the paradigm shift. Nearly all the DFDs were originally written for functional decomposition, and they have a tendency to create a top-heavy architecture of classes. With functional decomposition, there is a tendency to assume that the stem is an assembly of subassemblies at the appropriate level. Moreover, one tends to assign services at the corresponding level where the subassembly was found. This may cause objects to be identified in the wrong subassembly. Although false-positive identification of objects and classes is rare, not all the objects or classes are identified. The rareness of false-positive identification is totally dependent on the quality of the original DFDs. This is still an indirect method of finding objects and classes; it is based on data abstraction and not on object abstraction.

In many instances, an object or class contains more than one data store. Thus, their attributes may be mapped to objects and classes while their associated objects and classes remain unidentified.

Because the DFDs represent functional decomposition, pieces of an object may be scattered across several DFDs assigned to different persons. Thus, different variants of the same object may be redundantly and independently identified. Finally, transforms are not required to a service of an object; therefore, transforms are often compound operations that need to be assigned to multiple objects. If the objects are not properly identified, this leads to fragmented objects and classes.

Using Class-Responsibility-Collaboration (CRC) Cards

This technique was developed by Rebecca Wirfs-Brock et al. These developers observed that identifying objects and classes is a human activity that can be stimulated by the use of small pieces of paper (i.e., CRC cards or Post-it notes) to represent the objects/classes/interfaces. It was found that by letting the developers handle the CRC cards, developers with experience, creativity, and intuition can often identify new objects/classes/interfaces by noticing holes in the current set of cards. Thus, the cards served both as a vehicle to document the previously identified objects, classes, and interfaces and to stimulate the developers into finding iteratively and incrementally new objects, classes, and interfaces not currently documented.

For the classic version of this technique, do the following:

1. On a CRC card, document the name of the category/type (class/interface) and list both the responsibilities (i.e., services it provides) and collaborators (i.e., objects/classes/interfaces it needs to fulfill its responsibilities).
2. Identify missing categories (classes) and types (interfaces) that should be added to the existing set of CRC cards. Specifically, look for responsibilities that cannot be allocated to existing categories/types (classes/interfaces) and collaborators that have not yet been assigned to a category (class).

For the modern version of this technique, do the following:

1. On a Post-it note, document the name and list the responsibilities of the category/type (class/interface).
2. Position all the Post-it notes on a white board and draw association arcs between the categories (classes) to represent the collaborations.
3. Identify missing categories and types that should be added to the existing set of categories and types. Look for attributes and services that cannot be allocated to the current categories to identify new categories.
   Look at common service protocols to identify new types.

For a use-case version of this technique, do the following:

1. Start the effort as a brainstorming session for categories and types.

   • Identify some candidate categories/types by writing down a list of some of the "nouns" from the problem domain.

- Pick the nouns that have some responsibilities and write them on the cards (Post-it notes).
- Write a short description of the category/type for guidance.

2. Use your use cases to generate scenarios for the system.

- Assign a category/type to a participant
- Act out the scenario and discover the actual responsibilities of each of the category/type.
- Look for attributes and services that cannot be allocated to the current categories.
- Add missing categories to handle these situations as you run through the scenarios.
- Look for common service prototypes among apparent unrelated categories of objects.
- Add missing types to handle these situations as you run through the scenarios.
- Update the Post-it notes as to category/type name, responsibilities, and collaborators as you go through the scenarios.

3. Position all the classes on a white board and draw association arcs between the classes to represent the collaboration.

Some guidelines for using this technique are

- Limit the number of participants to three to six
- Scenarios must be concrete and specific (i.e., use cases must be expanded and real).
- Create a discard pile (not the garbage can; you may want to resurrect a discarded category/type).
- Record each scenario (we like to use sequence diagrams).
- Use a single pen to make changes (this ensures that everyone agrees before changes are made).
- Turn all objections into a concrete scenario (if you cannot show a scenario; it is not real).
- You can consider yourself done when you have a model that can handle all of the use cases.

This technique is inexpensive and easy to use. Little effort is invested in making the categories/types (classes/interfaces), and they can be easily discarded. Also, the method stimulates communication and is not intimidating to beginners.

Historically, this technique is better suited for thinking about and designing classes and interfaces than for identifying them. You must already have objects, classes, and interfaces to use this technique to identify additional objects, classes, and interfaces. Finally, the developers must have significant experience, creativity, and intuition for this technique to be consistently successful. However, the revised version based on use cases described above is very effective. It addresses many of the shortcomings of the original method. *It is this technique that we have been currently using in conjunction with use cases for inexperienced teams.*

RECOMMENDED APPROACHES

Which approach to use depends on the situation and the experience of your team. There is no one approach or one technique that is suitable for all, especially when you take into consideration time to market and cost. In spite of this caveat, we present here the most common preferences. If you have a tested relevant application framework as well as its associated repository developed, the "reusing application frameworks" technique is the best approach. If the frameworks do not exist, then there should be a separate effort using OODA. For the novice, however, this book presents a different approach that uses many of the above mentioned techniques (proven to be more usable by novices to this new object-oriented paradigm).[7]

We start by doing the following:

1. Because most analysts/developers are still given a requirements document in narrative English (native language) that uses the terms of the domain expert, it is not unreasonable to use the "Using Nouns" technique of Abbott/Booch with the caveat that this technique is used to find potential categories and types and will not find all the categories and types.

2. Identifying all candidates for objects, categories, and types in the problem domain by interactive dialog with the domain expert. Remember that both we and the domain expert are dealing with objects, categories, and types every day. Furthermore, "domain experts" make mental models and use abstraction to deal with the complexity of their respective businesses. We want to capture the objects, categories, and types that are in the mental model of the domain experts. If we can do this, we can deliver software to the marketplace faster and enhance that software package faster because it is consistent with the mental model of the domain experts. The goal of this step is to identify all the objects, categories, and types that the domain experts would identify.

---

[7] Many experienced object-oriented practitioners do not use CRC cards as presented in this approach. Instead, they rely on modeling tools that immediately construct UML diagrams for classes and objects. For experienced practitioners, that approach works well. However, after teaching many classes it is clear that the use of CRC cards has lead to greater success for beginners. Because this book is for experienced programmers that are new to this paradigm, we recommend the use of CRC cards until sufficient experience has been gained to move to the direct use of tools.

3. Use the "Using the Things to be Modeled" technique to elicit more potential objects, categories, and interfaces. In an attempt to help us in the identification, some object-oriented pundits have suggested this technique as a way to trigger our recognition of "potential" objects, categories, and interfaces. The categories as given by three leading teams of well-known experts are shown in Table 4-1, Table 4-2, and Table 4-3.

4. As a guide to help eliminate some potential false problem domain classes and interfaces, apply the definition test below. An object can be considered as

   - Any real-world entity
   - Important to the discussion of the requirements
   - Crisply defined boundary

5. If you have done a use-case analysis consider doing these additional steps

   - Use the use cases to generate scenarios
   - Use the scenarios to find missing categories and interfaces
   - Record the scenarios

Table 4-1 Categories According to Ross

Categories	Explanation
People	Human beings who carry out some function
Places	Areas set aside for people or things
Things	Physical objects
Organizations	Collection of people, resources, facilities, and capabilities having a defined mission
Concepts	Principles or ideas not tangible, per se
Events	Things that happen (usually at a given date and time), or as steps in an ordered sequence

Table 4-2 Categories According to Shlaer and Mellor

Categories	Explanation
Tangible	Cars, telemetry data, sensors
Roles	Mother, teacher, programmer
Incidents	Landing, interrupt, collision
Interactions	Loan, meeting, marriage
Specification	Product specification, standards

Table 4-3 Categories According to Coad and Yourdon

Categories	Explanation
Structure	"Kind-of" and "part-of" relationships
Other systems	External systems
Devices	Equipment
Events remembered	A historical event that must be recorded
Roles played	The different role(s) that users play
Locations	Places
Organization units	Groups to which the user belongs

A real-world entity attempts to keep the analysis in the problem domain and helps to eliminate implementation objects (design objects) such as stacks, keyboards, and programming languages. The phrase "important to the discussion of the requirements" helps exclude some of the objects that are not relevant to the present problem. For example, the space shuttle is a real-world entity, but it is hard to believe that it is important to our "mow the lawn" problem domain. The "crisply-defined boundary" comes from Booch and helps to exclude verb phrases such as "going to the store" from being considered an object.

EXAMPLE

Let us return to our lawn mowing example and apply our approach. In step 1, we apply the "using nouns" technique. Here is the statement of the "mowing lawn" example with nouns underlined.

We have a *family* with a *father*, *John*, a *mother*, *Jane*, two *sons*, *Peter* and *Paul*, and two *daughters*, *Elizabeth* and *Mary*. John is an *actor* and Jane is a *dentist*. All the *children* are *students*, and the *family dog* is *Lassie*. Their *family physician* is *Alice*. This family owns a *house* in the *suburbs* of *New York City* and though mowing the *family lawn* is normally a *chore* for the father, it can also be a *paid chore* for any one of the children. However, working within the *neighborhood* is *Jack*, a *professional lawn mower*.

If we now apply our domain knowledge, step 2, we may add lawn mower as a generalization of professional lawn mower, lawn as a generalization of family lawn, and dog as a generalization of family dog. In addition, we may add studio as a place where John works and office as a place where Jane and Alice practice their professions. In step 3, we may add "is_married" relationship and "mowing the lawn" to the list. Table 4-4 illustrates a typical result of applying the combined technique. This may have left us with some "false positives," for example, "mowing the lawn" might be better modeled as a service than as an object.

Table 4-4 Initial List of Candidates for Lawn Mower Example

LIST OF POTENTIAL OBJECTS/CLASSES/INTERFACES	
John	Jane
Peter	Paul
Elizabeth	Mary
Lassie	Family lawn
Jack	Alice
Family	Children
Lawn mower	Physician
Professional lawn mower	Family physician
Dentist	Actor
Mother	Father
Daughter	Son
New York City	Dog
Students	Family dog
House	Suburb
Chore	Paid chore
Office	Studio
Neighborhood	Lawn
"Mowing the lawn"	Is_married

The use cases presented in the previous chapter can be utilized to identify objects following the "using nouns" approach. The Check The Lawn use case shown in Figure 4-1, "Textual Description of the Check the Lawn Primary Low-Level Essential Use Case" is an example. Based on this use case, we would identify lawn, which has been identified above. With respect to the identification of Person, we recognize that it constitutes a good category for John, Jane, Alice, Peter, Elizabeth, and Jack. The use case also identifies a control object, namely a Message object, that captures how communications take place between members of the family.

SUMMARY

The standard four steps that we recommend are

1. Given a requirements document in narrative English (native language) that uses the terms of the domain expert, use the "using nouns" technique of Abbott/Booch with the caveat that this technique is used to find potential "objects" and it will not find all the objects, categories, and interfaces.
2. Identifying all the candidates for objects, categories (classes), and types (interfaces) in the problem domain by interactive dialog with the domain

Check the Lawn

Description: This use case deals with the situation in which a person observes the lawn to determine if it needs mowing.
Actor: System.
Specializes: Check environment.
Includes: None.
Extends: None.
Pre-Conditions: *Person* must be in the vicinity of the *lawn*.
Details:
>   **1.** The system sends a message to the person to check the lawn.
>   **2.** The person looks at the height of the lawn.
>   **3.** If the height is greater than some value, the lawn needs mowing, otherwise
>   it doesn't.
>   **4.** The person sends a *message* identifying the need to mow the lawn.

Post-Conditions: The need to mow the lawn is established (either it does or it doesn't).
Exceptions: None.
Constraints: None.
Variants: None.
Comments: Should have threshold for the height of the grass be particular to the person.

Figure 4-1   Textual Description of the Check the Lawn Primary Low-Level Essential Use Case.

expert. We want to capture the objects, categories, and types that are in the mental model of the domain experts.

3.   Use the "using the things to be modeled" technique to elicit more potential objects, categories, and types.

4.   As a guide to help eliminate some potential false problem domain objects, apply the definition test below. An object can be considered as (1) any real-world entity, (2) that is important to the discussion of the requirements, and (3) with a crisply defined boundary.

When you get more experience, we suggest the following steps for finding a list of candidate objects, categories, and types:

1.   Underline all the nouns in the requirements document or use cases.

2.   Filter the list of nouns to identify things outside the scope of the system. These are usually "external objects" to which the system interfaces. These external objects are useful for the use-case bundle diagram, but it is helpful to keep these objects in the use-case bundle diagram. Technically, they are not objects in the final model of the application/system, so are not objects that we want refined. We can then eliminate them from our list of candidates as part of the application/system.

3.   Usually several different nouns, or noun phrases are used to describe the same thing (concept or idea), a single term must be selected, and the alternative eliminated. For example, the "workplace" and the "office" are

probably the same concept in nearly all problem domains. If a different term is used to describe the same physical thing in a different semantic domain, (i.e., to capture a different concept), you need to capture both concepts. An example of this is if you used *mother* and *dentist* as problem domain terms that apply to Jane in our lawn mowing example. However, each term captures a different concept, so these terms represent two different categories or types. Specifically, *mother* captures a concept that has to deal with the parenting semantic domain, while *dentist* captures a concept in a work/health care semantic domain.

4. Sometimes the same noun is used to capture two different concepts; a new term(s) must be created to ensure that each concept, or "thing," is captured. For example, consider the term *floor*. There are two concepts that we can capture using this word: (1) we can refer to a floor as part of a room, and (2) we can refer to a floor (or a level) in a building. These are two separate concepts (or ideas), and they may not be represented by the same object. Remember that an object is a way of capturing a concept or idea.

5. Use the category list given by our experts to check if there are other concepts or ideas that we should add to the list.

6. As a guide to help eliminate some potential false problem domain objects, apply the following definition test; an object can be considered as (1) any real-world entity, (2) important to the discussion of the requirements, and (3) with a crisply defined boundary.

7. If you have use cases, you may want to use our modified version.

If you have developed use cases, we recommend using "modern version of the CRC card" technique, which is repeated below for your convenience.

1. Start the effort as a brainstorming session for categories and types.
   - Identify some candidate categories/types by writing down a list of some of the "nouns" from the problem domain.
   - Pick the nouns that have some responsibilities and write them on the cards (Post-it notes).
   - Write a short description of the category/type for guidance.

2. Use your use cases to generate scenarios for the system.
   - Assign a category/type to a participant.
   - Act out the scenario and discover the actual responsibilities of each of the category/type.
   - Look for attributes and services that cannot be allocated to the current categories.
   - Add missing categories to handle these situations as you run through the scenarios.
   - Look for common service prototypes among apparent unrelated categories of objects.

- Add missing types to handle these situations as you run through the scenarios.
- Update the Post-it notes as to category/type name, responsibilities, and collaborators as you go through the scenarios.

3. Position all the classes on a white board and draw association arcs between the classes to represent the collaboration.

5

Identifying Responsibilities

In the previous chapter we created a list of candidates for objects, classes, and interfaces as the starting point for building the analysis model. Now we need to determine if these candidates are "real constructs" that we want to keep in our model. Thus, we need to determine if there is any responsibility for these objects in our application/ system. Before we can do this, however, we have to know what an object is and what we mean by responsibility. In this chapter we do not make a distinction between object, category (class), or type (interface). For this step, the distinction is not used. In fact, we use the term *object* to refer to all three.

WHAT IS AN OBJECT?

In Chapter 2, we defined an object from multiple perspectives as it relates to the production of software. Now we want to use a more technical definition as it applies to analysis. A domain analysis view or definition of an object is:

> **Object.** An object is an abstraction of something in the problem domain, reflecting the capabilities of a system to keep information about it, interact with it, or both.

Humans have always formed concepts to understand the world. Each concept captures a particular idea or understanding that we have of the world in which we live. As we acquire and organize more concepts, we use them to help us make sense of and reason about things in our world.

An object is one of those things to which we apply our concepts. Examples include: invoice, employee, paycheck, train, train engine, boxcar, passenger car, dining car, computer, computer keyboard, joystick, screen, icon on a screen, mouse pad, organization, department, office, and the process of writing this line. Note from the examples, a train is composed of a train engine, boxcar, passenger car, and dining car. Thus, an object may be composed of other objects. These objects, in turn, may be composed of other objects and so on. For example, the passenger car is composed of doors, seats, windows, and so on. Another example is a machine that is composed of subassemblies that are made from other subassemblies. Moreover, the object may be a real thing (e.g., train, car, computer) or an abstract thing (e.g., mammal, marriage, time).

In object-oriented analysis and design, we are interested in an object for its business services. Remember that the way an object-oriented system works is by one object requesting the service of another object via the message passing paradigm. Thus, from an external (or system) perspective, an object is defined by its public services; that is, an object is defined by the services that it advertises. So technically, the protocol defines the class/object. However, we know as software developers, the protocol (collection of prototypes) alone is not adequate. During analysis, we expect to identify the business data and the associated business methods necessary to support the defined business services. For analysis, then, an object is an encapsulation of business attribute values (data) and their associated business methods (how services are provided). To preserve encapsulation and information hiding principles, an object also defines an external view of its public methods for access by other objects. This external view is its public business services. These public services are defined via prototypes and are the only vehicle by which another object may access its methods and thus its data. According to Wirfs-Brock, responsibility is the set of public services that an object provides and the associated data necessary to provide the services.

For most people, however, it is more natural to be able to relate attributes (i.e., data) to an object than to define its services, so we will look at identifying both attributes and services for an object together as one step.

WHAT IS AN ATTRIBUTE?

Things in the real world have characteristics. For example, a person can be described by her or his height, weight, hair color, eye color, and so on. Each characteristic that is common to all instances of the object/class is abstracted as a separate attribute. For example, Joe is 6 feet tall, weighs 175 pounds, has red hair and brown eyes, while James is 5'10" tall, weighs 160 pounds, has black hair and green eyes. For a person, potential attributes are height, weight, hair color, and eye color. Note that the characteristics that are abstracted into attributes are highly problem dependent. Consider the "person" object. Most of us can come up with a large number of characteristics for a "person" conceptually. When we limit our abstraction of a person to a specific problem domain or to a specific problem, we reduce the number of applicable characteristics.

Thus, for the purposes of analysis, an attribute is an abstraction of a single characteristic that is applicable to the business domain and possessed by all the entities that were themselves abstracted as objects. From a technical perspective, an attribute is some variable (data item or state information) for which each object (instance) has its own value. Each attribute must be provided with a name that is unique within the object. Because each attribute may take on values, the range of legal values allowed for an attribute should also be captured.

According to some object-oriented authors, there are a four types of attributes: descriptive, naming, state information, and referential. State-information attributes are used to keep a history of the entity; this is usually needed to capture the states of the finite state machines used to implement the dynamic aspect of behavior. Referential attributes are facts that tie one object to another object and are used to capture relationships. However, capturing states and relationships using attributes is an implementation issue. In this book, states and relationships are represented pictorially and not as part of the attribute list of an object. In this chapter, we address only descriptive attributes and naming attributes.

Descriptive Attributes

Descriptive attributes are facts that are intrinsic to each entity. If the value of a descriptive attribute changes, it means only that some aspect of an entity (instance) has changed. From a problem domain perspective, it is still the same entity. For example, if Joe gains one pound, from nearly all problem domain perspectives, Joe is still a person. More importantly, Joe is still the same person as he was before he gained one pound.

Naming Attributes

Naming attributes are used to name or label an entity. Typically, they are somewhat arbitrary. These attributes are frequently used as identifiers or as part of an identifier. If the value of a naming attribute changes, it only means that a new name has been given to the same entity. In fact, naming attributes do not have to be unique. For example, if Joe changes his name to James, that is all that is changed; his weight, height, etc. are still the same.

During analysis in the early days, many developers also required a unique naming attribute that was used as a key to map objects into a relational database. Better support for object-oriented technology exists today, so this requirement is no longer needed.

WHAT IS A SERVICE?

A service may be defined as work done for others. In a sense, the services of an object are the advertised or public work that an object is willing to perform when requested by another object via the message passing paradigm. These services are defined by prototypes. The prototype is made from four parts[1]: (1) name of the service (called the selector by some experts), (2) the arguments for the service (called the signature by some experts), (3) the data type of the return value, and (4) the exceptions that may be thrown by the service. Thus, every object must define its prototype for each service it plans to provide.

The defined collection of prototypes is the protocol of the object, which is the object's interface (i.e., all its advertised services). The selector (i.e., the name of the service) should be externally focused. For example, a service of a local restaurant may be "changing bills for coins." The "changing bills for coins" is defining a service from the user's perspective, while naming the service "changing coins for bills" is an internal perspective of the service. Naming services is very hard because we want names that reflect an external perspective and is consistent with the semantic domain in which the object resides.

WHAT IS A METHOD?

Technically, a method is a detailed set of operations that an object performs when another object requests a service.[2] However, a behavior by definition is a set of actions that an object is responsible for exhibiting — so alternatively, a method specifies a behavior of an object. A method is similar to a function in functional decomposition; however, there are some very important differences. Remember that these methods can only be accessed via the message passing paradigm, and these methods may only use its own data and data passed to it via its argument list.[3] Maybe most importantly, these services should be specified to a level of depth that is consistent with the semantic domain in which the object resides.

IDENTIFYING ATTRIBUTES

The key issue here is what data do we believe the object is responsible for knowing and owning. The following questions must be asked about each potential object:

---

[1] In fact, the four parts are insufficient to capture the semantics of the service. Ideally, one should at least add "pre" and "post" and invariant conditions to the components of a well-defined service.

[2] Conversely, a service of an object defines how another object may have access to a specific behavior (method/function).

[3] In a later chapter we will see that it also has access to other data via services of other objects with which its has relationships.

- How is this object described in general?
- What parts of the general description are applicable to this problem domain?
- What is the minimal description needed for this application?

If you take the Eastern or Taoist approach to object-oriented analysis, you will design your system by asking only the first two questions. You will not be concerned with the specific application that you are implementing. We have found that with this approach, there is a tendency, to produce a more flexible and robust model from a business perspective. You will then be able to respond to changes in the marketplace more quickly. This flexibility is usually at the expense of performance and space utilization.

If you ask all three questions and look only at the present application (Western approach), you will tend to produce a fine-tuned high performing system with good space utilization that makes more effective use of the hardware. However, it will be at the expense of having less reusable classes/objects and having less flexibility to respond to the marketplace.

Attributes are rarely fully described in a requirements document. Fortunately, they seldom affect the basic structure of the model. You must draw upon your knowledge of the application domain and the real world to find them.

Because most guidelines for identifying attributes do not help differentiate between false attributes from real attributes, Rumbaugh has offered the following suggestions to help eliminate "false" attributes:

1. **Objects**. If the independent existence, rather than just the value, of the attribute is important, then the attribute is an object and there needs to be a link to it. For example, consider a Person object. Is the address or city in which the person lives an attribute or another object? If, in your application, you do not manipulate the address without knowing to which person the address belongs, then it is an attribute. However, if you manipulate the address as an entity by itself, then the address should be an object with a link between it and the person.

2. **Qualifiers.** If the value of an attribute depends on a particular context, then consider restating it as a qualifier. For example, an employee number is not really an attribute of a Person object. Consider a person with two jobs. It really qualifies a link "employs" between the company object and the person object.[4]

3. **Names**. A name is an attribute when it does not depend on the context. For example, a person name is an attribute of Person. Note that an attribute, as in a person's name, does not have to be unique; however, names are usually qualifiers and not attributes. As such, they usually

---

[4] If is not important to the application that a person has a second employer, then making it an attribute of the Person object may be satisfactory.

either define a role in an association or define a subclass or superclass abstraction. For example, parent and teacher are not attributes of Person. Both are probably roles for associations. Another example is male person and female person. There are two ways to capture this: consider gender as an attribute of Person or make two subclasses.[5]

4. **Identifiers**. Make sure not to list the unique identifier that object-oriented languages need to unambiguously reference an object. This is implicitly assumed to be part of the model. However, do list the application domain identifiers. For example, an account code is an attribute of Account, while a transaction identification is probably not an attribute.

5. **Link attributes**. If the proposed attribute depends on the presence of a link, then it is an attribute of the link and not of the objects in the link. Make the link an associative object and make the proposed attribute one of its attributes. For example, let us assume that Jim is married to Mary. The date of their marriage is an attribute of the is_married association and not an attribute of Jim or Mary.

6. **Fine details**. Omit minor attributes that do not affect the methods.

7. **Discordant attributes**. An attribute that seems completely unrelated to all other attributes may indicate that the object may need to be split into two objects. A class should be coherent and simple (i.e., must represent a concept that operates in a single semantic domain).

To aid you in finding attributes, we suggest you begin by using the adjectives and possessive phrases in the requirements document. For example, *red* car, the *40-year-old* man, the *color* of the truck, the *position* of the cursor. Then, after identifying a few attributes, you should ask the above questions to identify more attributes.

SPECIFYING ATTRIBUTES

Coad and Yourdon stated it very well when they said, "Make each attribute capture an atomic concept." Atomic concept means that an attribute contains a single value or a tightly related grouping of values that the application treats as a whole. Examples of attributes include individual data items (such as age, salary, and weight) and composite data items (such as legal name, address, and birth date).

Issues on normalization, performance, object identification, and keeping recalculable information should be left to design and implementation. However, the form of the data (character, integer, string, color, etc.) should be specified. Its range, constraints, and invariants should also be captured. We recommend capturing constraints and invariants using declarative semantics. See Chapter 9 for discussions on Rules.

---

[5] Technically, making two subclasses is the most accurate model. However, if we never have services or relationships that are gender-specific, then it is appropriate to make gender an attribute during implementation.

Because identifying attributes is difficult, Shlaer and Mellor have offered properties to which an attribute must adhere. We have added an additional property, identified in this list as Property Zero.

Property Zero: An attribute must capture a characteristic that is consistent with the semantic domain in which this object (as a concept or idea) resides. For instance, consider the object Programmer, a characteristic of a programmer may be the years of experience in writing computer programs. However, age is probably not an attribute of Programmer; it is probably an attribute of Person, which is a different object from Programmer. Now if we make the dangerous assumption that all programmers are also people, then we can create a Human Programmer object by having it inherit the programmer's attributes (e.g., years of writing computer programs) from the Programmer object and the human attributes (e.g., age) from the Person object. Thus, Human Programmer is a composite of two objects.[6]

Property One: An instance (entity) has exactly one value (within its range) for each attribute at any given time. For example, we can choose eye color as an attribute of the Person object with the range of black, brown, blue, and green. If we discover that a person, Carey, which should be an instance of Person, has one green eye and one brown eye, then we cannot assign both green and brown as the eye color of Carey.[7]

Property Two: An attribute must not contain an internal structure. For example, if we made name an attribute of Person, then we are not interested in manipulating the given name and the family name independently in the problem domain.

Property Three: An attribute must be a characteristic of the entire entity and not a characteristic of its composite parts. For example, if we specify "computer" as an object that is composed of a terminal, keyboard, mouse, and central processing unit (CPU). The size of the screen is an attribute of terminal and not computer.

Property Four: When an object is an abstraction of a concept that interacts with other objects (especially tangible objects), the attribute of the object must be associated with the concept and not the other objects. For example, let us assume we want to transfer oil from a holding tank to a separator tank, and we define an Oil Transfer object to capture the concept about the body of liquid that moves. Then, if we assign the attribute

---

[6] Java is a single inheritance language; thus, we can implement multiple generalization/specialization by using aggregation (composition) and delegation or by using interfaces.

[7] This can be easily solved by having the eye color as an attribute of an object Eye and having Person own (has a referential attribute to) two eyes; however, this requires that the model be changed.

gallon to the object Oil Transfer, it must represent the number of gallons that are transferred. It may not be used to represent the number of gallons in the holding tank nor in the separator tank.

Property Five: When an object has a relationship with another object, especially an object of the same kind (class), the attribute must capture the characteristics of the object, and not the relationship or the other object(s) in the relationship. For example, if we add salary as an attribute and spousal relationship to Person, we cannot use the spouse's pay as the value for the salary attribute of a non-working spouse, and the date of their marriage is not an attribute of either spouse.

IDENTIFYING SERVICES

According to Coad and Yourdon, services may be categorized as either algorithmically simple and algorithmically complex. Within each of these categories, services can be broken down into various types. Each category and its types are given in Table 5-1 and Table 5-2. Coad and Yourdon believe that 80% to 90% of the services will be algorithmically simple. We believe that the number is closer to 60%.

Table 5-1   Algorithmically Simple Services

Create	creates and initializes a new object
Connect	connects an object with another object
Access	gets or sets attribute values
Disconnect	disconnects an object with another object
Delete	deletes an object

Table 5-2   Algorithmically Complex Services

Calculate	calculations that the object is responsible for performing on its values
Monitor	monitoring what the object is responsible for to detect or respond to external system or device or internal object
Query	computes a functional value without modifying the object

Algorithmically simple services are not usually placed in an object-oriented model. Every object is assumed to have these services. This makes the model simpler and will aid in reading large and complex models. In this step, we are only interested in identifying those business algorithmically complex services that must be provided by the object.

To aid us in finding services, we should use the verbs in our requirements document. Typically, an English sentence is in the form "subject—action verb—object." In this case, the verb is usually defining a method that must be provided by the object of the sentence. For example, "A person hit the ball." The tendency as a novice is to define a "hit" service for the Person object. In OD, the sentence is used to define a "receiving a hit" service for the Ball object. For the Person object to hit the Ball object, the Ball object must have a prototype service within its protocol to receive the "hit" message request from Person.

After using the verbs to identify services (application-specific case), we should consider generalizing the service name for the domain. Remember that the name should be given from an external perspective (user of the service). We want to use as generic a word as possible to give us an opportunity to find abstract classes, which are the most difficult constructs to discover.

SPECIFYING SERVICES

Specifying the service is done by defining the prototype for the service. If we remember from Chapter 3, the prototype is made from the name of the service, the signature of the service, the data type of the return value, and the exceptions that may be thrown. The name chosen should reflect either an external item or a user's view of the service. The signature is a list of arguments that need to be passed to the object for it to perform the named service. This is the additional data that an object does not have and expects to be given by the calling object. The return value is the results that the service return to the requester of the service. The exceptions[8] are the exceptions that the service expects the requesters to process.

Normally, it is good practice to specify no more arguments than what is necessary for the specific object to perform (execute) its method associated with the service. However, because we are trying to capture concepts and not technical definitions, the argument list may be adjusted to take advantage of polymorphism later. So during this step, the name of the service should be considered very carefully and we can be a little more lax about the arguments and the return value. Exceptions are usually ignored and added later during design.

RECOMMENDED APPROACH

Our approach for identifying responsibilities is:

---

[8] Exceptions are defined later in the book.

1. Identify attributes

   a. Look at all the adjectives and possessive phrases in the requirements document.
   b. Ask the following questions:

      1. How is this object described in general?
      2. What parts of the general description are applicable to this problem domain?

   If you want to follow the Western school, ask also the question

      1. What is the minimal description needed for this application?

   b. Use Rumbaugh's suggestions to eliminate false attributes.

2. Specify attributes

   a. Make each attribute an "atomic concept."
   b. Eliminate attributes that are calculable or derivable from the basic attributes.
   c. Eliminate attributes that address normalization, performance, or object identification during this step.
   d. Test that the attribute adheres to all the properties suggested by Shlaer and Mellor and that as a group the attributes are in the same semantic domain (good cohesion).

3. Identify services

   a. Look at the verbs in a requirements document. Remember the verb usually defines the services of the object of the sentence.
   b. Look at the user scenarios, which usually indirectly identify a lot of services.
   c. Look at each feature, which usually requires services from many objects.

4. Specify services

   a. Give a name to the service that is externally (relative to itself) focused.
   b. Define the signature of the service by identifying its argument list.

EXAMPLE

Let us return to our lawn mowing example. In this example, we have very few adjectives that would help us define attributes for the potential objects we identified in step 1a. However, we are dealing with objects that we all know, as well as with a problem domain that we can all readily understand. So we can start with step 1b, question number 1. Let us start with the eight Person objects: John, Jane, Peter, Paul, Elizabeth, Mary, Jack, and Alice. Examples of descriptive attributes that Person objects probably have are birth date, height, weight, hair color, eye color, and gender; naming attributes are GivenName and SocialSecurityNumber (see Table 5-3).

Table 5-3 Attributes and Values for a Selection of Objects in the Lawn Mower Example

Attribute Name	John	Jane	Peter	Paul
Birth date	9/12/40	2/24/42	8/30/69	3/5/71
Height	5'8'	5'10"	6'2"	6'6"
Weight	110 lbs	160 lbs	210 lbs	195 lbs
Hair color	Gray	White	Black	Blond
Eye color	Blue	Gray	Green	Black
Gender	Male	Female	Male	Male
Name	John Doe	Jane Doe	Peter Doe	Paul Doe
Social Security Number	123-45-6789	234-56-7899	345-67-1234	456-78-0123

Before moving to question 2, we have to decide on the problem domain. We can decide that we want to define our problem domain to cover everything. If that is true, our attribute list would have to be extended to cover the area of a person's health, employment, taxes, investments, social relationships, and so on. It will probably make the object very large and neither maintainable nor usable to any application, unless it has unlimited CPU and space resources. (There goes management's idea of one class/object definition for all usage.) However, it is not as bad as all that. Normally, every business is bound by the kind of domain for which they are in business.

Let us now limit our domain to home owner property care. We are interested in capturing applications like mowing the lawn, fertilizing the lawn, seeding the lawn, trimming the bushes, cleaning the pool, carpet cleaning, house painting, roof repair, gutter cleaning, chimney-sweeping, and so on.

If we think very carefully about the problem domain, we will probably realize that none of the attributes we have identified are applicable to our problem domain of "home owner property care." However, from the requirements description, we can see that the schedule of a person's time is useful and some state information (is Dad tired or not?) may be needed.

Furthermore, because family physicians are not within the domain of "home owner property care," we can drop Alice and FamilyPhysician from our list of potential objects. With similar logic, we can probably drop Studio, Dentist, Actor, Student, and Suburb from the list. It is also probably safe to drop Father, Mother, Son, and Daughter from the list,[9] especially in these modern days of equal opportunities of chores for all. We have kept Lassie and Dog on the list, because a dog may be an alternative to chemical fertilizer. The house is needed for other applications such as house painting. We are not sure about Chore and PaidChore. We suspect that we will need LawnMower, ProfessionaLawnMower, and FamilyLawn for our application.

After applying question 2, our revised attribute list now looks as follows:

> For John, Jane, Peter, Paul, Elizabeth, and Mary, there is one attribute: schedule.
> For Jack and ProfessionalLawnMower, the attributes are address, telephone number, and schedule.
> For Lassie and Dog, there is one attribute: schedule.
> For House, the attributes are address, telephone number, last painted date, last roof repaired date, and so on.
> For the FamilyLawn, the attributes are height of grass, last seeded, last fertilized, and so on.
> For Chore and PaidChore, no attributes were found.

Now, we are ready for question 3; our application is "mowing the lawn." If we restrict ourselves only to our application, we would eliminate the following potential objects from consideration: Lassie, Dog, Chore, PaidChore, and House.

After applying question 3, our revised attribute list now looks as follows:

> For John, Jane, Peter, Paul, Elizabeth, and Mary, one attribute—schedule.
> For Jack and ProfessionalLawnMower, attributes are address, telephone number, and schedule.
> For FamilyLawn, one attribute—height of grass.

In applying question 3, we have eliminated objects (and if we had a lot of attributes, probably some attributes) that are applicable to the general problem domain but not applicable to our specific application.

In Tao philosophy, the focus is on the path rather than on the destination or, in our terminology, the process rather than the goal. When we translate this into object-oriented modeling, the Tao philosophy tells us to focus on capturing the objects in the problem domain rather than on the objects that help us solve the immediate problem. It is the belief of the Taoist that focusing on the goal causes you

---

[9] This is actually incorrect. We will see in a later chapter that we need to use the father–child relationship. However, because "parenting" is a different semantic domain than "home owner property care," we have a tendency to eliminate these objects during this step.

to ignore valuable information, while focusing on the process lets the path show you the way. Translated to object-oriented technology, focusing on the specific problem or application causes you to ignore important concepts and, as a result, makes your classes (objects) less reusable.

If you are trying to produce flexible and reusable software, you should apply an Eastern or Taoist philosophy to problem solving and object-oriented modeling. In Eastern philosophy, we would not have asked question 3. We would expect that the proper modeling of the problem domain would automatically also contain our business solution to our application. This kind of philosophy is based on experimentation versus our classical Western thinking, which is based on planning.

Step 2 for attributes is left to the reader.

Now let us perform the step 3 and 4 for services. Since we have contrived a very simple example, the only service is "mow the lawn." If we look at people in general, the number of services that they provide is endless; but, we do not want to capture all these services. If we were to only consider services in the domain of "home owner property care," we will have added services such as house painting, lawn fertilizing, lawn seeding, house cleaning, gutter cleaning, sweeping the sidewalk, trimming the bushes, and racking the leaves. However, when we get back to our specific application, we are back to one service: "mow the lawn."

Thus, we have the following objects with a "mow the lawn" service: John, Peter, Paul, Elizabeth, Mary, Jack, and ProfessionalLawnMower.

Note that the family lawn already has a changeHeight or setHeight "height of grass" service because it is algorithmically simple.

As useful as the Eastern philosophy is in helping us perform better object specification, we still do not want to include in our final model either objects or services that are not needed for our specific application. So when all is said and done, we still need to apply the following tests to ensure that we have only the necessary objects:

1.   The object must provide some service for some other object in the application/system or an external interface service to some external object.
2.   In general, the object must have multiple attributes. In fact, an object can only provide services and have no attribute.[10]

Sometimes it is useful to keep an object (an abstraction) that may help us in organizing our structural model, which captures the relationships between objects. In such an instance, the only services of that object may its constructor and destructor.

SUMMARY

Our approach for identifying responsibilities is

---

[10] This kind of object, however, should be rare and usually is not discovered during this step.

1. Identify attributes
2. Specify attributes
3. Identify services
4. Specify services

This is a more Eastern approach to discovering responsibilities. If you were using use cases and CRC cards, then you can find the minimal services to support the application by

1. Mapping the CRC cards on to the class constructs. Categories (classes) map onto classes and the responsibilities map usually to services. Then the collaborators map either into relationships or into arguments of the service call that uses it.
2. To determine the arguments of the service call use the use-case scenarios. Walk through each use case and determine in detail how the system uses the model to provide the services necessary to support the use-case scenarios.
3. When you are walking through the scenarios, refine the argument list as you discover holes.
4. Add missing objects/classes as you discover them.
5. Use sequence diagrams to capture the details of the walk thorough.

This is a more Western approach to discovering of the responsibilities.

Specifying Static Behavior

In the previous chapter, we created a list of "real objects." In the process of finding these real objects, we identified attributes and services of these objects. However, while we did that, we took an external view of the service. More specifically, we did not concern ourselves with how the object will provide (perform) the service. Now we need to capture how each object provides the identified services. In the process of specifying these services, we may also identify additional services that must be provided by other objects.

WHAT IS BEHAVIOR?

In the previous chapter, we defined a service as "work done for others" even though an object can provide services to itself. Behavior can be defined as the set of actions that an object is responsible for exhibiting when it provides a specific service. Another object may access a specific behavior of an object only via the appropriate service. This behavior is usually captured as a method (function) in the object.

A behavior is defined when the following are specified: (1) all the inputs (arguments to the service), (2) all the outputs, and (3) how (from a domain perspective) the object will provide the service. Behavior can be either static or dynamic (see Chapter 1). In this chapter, techniques for capturing static behavior will be addressed. Techniques for capturing dynamic behavior will be addressed in Chapter 7.

In static behavior, the set of actions are captured by the operations (code) within the method. By definition, the operations within the method are not affected by any external or internal events[1] (actions). A good example of static behavior is the "square root" service for Number. If one requests the "square root" service from the number 4, which is an instance of Number, the result is always 2. There is no external or internal action that would cause the method of Number to change the algorithm for computing the square root and, thus, providing a different result.

It is possible that some behaviors allow concurrent actions to be performed. Intrinsic concurrency can be recognized in a requirements document by phrases such as

- At the same time
- Simultaneously
- Independently

Each of these terms indicates that more than one thing is occurring at the same time. At times, the presence of concurrency may make development of use cases somewhat complicated as use-case details tend to be written in a sequential fashion.

The most natural way to document behavior is to use any natural language. Unfortunately, all natural languages are rich in ambiguities and inconsistencies. When it is spoken, some clarification is provided by intonation, hand movements, and body language. In many situations, especially in specification, even spoken words will not alleviate the ambiguities or inconsistencies. The problem is that natural language is a set of atomic elements (words) that lack well-defined semantics (consistent and unambiguous definition in the problem domain). Thus, the resulting collection of words that form sentences or paragraphs becomes ambiguous or inconsistent; therefore, the behavior descriptions written in natural language becomes inconsistent and ambiguous.

One solution is to build a shell around the natural language with well-defined semantics. This technique is used in every field of endeavor. For example, in accounting, words such as *ledger*, *debit*, and *credit* have very precise and well-defined semantics. Similarly, in the computer world, words such as *input*, *output*, *bit*, and *byte* have well-defined semantics.

When we construct a shell around the English language to provide a richer set of semantically clear constructs, this is really modeling. The purpose of a model is to provide a richer, higher level, and more semantically precise set of constructs (usually words) than the underlying natural language. The model is designed to reduce ambiguities and inconsistencies, manage complexity, facilitate checks for completeness, and improve understandability. Associated with each of the models are techniques for capturing the behavior (function/method) of the model. Thus, the

---

[1] If they were true, we would model this with dynamic behavior.

techniques below for documenting behavior are based on a relatively formal under-lying model.

JAVA SERVICES (OPERATIONS) THAT AFFECT THE BEHAVIOR SPECIFICATION

There are specific constructs and mechanisms that were added to the Java platform (and more specifically, the Java language that affects the way we may choose to design the logic of our method for implementing a service). The new capabilities are

Basic Functions

1. There is native support for the capability to determine if two distinct objects have the same attribute values and have the same relationships with the same other objects. This is the equal service in the Object class.
2. There is native support for the capability to clone (i.e., make a duplicate and distinct copy) of an object. This is the clone service in the Object class.
3. There is native support for accessing a unique identifier for an object, that is an object has a unique identifier that is not an attribute; thus, having a unique key as part of the naming attribute is not a necessary requirement. This is the toString service in the Object class.

Runtime Type Identification (Reflection)

4. An object always knows of which category (ies) and types that it is an example.This is supported by the getClass service of the Object class and the many services of the Class class, that is, an object knows the classes and interfaces of which it is an instance. Thus, the object can be requested at runtime to identify the classes and the interfaces of which it is an instance.
5. An object always knows all the services that it supports. This is supported by services of the Class class and services in the reflection package, that is, an object knows the service name, it argument list, and its return value type of all its services. Thus, the object can be requested at runtime to provide the prototype of each of its services at runtime.

Multithreading

6. An object may have multiple and concurrent paths of executions. These paths are called *threads*.
   Thus, there is native support for concurrent programming in the Java pro-gramming language in the form of the Thread class and the Runnable interface.
7. There is native support to put a thread to sleep for a specific period of time. This is supported by the sleep service in the Thread class.
8. There is native support to suspend a thread and then to resume it under business logic control. This is supported by the suspend service and the resume service in the Thread class.

9. There is native support to suspend a thread and have it wait for an event to occur. This is supported by the wait service and the notify (notify and notify all) services in the Thread class.

10. There is native support for protecting the object's data integrity in a multithreading environment. Nearly all Java libraries are thread-safe and the "synchronized" feature is provided to the application programmer to implement methods (code) that are also thread-safe, that is, objects can be thread-safe in design and implementation.

Event-Response (Publish-Subscribe Pattern, Alias Observer Pattern)

11. There is native support for the ability for an object to notify other objects, which may be in very different categories, of an internal event. This is supported by the Event class, Listener classes, and the usage of the Observer Pattern, that is, we can have objects that are of different classes get notification of an event.

12. There is support for an object to subscribe for notification of an event at runtime.

13. There is support for an object to unsubscribe for notification of an event at runtime.

Exception Handling

14. There is native support for dealing with exception handling as a separate execution path. This is supported by the try-catch block mechanism.

15. There is native support to define your own exceptions to be processed as a separate execution path. This is supported by the extensibility of the Exception class.

TECHNIQUES FOR SPECIFYING STATIC BEHAVIOR

There are at least two ways of specifying static behavior[2]: (1) giving the before and after conditions on its execution and (2) decomposing the service into a series of activities and tasks that can be mapped to basic operations of the class or service class to other objects.

From a formal language perspective, the first way is preferred. In fact, UML uses this technique for operation specification, of which static behavior is a special case. However, we have found that analysts had a great deal of difficulty in recognizing the necessary preconditions and postconditions.[3] Furthermore, this technique does not help us to understand the business nor to find additional services

---

[2] This is called operation specification in the unified modeling language (UML).

[3] However, we advocate using pre-, post-, and invariant conditions as a way of documenting the information discovered by using business service analysis.

that are not identified in our process. Thus, we prefer to perform a business service analysis, which is the second way of specifying static behavior.

A service is comprised of a series of activities that perform the work of that advertised service. The discrete activities are, in turn, composed of tasks. Thus, an activity is a set of tasks that is organized and proceduralized to accomplish a specific subgoal. The tasks and activities are interdependent, and there is a well-defined flow of control between them. The definition of the behavior is the identification of the activities and tasks that are to be performed in support of the named service.

In capturing activities and tasks, the following questions should be answered:

- How are they performed?
- Why are they performed?
- What are their interrelationships?

For use in control specification and design, the following additional information should be gathered:

- Is it part of a transaction (if you are using the transaction paradigm)?
- Timing
- Frequency
- Volume
- Variants
- Business rules on verification and validation
- Processing algorithms
- Saved and/or stored data
- Reports
- Control points and check points, if any
- Error detection, correction, and recovery

The steps are very simple. Begin with the service trigger (the service call from some other object), document all the manual and mental steps that must be performed, document every decision point, document each test and calculation or change to the attribute, document all possible results from a decision point. Finally, consider exceptions and special cases.

The following three points of caution are appropriate:

1. Be careful with modeling manual processes. The ideal behind the object-oriented paradigm is that the object that has the data does the work. So, many manual processes should not be done by a conceptual human object in the system; these are done by the object itself. For example, a purchase order can fill itself. This may seem a little unnatural to a novice, but the purchase order has all the data needed to process itself. Similarly, a check in most banking application will process itself.
2. In many situations, only the activities are in the same semantic domain as the object—the tasks are in a different semantic domain. In such a

situation, the task needs to be services supplied by other objects. These other objects are usually related to the present object either through inheritance or aggregation. Capturing each service in the correct object is critical to having low coupling and good cohesion in the model. Remember that low coupling and good cohesion of objects lead to reusable and flexible software.

3. Operations allowed as part of service specification in object-oriented models are bounded. Operations can only change data that the object owns (i.e., its attributes) and have access only to the object's data and data passed to it via the argument list. Furthermore, it can only access services of other objects that it knows about. In the next chapter,[4] we will discuss how an object knows about another object.

TECHNIQUES FOR SPECIFYING CONTROL

Finding the services and describing each one as a sequence of actions that produce the intended result is one of the issues that is not well addressed in most object-oriented books or courses. We will attempt to give the reader some guidelines in this area.

We believe that just as we have borrowed techniques for documenting behavior from other methodologies, we need to borrow a technique from an existing method (McMenamin and Palmer) to help us specify the behavior of objects and capture the necessary services that meet all the requirements. This method was adopted and modified by Jacobson for capturing requirements in object-oriented analysis in his Objectory method. The steps described by McMenamin and Palmer are very simple.

1. List all the external and internal events to which the application/system needs to respond. The users and the interface system(s) are external to the system. A good way to get a list of external events is to perform a task analysis for the users and the external systems. In the terminology of the Objectory method, this would be called identifying the actors.

2. For each event, usually a message, determine how and in what sequence the necessary messages will be passed among objects to satisfy the request. This particular series of interactions among objects is called a scenario. A scenario shows a single execution of the application/system in time. When the scenario requires specific sequencing and synchronization beyond what is provided as part of the services of objects in the scenario, a task object should be created to capture the scenario controls. A scenario is equivalent to a transaction in many applications. Thus, a task is commonly used to capture the control aspects of a transaction.

---

[4] These constraints are consistent with the encapsulation and information hiding principles of the object-oriented paradigm. Fundamental to building good quality systems is the fact that the services of each object must be in the same semantic domain.

3. Capture the above sequences by drawing a sequence diagram for each scenario and its variations. These scenarios, or sequences of messages, are useful for understanding the application/system and for integrated testing. This step is different from both McMenamin/Palmer and Jacobson's Objectory method. In structured methods, usually a state machine for the whole system is designed to capture the scenarios; similarly, in the Objectory method, a state model is used to represent the system. This makes sense for both of the above methods because they are used in the early part of these methods before decomposition. We are using this technique after detail analysis (domain analysis) of the application/system to verify the validly of the domain analysis in addressing the specific application. This is a critical difference; we believe that using scenarios to validate our domain model is a better way to develop reusable classes than to start the modeling process for the application, as originally suggested by McMenamin and Palmer.

4. Capture the details of how each service is provided. By thinking through each scenario, the analyst/developer can specify precisely what must be done in each of the object services. Then the details of the actions that need to be taken within a service are captured. Again, this is different from the classical method, which would have taken a system view. We are not taking a decomposed view of the system.

5. Examine each service to establish if there are actions that occur concurrently.

6. If you haven't already done so, consider modeling the scenarios as use cases to reduce the number of scenario diagrams.

TECHNIQUES FOR DOCUMENTING CONTROL

Activity Diagrams

This technique uses processes or tasks as its building blocks.[5] The response is captured as a series of processes that operate on a set of data. From a technical perspective, one can argue that the activities and tasks are captured as "processes" (i.e., bubbles on the diagram) in lower-level diagrams. If we were performing functional decomposition, this would be correct. However, in object-oriented analysis, it is not always correct to map every activity or task to a service of an object. Often we map a task to an object. Mapping a task to an object is one technical

---

[5] Activity diagrams has always been a fuzzy item. It was intended originally to capture the processes at a higher level. It was used at a pre- or co-use-case level. Activity is not just like use cases. It is probably better to introduce activity as a way to document the process at the "domain"/business level. Then the activities or processes within which the "system will be used" will need to be objectified. Actually, you do not need everything to be object-oriented. What must be object-oriented is the system and the parts that interface with the system.

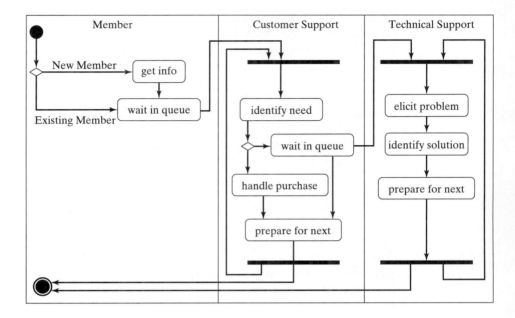

Figure 6-1   The UML Notation for a Generic Activity Diagram.

solution. A more correct approach would be to re-engineer the process so that it could be mapped to the service of a single object.

An activity diagram describes how activities are co-ordinated. Some authors consider activity diagrams to be a better mechanism for showing essential dependencies among activities performed by various entities. These diagrams provide direct representations for capturing concurrency within a service.

The UML notation for an activity diagram is illustrated in Figure 6-1. The solid circle represents the entry point. The diamond represents decision points. The rounded rectangles identify tasks that are to be performed. Arrows identify transitions from one task to the next. The solid lines are sychronization bars, which identify synchronization for ends of tasks (flows into the bar) and starts of tasks (flows out of the bar). Activities that are performed by different individuals can be expressed using partitions called **swimlanes**.

Collaboration Diagram

A collaboration diagram[6] shows the flow of control emphasizing the structural relationships among the instances in the interaction, as well as the messages passed

---

[6] The term in UML is *collaboration diagram*, but earlier object-oriented writings have used other terms. Many older sources refer to this diagram as an object interaction diagram.

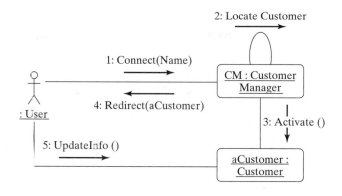

Figure 6-2   UML Notation for a Collaboration Diagram.

among them. It shows the objects and links that exist just before the service begins and also the objects and links created (and possibly destroyed) during the performance of the service. A collaboration diagram is much like the sequence diagram that is described in the next section; however, it captures additional information about how the objects are related to each other. The incorporation of additional detail is good, but it is harder to follow. While we prefer the use of collaboration diagrams, it is often the case that people do not read it as carefully as it deserves.

A message from one object to another is indicated by a label consisting of a sequence number, the name of the service requested, and the arguments list with an arrow showing the message-flow direction. In UML, there are additional options to handle sychronization with other threads of control, nested procedural calling sequences, concurrent threads, iteration, and possible conditional expressions. A collaboration diagram is illustrated in Figure 6-2.

Sequence Diagram

A sequence diagram[7] shows the flow of control by time ordering and emphasizes the passing of messages as they unfold over time. It shows the sequence of messages that implement a service or transaction. This technique uses objects as its building block. In this analysis technique, you trace the response of an event as a series of messages between objects. Each message is a request for services from another object. In using this technique, one must already have some idea about the objects that are in the system. This is one reason why we identify objects as the first step of our object-oriented method.

The UML notation for sequence diagrams is illustrated in Figure 6-3. A straight vertical line is used to represent an object. An event (external service

---

[7] Sequence diagrams were previously known as event trace diagrams and have origins predating object-oriented methodologies.

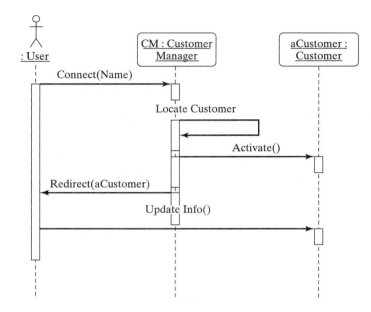

Figure 6-3   UML Notation for a Sequence Diagram.

request) is used to label the diagram. A service call to another object is represented by a direct arrow with the prototype of the service call as its label.

TECHNIQUES FOR DOCUMENTING STATIC BEHAVIOR

Pre-conditions and Post-conditions

In UML specifications, the recommended way of specifying pre-conditions and post-conditions is via textual specification. The textual specification would have the following sections: service name, inputs, output(s), elements of the object modified, pre-conditions, and post-conditions. We recommend adding invariant conditions to the list, if you choose this technique.

Flowcharting

A flowchart is the oldest technique for specifying a method/function. There are a large number of object-oriented methods that use this technique and have highly specialized notations for documenting the behavior.

A generic flowchart technique is described. A rectangle is used to capture the calculation or operations, and the diamond is used to capture the decision. Flow of control is shown by arrows. Words are placed on arrows from a diamond (decision point) as each arrow from the diamond represents one of the possible results.

Data Flow Diagrams

Data flow diagrams (DFDs) are an integral part of a number of methods (e.g., Rumbaugh). Each specific method uses a slightly different notation. A generic notation is described. Data flow (i.e., information) is represented by a labeled arrow. Operations (actions or transformations) are represented by labeled bubbles. Information sources or sinks are represented by labeled boxes. Attributes (stored information) are represented by a double horizontal line. The keywords *and* and *or* are used to link data flows.

Structured English

Structured English is also used with some methods. This method is widely used by system engineers who have no formal training in computers.

The generic guidelines for using structured English are

1. Use command verbs to describe operations, transformations, or actions.
2. Use attribute names for data to be manipulated.
3. Use prepositions and conjunctions to show logical relationships.
4. Commonly understood (semantically precise) mathematical, physical, business, and technical terms may be used.
5. Mathematical equations as well as illustrations such as tables, diagrams, and graphs may also be used for clarification.
6. Words other than the above should be used sparingly and only to help document the behavior.
7. Sentence or paragraph structures must be simple with single-entry, single-exit constructs. The constructs should consist only of the following:

   * Sequence: actions that occur in a specified time sequence.
   * Concurrence: more than one action taking place simultaneously.
   * Decision: a branch in the flow of actions is made based on the results of a test.
   * Repetition: the same action(s) repeated until some specified limit or result is reached.

Examples are given in Figure 6-4. Words that appear in all capitals are attributes (i.e., data) and lines that are indented represent subordination.

RECOMMENDED APPROACH

Although the use of activity diagrams may be more familiar to most of us, we do not recommend it. When they are used, analysts and developers have a tendency to map activities onto services of objects and to use the analysis as the specification of

1. Sequence Example
Find INTEREST DUE as
 RATE × INSTALLATION PERIOD × PRINCIPAL.
Next, subtract INTEREST DUE from ACCOUNT BALANCE.
Next, issue REMAINING BALANCE as ACCOUNT BALANCE.

2. Concurrency Example
Calculate NAVAID DISTANCE as great circle distance from
 AIRCRAFT POSITION to NAVAID POSITION.
Calculate ALT DIFFERENCE as
 AIRCRAFT ALTITUDE – NAVAID ALTITUDE.

3. Decision Example
If AMOUNT REQUESTED is greater than LIMIT.
then:
 return "NOT APPROVED"
else:
 subtract AMOUNT REQUESTED from LIMIT.
 Next, return "APPROVED"
endif:

4. Repetition Example
For each member of selected Accounts:
 ask each account to change its INTERESTRATE to NEWINTERESTRATE.
endfor:

Figure 6-4 Example of Structured English.

services. This is very bad practice because many of our activities violate the encapsulation and information-hiding principles of object-oriented technology. When these principles are violated, a system with high coupling and poor cohesion is created. A highly coupled system of objects with poor cohesion means that software is less maintainable and less flexible. We believe that the improper use of activity diagrams causes the development of poor software.

 We recommend using the existing method of McMennin and Palmer to specify the behavior of objects. The steps are very simple.

1. List all the external and internal events that the application/system needs to respond.
2. From each event, usually a message, determine how and in what sequence the messages will be passed between objects necessary to satisfy the request.
3. Capture the above sequences by drawing a sequence diagram for each scenario and its variations. These scenarios or sequence of messages are useful for understanding the application/system and for integrated testing.
4. (Added by the authors) If you have not already created a use-case model, create a use-case model for the scenarios. This is almost necessary for large systems, as the number of actual scenarios or sequence diagrams would be overwhelming.

5. Capture the details of "how each service is provided." By thinking through each scenario, the analyst/developer can specify precisely what must be done in each of the object services. Then, the details of the actions need to be taken within a service and captured using structured English.[8]

EXAMPLE

Based on earlier analysis, we have the following objects with a mowTheLawn service: John, Peter, Paul, Elizabeth, Mary, Jack, and professional lawn mower. Remember that we are assuming that the family lawn already has a change or set heightOfGrass service because it is algorithmically simple.

For this model to work, we need an external object (cron job) that periodically (i.e., every 15 minutes) asks each object, including John, to start the service/task that is on their schedule. This is a very common external event; many services are called based on a predetermined schedule. Let us presume that John's mowTheLawn service has scheduled the actual mowing (mowFamilyLawn service) to occur at 7 PM. When John comes home, he will immediately perform the mowFamilyLawn service. Figure 6-5 defines the mowFamilyLawn service.

We have not refined the actual mowing the lawn. We have also assumed that John has a way of contacting all his children. We will show how contacting his children can be accomplished in a later chapter.

Now, let us look at the mowTheLawn service for the children. All of the children, with the exception of Peter, will delegate any lawn mowing request that pays over five dollars to Jack, who will mow any lawn for four dollars. Their service is defined in Figure 6-6. Peter always mows the lawn, regardless of the pay. His service is defined in Figure 6-7.

The children have a mowLawn service instead of a mowFamilyLawn service, as the children will mow any lawn. Because of this flexibility, we needed to associate a lawn address with that service. In the case of John, we did not do this as John will only mow the family lawn. Also, for the children to be able to get access to Jack, it is assumed they have access to his telephone number via the telephone book. In a later chapter, we will discuss the various vehicles by which one object has access to another object's services. The definition of the mowTheLawn service for Jack and for the ProfessionalLawnMower is left to the reader.

---

[8] Although there are advantages and disadvantages to all three techniques of documenting the behavior, we recommend using structured English for the following reasons: (1) in many organizations the analysis is performed by non-computer scientists/programmers and for them, structured English is easier to understand than either data flow diagram or flow charts; (2) DFDs and flowcharting should be used with a computer-aided software engineering (CASE) tool. Unfortunately, most CASE tools today do not provide satisfactory end-to-end support; (3) furthermore today, CASE tools for object-oriented methods are neither easy to use nor conducive to the way we really do analysis and design; and (4) many of us still assume that when we use DFDs or flowcharts, we can revert back to functional decomposition. When we do this, we negate the benefits of going to object-oriented technology. Again, most CASE tools have not enforced the additional semantic constraints on DFDs and flowcharts that are really implied by using these same techniques for documenting object (class) behavior.

OBJECT NAME	John

SERVICE: "mowFamilyLawn (no arguments)"
If **MYCONDITION** is equal to "tired,"
then:
for each child in selected Children
ask each child to "mow the lawn" for five dollars.
if answer is "yes,"
then:
remove "mowFamilylawn" from SCHEDULE.
return;
else:
endif:
endfor:
perform mowing the lawn.
else:
perform mowing the lawn.
endif:

Figure 6-5   Service Provisions of John for Mowing the Lawn.

OBJECT NAMES	Paul, Elizabeth, Mary

SERVICE: mow the lawn (ADDRESS_OF_LAWN, DOLLAR_AMOUNT)
if DOLLAR_AMOUNT is less than five dollars,
then:
get SCHEDULE for evening (7 PM–9 PM)
Next, if SCHEDULE has open slot,
then:
place mowLawn in slot.
associate ADDRESS_OF_LAWN with mowLawn.
return "yes, I will mow lawn this evening."
else:
return "no, I cannot mow the lawn."
endif
else:
get Jack's TELEPHONE NUMBER from Telephone Book.
ask Jack to mow the lawn (ADDRESS_OF_LAWN, self, ADDRESS)
if Jack's response is "yes,"
then:
return "Yes, I will mow lawn this evening."
else:
return "No, I cannot mow the lawn."
endif:
endif;

Figure 6-6   CRC Card for Paul, Elizabeth, and Mary in the Lawn Mowing Example.

OBJECT NAME	Peter

SERVICE: "mow the lawn (ADDRESS_OF_LAWN, DOLLAR_AMOUNT)"
get SCHEDULE for evening (7 PM–9 PM)
Next, if SCHEDULE has open slot,
then:
place mowLawn in slot.
associate ADDRESS_OF_LAWN with mowLawn.
return "Yes, I will mow the lawn this evening."
else:
return "No, I cannot mow the lawn."
endif

Figure 6-7   CRC Card for Peter in the Lawn Mowing Example.

If we think about when a person performs a service that is a sequence of actions, we quickly realize that most of our behaviors have to do with time or elapsed time. For example, we wake up after having slept for x number of hours, go to sleep at y o'clock, and eat at a certain time. Thus, the only external event in this application is time elapsed. A reasonable model of this "real-world" situation is to assume that it only needs to be modeled at 15-minute intervals, so that a person scheduling her/his life at 15-minute intervals and at no finer granularity. Thus, the high-level sequence diagram may look like the one illustrated in Figure 6-8.

The Scheduler is a new object; its sole purpose is to ask an object that uses scheduling to perform a required task based on what the time is now. Each object operates as if it can perform some service (function) every 15 minutes. If one of the objects were scheduled to "mowLawn" at 7 PM, the schedule will send a message to that object to execute its callSchedJ with the argument of 7 PM. In each object, the callSchedJ method is the same; it checks its schedule to see what service (function) needs to be performed. In this case, it would be the mowLawn service.

SUMMARY

Below are the detailed steps of our approach for specifying static behavior and for identifying additional services:

1. List all the external and internal events to which the application/system needs to respond.
2. From each event, usually a message, determine how and in what sequence messages are passed between objects necessary to satisfy the request.

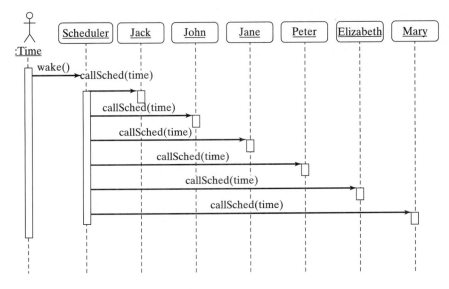

Figure 6-8   Scheduler's Sequence Diagram from the Lawn Mower Example.

3. Define and draw a sequence diagram for each scenario and its variations.
4. If the number of scenarios is large (and you aren't already using use cases), consider creating a use-case model to reduce the number of diagrams.
5. Capture the details of each service associated with the sequence diagram by using one of the documentation techniques given in this chapter.

7

Dynamic Behavior

This chapter presents techniques for capturing dynamic behavior. For applications that are not control-based, most objects (i.e., classes) do not undergo significant state changes, so that only a few (if any) require state diagrams. In many control-based applications, however, the state diagrams may be the dominant aspect of the model.

Technically, state diagrams are the formal specifications of the behavior of a class and, thus, of an object. Static behavior is really a special case of a modeless state diagram. A modeless state diagram occurs when an object (class) always responds the same way to external and internal events (stimuli). Note that scenarios are not state diagrams; they are examples of execution of the system. They involve usually several objects playing various roles. Thus, they are instances of behavior, and as such they can only illustrate behavior; they cannot define it. Technically, when all state diagrams have been created, all scenarios can be derived from this entire set of state diagrams. In fact, many developers employ scenarios to check the sanity of the model. Similarly, because a scenario is an instance of a use case, a use case is a "slice" of the system behavior across state diagrams from multiple classes.

INTRODUCTION

Object-oriented analysis is often described in terms of structure, behavior, and rules. The structural analysis captures the static vision of how the objects are related to each other; it essentially captures the data semantics of the application. A visual, spatial metaphor is used to document these relationships. In all of the previous analysis chapters, we have focused on capturing the structural aspects of the application. In contrast, behavior analysis captures the time-dependent aspects of the application. For example, it is used to specify how to hire employees, dismiss employees, add diagrams to a document, or delete a word from a document. Thus, whether the behavior is static or dynamic, the method description captures the procedural semantics of the application over time. Rules, which are discussed in a later chapter, capture the declarative semantics of the application.

If the application has no time-dependent[1] behavior, then capturing the structural aspects of the system and performing static behavioral analysis is sufficient to build the application. This is the situation with our case study so far. However, the world we live in is not static; it changes over time. Dynamic modeling mechanisms provide us with a way to capture the behavior of objects, thus, the behavior of the application, over time.

Temporal relationships are difficult to capture. Most applications are best understood by first examining its static structure (data semantics), that is, the structure of its objects and their relationships (inheritance, association, aggregation) to each other in a moment of time. After capturing this aspect of the application, we want to examine the changes to the objects and their relationships over time. Those aspects (which are parts of the procedural semantics) of an application that are concerned with these changes over time are captured in the *dynamic* model. Thus, this chapter presents mechanisms that help us capture flow of control, interactions, and sequencing of operations in an object oriented application. The major concepts of dynamic modeling are *events*, which are the stimuli, and *states*, which is an object configuration that exists between events. Thus, an application can be described in terms of object behaviors, that is, an orderly sequence of state changes of objects over time, and the behavior of an object is captured as a chain (or probably a network) of cause (stimuli) and effect (state change) over time.

For example, the chain of cause and effect for an Order object in an order processing system may be as follows: at placing the order: requisition state; at filling a line item of the order: partially filled state; at shipping of line item: partially shipped state; when all the line items have been filled and shipped: shipped state. When the order is shipped, an Invoice object is created and the Order object's data is archived and the object is deleted from the system.[2] Figure 7-1 shows a chain diagram depicting this.

---

[1] The behavior that is being discussed is not truly time-dependent; it is actually dependent on the past history of the system.

[2] Archiving the data associated with the order object will allow one to reconstruct the order object in the event that the customer contests the invoice.

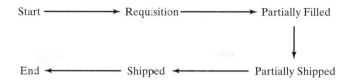

Figure 7-1 Chain of Cause and Effect for an Order Object.

TECHNIQUES FOR IDENTIFYING DYNAMIC BEHAVIOR

An object in the real world normally has a lifetime. Often it is created or comes into existence, progresses through certain stages, and then dies or vanishes. For example, a human being is conceived by her or his parents, processes through stages (baby, child, pre-schooler, grammar school, teenager, young adult, mid-age, senior citizen), and eventually dies. Some individuals do not visit all stages, and others appear to have reverted back to an earlier stage. However, all human beings follow this basic pattern of dynamic behavior throughout their lifetimes.

From our general observations on behavior patterns for different things in the real world, we conclude as follows:

- Most things go through various stages during their lifetimes.
- The order in which a thing progresses through its stages forms a pattern that helps in classifying the kind of thing it is.
- In a pattern, not all progressions between stages are allowed. Some progressions are forbidden by the laws of physics, some by statute, etc.
- There are incidents and events in the real world that cause a thing to progress (or indicate that it has progressed) between stages.

For technical reasons, we also add the following assumptions:

- A thing is in exactly one and only one stage of its behavior pattern at any given time.
- Things progress from one stage to another stage instantaneously.

Note that the granularity of time depends on the degree of abstraction and can vary at different levels of the application. Basically, however, the progression (transition) must be treated as atomic, that is, non-interruptible, at the given level of abstraction. Thus, the incident or event that causes the progression must be treated as atomic. For an incident occurs at a point in time, while a stage (state) is a configuration of objects that exists between incidents.

Let us now test these observations and assumptions on a second example. Figure 7-2 shows the behavior pattern for an airplane: In this example, the airplane goes through numerous stages that are shown by the bold text. They include parked

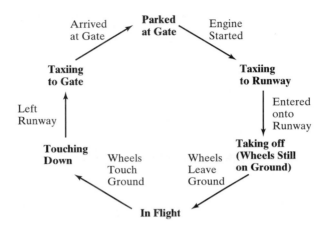

Figure 7-2   Behavior Pattern for an Airplane.

at the gate, taxiing to runway, and so on. The pattern is simple and is shown in the figure by using arrows. The pattern of progressing through stages applies to all instances of airplane. Not all progressions between stages are allowed as the law of physics prevents an airplane from progressing from parked at the gate to being in flight. There are incidents/events that signal the progression between states. These incidents/events are shown as labels on the arrows. For example, when the airplane is in the "taking-off" stage, "wheels leaving the ground" signals the progression from the "taking-off" stage to the "in-flight" stage. The wheels leave the ground instantaneously, and, at any given instance of time, we can assume that the airplane is in one of the above stages.

The stages are defined by our perception (model) of reality and that some of the incidents/events are really indicators of the progression (change of state) from one stage to another stage. We will see later that the progressions (changes of state) are used as a vehicle to cause an action (execution of code) to occur during the "instantaneous" progression from one stage to another stage. Thus, stages are defined because the thing may need to take some action when the incident/event occurs. For instance, in the airplane example, when the "wheels leaves the ground," the wheels need to be lifted back into the airplane. Also, when the airplane "touches down," the brakes are applied, and usually the engines are reversed.

Common Lifecycle Forms

The pattern that characterizes a *Class* is called its *lifecycle form*. While any pattern/form is possible, two forms appear to dominate the modeling of computer applications at this time. Sally Shlaer and Stephen Mellor have given names to these patterns. They are

- *Circular Lifecycle.* Circular lifecycle generally applies when the object/class has an operational cycle for its behavior.
  Examples include the airplane, a microwave oven, and a robotic drill.
- *Born-and-Die Lifecycle.* When an instance gets created and deleted (or rest in a final state) during the life of the system being analyzed, the class is a good candidate for this form. Examples include a human in the history of mankind, an account in a banking system, a logging record, and a bar of candy in the course of a few days.

Models for Capturing Lifecycle

Historically, state models were used with structured methods to show how a system behaves when it receives external events from objects outside of the system. One of the weakness of this technique was that we lumped the system into one large object and the number of states needed exploded. Today, we assign a state model (machine) per object (i.e., the state model is part of the class definition of an object). This would reduce the state explosion problem and assign the state to the appropriate objects that exhibit the dynamic behavior for the system. This also makes managing the complexity of dynamic behavior much more maintainable and flexible.

A *state model* establishes relationships among *states* of an object, *events*, *transitions* between states as a result of *events*, *actions*, and *activities* performed by the object.

- *State Model.* This is a sequence of states that an object goes through during its lifetime in response to events. It also includes the responses to events.
- *State.* This represents a stage in the lifecycle of a typical object. A state is technically a period of time during which an object is waiting for an event to occur. [The complete internal state for an object is the combination of the data values of the attributes within the object. Because this may lead to thousands or millions of states, the state we choose to describe in a state model usually depends either on a grouping of data values and ranges, or they depend on the group of operations permitted (based on attribute values) on the object during different parts of its lifecycle. Thus, a state is an abstraction of the attribute values of an object.]
- *Event.* An event is a condition that can be detected by the object. Events can cause a transition to another state and/or they can cause one or more actions to be triggered. Technically, an event is an occurrence at a point in time where granularity of time depends on the degree of abstraction. Though the granularity of time may vary at different levels of the same application, an event must be atomic (i.e., non-interruptible) at the given level of abstraction. An event is a one-way asynchronous transmission[3] of

---

[3] Two-way information flow (e.g., call-and-return) can always be modeled as two one-way information flows.

information from one object to another. It may have parameters with names and types as part of the message sent.

- *Transition.* A transition is a response by an object to an event received by it. The response produces a change in the object that can constitute a change in state. Recall that we can choose our states to reflect ranges on attributes rather than individual data values to limit the number of states. Hence, a change in attribute may not be sufficient to cause a change in state. The mechanism for identifying if a change in state occurs is a *guard condition.*[4] A guard condition is a Boolean expression in terms of event parameters and the state variables and functions of the object to which the state diagram belongs. When an event triggers the transition, the value of the guard condition is evaluated. If the value evaluates to true, the transition occurs; otherwise, the transition does not occur. Not all transitions have an associated guard condition although we can say that the guard condition is simply the Boolean value true.

- *Action.* An action is an activity or an operation that is done inside of a state or on a transition. An action is atomic and instantaneous; that is, it is not interruptible at the abstraction level of the associated state. An action might set or modify one of the data members of the object, trigger an event in another object, execute one of the operations on the object, or call one of the public operations of another object. An action can occur during a transition, on entry into a state, during the entire period an object is in a state, on exit from a state, or on arrival of an event that does not cause a state transition.

- *Activity.* An activity is an operation or set of operations that is executing during the entire period an object is in a state. An activity is not atomic and may be interrupted by an event while it is executing.

Four forms of state models are widely used in analysis: (1) Mealy, (2) Moore, (3) Harel, and (4) modified Harel. The unified modeling language (UML) state model is based on the modified Harel. These models differ in terms of where actions are placed in the model. In the Mealy model, an action is performed when the transition is occurring. In the Moore model, an action is performed when an object enters into the state. In the Harel model, an action is performed when the transition is occurring, but it adds substates and other powerful constructs. In the modified Harel, an action can be performed when the transition is occurring, when an object enters a state, and when an object exits a state. UML has also allowed activities that occur while an object is in a state. Thus, UML represents a generalized case and can encompass all of the accepted state models.[5] State models are usually documented graphically using *state transition diagrams* as is shown later in this chapter.

---

[4] Guard conditions on transactions is a UML notation. Historically, such conditions in state machine models were called transition rules.

[5] This allows individuals familiar with Mealy, Moore, or Harel to capture their state models using UML.

In UML, three additional constructs are added: *history state*, *activity*, and *timing mark*. A *history state* is used to capture the concept that a state must "remember" its substate when it is exited and be able to enter the same substate on subsequent reentry into the state. An *activity* is an operation or set of operations within a state that takes time to complete; thus, it is not instantaneous and can be interrupted. Some activities continue until they are terminated by an external event (usually a state change), and others terminate on their own accord. A *timing mark* construct is used to capture real-time constraints on transition. The most common use of a timing mark is to capture the maximum limits on the elapsed time between events.

IDENTIFYING AND SPECIFYING EVENTS

From the above discussion of the lifecycle model, one of the key components that we need to identify is event(s). In this section, we learn techniques to identify and specify events.

Use Case and Scenario

As described in Chapter 4, a *use case* is a generic description of an entire transaction involving several objects. A *scenario* is an instance of a use case. It shows a particular series of interactions among objects in a single execution of the system. This single execution of the system typically constitutes a transaction (from the external object's perspectives) between the external object and the application/system.

Scenarios can be shown in two different ways:

1. *Sequence Diagram*. This shows the interaction among a set of objects in temporal order, which is very useful in understanding timing issues. An alternate form is a text dialog; a form that is widely used by non-technical requirement writers.
2. *Collaboration Diagram*. This shows the interactions among a set of objects as nodes in a graph, which is helpful in understanding software structure as all the interactions that affect an object are localized around it.

Sequence Diagram

Of the two ways to show scenarios, we will only discuss the sequence diagram in this book.[6] The basic elements of a *sequence diagram* were introduced previously. There is a form of the sequence diagram that captures procedure-calling sequences in situations where there is a single point of control at any given time. In this scheme, a

---

[6] While a collaboration diagram provides greater detail about the relationships among objects, they tend to be more complicated and most novices overlook or misinterpret them.

double line is used to show the period of time an object has a thread of control. Thus, a single line indicates that the object is blocked (not in control) and is waiting for an event to give it control.

EXAMPLE

For better understanding, let us borrow an example from Shlaer and Mellor. Suppose we want to model a scaled-down microwave oven, the One Minute Microwaver. The product requirements are as follows:

1. There is a single control button available for the users of the oven.
2. If the oven door is closed and a user pushes the button, the oven will cook (i.e., energize the tube) for one minute.
3. If user pushes the button at any time when the oven is cooking, user gets an additional minute of cooking time. For example, if the user has 31 seconds more cooking time to go and he/she pushes the button twice, the cook time is now for 2 minutes and 31 seconds.
4. Using the button with the door open has no effect.
5. There is a light inside the oven.
6. Any time the oven is cooking, the light must be turned on (so that the user can peer through the window in the oven's door and see if her/his food is boiling over.)
7. Any time the door is open, the light must be on (so that the user can see the food or have enough light to clean the oven).
8. User can stop the cooking by opening the door.
9. If user closes the door, the light goes out. This is the normal configuration when someone has just placed food inside the oven but has not yet pushed the control button.
10. If the oven times out (cook until the desired preset time), it turns off both the power tube and the light. It also then emits a warning beep to tell the user that the food is ready.

From the textual requirements, the following pertinent incidents are identified:

- Opening the door
- Closing the door
- Using the control button
- Completion of the prescribed cooking interval

These incidents are events that may cause the oven to have to perform some operations, as well as cause a change its state. These incidents are abstracted or captured as events. With those external events, we can create the following set of sequence diagrams for the microwave oven using use cases and scenarios: scenario 1 is the normal case and is shown in Figure 7-3. Please note that all scenarios are developed from an external (user's) perspective. In scenario 2, no additional time was added. This is shown in Figure 7-4. In scenario 3, the user opens the door while food is cooking. This is shown in Figure 7-5.

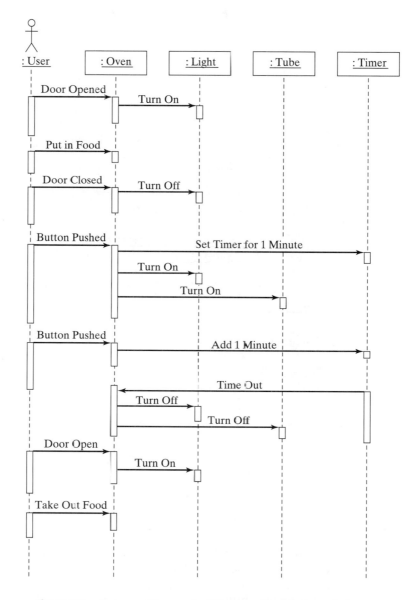

Figure 7-3   Sequence Diagram for Microwave Oven in Scenario 1.

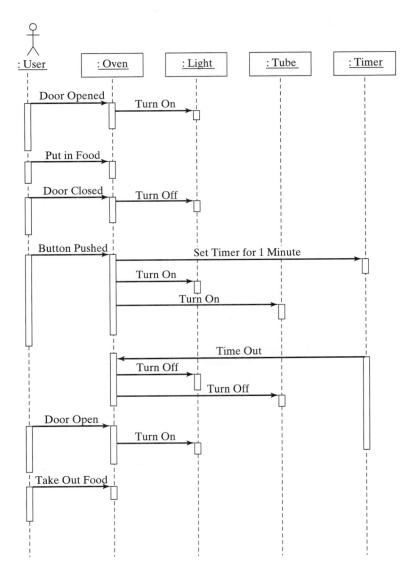

Figure 7-4   Sequence Diagram for Microwave Oven in Scenario 2.

These scenarios cover all the various sequences that are pertinent to the building of the state model. Technically, the user opens the door and the door notifies the oven that the door is open; similarly for the closing the door. The user also pushes the button and the button notifies the oven that the button has been pushed.

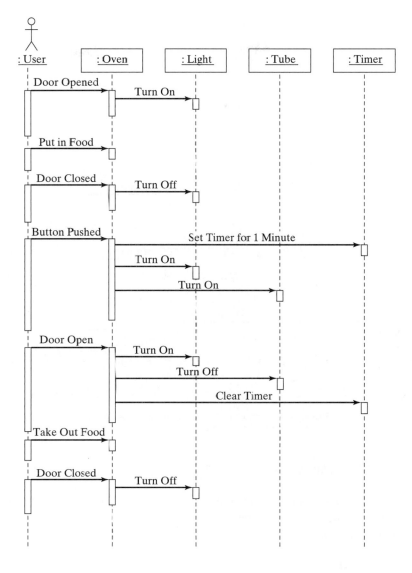

Figure 7-5   Sequence Diagram for Microwave Oven in Scenario 3.

However, neither the button nor the door takes any action on its own from these incidents. We modeled it as if the user opens the door is sending a signal to the oven directly; this simplifies the model with no loss of information for our purposes. This is shown in Figure 7-6.

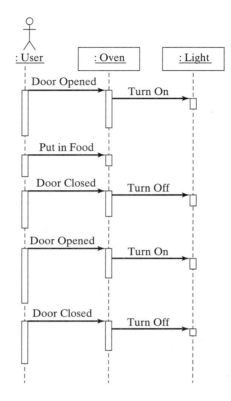

Figure 7-6   Sequence Diagram for Microwave Oven in Scenario in Scenario 4, the User
is Opening and Closing the Door.

SPECIFYING DYNAMIC BEHAVIOR

Use cases and scenarios are not sufficient documentation for the development. We
now look at ways of documenting the events and documenting the dynamic behavior
in a form more suited for programming.

Event List

An *event* is the abstraction of an incident or signal in the real world that tells some
object of the system that it is (or maybe) moving to a new state. In the abstraction
process, four aspects of an event should be specified:

1. **Meaning.** The meaning of an event is usually captured in a short phrase
    that tells what is going on in the real world. For example, "wheel leave
    ground" in the airplane example and "door open" in the microwave
    example.

2. **Destination.** The object[7] that receives the event. By convention, the event is sent only to one receiver. (If more than one object is to respond to the event, we can treat it as if each object receives its own copy of the event.)

3. **Label.** A unique label must be provided for each event. This distinguishes different events from each other. This is very important when there are distinct events with similar meanings. Though the label is arbitrary, the suggested format for labeling is to use a letter-number combinations. A convenient convention is to use destination-based labeling where all the events that are received by the same class begin with the class's key letter(s).[8]

4. **Event Data.** An event should be thought of as a service request; thus, it can and usually will carry data. This data is given to the object as parameters of the service request.

An *event list* is simply a listing of all the events from the scenarios that are applicable to the definition of the state models for the objects within the application/system. The event list for the microwave oven is shown in Table 7-1.

Table 7-1 Event List

Label	Meaning	Source	Destination	Data
V1	Door open	User	Oven	None
V2	Door closed	User	Oven	None
V3	Button pushed	User	Oven	None
V4	Timer timeout	Timer	Oven	None
L1	Turn on light	Oven	Light	None
L2	Turn off light	Oven	Light	None
P1	Turn on tube (energize Tube)	Oven	Tube	None
P2	Turn off tube (de-energize Tube)	Oven	Tube	None
T1	Set timer for one minute	Oven	Timer	None
T2	Add a minute to timer	Oven	Timer	None
T3	Clear timer	Oven	Timer	None

---

[7] The state model is part of an object. Because lifecycle patterns are by class, we define the state model for the entire class.

[8] The classes key letter(s) is a developer defined way to refer to a class with an abbreviation rather than the full class name. For example, a class named Microwave could use mw as the key letters. The use of key letters is an artifact of the C programming roots of C++ where functions that operated on specific data structures used key letters to allow programmers to remember an association between the function and the data structure on which it was to operate.

Without the sequence diagram, most of us would consider "putting in the food" and "taking out the food" as important incidents. However, the sequence diagram shows that they do not cause any action to occur and, thus, are not material to the modeling process. This may seem strange to the novice as the primary purpose of the microwave is to heat food. In reality, the microwave works with no food in it; we can turn on our microwave with nothing in it. So our model does capture accurately how a microwave is actually designed and built. Also the warning beep is an incident, but the processing of that event is handled by the external object (user). Thus, it is not an event that the system will process and thus not on our event list.

State Transition Table

In dynamic behavior modeling, a *state* is given a number and a name that is unique within the state model. The number is used in the state transition table to depict the next state and does not prescribe the order in which an object would occupy the states. An *action* is a set of operations that must be done when the transition occurs. The following operations are allowed:

- Read and write operations involving its own attributes.
- Generate an event to be sent to any other object, including itself.
- Generate an event to something outside the scope of analysis (e.g., an operator, a hardware device, or an object in another system/subsystem).
- Create, delete, set, reset, read a timer.
- Access services of another object, including objects in its same class.

Because the operations allowed are very liberal in an action, it is the responsibility of the analyst/developer to ensure the consistency of the state model as a whole. Thus, analysts should ensure the following:

- *Leave the object consistent.* If an attribute gets updated, any attribute that computationally depends on it must be updated.
- *Ensure consistency of relationship.* If the action creates or deletes an object, it must ensure that any relationship involving those objects are made consistent with the rules stated on the model.
- *Leave subtypes and supertypes consistent.* If action migrates an object from one type to another type, it must ensure that all the proper objects and relationships are managed.

In a *state transition table*, each row represents one of the possible states (stages) of the state model,[9] and each column represents an event that has this state model as its destination. The cells of the table are filled in with the specification of what happens when an instance of class (e.g., your specific microwave oven) is in a given state (row in the table) receives a particular event (the column).

---

[9] A state model belongs to an object.

The process of creating the state transition table for each class[10] is

1. Place all the events that have the same destination on the columns of the table.
2. Start with one row if you have not identified any stages or use your stages as possible states.
3. Take each scenario and start filling in the cells in the table, showing the next state above the line and the action below the line.
4. When you run into a conflict (i.e., a cell has to respond to an event differently for two different scenarios), add a new state to the model as this means that there was a change in state (stage) that has not been captured in the original analysis.[11]
5. Keep doing steps 3 and 4 until all the scenarios are captured in a consistent manner in the table.
6. Now check the empty cells and decide if these are events ignored or can't happen situations.
7. Finally, reduce any identical rows to one row, if you are using the Mealy model.

Steps 6 and 7 are very important as they ensure the completeness of the analysis. The state transition tables for the microwave oven are shown in Table 7-2, Table 7-3, Table 7-4, and Table 7-5.

Table 7-2 Light

States	L1: Turn On	L2: Turn Off
1. On	Event ignored [4]	2 None
2. Off	1 None	Event ignored[1]

1. When light is on, ignore "on" request; similarly for off.

Table 7-3 Microwave Oven

States	V1: Door Open	V2: Door Closed	V3: Button Pushed	V4: Timer timeout
1. Idle with door open	Can't happen [1]	2 Turn off light	Event ignored	Can't happen[2]

---

[10] Because patterns of behavior hold over an entire class, we define a state model for the class. Each object gets its own state model, just like attributes.

[11] This is usually seen as the need to perform different actions when the event is received in the different scenarios.

Table 7-3 Microwave Oven (*continued*)

States	V1: Door Open	V2: Door Closed	V3: Button Pushed	V4: Timer timeout
2. Idle with door closed	1 Turn on light	Can't happen[3]	3 Set timer to one minute; turn on light; turn on tube	Can't happen [2]
3. Initial cooking period	6 Turn off tube: clear timer	Can't happen [3]	4 Add one minute to timer	5 Turn off tube; turn off light; sound warning beep
4. Extended cooking period	6 Turn off tube: clear timer	Can't happen [3]	4 Add one minute to timer	5 Turn off tube; turn off light; sound warning beep
5. Cooking complete	1 Turn on light	Can't happen[3]	Event ignored	Can't happen[2]
6. Cooking interrupted	Can't happen[1]	2 Turn off light	Event ignored	Can't happen[2]

1. Door is already open.
2. Timer is not running.
3. Door is already closed.

Table 7-4 Timer

State	T1: Set Timer	T2: Add Time	T3: Clear Timer	T4: Clock Tick	T5: Fire
1. Idle	2 Set time remaining to 1 minute; set up ticking mechanism	Can't happen[1]	Can't happen[1]	Can't happen [2]	Can't happen[4]
2. Set	Can't happen[3]	5 Add 1 minute to time remaining	1 Clear time remaining: unset tick mechanism	3 Subtract one time tick from remaining time	Can't happen[4]

Table 7-4 Timer (*continued*)

State	T1: Set Timer	T2: Add Time	T3: Clear Timer	T4: Clock Tick	T5: Fire
3. Counting down	Can't happen[3]	5 Add 1 minute to time remaining	1 Clear time remaining: unset tick mechanism	3 Subtract one time tick from remaining time; check if time remaining is ≤ 0; if so, generate internal T5 signal to cause transition to firing state.	4 Generate T3 signal to effect transition from firing to idle
4. Firing	Can't happen[3]	Event ignored[5]	1 Clear time remaining: unset tick mechanism	Event ignored[5]	Can't happen[4]
5. Adding	Can't happen[3]	5 Add 1 minute to time remaining	1 Clear time remaining: unset tick mechanism	3 Subtract one time tick from remaining time	Can't happen[4]

1. Timer is not active.
2. Tick mechanism is not active.
3. Timer is already set.
4. T5 is an internal signal that is generated only when it is in state 3.
5. Too late.

Table 7-5 Power Tube

States	P1: Turn On	P2: Turn Off
1. On	Event ignored[1]	2 None
2. Off	1 None	Event ignored[1]

1. When tube is energized, ignore "on" request; similarly for off.

Observe that in Table 7-3 states 1 and 6 are identical state transitions; states 3 and 4 are also identical. However, in each case, the pre-condition for entering each state is different. For instance, you can only get into the cooking interrupt state from prior states when the power tube is on and the timer is turned on. While a person can open and close the microwave door to cause the state model to move from state 1 to state 2 and back to state 1, this would not require that the timer be cleared and the tube to be de-energized. When we get to diagramming the state models, we will see the impact of these pre-conditions on the different state models.

We can assume that these objects have methods that really turn on and off the physical devices.

DOCUMENTING DYNAMIC BEHAVIOR

We will look at a graphic form, the state diagram, for documenting the state model in a class. Though each object has its own state model, we define the template for the state model in the class. Remember all objects in the same class have copies of the same state model.

State Diagrams

A *state diagram* is a graphic form of documenting a state model. It describes in pictorial form all the possible ways in which the objects respond to events without respect to whether they are sent by other objects or are purely internal. A simple UML state diagram for an object with two states is illustrated in Figure 7-7. The start state is indicated by a transition into it from a solid circle. The solid circle is often interpreted as the initial creation of the object with the transition into the start state a result of completing the initialization of the object. This perspective allows us to deal with situations where an object may not be in a consistent state until the initialization has been completed. The transition into the initial state is an indication that the object has reached consistency. The final state of the object is indicated by a solid circle within a circle. The final state is a state that has no exit transition (i.e., you can enter and cannot leave). This does not mean that an object is destroyed.

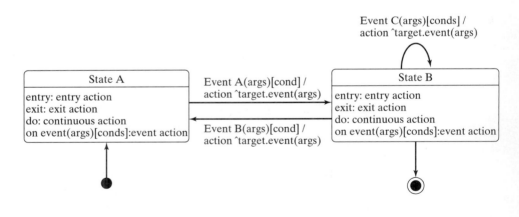

Figure 7-7   Simple State Diagram.

A state is composed of

- *Name*. A textual string that distinguishes this state from other states. A state may be anonymous (have no name).
- *Entry Action (Keyword: entry)*. Action executed on entry into the state.
- *Exit Action (Keyword: exit)*. Actions executed on exit from the state.
- *Internal transitions (Keyword: on)*. Transitions that are handled without causing a change in state.
- *Activity (Keyword: do)*. An ongoing computation that occurs the entire time the object is in a state.
- *Substates*. A nested structure of the state. It may involve disjointed sequentially active substates or concurrently active substates.
- *Deferred Events (Keyword: defer, NEW)*. A list of events that are not handled in that state. These events are postponed and queued for handling by objects in another state.

States are represented in UML by rounded rectangles with a horizontal line that separates the name of the state from the other components of the state. Transitions are directed arrows that link the initial state to the final state. In UML, when an action is listed within a state, it is preceded by a label that indicates when the action is supposed to happen. There are four possible kinds of labels:

- **Entry**. The action is performed when the state is entered.
- **Exit**. The action is performed just before the transition to the new state.
- **Do**. The action is performed continuously during the entire period that the object is in this state.
- **On** *any event name*. The action is performed when the event occurs and the object stays in the same state.

A transition is composed of

- *Source State*. The state affected by the transition (i.e., the active state). The transition fires when an event is received and guard condition, if any, is satisfied (obviously the object must also be in the source state at the time).
- *Event*. Its reception makes the transition eligible to be fired.
- *Guard Condition*. A Boolean expression that can be evaluated when a transition is triggered. If the evaluation is true, the transition is fired. If the evaluation is false, the transition may not fire, and if no other transition may be triggered by the event, the event is lost.
- *Action*. An executable atomic computation. In this context, it is executed during the transition.
- *Target State*. The state that is active after the completion of the transition.
- *Signals*. A list of events (signals) that may be generated during the transition.

In UML, a transition is labeled by

- The event that causes the transition (mandatory)
- Any guard condition (optional)
- Any action that is performed during the transition (optional)
- Any event that is generated by the transition (optional)

The event associated with the transition is identified by a label followed by the event data enclosed within parentheses. If there are not any event data, the parentheses are empty. Any guard condition will appear after the event enclosed within square brackets. Any action performed during a transition appears in the diagram after triggering event and condition separated from them by a /. An event generated appears after the transition action and is preceded by a carot, ^, the target of the event by a label separated from the event name by a period. The generated event has its associated arguments. A transition must have an associated event but does not necessarily have an associated guard condition, action, or generated event.

The simple state diagram also illustrates one additional feature: a *transition to self*. A transition to self is a transition from an initial state back to the initial state. There is distinction between handling an event within a state and as a transition to self. In the case where an event is handled within the state, the entry and exit actions are not performed. However, on a transition to self both the entry and exit actions are performed as well as any actions specified in the transition.

The simple state diagram illustrated in Figure 7-7 is sufficient for simple state models. More complex state models incorporate nested states (i.e., substates). The UML diagram for illustrating a nested state diagram is illustrated in Figure 7-8. The transition from the nested solid circle identifies the entry substate. Actions are associated with the nested states rather than the encompassing state.

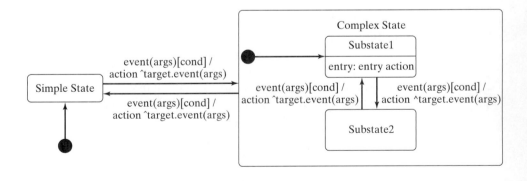

Figure 7-8   Nested State Diagram.

UML supports even more complex state models by allowing concurrent sub-states. Concurrent substates are viewed (for modeling purposes) as having separate threads of control. That is, each substate can act independently of the other. An example of concurrent substates for filling out a section of course registration request is illustrated in Figure 7-9. In this example, a transition to the next state occurs only when all nested concurrent states have reached the exit conditions. This should be contrasted with the situation illustrated in Figure 7-10.

As stated previously, UML supports both Mealy and Moore state diagrams. The choice of how a state model is captured depends on analyst preference. In the case of our example, either approach is acceptable. Below are the state diagrams (Mealy and Moore) for the state transition diagram of the microwave oven. One of the powerful aspects of UML is that it can support both the Mealy and Moore models. In the Mealy model, states from the transition table were collapsed because the actions are associated with the transition.

In the Moore model, the action is associated with the state. We cannot eliminate identical rows from the model. In our model, the action is associated with the entry into the state. There are models that allow associate action with exit from a state also. UML supports a model that allows action with transition, entry into a state, and exit from a state. However, in practice, we normally associate the action with the transition. The Harel model also associates the action with the transition, but it also allows substates and other powerful capabilities. State models are not the only model that can be used for capturing dynamic behavior; other models such as Petri Nets exist to handle more sophisticated dynamic behavior. The state model is usually sufficient for most practitioners.

Course registration request

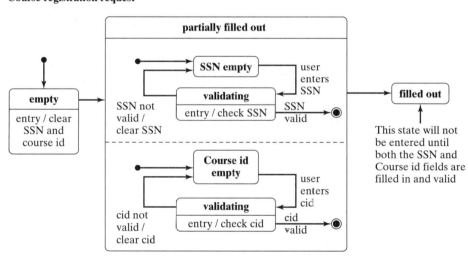

Figure 7-9 Nested Concurrent Substates with Exit Requiring Both Concurrent Substates to Reach Exit States before Exit from the Enclosing State.

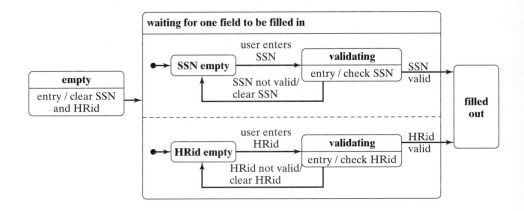

Figure 7-10   Nested Concurrent Substates with Exit Requiring Satisfaction of Either of the Substates.

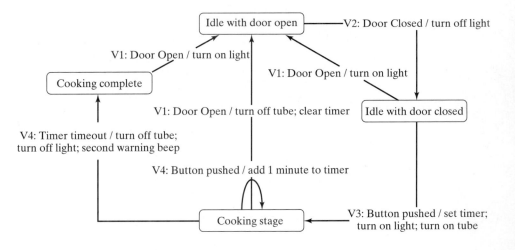

Figure 7-11   UML Notation for Mealy State Diagram for Microwave Oven.

RECOMMENDED APPROACH

The steps we recommend for performing behavioral analysis are

1. Prepare scenarios of all the typical interaction sequences.
2. Prepare scenarios of all the accepted business exception cases.
3. If appropriate, prepare scenarios of all the failure and rare cases. Failures includes error conditions, equipment failures, and undesirable and unusual

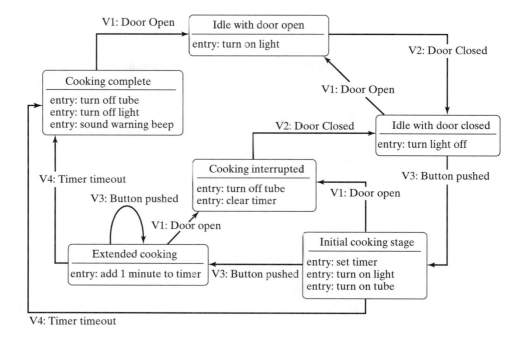

Figure 7-12   Moore State Diagram for Microwave Oven.

behaviors.[12] In object-oriented methods, the failure conditions that are to be processed by the application/system should be formalized into the analysis model just as normal behaviors.[13]

4. Develop sequence diagram for all cases that help identify events.
5. Use the sequence diagram to generate an event list. Note that in the example, we assumed that the transition is only dependent on the recep-

---

[12] Many of us (real-time process control) know this as failure analysis and understand that proper analysis is highly problem dependent. The purpose of failure analysis is to take into account the effect of certain kinds of malfunctions and errors and to evaluate strategies for dealing with them. In process control, the goal is to either maintain control, or recover control, or have a graceful and safe shutdown of an industrial or external process. Frequently, the failure analysis leads to additional requirements, installation of new sensors, addition of electrical/mechanical safeguards, writing of emergency procedure instruction book, etc.

[13] A word of caution to the meticulous thinker; it is very easy to get carried away and investigate a myriad of possible failures. Economics and time constraints, but balanced with safety, should be applied to limit the failure analysis to real and reasonable scenarios. Far-fetched scenarios should not be designed into the system. However, if there is a safety or economic damage concern, it is strongly recommended that a manual procedure be written to handle these situations. For abnormal behaviors are usually extremely complex and can cause the model to grow larger and more complex. This will make the system more difficult to maintain and to modify.

tion of one event. In some situations a transition may depend on the arrival of two or more events from different sources. There are two ways you can handle this situation. First, you can create an intermediate state to hold the reception of one of the event and use it as a holding state for reception of the other event(s). The other choice is to add an attribute or object to hold the data. This would require the programmer to initialize and clean up the attribute or object at the appropriate times.

6. Use the event list and your knowledge of classes to create state transition tables.
7. Use the state transition table to create your state diagrams.
8. Check the state diagrams by testing the scenarios against the diagram.

SUMMARY

Historically, capturing the changes to objects and their relationships over time has been very difficult to manage. In this chapter, we presented a concept and its associated mechanisms to capture this aspect of the application/system. This concept is called dynamic behavior. We learned the following about dynamic behavior:

- How to identify it by recognizing common lifecycle forms: circular and born-and-die.
- How to identify and to specify events that are the key stimuli to cause objects to change state.
- How to use the events to help us identify and specify the dynamic behaviors using state transition tables.
- How to document this specification in a graphical form by using a state diagram.
- A couple of types of finite state machines that may be used to implement the dynamic behavior captured using the state transition table.

8

Identifying Relationships

In the previous two chapters, we captured how each object provides services. In the process of specifying how it was done, we also demonstrated that some objects need access to services (functions) of other objects to perform the necessary operations to supply the original service. However, in the object-oriented paradigm (unlike the procedural paradigm), an object cannot just call a service (function). The message passing paradigm requires that a service request be directed to an object. In this chapter, we address how an object accesses the services of another object.

ACCESSING ANOTHER OBJECT'S SERVICES

One of the fundamental differences between the object-oriented paradigm and the procedural paradigm is that in the object-oriented paradigm every service request (function call) must be sent to a specific object, while in the procedural paradigm a function can be called directly. For example, for object A to send a message to object B, object A must have a "handle" to object B. Thus, in object-oriented technology, the analysts/developers should understand the various vehicles available to give an object access to the handle of another object.

There are four basic ways that one object accesses another object's services:

1. The calling object, which somehow has a handle, passes the handle of the other object as one of the arguments of the function (message) signature.
2. The called object has a relationship (aggregation or link[1]) to the other object. A relationship gives handle(s) to other objects in the relationship.
3. The needed service belongs to an "ancestor" class.[2]
4. Access to static class functions, which may be considered a managed global function.

RELATIONSHIPS

In a world of perfect reuse and portability, each object and/or class would be independent of every other object and/or class. Then during step 3 (when we captured how each object provides services), we would have been able to specify all the operations of every method with operations that only use data belonging to the object and/or is passed to the object from the calling object. In this perfect world, all services would be provided using only data associated with itself and the calling object. This would make reuse and portability a very easy issue.

There are object-oriented experts who argue that the use of relationships (association and aggregation) violate the encapsulation and information hiding principles. This is a correct statement. Unfortunately, all relationships, including generalization (a.k.a. inheritance), violate the encapsulation and information hiding principles; there are very few experts who would argue against inheritance and polymorphism. We take a more practical approach to object-oriented technology. If a mechanism helps us manage complexity, then we are willing to use it. In practice, one or more groups of collaborating objects are needed to implement a large number of the services. Experience has shown that all the mechanisms/constructs (and then some) that we will be discussing are needed to implement any application/system of any significant capability.

Unfortunately, *No object is an island, independent of all others*. Objects typically depend on other objects for services and possibly for error handling, constant data, and exception handling. Some objects are components of other objects, and some objects are used to join other objects. Moreover, objects are, by definition, instances of classes, and classes may inherit attributes and services from other classes. In most applications, the model needs to capture these interdependencies of the various objects.

These interdependencies are called relationships. A relationship is not merely a link that ties one object to another object so that it can access the other object's

---

[1] Link is a relationship between objects and an association is a relationship between classes.

[2] The standard object-oriented term for ancestor class is *superclass*. In brief, the service is inherited from the ancestor.

services. A relationship also carries a semantic meaning. Object-oriented technology gives both analysts and developers a very rich set of mechanisms or constructs to capture these semantic relationships.

In this chapter, we discuss three very important relationships: generalization, links, and aggregation. These are certainly not new concepts; we work with them everyday. For example, we all learned generalization when we studied taxonomies in biology class. An excellent example of a link is marriage, and an example of aggregation (whole-parts) is a car. Moreover, links in the form of associations have been widely used for years in the database modeling community.

Some object-oriented authors believe that every piece of information should be attached to a single class; thus, a link violates the encapsulation principle and should not be allowed. However, most of us who have developed large and complex applications/systems believe that some information transcends a single class, and that the failure to treat a link on an equal footing with objects leads to a model (program) that contains hidden assumptions and dependencies. Thus, during analysis one should model a link to indicate that the information it contains is not subordinate to a single object (class) but dependent on two or more objects (classes).

Part of the problem is that most object-oriented languages do not directly support relationships. That is, they emphasize the object and not the fact that objects stand in relations with each other. This is not a problem with the object-oriented paradigm, but a problem with how the language that we use to implement the paradigm affects our thinking about the paradigm.

GENERALIZATION

Generalization, as we will use it, has its roots in the knowledge representation paradigm used in artificial intelligence. Ross Quillian's psychological model of associative memory is one example. In that representation, Quillian introduced the node-link model for representing a semantic knowledge network. The nodes represented classes and the links represented relationships between objects in the respective classes at the nodes. In a semantic network, both the node and the link had labels. One of the most powerful labels represented the generalization relationship. That link was called the *is_a*. The concept of the is_a relationship is quite simple. If object A has an is_a relationship with object B, then all the attributes and services of object B are the attributes and services of object A. For example, consider the situation where we have two objects: Person and Employee. Reasonable attributes for Person could be: name, age, weight, and height, but an Employee is_a Person. By the definition of the is_a relationship, the attributes of Person are also the attributes of Employee. Note that normally the Employee has additional attributes such as salary, position, organization number, and employee identification number. In this example, the Person object is referred to as the *ancestor* (or parent) node and the Employee object as the *descendent* (or child) node. The ancestor is a generalization of the descendent, and, conversely, the descendent is a specialization of the ancestor.

Generalization relationships pose some important properties that differentiate it from other relationships.[3] These properties are the following:

1. Structural Properties

   a. Attributes
   The descendent has all the attributes of the ancestor. For instance, Employee has the age attribute because it is a descendant class of Person.
   b. Non-generalization relationships
   The descendent has all the non-generalization relationships of the ancestor. For example, if we add a marriage link[4] between two Persons, Employee will also have a marriage link because it is a descendent of Person.

2. Interface Properties
All services provided by the ancestor must also be provided by the descendent.[5] For instance, if the Person object had an addWeight service, then Employee will also have an addWeight service because Employee is a descendent of Person.

3. Behavior Properties

   a. Generalization without polymorphism (good child)
   In generalization without polymorphism, all methods supplied by the ancestor for its services are also used by the descendent to provide the corresponding services.
   b. Generalization with polymorphism (bad child)
   In generalization with polymorphism, some methods supplied by the ancestor for its services are also used by the descendent to provide the corresponding services. For the remaining services of the ancestor, the descendent supplies its own customized methods that replace the appropriate corresponding methods.[6]

---

[3] In theory, all three aspects (attribute, service, and behavior) can be redefined in the subclass, We have limited the redefinition for a very practical purpose and consistent with the implementation of inheritance in Java. Other languages may give you more flexibility in redefinition, and this may seem more powerful; however, there can be too much flexibility. In most languages, the additional flexibility results in software that is less safe as we cannot guarantee that the software is well tested.

[4] A *link* is a relationship between two objects. We will learn later that Person is really a class, and, as such, the relationship is really an association.

[5] Even if the service of a descendent effectively removes the behavior, it must still provide the interface for that service.

[6] This is perhaps a good time to remind the reader that the "bad" child is often an excellent model in object-oriented analysis and design.

4. Mathematical Properties

a. Antisymmetry
If object A is_a descendent of object B, then object B may not have an is_a relationship with object A (object B is not a descendent of object A). For example Employee is_a Person, but not all persons are employees.

b. Transitivity
If object A is_a object B and object B is_a object C, then object A is_a object C.[7] For example, if we add the fact that a SalesPerson is_a Employee to our example, then SalesPerson is also a Person. Furthermore, it also has the age attribute because of properties 1a and 4b.

Generalization/specialization is a critical mechanism to the object-oriented paradigm because finding the correct ancestor(s) to assign the services and attributes is crucial to designing a good model. Unfortunately, it is very difficult for novices to realize that most of the objects with which they work are composites of other objects.

To overcome this difficulty, novices should consider every object as a complex object that may be viewed as many different subobjects, each subobject represents that complex object in a single semantic domain. For example, we are (1) employees in the work domain, (2) taxpayers in the governmental domain, (3) parents and/or children in the family domain, and (4) members in the social club domain.[8] The services we provide and the relationships we have are different for each domain. For example, consider the services *hire*, *promote*, *retire*, and *fire*. All these services are intimately tied to the fact that each of us is also an employee. When a person is unemployed, these services would not apply. As a taxpayer, a tax audit relationship with a tax-auditor may exist. This is a relationship that is very intimately tied to each of us being a taxpayer. It would be improper to use this relationship in the other domains. For instance, a taxpayer does not want his auditor known by her/his employer or by her/his social club.

The proper use of generalization helps us represent composite objects in a manner that manages complexity and, thus, makes software more maintainable and flexible to change. Although a descendent can be thought of as having all the attributes, non-generalization relationships, and services of all its ancestors, it is better to consider the descendent as having access to all these things via the appropriate subobject of which it is a specialization. This forces us to keep the attributes, relationships and services in the appropriate semantic domain, which reduces coupling

---

[7] Transitivity makes it possible to organize the objects in a hierarchical manner. Because of this property, generalization is diagrammatically shown as an acyclic directed graph. Because Java does not support multiple inheritance within category, generalization is shown diagrammatically as a tree.

[8] Although some of these names may also be role names in some applications, we will assume that we want to capture these concepts as objects.

and provides higher cohesion. Lower coupling and higher cohesion lead to more maintainable and more flexible software.

IDENTIFYING AND SPECIFYING GENERALIZATION/SPECIALIZATION

We recommend using the original list of potential objects minus the objects external to the application as our list of objects that may potentially be used in an is_a relationship. With this list, we apply the following test to each possible pairing of the objects. We ask: Is object A an object B? and Is object B an object A? The allowable answers are: *always*, *sometimes*, and *never*. If the answer to both questions is *never*, the two objects are not in an is_a relationship with each other. If both answers are *always*, object A and object B are synonymous. These objects will either be instances of the same class or their are two different names for the same class. If the answer to "Is object A an object B?" is *always* and the answer to "Is object B an object A?" is *sometimes*, then object A has an is_a relationship with object B. The only remaining combination will mean that object B has an is_a relationship with object A.

For example, let us look at the following list of objects: Officer, Manager, Supervisor, Advisor, Engineer, Contractor, and Representative. We apply our test to these objects in a typical corporate environment. The answers are illustrated in Table 8-1.

Table 8-1 An is_a Analysis Table.

Is A a B	O	M	S	Ad	E	C	R
Officer	X	a	n	n	n	n	a
Manager	s	X	s	n	n	n	a
Supervisor	n	a	X	n	n	n	a
Advisor	n	n	n	X	n	n	a
Engineer	n	n	n	n	X	s	n
Contractor	n	n	n	n	a	X	n
Representative	s	s	s	s	n	n	X

A is the row, B is the column, O=Officer, M=Manager, S=Supervisor, Ad=Advisor, E=Engineer, C=Contractor, and R=Representative. In the cells, a = always, s = sometimes, and n = never.

To use this table effectively, we look at the columns with at least one a and then start with the columns containing the smallest numbers of a's. In this example, it would be the Engineer column. From the table, a Contractor is_a Engineer. The next column with the least a's is Manager. From the table, Supervisor is_a Manager and Officer is_a Manager. Finally, we are ready for the representative column. If we use the results of the table directly, we have four is_a relationships:

- Officer is_a Representative
- Manager is_a Representative
- Supervisor is_a Representative
- Advisor is_a Representative

However, from earlier is_a relationships, we know that both a Supervisor and an Officer are also Managers. So probably the proper semantics are that the Manager is_a Representative and an Advisor is_a Representative. The Supervisor and the Officer inherit this relationship from Manager.

As an exercise for the reader, consider adding the following three objects to the Table 8-1: (1) Jim who is an Officer, (2) Jack who is a Supervisor, and (3) Joe who is an Engineer. When doing this exercise, you should note that the three objects (Jim, Jack, Joe) all satisfy the is_a test.[9]

OBJECT AGGREGATION

To view an object as subobjects, each of which operates in a single semantic domain[10] is not the same as viewing an object as consisting of components of objects. To support this second view, another mechanism, *aggregation*, is provided in the object-oriented paradigm. *Aggregation* (or *whole-parts*) is not a new concept to us. Analysts and developers are constantly dealing with aggregate entities consisting of component entities. The aggregate constitutes the whole and the components are the parts. For example, a purchase order is composed of line items, a weekly timesheet is composed of numerous daily time accounting, and a system is composed of subsystems made from hardware, software, and so on.

Aggregation, like generalization, possesses some important properties.

1. *Structural Properties.* The parts must have some structural or functional relationship to the whole for which they are constituents.
2. *Mathematical Properties*

- *Antisymmetry.* If object A is a part of object B, then object B cannot be a part of object A. For example, a purchase order is composed of line items. By antisymmetry, a purchase order is not part of a line item. Note that the line item may be composed of sub-line items. Even in this case, a line item may not be part of a sub-line item.
- *Transitivity.* If object A is a part of object B and object B is a part of object C, then object A is a part of object C. For example, a purchase

---

[9] We will learn in a later chapter that generalization/specialization is really applied to classes. Jim, Jack, and Joe are instances. Although a case can be made for an instance being a specialization of a class object, in the object-oriented paradigm, a different mechanism is used to capture this special case—instantiation.

[10] For example, the generalization/specialization view of an object.

order is composed of line items which may be composed of sub-line items. By transitivity, a sub-line item is also part of the purchase order.

These properties must be satisfied by all instances of an aggregation. Furthermore, when these aggregations are implemented, these properties should be managed. Unfortunately, this is rarely done as most programming languages do not provide the language mechanisms to directly support aggregation.

Attributes, relationships, services, and methods are not inherited in aggregation, in contrast to generalization. Because the properties of an aggregation are very weak, aggregation may be either static or dynamic, and a component of an aggregate may also be conditional. A *static aggregation* has fixed (invariant) components and cannot be changed. A *dynamic aggregation* has components that may vary over time. A *conditional component* either is or is not a component of an aggregate, depending on whether a specific condition holds.[11]

Aggregations are very useful. They reduce complexity by treating many objects as one object. They provide a construct or mechanism that better models specific application domain entities (e.g., purchase order) than does a link. Aggregations also ensure the proper visibility (information and service hiding) of the interactions among the components. For example, the individual lights of a traffic signal must be turned on and off in a specific sequence. Thus, the creation of a traffic light object that aggregates the three traffic lights as components allows modeling the control of the individual components via the aggregate. This is very powerful, as it hides all the complexity from the users of the traffic signal.

CLASSIFICATION OF AGGREGATION

Unfortunately, because the object-oriented paradigm has not defined the aggregation mechanism very well, most of us have difficulties applying this mechanism properly in practice. The latest literature on this topic argues that this is because of the fact that aggregation, itself, is an "ancestor" concept. It is our belief that we need to use the "descendent" concepts (more specialization) to be able to use this mechanism effectively. These descendent concepts, or different kinds of aggregation, capture additional properties, which help us better manage complexity.

Unified modeling language (UML) identifies two types of aggregation relationships: aggregation and composition. In UML parlance, aggregation refers to collections in which the objects that make up the collection do not stand in static structural relationships with each other. Examples of aggregations include flocks of birds and a pile of sand. Composition represents collections in which the objects that make up the collection exist in structural relationships with each other. An example

---

[11] Novices should be very careful with conditional components. They should rarely be used; normally, it is better to capture a variation by specialization (subclassing).

of a composition is the motor of a car, which is made up of motor parts that exist in specific relationships with each other.

From a theoretical perspective, linguists, logicians, and psychologists have studied the nature of relationships. One of the relationships that has been studied reasonably well is the relationship between the parts of things and the wholes that they make up.[12] In a joint paper, Morton Winston, Roger Chaffin, and Douglas Herrmann discussed this whole-parts relationship. They described several kinds of aggregation (composition or meronymic relationships). In their study, the kind of relationship is determined by the combination of the following basic properties:

- *Configuration*—whether the parts bear a particular functional or structural relationship either to one and another or to the whole that they constitute
- *Homeomorphic*—whether the parts are the same kind of things as the whole
- *Invariance*—whether the parts can be separated from the whole

The paper identified six types of aggregation; we have added a seventh.

1.   Assembly-parts (Component-integral composition)
2.   Material-object composition
3.   Portion-object composition
4.   Place-area composition
5.   Collection-members composition
6.   Container-content (Member-bunch composition)
7.   Member-partnership composition

Assembly-Parts (Component-Integral) Composition

In this assembly-parts aggregation, the whole comprises components that maintain their identity even when they are part of the whole. To be an aggregation of this kind, the parts are required to have a specific functional or structural relationship to one another as well as the whole that they constitute. For example, frames are part of a roll of film, bristles are part of a brush, wheels are part of a car, analytical geometry is part of mathematics. In addition, an integral object (whole) is divided into component parts, which are objects in their own right. Furthermore, the components may not be haphazardly arranged but must bear a particular relationship, either structurally or functionally, with one another and with the whole. Thus, the whole exhibits a patterned structure or organization. Examples include traffic signals, cars, airplanes, toys, machines, and computers.

---

[12] The study of aggregation (particularly whole-parts relationships) is referred to as mereology. The accepted formal theory of whole-parts is typically presented within one of two frameworks: the Calculus of Individuals of Leanard and Goodman and the Merology of Lesniewski.

These items are assembled from parts because, in an assembly-parts aggregation, the assembly does not exist without parts. The whole may be tangible (car, toothbrush, airplane, printer), abstract (mathematics, physics, physiology, accounting, jokes), organizational (NATO, United States of America, Exxon), or temporal (musical performance, film showing).

However, when a component ceases to support the overall pattern of the object, a different relationship is established. For example, if a memory card is taken out of a computer, the memory card is no longer considered part of the computer. However, the memory card is still considered a computer part or a piece of a computer. Unlike a component, a part or a piece does not participate in the overall pattern of the whole and provides no functional support for the whole. In a component-integral object, a component of the whole can be removed without materially affecting the concept of the whole.

When looking for component-integral object composition in a requirements document, look for the keywords "is part of" and "is assembled from." Examples of this are

- A keyboard is part of a computer.
- Nuclear physics is part of physics.
- Windows are parts of a house.
- A piano recital is part of the performance.
- Chairs are parts of the office.
- A telephone is assembled from its parts.
- An orchestra is assembled from its various instrument sections.

As these examples show, it is not difficult to identify assembly-part relationships from a requirements document.

Material-Object Composition

In the material-object aggregation, the parts (materials) lose their identity when they are used to make the whole. In fact, the relationship between parts is no longer known once they become part of the whole. Thus, a material-object composition relationship defines an invariant configuration of parts within the whole because no part may be removed from the whole. Examples are "Bread is made from the following ingredients: flour, sugar, yeast," and "A car is made from materials such as iron, plastic, and glass."

Note that while material-object composition defines what the whole is made of, a component-integral object defines the parts of the whole. For example, to describe a component-integral object relationship we would say "A car has the following clearly identifiable parts: wheels, engine, doors, and so on." Thus, components can be physically separated from the whole because the relationship is extrinsic. Note that the relationship in a material-object relationship is not extrinsic as you cannot separate the flour from the bread once the bread is made.

When looking for material-object composition in a requirements document, look for keywords as "is partly" and "is made of." Some examples follow:

- Cappuccino is partly milk.
- A chair is partly iron.
- A table is made from wood.
- A high-rise building is partly steel.
- Candy is made partly from sugar.
- Bread is made from flour.

Note that "partly" is not necessary for a material-object relationship. For instance, a mirror may be made of all glass (not "partly" of glass). Furthermore, whether you choose to use the material-object or component integral object to represent a relationship may be domain-dependent. For example, in most situations one would model the ceramics of a sparkplug as material-object composition. However, if in your problem domain you can separate the ceramic from the spark plug, you will need to use the component-integral object composition to capture the relationship.

Portion-Object Composition

In the portion-object aggregation, the relationship defines a homeomorphic (same kind of thing as the whole) configuration of parts as the whole. Usually, portions of the objects can be divided using standard measures such as inches, millimeters, liters, gallons, hours, or minutes. In this manner, the portion-object composition supports the arithmetic operations of subtraction, addition, multiplication, and division.

When looking for portion-object composition in a requirements document, look for such keywords as "portion of," "slice," "helping of," "segment of," "lump of," "drop of," and "spoonful of." Examples of this are as follows:

- A slice of bread is a portion of a loaf of bread.
- A spoon of cereal is a portion of a bowl of cereal.
- A second is part of a day.
- A meter is part of kilometer.
- A cup of coffee is usually part of a pot of coffee.

When the word "piece" is used, however, care must be taken to ensure that the pieces are similar in nature. For example, a piece of candy is candy and a piece of rotten apple is apple, but a piece from an exploded car is not a car.

Note that each slice of bread is considered bread and each cup of coffee is considered coffee. Moreover, both second and day are units of measurement on which you can perform a mix-and-match for the basic arithmetic operations. This observation also holds true for the meter and kilometer units of measurements. However, you may not mix and match seconds with kilometer as they are different semantic concepts. This similarity between a portion and the whole permits the analyst/

designer to allow a portion to selectively inherit properties from the whole. For example, the kinds of ingredients in a loaf of bread are the same as it is in a slice of bread. The component-integral object composition also allows certain properties of the whole to apply to its parts. For example, the velocity of a ball can also be used to imply the velocity of each of its parts.

Place-Area Composition

In the place-area aggregation, the relationship defines a homeomorphic (same kind of thing as the whole) and invariant configuration of parts as the whole. This relationship is commonly used to identify links between places and particular locations within them. Like the portion-object composition, all the places (pieces, slices) must be similar in nature, but differ in that the places cannot be separated from the area of which they are a part.

When looking for place-area composition in a requirements document, look at the preliminary portion-object composition and ask if this relationship is invariant. If it is, then it is a place-area composition instead of a portion-object composition. Also look at the container-content relationships (see below) and ask "Are all the content homeomorphic and also non-removable." If the answer is yes, again it is a place-area composition instead of a container-content relationship. Some examples follow:

- New York City is part of New York State.
- Los Angeles is part of the United States of America.
- A peak is part of a mountain.
- A room is part of a hotel.
- Yosemite is part of California.

Spend a little extra time to convince yourself that a room as part of a hotel is an example of a place-area composition.

Collection-Members Composition

Collection-members composition is a specialized version of place-area composition. In addition to being a monomeric and invariant configuration of parts within a whole, there is an implied order to its members. One example is an airline reservation with its various flight segments. Here, the order of each flight segment in the itinerary is a very important part of the reservation. Other examples include: monthly timesheet—daily timesheets, monthly planner—daily plans, people—organization chart, name—telephone book, name—Roledex, and file—file cabinet.

When looking for collection-members composition in a requirements document, look at the preliminary place-area composition and ask if this relationship has an implied order. If it does, then it is a collection-members composition instead of a place-area composition.

Container Content (Member-Bunch) Composition

The member-bunch composition defines a collection of parts as a whole. The parts (contents) bear neither a functional nor a structural relationship to each other or the whole. Furthermore, the contents are neither homeomorphic nor invariant. The only requirement is that there is a spatial, temporal, or social connection for determining when a member is part of the collection. The container exists and has properties and behaviors of its own. That is, it exists even if there are no contents.

Examples are purchase order—line items, bag—contents of bag, box—contents of box, union—members, company—employees, and so on. In the first example, it is very common for one to place a "blanket" purchase order with no line items. The specific items/works (line items) are added later, and there is no implied order in the line items. Furthermore, note that the organization-chart relationship for employee has an implied order and invariant property; while the company-employees relationship is not invariant nor does it capture any implied order.

This type of aggregation should not be confused with inheritance (classification). For example, "Jason is a human" and "airplane is a transport vehicle" are classifications. Jason possesses all the attributes and provides all the services of a human. Similarly, airplane has all the attributes and provides all the services of a transport vehicle.

The container-content relationship is different. It is usually based on spatial or social connections. For example, a shrub is part of a garden implies that it is within the geographical confines of the garden and probably in close proximity to other plants within the garden. Similarly, an employee's membership in a club implies a social connection. However, for a shrub to be classified as a garden, every shrub would have to be a garden. Similarly, every employee would have to be a club. This relationship has a tendency to be a catch-all for aggregation-type relationships.

Member-Partnership Composition

The member-partnership composition defines an invariant form of the container-content relationship. It defines an invariant collection of parts as a whole.

Examples of this type of relationship include the following:

- Ginger Rogers and Fred Astaire as a dance couple
- Laurel and Hardy as a comedian team
- Jacoby and Myers as attorneys at law
- Lee and Tepfenhart as authors of this book

Members in this relationship may not be removed without destroying the relationship (partnership). For instance, if Laurel leaves Hardy, the comedy team of Laurel and Hardy no longer exists. Hardy can now form a new comedy team with a new partner, but it will a different partnership.

When looking for member-partnership relationships, review the preliminary list of container-content relationships for invariance. If the relationship is invariant, then make it an member-partnership relationship.

Objects and Aggregation Relationships

Now that we understand aggregation better, we should make two observations about them. In particular, we should recognize the following:

1. An object can be viewed as more than one aggregation. For example, a loaf of bread may be viewed as an aggregate of slices of breads (portion-object composition) and it may be viewed as being made from flour, sugar, yeast, etc. (material-object composition). Both views can be supported simultaneously in the object-oriented paradigm.

2. Transitivity holds only for aggregation of the same kind. For example, the microwave oven is part of a kitchen (component-integral composition) and the kitchen is part of a house (place-area composition). However, the microwave oven is not part of the house. Furthermore, a computer can be an aggregation of a terminal, hardware box, keyboard, and mouse. The hardware box usually comprises a CPU, memory, hard disk drive, and floppy disk drive. By transitivity, a CPU is part of the computer. However, a terminal is made of glass, silicon, steel, and plastic. This decomposition of the terminal is not the same as the above decomposition[13] of the hardware box. Most of us would not apply the transitivity or antisymmetric properties to the material composition of the terminal in conjunction with the component-integral composition of the computer. At best we would say that the material-composition of the computer is a union of the material composition of the parts.

LINKS BETWEEN OBJECTS

Generalization and aggregation help us capture relationships between objects when we want to view an object as being a set of other objects. There are relationships between objects that are not generalizations or aggregations. For example, the marriage relationship between a person and his/her spouse. Certainly, this relationship is not viewed as a generalization. If it were, a person would have to inherit all the in-law relationships of his/her spouse. It is also not an aggregation, in spite of the religious ceremony, as divorces are legal. Thus, we need another mechanism to capture all these other relationships between objects. In the object-oriented paradigm, this "catch-all" relationship is called a *link*.

---

[13] Both of the earlier aggregations are component-integral compositions.

From a technical perspective, a *link* is a relationship (physical or conceptual) between objects that lets one object know about another object so that one object may request the services of another object. However, a link should also have a semantic meaning that is consistent with the semantic domain within which the object resides.

In object-oriented modeling, all links are considered bidirectional.[14] Thus, once a link is established between two objects, each object may request the services of the other object. A *role name* uniquely identifies one end of a relationship and provides a vehicle for viewing a relationship as a traversal from one object to a set of associated objects.[15]

The role name allows an object at one end of the relationship to traverse the relationship without explicitly using the relationship name. Role names are necessary for a link (association) between two objects of the same class. For example, in a *supervise* relationship between employees in the class **Employee**, the role names Supervisor and Subordinate would help distinguish between two employees participating in the supervise relationship. Role names are also useful to distinguish between multiple links between two objects. For example, consider a manual car wash. The role names from car to employee could be *washer*, *dryer*, *waxer*, *polisher*, and *buffer*. For a specific instance (object) of a car (class), Joe (an instance of **Employee**) is the washer and the buffer, because he both washes and buffs the car. Furthermore, a link can be binary (between two objects), ternary (between three objects), or higher. In practice, it is rare to find links with a semantic meaning that tie together objects of three different object types (classes).[16]

An *association* describes the set of links between two (or more) objects of a single class or of different classes with the same semantic meaning. Thus, a link may be viewed as an instance of an association. Examples of associations between the same class for class **Person** are married_to and works_for. Today, with the two-income family, two persons may be married to each other with one of them also being the supervisor of the other in the workplace. We cannot use one link to capture this situation as the two relationships have different semantic meanings. The couple can get a divorce but still maintain the same work relationship. An example of an association between two classes is the employment relationship as applied to the classes Company and Person. That is, "Joe is employed by Exxon" is an instance of a link in this association. Because every link (and, thus, the corresponding association) is bidirectional, "Exxon employs Joe" is the link in the reverse direction.

---

[14] All links are considered bidirectional during modeling; however, in implementation it is not uncommon practice to drop one direction of a link.

[15] Set means one or more objects. From an object's perspective, traversing a relationship is an operation that yields the related (associated) objects. Thus, in implementation the role name is a derived attribute (attribute, which is derived from the association rather than intrinsic in the object) whose value is a set of related objects.

[16] An example of a ternary link would be the relationship between concert, concert tickets, and attendee.

Because an association is an abstraction of a concept, it may also have attributes and services. It may have the same properties and capabilities as a class.[17] Because we normally do not think of a link as an object, novices should be very careful not to assign attributes of the relationship to one of the class in the relationship. For example, consider a person's salary. It is normally modeled as an attribute in the class **Person**. However, it is actually an attribute of the employment relationship between the classes **Person** and **Company**. If you still have doubts, consider the case in which a person has two jobs with two different employers.

The last example raises a pragmatic point: When does one make salary an attribute of **Person** and when does one make it an attribute of the association. Theoretically, the correct answer is that salary is an attribute of the association. From a modeling perspective, we recommend that you use what is appropriate for your business situation. To decide which is appropriate requires good engineering judgement. We recommend that you consider the problem domain, future direction of product, and next release features as factors during the analysis phase.[18]

IDENTIFYING AND SPECIFYING LINKS AND AGGREGATIONS

The best source for initially identifying some of the links (associations) and aggregations is the requirements document. Reread the requirements document and look for the possibilities of one object being part of another object. These are potential aggregations. Use the suggestions of key phrases and tests described above.

Also, look for links in the requirements document. Links, like services, are often seen as verbs in a requirements document. Phrases that usually imply a link include "which it gets from," "keeps track of," "changes with," and "depends upon." Furthermore, the detailed description of a service is also a source of identifying links. Most objects that need to collaborate (i.e., use services) with other objects and to access these other objects usually require a link.

Other sources to help find links are the sequence diagrams and the behavior specification documents. Each service request from another object must be supported by some access vehicle. If the "handle" is not passed as an argument, then a relationship must be established between the two objects. Care should be given to naming the relationship, usually a link, in a manner that captures the semantic meaning of the relationship.[19]

---

[17] In many situations, however, neither the attributes nor the services of the relationship need to be captured in the model.

[18] In design, modifiability, reusability, simplicity, and performance need to be considered.

[19] If CRC cards are used and use cases drove the design of the CRC cards, you have a collection of collaborators. Finding the associations and aggregations are much easier as the collaborators give you a big clue. If the collaborator is transient, then the object probably wants a pointer to the object passed to it from the caller. If the collaborator is persistent, then the object has to have a relationship (either association or aggregation) with the object.

When you are studying the behavioral specification document, only put in links that have semantic meaning. If you cannot find a good name for the link, consider whether this handle should have been part of the signature (should have been passed to this object from the calling object).

Remember the following rules to determine whether you have found a link or an object aggregation:

1. An aggregation may not connect an object to itself. This would violate the antisymmetric property of aggregation. In many circumstances, this rule is extended to the idea that an aggregation should not connect an object of one class to an object of the same class as a mechanism to absolutely prevent an aggregation from connecting an object to itself. On the other hand, a link may connect two objects of the same class. For example, supervise is a relation between two employees (instances) of the class **Employee**. The most common example given is marriage between two persons. However, this example is flawed because our society does not legally recognize the union of two persons of any gender as a marriage. Marriage in most societies today is a relationship between an instance of class **Female** and an instance of class **Male**. This example, therefore, captures the constraints on the relationship as defined by present societal standards and shows the importance of capturing the link/association on the correct object or abstraction. Thus, we see how difficult it is to model properly and capture all the implied constraints.

2. Multiple connections between objects are legal. Each connection should be used to capture a distinct semantic meaning. For example, consider sending a car through a nonautomated car wash. Employees are needed to wash, dry, wax, polish, and, finally, buff the car. Every task may be performed by one employee or each task may be performed be a different employee. If we model these as links to the employees who performed the various tasks, we would have multiple links for an instance (object) of **Employee** (class). For example, Joe could have both washed and buffed the car.

3. Self-associations are possible and common. In this case, role names are essential to capture the relationship accurately.

4. Multiple association does not imply that the same two objects are related twice.

MANAGING RELATIONSHIPS

One of most difficult tasks in building an object-oriented model is to determine whether a potential relationship is better captured as either an argument in the signature of the service (function), link, aggregation, or generalization/specialization.

The following are some guidelines for this task:

- If the relationship is permanent (static), then it must be captured as a relationship. Now, what does *permanent* mean? If you consider a scenario as a unit of time, then *permanent* means that the relationship needs to be known across scenarios. Note that *permanent* is a relative term. Basically, if it has to be stored in memory for use by some other independent process, then it is permanent.

- A relationship must capture some concept that applies to the problem domain or some subdomain that is needed for implementation. In other words, there must be a semantic meaning to the relationship. A service should only traverse (use) the relationship when its usage is consistent with that semantic meaning. For example, consider the link for two **Person** objects: married_to. Today, with two income families, it is possible for one spouse to work for another spouse. It would be improper and poor modeling to use the married_to relationship to get to work domain services of the other spouse. A second link (works_for) needs to be established to capture this different semantic relationship.

- If you think you have an aggregation, make sure that all the parts are in the same domain and provide the same functional or structural configuration to the whole. Apply transitivity and antisymmetric tests to check for consistency. Note that transitivity is possible only with aggregations of the same kind. It is very common for novices to mix parts of different kinds of aggregation in one aggregation. This will cause the transitivity test to fail. When this happens, you probably need to look at the parts to see if the are different types of aggregates. For example, consider a building that has the following parts: windows, floors, offices, elevators, ceilings, walls, stairs, meeting rooms, cafeteria, atrium, and sundry shop. If you put all these parts into one aggregation, you have mixed parts from two different semantic aggregations. The offices, floors (meaning one level in a building), meeting rooms, cafeteria, atrium, and sundry shop are defining a functional configuration of the building; while the windows, floors (meaning the physical floor), ceilings, and walls are defining a structural configuration of the building. These parts must be captured in two different aggregations as they have different semantics.

- An aggregation may not connect two objects of the same kind to each other. This would violate the antisymmetric property of aggregation. For example, a person may not be an aggregate of other persons. However, a link may connect two objects of the same kind. For example, supervise is a relation between two employees (instances) that is valid.

- Aggregation is often confused with topological inclusion. Topological inclusion is a relationship between a container, area, or temporal duration and that which is contained by it. Examples are (1) the customer is in the room, (2) the meeting is in the evening, and (3) Monument Valley is in Arizona and Utah. In each case, the subject is surrounded by the container; however, it is not part of the container in any meaningful semantic domain. For example, a customer is not part of a room, nor is a meeting part of an evening. Furthermore, no part of Monument Valley is Arizona or Utah, because it is part of the Navajo reservation. Topological inclusion is most commonly confused with place-area composition. Note that every part of Dallas is in Texas, while no part of Monument Valley is in Arizona.

- Sometimes, novices confuse attributes with aggregation. Attributes describe the object as a whole (a black-box approach); aggregation describes the parts that makes the whole (white-box approach). Thus, a house may have attributes as width, length, and height but is made from wood, glass, bricks, etc.
- Attachment of one object to another object does not guarantee aggregation. Certainly toes are attached to the feet and they are part of the feet; however, earrings are attached to the ear, but they are not part of the ear. Toes provide functional support to the feet, but earrings do not supply any functional or structural support.
- Ownership may also be confused with aggregation. Certainly a car has wheels, and wheels are part of a car. However, the fact that James has a car does not imply that the car is part of James. Thus, ownership is captured by a link.
- Multiple links between objects are legal. Each link should be used to capture a distinct semantic meaning. (See the car wash example for Joe.)

DOCUMENTING RELATIONSHIPS

In the past, nearly every major object-oriented methodologist had his/her own way of documenting classes, objects, relationships, and behaviors. Such is not the case today; the majority of authors employ UML to document relationships. The notation templates for documenting relationships in UML are shown Figure 8-1.

In a generalization diagram, we see that a class is represented by a rectangular icon, and the generalization/specialization is drawn as a solid line from the specialized class to the generalized class with a large triangular arrowhead on the generalized class end. Normally, the specialization classes of the same parent are different alternatives in the same semantic domain and provide for a partitioning of the parent class; however, some applications require that we specialize in several dimensions simultaneously; in these cases, UML allows a discriminator label to be attached to a generalization arc. Arcs with the same label represent specialization in the same dimension. Different dimensions represent orthogonal abstract ways of describing an object of the parent class. Though UML notion doesn't preclude the concepts of multiple classification and dynamic classification, it does not explicitly support these concepts.

Aggregation is a special form of association that deals with the composition of the aggregator class. In an aggregation diagram, a class is represented by a rectangular

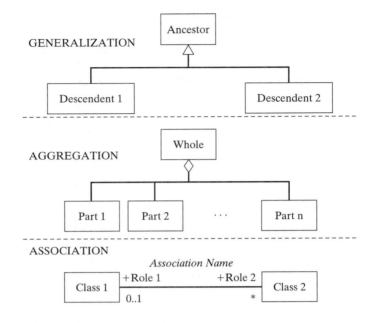

GENERALIZATION

AGGREGATION

ASSOCIATION

Figure 8-1   UML Notation for Object Generalization, Aggregation, and Association.

icon, and the aggregation is drawn as solid lines from the aggregates (parts) to the aggregator (whole) with a diamond arrowhead on the aggregator's end. In UML, two forms of aggregation are recognized. The first form is one in which the parts may exist independently of the whole; this is represented by the use of the unfilled diamond and is called *aggregation* in UML. The second form is one in which the parts may only exist as part of the whole; this is represented by the use of a filled diamond and is called *composition* in UML. The multiplicity of the aggregator may be one, many, and optionally one. Multiplicity is captured by using a text expression. The expression is a comma-separated list of integer ranges. A range is indicated by an integer (the lower value), two dots, and an integer (the upper value); a single integer and the symbol "*" are also legal ranges. The symbol "*" indicates any number, including none.

In an association diagram, classes are represented by rectangular icons, and a binary association is represented by a straight solid line between two rectangular icons.[20] An association may have a name with an optional small "direction arrow" (solid triangle with no tail) showing how to read the association. The name is placed

---

[20] Ternary relationships are drawn using an additional diamond icon to tie the lines together. This diamond icon is also used for all other higher-order relationships. An association that needs to be a class is captured as a class, and its association with the relation is shown with a dashed line from the class icon for the association to the association (solid line) between the two classes participating in the association.

on or adjacent to the association line.[21] The association name may be omitted if role names are used. At each end of the association is a role. Each role may have a name that describes how its class is viewed by the other class(es); this is called the role name. The role names opposite of a class must be unique. The role name also determines the multiplicity of its class, that is, the number of instances of the class that can be associated with one instance of the other class. Multiplicity is captured by using a text expression. The expression is a comma-separated list of integer ranges. A range is indicated by an integer (the lower value), two dots, and an integer (the upper value); a single integer and the symbol "*" are also legal ranges. The symbol "*" indicates any number including none. If the multiplicity is more than one, the keyword {ordered} may be placed on the role, indicating that the instances in the association have an explicit order.

RECOMMENDED APPROACH

Our steps for finding relationships are as follows:

1. Get a list of potential objects that may be involved in generalization.
2. Create a table of these objects for the "is_a" test.
3. Fill in the cells of the table, using only *always*, *sometimes*, and *never*.
4. Use the table to find all the generalizations. Remember to eliminate the "instantiations."
5. Draw a hierarchical diagram of the generalizations between classes using UML notation.
6. Reread the requirements document and look for aggregations and links (associations). Use the key phrases given earlier as clues to finding these relationships.
7. Look for role names, which appear as nouns in most requirements documents. Although many object-oriented authors have stated that role names are optional, we strongly recommend its usage as it is often easier and less confusing to assign role names instead of, or in addition to, relationship names.
8. Reread the specifications for all the services and identify the relationships needed to support those services. By rereading each service, the analyst/developer can refine what must be done in each of the object services.
9. If the sequence diagrams, use-case model, and the behavior specifications are documented, read these documents to find additional links.
10. Determine whether each potential relationship is better captured as an argument in the signature of the service (function), as a link, aggregation, or generalization/specialization.
11. Document the results using UML notation.

---

[21] In theory, an association may have different names in each direction. We do not recommend trying to name associations in both directions.

EXAMPLE

Let us return to our lawn mowing example. Based on the previous analysis, we have the following objects: John, Jane, Peter, Paul, Elizabeth, Mary, Jack, and ProfessionalLawnMower. We will discuss generalization in the next chapter. So now after reviewing the requirements document and the behavior specifications, we realize that capturing the family and its relationships are useful to this application. Figure 8-2 and Figure 8-3 illustrate object aggregations and links that we consider useful in our example. The objects are represented by underlining the name in compliance with the UML specification.[22] The design of the UML association diagram and aggregation diagram is described in the next chapter.

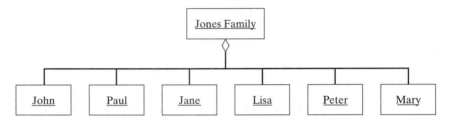

Figure 8-2   Aggregation Diagram for the Lawn Mower Example.

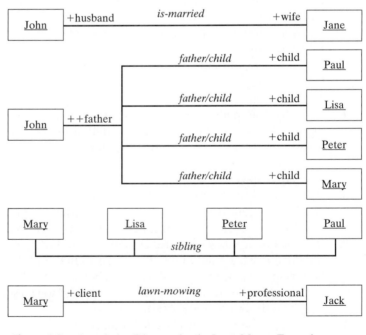

Figure 8-3   Association Diagram for the Lawn Mower Example.

---

[22] Many of the tools available on the market do not support construction of such object diagrams.

In this example, Jane has access to John's services via the is_married link. John has access to all the children's services via the father/child links. Mary has access to Jack via the lawn_mowing link. Mary's sibling link, mother/child link, and father/ child link are permanent. It is always applicable over time. These are called *static* (and invariant) *relationships*.

Mary's lawn-mowing link with Jack, however, is less permanent. Mary may choose to change to another professional lawn mower at any time. Her relationship with a professional lawn mower, however, may be permanent in that there is some professional lawn mower that she uses. In such a case, we consider the link static and variant. In the next chapter, we will use the links to define associations, and we will use the object aggregation to define class aggregation.

SUMMARY

Our steps for finding relationships are as follows:

1. Get a list of potential objects that may be involved in generalization.
2. Create a table of these objects for the is_a test.
3. Fill in the cells of the tables, using only *always*, *sometimes*, and *never*.
4. Use the table to find all the generalizations. Remember to eliminate the "instantiations."
5. Draw a hierarchical diagram of these generalizations between classes using the UML notation.
6. Reread the requirements document and look for aggregations and links (associations). Use the key phrases given earlier as clues to finding these relationships.
7. Look also for role names. They appear as nouns in most requirements documents. Although many object-oriented authors have stated that role names are optional, we strongly recommend its usage as it is often easier and less confusing to assign role names instead of, or in addition to, relationship names.
8. Reread the specifications for all the services and identify the relationships needed to support those services. By rereading each service, the analyst/ developer can refine what must be done in each of the object services.
9. If the sequence diagrams, use-case model, and the behavior specifications are documented, read these documents to find additional links.
10. Determine whether each potential relationship is better captured as an argument in the signature of the service (function), as a link, an aggregation, or a generalization/specialization.
11. Document the results via the UML notation.

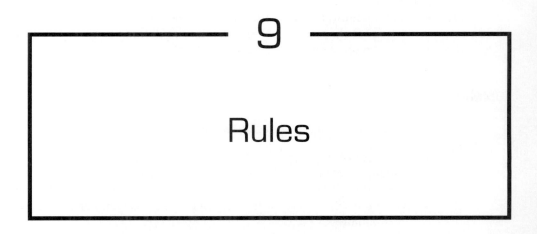

9

Rules

What has been presented so far is a collection of mechanisms integrated into a consistent paradigm that helps manage the complexity of the procedural aspects of functional modeling.[1] However, there are aspects of an application/system that are non-procedural (declarative) and are better modeled using other mechanisms. In this chapter, we discuss how the object-oriented paradigm can be extended to include the capability to manage declarative aspects of an application.

INTRODUCTION

The concepts of abstraction, encapsulation, inheritance, relationship, and polymorphism in object-oriented methods support the design and implementation of sophisticated procedural applications. Most object-oriented methods are presently based on the assumption that all aspects of the application/system are modeled within the procedural paradigm.

---

[1] Functional modeling has two aspects: procedural and declarative.

Some applications, however, have many requirements that are given in a declarative manner.[2] For example, the requirements might state that the input voltage into the device can never exceed three volts. When such requirements are employed, the handling of the declarative semantics (rules and facts) is left to the analyst/developer. One of the most difficult tasks for developers is transforming declarative statements into the procedural paradigm. It is very natural for developers to incorporate these declarative statements across the methods of various classes. However, when a declarative statement affects several methods, especially across multiple classes, it must be written in several places. This is not a good practice because (1) there is a transformation of declarative semantics into procedural semantics, and (2) it creates hidden coupling between methods. The first reason makes the model less readily understandable and violates the goal of modeling reality the way the domain experts see it. The second reason makes maintaining and changing the model very difficult.

Applications tend to grow; as they grow, developers encounter more situations in which declarative statements have been distributed across methods. Soon, the model becomes unmaintainable. For example, maintaining an invariant involving two objects may require similar but not identical tests be inserted a variety of places within the code. This leads to errors of omission and logic by analysts, designers, and programmers as the application is extended. Because the invariant is not in one place, it is never explicitly stated. Unstated assumptions make modifications of code difficult and error-prone. We need both a method and a mechanism to handle declarative statements.

The needed implementation mechanism is a *data-driven mechanism*. This mechanism simplifies the task of maintaining model integrity in two important ways. First, it enables invariants and constraints to be stated explicitly in a single place, rather than having them scattered in multiple places. This makes the model (and thus code) easier to understand and modify. Second, because it is data-driven, invariants and constraints are reevaluated *automatically* whenever relevant changes are made to an object's attribute. This relieves the analyst/programmer of the burden of explicitly incorporating data integrity rules into their procedural logic. The application's procedural logic is no longer cluttered with code for maintaining model integrity.

The data-driven mechanism is important because many of our declarative requirements are given to us in a data driven manner. This gives us a way to capture reality as domain experts see it—without the need to transform a declarative requirement (or solution) into a purely procedural model. Declarative statements are usually written at a higher level of abstraction than procedural statements. Implementing declarative statements using this mechanism frees the analyst, designer, and programmer from having to manage flow of control for these statements.

---

[2] We can distinguish between declarative and procedural languages or statements. Most of us have worked with procedural programming languages. They give us the constructs so that we can write a set of instructions that must be executed sequentially. The sequence may vary depending on conditions tested and group of instructions may be executed repetitively. However, declarative languages declare a set of facts and rules. They do not specify the sequence of steps for doing the processing.

Rules

Rules capturing declarative semantics are employed for a variety of purposes, such as enforcing invariants in a domain model, auditing complex data structures, monitoring the state of a state machine, or checking constraints while a user inputs data. There are all kind of rules: some are best captured directly in the classical object-oriented paradigm while others are better captured via other mechanisms.

One kind of rule that is better captured via another mechanism is the *data driven rule*. This is due to the property that it requires a mechanism to act as a "monitor" of the model that observes changes to an object's attributes and reacts when a condition is satisfied. Many applications naturally require this capability. Examples are (1) applications that monitor a physical system, (2) applications that apply business policies or engineering guidelines, and (3) software development tools.

The data driven mechanism is well-suited to handling rules that monitor things. It supports the situation–action directive without complicating an application's procedural logic. It also satisfies two very important goals of the object-oriented paradigm: (1) the model should be built to reflect the way the domain experts see reality, and (2) whenever possible, the code for the application should be generated from a model that is easy for the domain experts and the end users to understand.

To satisfy the above two goals, declarative statements (including rules) need to be rigorous. They must be understandable to the end user so that they can verify that the rules correctly represent business policies and desired application/system behavior. Thus, declarative statements, including rules, should be written in structured English.

IDENTIFYING DECLARATIVE STATEMENTS

Declarative statements are different from procedural statements. Identifying declarative statements in a requirements document is relatively simple. While procedural statements are always part of a specified sequence (e.g., a procedure, an activity, or a task), a declarative statement stands alone. A declarative statement is independent of any sequence of other statements. It declares a *fact* or a *rule*.

A fact statement may be expressed in various ways. The following are all examples of facts:

- A record

Book	Author(s)	Publisher
Object-Oriented Analysis	Coad/Yourdon	Yourdon Press
Poor Developer's Guide to Object-Oriented Programming in C++	Lee/Tepfenhart	Prentice Hall

- A set of values in a spreadsheet
- A plain statement (e.g., all surgeons are medical doctors)
- A stand-alone equation:

MIN_MONTHLY_PAYMENT = (PRINCIPAL * INTEREST_RATE)/ 12

Rules usually capture information about how the business should operate. Rules encapsulate business knowledge. Common key words in declarative statements that indicate a rule are:

- It must always hold that . . .
- It must always be true that . . .
- Under all conditions, when . . . then . . .
- Under all conditions, if . . . then . . .
- When . . . if . . . then . . .
- . . . if only . . .
- . . . is correct only if . . .

Situations where a rule may be used as a declarative requirement to

- enforce *"things that should always be true"* (invariants)
- detect *"things that should never be true"* (constraint violations)
- maintain the integrity of your domain model
- monitor for and react to important events
- express domain knowledge (*business policies, engineering rules,* and *situation–action heuristics)*
- specify an operation (function) that would have to be used in many methods
- exploit the data-driven or event-driven nature of rules

SPECIFYING AND DOCUMENTING RULES

When a requirement is written as a declarative statement, the best practice is to specify it as a rule.[3] Ideally, we want a technique that captures rules explicitly in a manner that is easy to read and generates the correct code. A technique that captures rules explicitly and makes them easy to read is structured English. The details of the constructs available in structured English must wait until after the classification of (business) rules.

---

[3] Facts can be expressed as rules very easily. They will be derivation rules. Derivation rules are explained in the record of martin's categories and our third.

James Martin has constructed the following classification scheme for rules. His scheme describes the following types of rules:

- *Integrity rules* state that something must always be true (e.g., a value for an attribute must be in the integer range from 1 to 5).
- *Derivation rules* state how a value (or set of values) is computed (e.g., tax withheld = federal income tax + state income tax).
- *Behavior rules* describe the dynamic aspects of behavior, such as what conditions must be true for an action to performed (e.g., when the door is open, the light in the oven is turned on).

To facilitate mapping these rules into the object-oriented paradigm, we can further refine James Martin's rule categories. Our categories are

1. *Data integrity* rules state that something must be true about an attribute(s) (e.g., a value for an attribute must be in the integral range from 1 to 5).

2. *Relationship integrity* rules state that something must be true about a relationship (e.g., a manager may not supervise more than 10 employees).

3. *Derivation* rules, including facts, state how a value or set of values is computed (PRICE = 1.5 × COST).

4. *Service precondition* rules state that something must be true before a service is performed (e.g., a cash advance will not be given unless it is past the fifth of the month).

5. *Service postcondition* rules state that something must be true after a service is performed (e.g., order form is stored once it is correctly completed).

6. *Action trigger* rules define the causal relationship between events and actions (e.g., when an order is accepted, send the bill immediately).

7. *Data trigger* rules define the causal relationship between an attribute's condition and an action (e.g., when the stock is below reorder level, then reorder).

8. *Control condition* rules handle situations in which multiple triggers are involved in the rule (e.g., if the product has been sent and the money received or if the purchase order has been canceled and the deposit returned, then the purchase order is closed).

Based on our classification scheme, the constructs in structured English shown in Figure 9-1 capture the rules. In these constructs, a condition is a Boolean expression, an event is a stimulus (signal), and an action is an invocation of a procedural statement.

1. For triggers and control conditions,
   IF condition THEN action
              or
   WHEN event IF condition THEN action

2. For integrity rules,
   IT MUST ALWAYS BE THAT statement of fact
              or
   IT MUST ALWAYS BE THAT IF condition THEN action

3. For service precondition,
   BEFORE service that is to be performed IT MUST BE THAT fact

4. For service postcondition,
   AFTER service that has been performed IT MUST BE THAT fact

5. For derivation rules, fact, usually an equation
              or
   WHEN condition or event THEN action
              or

Figure 9-1   Structured English Constructs.

MAPPING RULES TO THE PROPER OBJECT-ORIENTED CONCEPTS

In the 1980s artificial intelligence systems became highly fashionable. The mechanism on which these systems were built was primarily an *inference engine*. An inference engine processes a collection of facts and rules to make deductions using logical inference. The rules an inference engine processes are called *production rules*. Most of us understand declarative semantics from this perspective. However, the rules talked about in this chapter are not production rules.[4] They are rules linked with the object-oriented model to provide a meaningful and useful model for implementation.

The mapping guidelines for taking a rule into an object-oriented concept are as follows:

1. *Service pre-condition*. A service pre-condition is mapped onto a service. As suggested by Meyers, the pre-condition is a requirement that should be guaranteed by the calling object.
2. *Service post-condition*. A service post-condition is also mapped onto a service. It is a rule that must be checked by the author of this service. The service must guarantee that the post-condition is satisfied.
3. *Control condition*. A control condition is mapped onto a finite state machine. It is usually a condition needed for a change of state.
4. *Action trigger*. An action trigger is mapped onto a finite state machine. It is usually an event in a state transition diagram.

---

[4] An inference engine may be used to implement a method in a class; however, we do not recommend this technique.

5. *Relationship integrity.* A relationship integrity is mapped onto a relationship. It normally affects the instantiation, deletion and addition to a relationship.

6. *Data integrity or data trigger.* Data integrity and data triggers are mapped onto an attribute. Normally, it is checked every time the attribute changes value.

7. *Derivation.* A derivation is difficult to map. It is usually used as part of a method. However, there are situations where it is implemented as a trigger. Care must be taken when you have a derivation rule.

DOCUMENTING THE RULES USING UML

The documenting guidelines for the various rules are as follows:

1. *Service pre-condition.* A service pre-condition is mapped onto a service. This needs to be captured as part of the entrance criteria. If there is an operation specification for the service, use the precondition section of the *operational specification* to document this. If not, include this as a comment in the method specification.

2. *Service post-condition.* A service post-condition is also mapped onto a service. If an operations specification is written for the service, use the post-conditions section to document this. The post-conditions must also be included in the method description.

3. *Control condition.* A control condition is mapped onto a finite state machine. It is usually a condition needed for a change of state. This is documented as a guard condition in unified modeling language (UML).

4. *Action trigger.* An action trigger is mapped onto a finite state machine. It is usually an event in a state transition diagram. This is documented as an event in UML.

5. *Relationship integrity.* A relationship integrity is mapped onto a relationship. It normally affects the instantiation, deletion of, and addition to a relationship. This is documented as a constraint in UML.

6. *Data integrity or data trigger.* Data integrity and data triggers are mapped onto an attribute. Normally, they are checked every time the attribute changes value. This is best documented by creating a new stereotype, called "data trigger," which is used to capture the actions associated with the rule(s). Then artificial associations are drawn between the classes that need data triggers and the data trigger class.

7. *Derivation.* A derivation is documented as part of the method.

IMPLEMENTING RULES

The mapping guidelines given above show that service pre-condition rules, service post-condition rules, control condition rules, action triggers, and derivation rules map very nicely into the classical object-oriented model. However, relationship integrity rules, data integrity rules, and data triggers are not well supported in our model. To handle these rules, a data driven mechanism is needed. There are two ways to supply a data driven mechanism:

1. *Use the triggers in the database system.* Using triggers in the database system is the classical way of handling data integrity and data trigger rules. Every time the database recognizes a change in data value, it triggers a routine written by the user. The appropriate rules are implemented in that routine. This is reasonably straight forward for simple data driven rules, but it is a little more tricky for complex rules (such as relationship constraints).

2. *Using an object that includes rule functionality.* Jess is an expert system shell derived from CLIPS.[5] It uses the Rete algorithm written in Java to fire rules against a set of facts. Jess can be incorporated as Java program to provide a rule mechanism derived from CLIPS and can create and operate on Java objects. This enables an application to directly employ data-driven computations.

RECOMMENDED APPROACH

When declarative statements appear in the requirements document, the following steps are recommended:

1. Separate the declarative statements from the procedural statements.
2. Restate the declarative statements using structured English as rules, taking care that the rules are rigorous and implementable.
3. Map the rules onto the appropriate object-oriented mechanism.
4. If data driven rules are used, employ a data driven mechanism to model these rules. We recommend Jess over using database triggers.

SUMMARY

Declarative statements, or rules, are another natural form in which domain experts and end users state their requirements. We, as analysts and developers, should accept declarative statements as a natural part of textual requirements. It follows that declarative statements should be captured within a model. To do this, we must translate the textual declarative requirements into structured English to assure that we have rigorous and implementable requirements. After stating all the declarative

---

[5] Jess was originally conceived as a Java clone of CLIPS but has been extended significantly beyond CLIPS.

requirements in structured English, we should then map each declarative statement into a rule category. The rule category allows it to be properly assigned to the appropriate object-oriented mechanism in the model.

Because not every rule category could be assigned to a classical object-oriented mechanism, we introduced the data-driven mechanism. This mechanism supports rules triggered by a change in the value of an attribute. As discussed, this is a very valuable extension to the object-oriented paradigm. Historically, triggers in a database system were used to implement this mechanism; However, documenting database trigger functions and getting people to read it were not easily accomplished. An alternative approach was developed at the Sandia National Laboratories in the form of a expert system shell written in Java that can be incorporated within a Java program. This solution is highly desirable because we can see all the code in one place.

As with any tool, data-driven rules are good for some tasks and not as effective for other tasks. We recommend them for

- enforcing invariants
- maintaining data integrity
- maintaining relationship integrity
- detecting constraint violations
- stating business policies and engineering guidelines

A data-driven rule is like a demon that constantly monitors attributes and reacts when appropriate. The action portion of the code sits apart from the routine procedural code and is automatically triggered by relevant changes in the objects that the rule monitors. This relieves the analyst/developer from designing and programming explicit control for the data-driven rule.

10

The Model

In the previous chapters we have actually built an integrated model of the system. If we had executed the activities in each chapter perfectly, we would have our model. Unfortunately, the guidelines presented here are not adequate to guarantee this result. In fact, the weakness in our method is its inability to help an analyst/developer identify abstract classes.[1] At this point we need to find these classes. This is the refinement phase of our method.

CONCEPTS

Although most of us will tell you that the strength of object-oriented technology is that it gives you the mechanism to model reality, in fact it is not an approach that models reality. For anybody who has studied philosophy, reality is the state of mind of each individual. So what is object-oriented technology really doing? It models

---

[1] This is the inherent weakness in all object-oriented methods. Now, we know why people say objects are hard to find. Because abstract classes capture concepts from our mind, we do not anticipate a technique in the foreseeable future that will help us capture conception.

people's understanding and processing of reality by capturing the concepts they have acquired. Thus, a vital part of learning this technology is acquiring an understanding of what a concept is and how it is used in object-oriented analysis.

Each concept is a particular idea or understanding that a person has of the world. The person knows he or she possesses a concept when he or she can apply it successfully to surrounding things/objects. For example, a car and a telephone are widely held and understood concepts. We can certainly apply it to things/objects and determine if that thing/object is an instance of either a car, telephone, or neither.

The formation of concepts helps us organize our reality of the world. Psychologists believe that babies start life in a world of confusion and gradually acquire concepts to reduce the confusion. For example, at a very young age a baby learns to differentiate between the sounds of its mother and father.

Human beings seem to possess an innate ability to perceive regularities and similarities among the many objects in our world. Every time we recognize these regularities and similarities, we create a concept to organize them. Eventually, we develop concepts (e.g., red and car) and learn to combine concepts to form new concepts (i.e., red car). As we grow older, we construct more elaborate conceptual constructs that lead to increased semantic meaning, precision, and subtleties.

Because we define them, the concepts we form and use are indeed varied. Concepts may be *concrete* (person, car, table, house), *intangible* (time, quality, company), *roles* (mother, programmer, teacher, student), *relational* (marriage, partnership, supervision, ownership), *events* (sale, interrupt, collision, take-off), *displayables* (string, icon, video), *judgements* (high pay, good example, excellent job), and others (signal, atom, gnome, tooth fairy).

These concepts serve as mental lenses with which we try to make sense of and reason about objects in our world. For example, the concept of person helps us reason about several billion objects on this earth. New concepts may (1) help us perceive the same objects in a different way, (2) help us reason about an existing object in a different manner, and (3) add new objects to our awareness. For example, the concept of employee helps us reason in a new way about the several billions of objects. The concept atomic particle adds new objects to our awareness, and particle spin as it applies to an atomic particle helps us reason about an existing object in a different manner.

People can possess concepts about things that have existed, do exist, may exist, and probably will not exist. Two concepts, Santa Claus and Fairy Godmother, have objects for some people, yet they are not for others. Concepts like total world peace and solar-powered car do not apply to anything today, but this may not be so in the future. It is highly unlikely that the concept of perpetual motion will apply to anything today or in the future. People also form concepts for which no objects exist. For example, many people have a concept of a perfect mate, yet there is no object that has passed the concept's test.

CONCEPTS AND OBJECT-ORIENTED MODEL

By definition, a privately held idea or understanding is called a conception. When that idea or understanding is shared by others, it becomes a concept. To communicate with others, we must share our individually held conceptions and arrive at mutually agreed upon concepts. For example, if your conception of a car is only a 1970 silver Lamborghini and your spouse's conception of a car is a family station wagon, you may want to come to a common understanding on the concept of a car before the family goes car shopping.

The process of object-oriented analysis is really the process of capturing a set of shared concepts among domain experts, users, managers, and developers. These concepts underlie every organizational process, define a shared organizational reality, and form the basis for an organizational language that is used for communication.

To help specify these concepts, the object-oriented paradigm has the following basic mechanisms: class, association, aggregation, generalization/specialization, polymorphism, and instantiation. In later chapters, we will add mechanisms to support concepts that deal with dynamic behavior and to deal with rules. Because this is a living technology, more mechanisms are being developed to provide better support for modeling concepts that are needed to help us better manage complexity. In this section of the book we review these basic mechanisms.

Class

A class describes a category; a group of objects with identical attributes, common behavior, common relationships (link and aggregation), and common semantics. Examples of classes are person, employee, timesheet, company, and department. Each object in a class has the same attributes and behavior patterns. Most objects get their individuality by having different values for their attributes and having different objects in their relationships. However, objects with identical attribute values and/or identical relational objects are allowed.

The important key to two objects being in the same class is that they share a common semantic purpose in the application domain, beyond the fact that they have the same attributes, common relationships, and common behaviors. For example, consider a grain silo and a cow. If these were objects in a financial application, the only two attributes of importance may be age and cost, and both the silo and the cow may actually be in the same class of farm assets. However, if the application were a farming application, then it is unlikely that the silo and the cow would be in the same class. Thus, interpreting the semantics depends on the application and is the judgement of the domain expert.

Interface

An interface describes a type, a group of objects with possibly different attributes and existing in different relationships but exhibiting a set of common behaviors in special circumstances. Each object that shares an interface is able to respond to the same set of messages. That is, they all provide a shared set of services even though they may belong to very different categories.

The important key to two objects having the same interface is that while they may have a different semantic purpose in the application domain, they also have a common role in some limited part of the application domain. For example, take a grain field and cow. If these were objects in an agricultural application, then the objects might have very different descriptions. We could describe the grain field in terms of acreage and the crop being raised on it. The cow would be described in terms of age and weight. The activities associated with managing the field and the cow would be quite different. We would have to till the land, fertilize it, and harvest the grain. We would have to feed the cow, have it treated by the vet, and milk it. At the same time though, both objects produce a product for the farmer that has some monetary value, namely grain and milk. Hence, these two objects can be described by a common interface associated with annual yield of product.

Association

An association describes a group of links with common structure and semantics. An association is a way to capture the links between objects in a meaningful way via their classes (object types). An association describes a set of potential links in the same way that a class describes a set of potential objects. In object-oriented modeling, all links, thus all associations, are considered as bidirectional. Once a link is established between two objects, each object may request the services of the other object. However, the proper usage of the association should require that the association (i.e., the links) be used only to access services consistent with the semantic meaning of the association. In theory, an association can be binary (between two classes), ternary (between three classes), or some higher order. In practice, most associations are binary.

Class Aggregation

A class aggregation describes a group of *object aggregations* with common structure and semantics. Thus, class aggregation is a way to capture the object aggregations between objects in a meaningful way via their classes (object types). Examples of aggregation are purchase order, with its associated line items, and a timesheet with its associated hourly accounting. Although many aggregations are implemented as unidirectional, in analysis these relationships should be considered as bidirectional.

An aggregation may be either static or dynamic, and a component of an aggregate may also be conditional. A *static aggregation* has fixed components that cannot be changed. A *dynamic aggregation* has components that may vary over time. A *conditional component* either is or is not a component of an aggregate, depending on whether a specific condition holds.

Aggregation has become such a useful mechanism for analysis that seven distinct kinds of aggregation have been identified. They are as follows:

- Assembly-parts (component-integral composition)
- Material-object composition
- Portion-object composition
- Place-area composition
- Collection-members composition
- Container-content (member-bunch) composition
- Member-partnership composition

These were described in Chapter 9.

Generalization/Specialization of Classes

Generalization is an abstraction mechanism for sharing similarities among classes while their differences are preserved.[2] Generalization is the relationship between a class and one or more refined versions of that class. The class being refined is called the *superclass*[3] and each refined version is called a *subclass*.[4] For example, an aircraft has a manufacturer, identification number, weight, and cost. A helicopter, which also has propellers, and a jet fighter, which also has missiles, are refined versions of an aircraft.

Generalization gives us the capability to define the features of an aircraft once and then just add the additional features for helicopter and jet fighter. In our example, the aircraft is the superclass, and the helicopter and jet fighter are the subclasses.

Attributes, relationships, and services with the same semantic meaning are attached to the superclass and inherited by the subclasses. Each subclass inherits all the attributes, services, and relationships of the superclass. For example, the jet fighter inherits the attributes, manufacturer, identification number, weight, and cost from the aircraft. *It inherited the attributes and not the values.* The jet fighter must determine its own values for these attributes. Generalization is commonly called the "is_a" relationship because each instance of a subclass is also an instance of the superclass.

Generalization is transitive across any number of levels of generalization. The term *ancestors* refers to the generalization of classes across multiple levels. An instance of a subclass is simultaneously an instance of all its ancestor classes. Furthermore, the subclass includes values for every attribute of every ancestor class and relational objects for each relationship in its ancestral classes. In addition, all the services and associated methods of all the ancestral classes may be applied to the subclass.

Each subclass not only inherits all of the above but usually adds specific attributes, relationships (associations and maybe aggregations), and services with its

---

[2] In most object-oriented languages, including C++, this is implemented using inheritance.

[3] Called a base class in C++.

[4] Called a derived class in C++.

associated methods as well. In our example, the jet fighter added missiles as an attribute and probably fireMissile as a service. This attribute and service are not shared by other aircraft.

Polymorphism

One of the goals of object-oriented technology is to reuse code; generalization is one of the most effective vehicle to facilitate code reuse. However, some methods may need to be tailored to meet business needs. When such tailoring is required for a subclass, object-oriented technology has a mechanism, called *polymorphism*, in which the subclass can have a method (behavior) that replaces its superclass' method for a specific service. Thus, when that service is requested from an instance of the subclass, the subclass method is invoked. However, when the service is requested from other instances (assuming no other subclass has also made a replacement for this service), the superclass method is invoked.

For example, consider this simple example. We have a class Employee that has a subclass Executive. From a modeling perspective, an executive is also an employee. One of the services that applies to all employees is payRaise. For all employees, the pay raise is the employees' salary multiplied by the annual inflation. This has been the corporate policy for the last 10 years. With generalization, this has worked very well. Each year at raise time, the payRaise service is invoked for all employees, including the executives. Even though executives are employees, the directors of the corporation decide that executive pay raises should be computed differently than the rest of the employees. It is decided that executive pay raises will be five times the annual inflation rate plus a bonus of 15% of the gross revenue.

What mechanism does object-oriented technology have for handling this situation? In this situation, the subclass "executive" can have a method that replaces the employee's payRaise method every time this service is requested for an executive. Although these methods are different, they accomplish the same business purpose (have the same semantics of payRaise). This phenomenon is known as *polymorphism*. The method that gets invoked depends on the class of the object. Thus, the employee and executive example can be captured by making the payRaise service polymorphic.[5]

Instantiation

Instantiation is a mechanism in the object-oriented paradigm where we can create instances of a class. These instances (objects) are the keepers of the data that make our application/system work. This mechanism is one of the vehicles that we use to make our model dynamic.

---

[5] Note that the name and signature of the service are preserved. This differs from C++ function overloading where the name of the function or the operator is reused, but the arguments are different. Thus, function overloading is not a vehicle for implementing polymorphism in C++. Polymorphism is implemented in C++ by using virtual functions.

DOCUMENTING CONCEPTS USING UML

In earlier chapters, we have informally shown how to document some of the constructs discussed in the previous section. Now, show each of the constructs in a more formal and complete form.

Class Concept

In UML, there are four constructs that can be used for describing the class concept:

- Basic class and object construct
- Parameterized class and bound class constructs
- Interface construct

Basic Class Construct

In UML, the icon for a class or an object is a solid rectangle containing the name of the *class* (object).[6] The rectangle can be broken into three compartments[7] to identify more than just class name. The top compartment shows the class name. The center compartment shows the attributes. An attribute can be documented to several degrees of completeness: the attribute name; the attribute name and type; and the attribute name, type, and default value. The bottom compartment shows the operations. An operation is documented by stating its signature, covering the name, type and default value of all parameters and return type (if it is a function). Because a class may appear in many different diagrams it is not necessary to show every attribute and operation every time it appears. In some cases, it may make sense to show just a subset of them. An empty compartment does not imply that there are no attributes or operations, just that they have not been identified in that particular diagram. One can use ellipsis, ("..."), to denote that there are entries that have not been shown in this particular diagram. An example of representing class (with and without attributes and operations) is given in Figure 10-1.

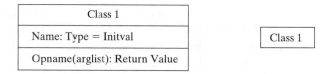

Figure 10-1   Expressing Class Information in UML.

---

[6] To distinguish between class and object, objects have their names underlined.

[7] A seldom used feature of UML is the presence of a fourth compartment to be used for documenting responsibilities.

Parameterized Class and Bounded Class Construct

UML can also deal with *parameterized* (templated) classes and *bound* classes. Parameterized classes are classes that define a basic class in which the data types of one or more of the attributes are a parameter of the class definition. A bound class is created when the parameters of a parameterized class are bound to a data type. The notation is illustrated in Figure 10-2. It should be noted that Java does not support parameterized classes as this is primarily a C++ construct.

Interface Construct

UML supports representing interfaces. Interfaces can be classes that serve as proxies or stubs or they can be pure abstract classes used to separate interface from implementation. There are two basic representations, one in which the interface is shown as a circle attached to the implementing class and the other in which the interface class is documented using the standard class icon with the <<interface>> prototype specified. The implementing class is shown connected to the interface with a dashed line terminating with an unfilled triangle pointing at the interface. Examples of representing interfaces are illustrated in Figure 10-3.

Association

In UML, an association is documented by a line drawn between the classes participating in it (illustrated in Figure 10-4). Centered and above the line is the name of the association. At the ends of a line, the roles that objects (of the class) hold within the association are identified by role names. The role names may appear above or below the line. The multiplicity of the role is identified by the appropriate marker at the end of the line. Appropriate markers are shown in Figure 10-4. Relation 1 illustrates an association where Class 1 has a multiplicity of 0 to many and Class 2 has a multiplicity of 1. Relation 2 illustrates an association where Class 1 has a multiplicity of 1 to many and Class 2 has a multiplicity of 0 or 1. Relation 3 illustrates an association where Class 1 has a multiplicity of many while the multiplicity of Class 2 is not specified. In this case, one normally assumes that the multiplicity is 1. A qualified association has a box at the end of the line identifying the qualifier. This is illustrated in relation 4 in the figure. Associations are assumed to be bidirectional, meaning that they can be traversed in either direction. In some cases, the association can only be traversed in a single direction. UML denotes this by using a line with an arrow head that indicates the direction of traversal. This is illustrated in relation 5 in the figure. Relation 6 illustrates a dependency relation. UML also provides a mechanism for associating attributes with an association. This is accomplished by linking an association class with the line for relation with a dashed line. This is illustrated by relation 7 in the figure.

Figure 10-2   UML Templated Class and a Bound Class.

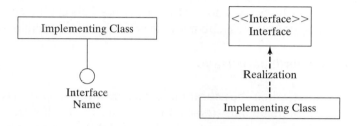

Figure 10-3   UML Diagrams for Representing Interfaces.

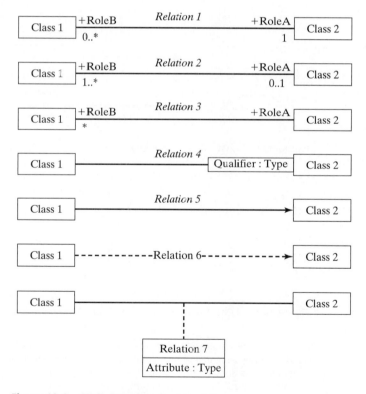

Figure 10-4   UML Notations for Associations.

Class Aggregation

UML distinguishes between two different kinds of aggregations (aggregation and composition) as illustrated in Figure 10-5. The UML concept of aggregation captures the idea of part-whole. UML aggregation is illustrated as an empty diamond on the end that constitutes the whole. The UML concept of composition is that the part object can only belong to one whole and that the parts are usually expected to live or die with the whole. UML composition is illustrated as a filled diamond on the end that constitutes the whole. Multiplicity markers can be employed on the many end of the aggregation. These markers are the same as used in associations.

Generalization/Specialization of Class

Class generalization/specialization is documented in UML using a line with an empty triangle that points towards the generalization as illustrated in Figure 10-6. In the example, Class 1 is superclass for Class 2. UML allows one to document multiple generalizations[8] by establishing multiple generalization/specialization relations from a class to multiple parent classes. Java, however, only supports single generalization/specialization relations.

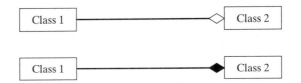

Figure 10-5   UML Notation for Aggregation and Composition.

Figure 10-6   UML Notation for Generalization/Specialization.

---

[8] In older parlance, this was often referred to as multiple inheritance because generalization/specialization is typically implemented using inheritance. Interfaces are also implemented using inheritance. As a result, the statement that Java does not support multiple inheritance is not entirely correct as a Java class may inherit from a single parent class and from multiple interfaces. Complicating this further is the fact that interfaces may have multiple generalizations.

Generalization/Specialization of Interface

Interface generalization/specialization is documented in UML using a line with an empty triangle that points towards the generalization as illustrated in Figure 10-7. In the example, Interface 1 is a superclass for Interface 2. UML allows one to document multiple generalizations by establishing multiple generalization/specialization relations from a class to multiple parent classes. While Java only supports single generalization/specialization relations for classes, it does support multiple inheritance for interfaces.

Polymorphism

In UML, polymorphism is documented by showing the service (operation) in both the superclass and the subclass.

Instantiation

UML allows one to document objects as well as classes. An object is denoted using the notation for class with the object name underlined. The object name is denoted by a label separated from the class name by a colon. An example is illustrated in Figure 10-8. If a class creates instances of another class, this can be shown using a dashed arrow illustrating the instantiation dependency between the class and an instance. This is also shown in the figure.

Refining the Model

The steps for refinement are as follows:

1. Group all objects with the same attributes, similar relationships, and common behavior. If there is a concept within the application domain that defines these objects, use that name for the class. If not, ask the domain expert what concept this may resemble. Use the class that the domain expert provides and regroup your objects.

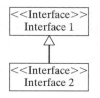

Figure 10-7   UML Notation for Generalization/Specialization.

Figure 10-8   UML Notation for an Object.

2. Group the links and object aggregations into associations and class aggregations. Remember that all the members of the group must carry the same semantic meaning.
3. Determine whether the classes are specializations of a common superclass. Look for identical attributes, relationships, services, and behaviors across classes and, with them, try to form a class. Again, ask the domain expert if these properties capture a useful domain concept. Remember that these new objects must operate in a useful semantic domain.
4. Look for polymorphism. See if there are services of objects that are the same or similar, but differ in behavior (how the service is provided). If these objects operate in the same semantic domain, make the service polymorphic.
5. Look for interfaces. See if there are subsets of services of objects of different classes that are common. Perform all the above steps again until no new superclass is found.

SUBSYSTEMS

In building large applications/systems, the analyst/developer has to deal with a number of interesting and different subject matters. For example, in a typical application, we have the following subject matters: the application, interface to external systems, user interface, alarm subsystem, and logging subsystem.[9] This is normally too much material for most of us to deal with as a whole. Consequently, we need a strategy for organizing these different matters into more manageable subsystems. The strategy or technique we shall use is based on the work of Shlaer and Mellor. Their strategy relies on the concept of domain.

Domain

A domain is a separate real, hypothetical, or abstract world inhabited by a distinct set of objects that behave according to rules and policies that characterize that domain. For example, an Airline Management domain would be concerned with airplanes, air routes, airports, and gates, as well as with the operating policies and FAA regulations governing their use. However, the User Interface domain is

---

[9] In design, we add the screen subsystem, database subsystem, etc. The operating system, programming languages, software packages, and development environment are all considered part of design.

concerned with windows, pull-down menus, dialog boxes, and icons together with a different set of operating policies.

Each domain forms a separate but cohesive whole. The principle of cohesion helps us keep closely related ideas together and unrelated ideas separate. Because a domain represents a set of closely related objects, rules, and policies, it can be treated as a unit (subsystem) for the purpose of analysis.

To better understand domain, we can look at this concept in terms of objects:

1. An object is defined in one domain.
2. The object in a domain requires the existence of other objects in the same domain.
3. The objects in one domain do not require the existence of objects in a different domain.

For example, consider an airline management application. (1) The air route should be only in the Airline Management domain. (2) Air Route by itself is not much use to us with airplanes and airports. (3) Air routes and airplanes can exist without windows or dialog boxes. Conversely, windows and icons can exist without air routes and airplanes.

Although an object in one domain does not require the existence of an object in another domain, it is very common for an object in one domain to have a counterpart instance in another domain. For example, an airplane in the Airline Management domain may have a counterpart airplane icon in the User Interface domain.

To help us recognize domains, Shlaer and Mellor have given us a classification scheme:[10]

1. *Application Domain*. This is the subject matter from the customer/user perspective. This is what we normally call business requirements analysis.
2. *Service Domain*. This domain provides generic mechanisms and utility functions to support the application domain. These are the domains that are hard for us to identify.
3. *Architectural Domain*. This domain provides the generic mechanisms and structures for managing data and control for the system as a whole.
4. *Implementation Domain*. This domain includes the programming language, operating systems, networks, and common class libraries.

Bridge

According to Shlaer and Mellor, a bridge exists between two domains when one domain needs to use the mechanisms and/or capabilities provided by the other domain. The domain that requires the capabilities is known as the *client*, while the

---

[10] In analysis, we are concerned only with Application Domains and Service Domains. In design, Architectural Domains and Implementation Domains are considered.

domain that provides them is called the *server*. For example, the Airline Management domain (client) may use the User Interface domain to display the air routes to the user. During analysis, the bridge defines a set of external services (from the client's perspective) and a set of requirements (from the server's perspective). For instance, in our airplane example the airplane icon must be able to derive its position from the position of the airplane object in the Airline Management domain.

ORGANIZING SUBSYSTEMS

According to Rumbaugh et al., the decomposition of a system into subsystems may be done both horizontally and vertically. Although most of us have numerous ways to decompose a system, any decomposition reduces to one or the other or a combination of these two kinds.

Horizontal Layers

A layer system is a set of semantic domains (virtual reality), each built in terms of the ones below it and providing the basis of implementation for the ones above it. Examples of this approach are the protocol layers of OSI and the TNM layers for telecommunication operating support systems. For the non-telecommunication technologist, an interactive graphic system is another example. Here, windows are made from screens that are made from pixels driving some I/O device. The layers are the application domain, window domain, screen domain, pixel domain, and hardware domain.

The goal is to make each layer as independent as possible. Although there is usually some correspondence between objects in different layers, the communication between layers is basically one-way. A subsystem knows about the layers below it[11] but has no knowledge of the layers above it. Thus, a client-server relationship exists between the layers.[12]

Usually, only the top layer, which is the application domain, and the bottom layer, which is the hardware domain, are specified in the requirements document. One of the purposes of analysis is to find all the intermediate layers. It is good practice to have at least one layer (service domain) between the application layer and the hardware layer as this facilitates porting to other hardware/software platforms.

---

[11] In some paradigms, the communication may only be to the layer immediately below it. This restriction preserves the information hiding and encapsulation principles between layers and makes software more maintainable as a designer only needs to check the layer below it. However, in practice this is too restrictive. During design, performance considerations usually force us to allow the upper layer to access all the services in any lower layer.

[12] The upper layers are the clients for the lower layers.

Vertical Partitions

Vertical partitions divide a system into several weakly-coupled subsystems,[13] each of which provides one kind of service. For example, consider a computerized work management system for maintenance personnel. There may be a separate subsystem for routine work, troubleshooting, time reporting, and salary administration. There is only a very weak coupling between these subsystems. Routine work is only coupled to time reporting as to the hours worked. Salary administration uses time reporting to determine how much to pay; however, it has neither coupling to routine work nor troubleshooting.

Combination

A system can be successively decomposed into subsystems using both vertical partitions and horizontal layers in various combinations. Horizontal layers may be partitioned and vertical partitions may be layered. Most large systems require this kind of mixture.

IDENTIFYING SUBSYSTEMS

To identify subsystems, we are going to use the fact that there should be coupling between objects in the same domain and low coupling across domains. If we draw a model that captures only the associations and class aggregations, we would find a clustering of classes. We will use each cluster as a potential subsystem. To help us determine if the cluster is a subsystem, Shlaer and Mellor have the following suggestion:

1. Give the domain a name and prepare a mission statement for it.
2. Find the bridges (services to other subsystems) for the domain.
3. See if these services are consistent with the mission statement.
4. Determine if you can replace these set of objects with a different set of objects with the same mission.

If all the above are true, the cluster is a subsystem. If you find a number of intersubsystem relationships defined between the same two subsystems, a cluster may have been split improperly. Look again at your class definitions, see if you can redefine the classes to make the clusters better behaved.

Documenting Subsystem

Subsystems can be documented in UML utilizing packages. A package diagram identifies a grouping of software elements, typically a collection of classes. UML

---

[13] If the subsystems are independent of each other, then it is more effective to consider them as separate systems.

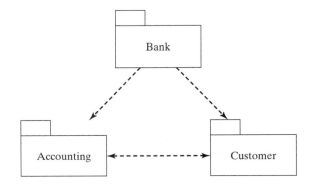

Figure 10-9   Package Diagram Illustrating Subsystem Interactions.

uses a stylized folder to represent a package. A package diagram is illustrated in
Figure 10-9. In this diagram, the accounting and customer subsystems communicate
with each other as indicated by the double arrowed line between them. The Bank
package exists in a layer above the Accounting and Customer packages. The Bank
package communicates with the packages below it, but they can not make requests
to it as evidenced by the single direction arrows.

RECOMMENDED APPROACH

Our recommended approach consists of the following steps:

1. Group all the objects with the same attributes, similar relationships, and
    common behavior. If there is a concept within the application domain
    that defines these objects, use that name for the class. If not, ask the
    domain expert what concept this may resemble. Use the class that the
    domain expert provides and regroup your objects.
2. Group the links and object aggregations into associations and class aggre-
    gations. Remember that all the members of the group must carry the
    same semantic meaning.
3. Determine whether the classes are the specialization of a common super-
    class. Look for identical attributes, relationships, services, and behaviors
    across classes and try to form a class. Again, ask the domain expert if
    these properties capture a useful domain concept. Remember that these
    new objects must operate in a useful semantic domain.
4. Look for polymorphism. See if there are services of objects that are the
    same or similar but differ in behavior (how the service is provided). If
    these objects operate in the same semantic domain, make the service
    polymorphic. Perform all the above steps again until no new superclasses
    are found.

5. Draw a model that captures only the associations and class aggregations.
6. Identify the cluster of classes and assume they are potential subsystems.
7. Give this cluster a name and a mission statement.
8. Use the bridge and replacement test to determine if it is a subsystem (separate domain).

EXAMPLE

Let us return to our lawn mowing example.

Refinement

In this section, we will refine our model in the one semantic domain: home care.[14] Based on the analysis, we have the following objects: John, Jane, Peter, Paul, Elizabeth, Mary, Jack, FamilyLawn, and ProfessionalLawnMower.

We start by trying to group objects together. First, Paul, Elizabeth, and Mary are objects that have the same attributes, common relationships, and common behavior. Jack and ProfessionalLawnMower also appear to be in the same class. In fact, ProfessionalLawnMower is a class and that Jack is an instance of that class.

Although we have identified ProfessionalLawnLower as an object, it is also a class. This is one of the difficulties in reading a requirements document. In one usage, a name of a class is used to refer to itself as an object and in another usage, the name is used to refer to itself as a collection of instances of an object type. Now you understand the problem with step 1; when you list objects, you are also listing classes.[15] Our first cut at listing objects is shown in Figure 10-9.

Class	Instance(s)
Family	Jones
ProfessionalLawnMower	Jack
ChildA	Mary, Elizabeth, Paul
ChildB	Peter
Father	John
Mother	Jane
Lawn	Family lawn

Figure 10-10   List of Initial Classes Instances for the Lawn Mower Example

---

[14] The subsystem identification steps are shown in the case study.

[15] This cannot be wrong, for every class is also an object; however, the reverse is not true (i.e., there are objects that are not classes).

If we review all the classes above, we notice that class **childA** and class **childB** are almost identical. The difference is that the two classes have different methods for the "mow the lawn" service. Because the semantic meaning and signature for the service are the same, this situation is best captured using polymorphism. Thus, we can create a superclass **Child** for subclasses **ChildA** and **ChildB**. This model is adequate if we presume that we deal only with one generation of a family and ignore the fact that professional lawn mower can also be in a family. This more flexible and more accurate model is left as an exercise for the reader. The model shown in Figure 10-10 through Figure 10-12 is adequate for our limited application. The class descriptions are illustrated in Figure 10-14 through Figure 10-18.

In this example, we introduced a second form of polymorphism. In the earlier example, the superclass **Employee** had a method specified for the service payRaise; the subclass **Executive** then specified its own method for payRaise. However, we could have added another subclass, **Supervisors**, that does not specify its own method for payRaise. In that event, instances of **Supervisors** use the method specified in the superclass **Employee**. Here, the superclass **Child** defines the prototype for the service mow_the_lawn but did not specify a method for performing the service. When this is done, every subclass must specify its own method for handling the service. There is no default specification in the superclass. Both subclasses **ChildA** and **ChildB** must have methods for the service mowTheLawn.

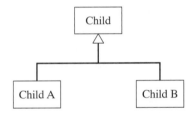

Figure 10-11   Class Generalization Diagram for Lawn Mowing Example.

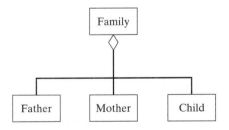

Figure 10-12   Class Aggregation Diagram for Lawn Mowing Example.

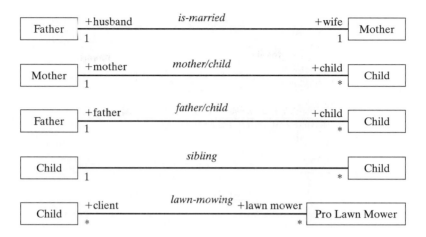

Figure 10-13   Class Association Diagram for Lawn Mowing Example.

You should also recognize that the differences between **ChildA** and **ChildB** are that they have different methods for implementing the service mowTheLawn, and that only **ChildA** has an association with **ProfessionalLawnMower**. The rest of the class descriptions are left as an exercise for the reader.

Subsystems

Since Chapter 4 and including our work on refinement, our emphasis has been on the modeling the semantic domain: home care. Thus, we been focused on the objects that support the system in performing the Look For Work Conditions and the Run Simulation Forward One Time Unit use cases. These use cases are driven by the Asynchronous Event Daemon and the Simulation Clock respectively. The result is a subsystem, the lawnMowing Model, which is a specialized version of Home Care.

However, our model is not complete. First, we have not incorporated into our model the generation of events for the observer watching the simulation as dictated by the Run Simulation Forward One Time Unit use case. Furthermore, there are two other use cases, Subscribe To Simulation Information and Set Simulation Parameters, that are driven by the observer and director actors respectively and which we have not addressed at all.

Developing the model for these two use cases is not instructional, and there are standard Graphical User Interface (GUI) libraries (e.g., Microsoft's Microsoft Foundation Class [MFC]). Thus, we are not going to develop the model necessary to support these other two use cases. However, these two use cases introduce two additional subsystems: the user interface and the controller. The user interface is the subsystem by which the observer and the director interact with the system. The user interface

CLASS NAME	Father

ATTRIBUTES
Schedule, mycondition

SERVICES
Prototype: mow_the_lawn (no arguments)
{
get SCHEDULE for evening (7 PM–9 PM)
Next, if SCHEDULE has open slot,
then:
place mowFamilyLawn in slot.
return "Yes, I will mow the lawn this evening"
else:
return "No, I cannot mow the lawn"
endif
}
Prototype: mowFamilyLawn (no arguments)
{
If MYCONDITION is equal to "tired,"
then: //get children via father/child association
for each child in selected Children
ask each child to "mow the lawn" for 5 dollars.
if answer is "yes,"
then:
remove "mowFamilylawn" from SCHEDULE.
return;
else:
endif:
endfor:
perform mowing the lawn.
else:
perform mowing the lawn.
endif:
}

Figure 10-14   Example of a Class CRC Card from the Lawn Mower.

CLASS NAME	Family

ATTRIBUTES
None

SERVICES
Constructor will create the family (see Chapter 17)

Figure 10-15   Example of a Class CRC Card from the Lawn Mower.

CLASS NAME	Child
SUBCLASSES	ChildA, ChildB

ATTRIBUTES
Schedule

SERVICES

Prototype: mow_the_lawn (address_of_lawn, dollar_amount)
    // there is no method specified, we will require that each
    // subclass specify a method for providing this service.

Figure 10-16   Example of a Class CRC Card from the Lawn Mower.

CLASS NAME	ChildB
SUPERCLASS	Child

ATTRIBUTES
No additional attributes; remember, it will inherit schedule from child

SERVICES
Prototype: mow_the_lawn (address_of_lawn, dollar_amount)
{
get SCHEDULE for evening (7 PM–9 PM)
Next, if SCHEDULE has open slot,
then:
place mowLawn in slot.
associate ADDRESS_OF_LAWN with mowLawn.
return "Yes, I will mow the lawn this evening."
else:
return "No, I cannot mow the lawn."
endif:
}

Figure 10-17   Example of a Class CRC Card from the Lawn Mower.

model consists of classes and objects associated with windows, buttons, menus, and other interface classes. The controller is the subsystem that handles subscriptions

SUPERCLASS	Child
CLASS NAME	ChildA

ATTRIBUTES
No additional attributes; remember, it will inherit schedule from child

SERVICES
Prototype: mow_the_lawn (address_of_lawn, dollar_amount)
{
if DOLLAR_AMOUNT is less than $5,
then:
get SCHEDULE for evening (7 PM–9 PM)
Next, if SCHEDULE has open slot,
then:
place mowLawn in slot.
associate ADDRESS_OF_LAWN with mowLawn.
return "Yes, I will mow the lawn this evening."
else:
return "No, I cannot mow the lawn."
endif
else:
use lawn-mowing association to get
a professional lawn mower: plm
ask plm to "mow the lawn (ADDRESS_OF_LAWN, self, ADDRESS)."
if plm's response is "yes"
then:
return "Yes, I will mow the lawn this evening."
else:
return "No, I cannot mow the lawn."
endif:
endif:
}

Figure 10-18   Example of a Class CRC Card from the Lawn Mower.

and setting simulation parameters. The controller consists of classes and objects associated with keeping time, subscriptions, and events.

With these two subsystems, our design is complete. Figure 10-19 illustrates how the three subsystems interact. In this figure the controller subsystem drives the LawnMowing Model through the time simulation and establishes subscriptions to LawnMowing Model elements. The user interface subsystem does not communicate directly with the LawnMowing Model subsystem. It sends the subscription requests to the controller, which then forwards them to the LawnMowing Model subsystem. During the simulation, the LawnMowing Model subsystem generates events. These events are forwarded to the appropriate subsystem based on subscriptions. This includes the user interface and the controller subsystems.

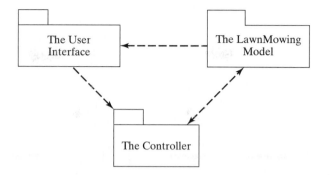

Figure 10-19   The Three Subsystems Constituting Our Home Care
Simulation System.

SUMMARY

The substeps of model refinement and subsystem identification are as follows:

1. Group all objects with the same attributes, similar relationships, and common behavior. If there is a concept within the application domain that defines these objects, use that name for the class. If not, ask the domain expert what concept this may resemble. Use the class that the domain expert provides and regroup your objects.

2. Group the links and object aggregations into associations and class aggregations. Remember that all the members of the group must carry the same semantic meaning.

3. Determine whether the classes are specializations of a common superclass. Look for identical attributes, relationships, services, and behaviors across classes. With these common attributes, relationships, services, and behaviors, try to form a class. Again, ask the domain expert if these properties capture a useful domain concept. Remember these new objects must operate in a useful semantic domain.

4. Look for polymorphism. See if there are services of objects that are the same or similar but differ in behavior (how the service is provided). If these objects operate in the same semantic domain, make the service polymorphic. Perform all the above steps again until no new superclasses are found.

5. Now draw a model that only captures the associations and class aggregations.

6. Identify the cluster of classes and assume they are potential subsystems.

7. Give this cluster a name and a mission statement.

8. Use the bridge and replacement test to determine if it is a subsystem (separate domain).

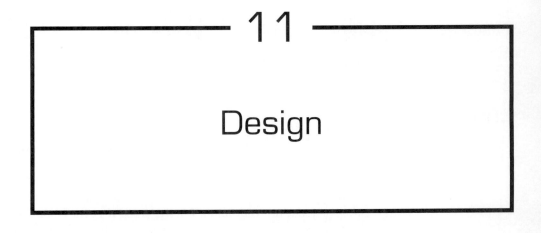

11

Design

At the end of the last chapter, we completed the analysis model of the application domain. Now we are ready to consider the technology necessary to implement the model. In this chapter, we add to the model all the technology-dependent objects (classes) to make the application implementable. The result of this activity is the design model.

We do not discuss or describe object design patterns in this book, despite the large degree of interest this topic area has generated. We justify this by our observation that the use of design patterns by people without significant experience in object-oriented methods has led to considerable problems. Design patterns, although simple and easy to understand in themselves, can be very difficult for inexperienced people to apply correctly. We have observed that novices tend to warp their object models into the patterns that they understand best. Instead we have chosen to give a few general rules on how to map an object model into a good and usable design that can be easily implemented. We are leaving design patterns to an advanced book on design.

INTRODUCTION

After you have modeled a business solution to your application/system, you must decide on an approach to implement the business solution using available technology. *System design* is the high-level strategy for implementing the business solution and *detailed design* is the low-level strategy of the implementation of the application/system.

In system design, the developer must do the following:

- Organize the system into subsystems
- Identify concurrency inherent in the model
- Allocate the subsystems to processors and tasks
- Choose a vehicle and an approach for data storage
- Determine a control strategy for accessing global resources
- Choose an implement of control for the software
- Consider start-up, shut-down, and failure strategies

In detailed design, the developer must do the following:

- Add the objects/classes from the architectural and implementation domains
- Design efficient algorithms for complex services
- Optimize the design of the application/system
- Maximize the use of inheritance
- Redesign the associations for efficiency
- Determine the best representation of classes
- Package the classes and associations into reusable units

Obviously, detailed design follows system design.

SYSTEM DESIGN

Although all the issues and decisions a developer must make in system design are critical to the success of the project, we will only discuss dividing the system into a small number of components and the control strategy for the software.

Subsystems

Each major component of the system is called a *subsystem*.[1] Each subsystem should deal with a separate subject matter called a *domain*. Each domain can be

---

[1] This is the same concept as discussed in the previous chapter. In analysis, we use subsystem to manage complexity in the application domain. Now, in design, we use subsystems to manage the complexity in the architectural and implementation domains.

independent of the rest of the system.[2] A good clue to a domain is that it has its own terminology with a different semantic meaning; it is a separate real, hypothetical, or abstract world that is inhabited by a distinct set of objects that behave according to the rules and policies of the domain. A subsystem is neither an object nor a function but a package of classes, associations, operations, events, and constraints that are interrelated and that has reasonably well-defined and hopefully a small number of interfaces with the rest of the system.

A subsystem is usually defined by the services it provides, just like an object or class is. The relationship between the rest of the system and the subsystem can be peer-to-peer or client/server.

In a peer-to-peer relationship, either side may have access to the other's services. Communication is not necessarily done by a request followed by an immediate response, so there can be communication cycles that can lead to subtle design errors.

The client/server relationship, however, is much simpler; the client calls on the server that performs some service and replies with the results. The client needs to know the interface of the supplier, but the supplier does not need to know the interface of the client. All the interactions are done through the supplier's interface.

There are all kinds of suggestions on how to decompose a system. The decomposed system can be organized in two ways: by horizontal layers or by vertical partitions.

A layered system is an ordered set of subsystems in which each of the subsystems is built in terms of the ones below it and provides the basis for building the subsystem above it. The objects in each layer can be independent, although there is some correspondence between the objects of various layers. However, knowledge is only one way; a subsystem knows about the layers below, but it does not know about the subsystems above it. Thus, a client/server relationship exists between layers. An example of a layered system is a windowing system for a computer user interface.

A vertically partitioned system divides a system into several independent or weakly coupled subsystems, each providing one kind of service. For example, an operating system includes a file subsystem, device controller, virtual management subsystem, and an event interrupt handler. In a vertical partition system, a peer-to-peer relationship exists between subsystems.

A real system may be successfully decomposed into subsystems using both layers and partitions in various combinations; a layer can be partitioned and a partition can be layered. Most large systems require a combination of layers and partitions.

Architectural Frameworks

In reality, because many of the decisions that should be made at the system design stage are given to the developers, much of the design process is figuring out how to

---

[2] It is our opinion that effective reuse is not at the object/class level as proclaimed by most experts but at the domain level. An example of successful domain reuse is seen with the many application service domain packages available.

integrate these givens into a working system. One of the major improvements in software development is that software vendors have given developers a subsystem that performs specific services very well for applications. Thus, developers should take advantage of written and tested subsystems when possible. Moreover, most developers have built certain architectural frameworks that are well suited for certain kinds of applications. If you have applications with similar characteristics, you should use these corresponding architectures as a starting point for your design.

The kinds of systems are as follows:

- **Batch**. A data transformation is done on an entire set of inputs.
- **Continuous**. As input changes in real-time, a data transformation is performed in real-time.
- **Interactive**. External interactions dominate the application.
- **Transaction**. The application is concerned with storing and updating data, often including concurrent access by many users and from many different locations.
- **Rule-based**. The application is dominated by concern about enforcing rules.
- **Simulation**. The application simulates evolving real-world objects.
- **Real-time**. The application is dominated by strict timing constraints.

The steps for performing an object-oriented system design for the first four architectural frameworks are below.

Batch Architectural Framework

1. Break the transformation into subtransformations, so that each subtransformation performs one part of the transformation.
2. Define temporary objects for the data flows between subtransformations. Then each subtransformation only needs to know about the objects on each side of itself (i.e., its inputs and outputs).
3. Expand each subtransformation into other subtransformations until the operations are straightforward to implement.
4. Restructure the pipeline for optimization.
5. Use the new set of objects to form classes that loosely couple to the original object model.

Continuous Architectural Framework

1. Identify all the objects that need continuous updates.
2. Draw a sequence diagram for the continuous transformation.
3. Make the inputs and outputs of the services temporary objects that contain the values that change continuously.
4. Refine or define methods for each object/class that will process the incremental changes for the object.
5. Add any additional objects needed for optimization.

6. Use the new set of objects to form classes that loosely couple to the original object model.

Interactive Architectural Framework

1. Separate the objects that form the interface from the objects that define the semantics of the application; they are in two different domains.
2. Use predefined (library) objects to interface with external agents. For example, most windowing systems have libraries that give developers the windows, menus, and buttons for usage.
3. Use an event-driven (callback) approach to decomposition.
4. Separate physical events from logical events and assign them to the correct objects. Logical events are part of the application and physical events are probably part of the interface domain. Be careful, because many times a logical event corresponds to multiple physical events.

Transaction Architectural Framework

1. Map the object model into a database.
2. Determine the resources that cannot be shared.
3. Determine the unit of a transaction (the objects that must be accessed together during a transaction) using an sequence diagram.
4. Design the concurrency control for the transactions. Most database systems support this.

Software Control Within a Framework

There are two kinds of control flows within a software system: external and internal. External control is the flow of externally visible events among the objects in the system, while internal control is the flow of control within a method.

There are three ways to control external flows: procedural-driven sequential, event-driven sequential, and concurrent. Similarly, the three ways to control internal flows are: procedure calls, quasi-concurrent intertask calls, and concurrent intertask calls. Both the internal and external control strategies chosen are highly dependent on the resources (language, operating system, etc.) available and the pattern of interactions in the application.

Because all the major object-oriented languages, such as Smalltalk, C++, and Objective C, are procedural languages, procedural-driven sequential is the most common way to control external flow. In this style, the control resides within the application code. The application code issues requests for external inputs and waits for it to arrive. When it arrives, control is resumed within the procedure that made the call. Although this style is easy for most developers to implement, the developer must convert the events in a sequential flow of operations (methods) between objects. This is done using an sequence diagram.[3] This style of control is useful when there is a regularity of external events. However, this style is not very good for handling asynchronous events, error conditions, flexible user interfaces, and process control systems.

In the event-driven sequential style, the control resides within a dispatcher or monitor provided by either the language, subsystem, or operating system. Application procedures are attached to events and are called by the dispatcher when the corresponding events occur (callback). The application makes procedure calls to the dispatcher for input/output but does not wait for it in-line. Events are handled by the dispatcher, and all application procedures return control to the dispatcher instead of retaining control until input arrives.

Event-control style is more difficult to implement with standard programming languages (Smalltalk, C++, or Objective C). This style permits a more flexible pattern of control than the procedural style. Because it simulates cooperating processes within a single multithreaded task, a single errant method can block an entire application. However, event-control style produces more modular design and can better handle error conditions.

In the concurrent style, control resides in several independent objects where each is a separate task. A task can wait for input, but other tasks continue to execute. There is a queuing mechanism for events, and the operating system resolves scheduling conflicts among tasks. Java is an object-oriented language that directly supports tasking and concurrency.

Documenting System Design

Diagrammatically a system architecture, the system design, is documented in Unified Modeling Language (UML) utilizing three different diagrams: a package diagram, a component diagram, and a realization diagram. A package diagram shows software partitioning. A component diagram describes relationships among the software components of the system. A realization diagram places the components on hardware platforms. These diagrams are typically accompanied by textual descriptions of the components, connections, and hardware.

As was introduced in the previous chapter, a package diagram identifies a grouping of software elements, typically a collection of software classes. A simple package diagram is illustrated in Figure 11-1. One can explicitly include in the package icon all of the classes that are members.

The component diagram identifies the components that form the system along with the connections among individual components, as illustrated in Figure 11-2. The UML specification identifies five prototypes for components, namely (1) application, (2) library, (3) table, (4) file, and (5) document. According to the UML specification, a component is drawn as a rectangle with two smaller rectangles overlaid on one side of it. However, the UML specification does suggest alternative

---

[3] Sequence diagrams are discussed in Chapter 6 on behavior.

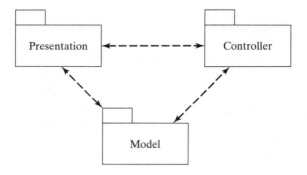

Figure 11-1   Simple Package Diagram for a Model-Controller-View System.

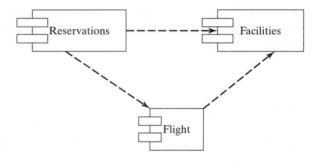

Figure 11-2   Component Diagram for an Airlines Reservation and Flight Scheduling System.

representations for the later four prototypes. Dependencies are illustrated as dotted arrows. One can include within the component diagram explicit identification of the classes that a component realizes (implements). This is illustrated by a dotted arrow to the UML representation for a class.

The deployment diagram captures relationships between components and the hardware on which they are hosted. Components are captured in the deployment diagram using the same graphical mechanism as in the component diagram. However, components are placed inside graphical boxes that represent hardware devices (nodes) in the system. A node does not have to be a generalized processing computer but can include sensors, RAID disk arrays, and other devices that are an integral part of a system. Solid lines are used to indicate hardware connectivity between nodes. A simple deployment diagram is illustrated in Figure 11-3.

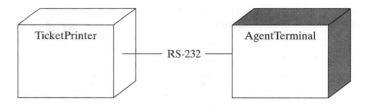

Figure 11-3 Deployment Diagram Illustrating an Agent Terminal Connected to a Specialized Printer for Printing Tickets.

DETAILED DESIGN

During analysis, we determined the objects/classes, their associations, and their structure from an application perspective. During design, we have to add the implementation objects and optimize data structures and algorithms for coding.

There is a shift in emphasis from application domain concepts to computer concepts. Given the classes from the application, the designer must choose among different ways to implement them. Factors that may be important include execution time, memory usage, and disk Input/Ouput (I/O) access. However, optimization of design should not be carried to excess, as there must be a practical trade-off between optimization and ease of implementation, maintainability, and extensibility of the final product.

Usually, the simplest and best approach is to take the classes found in analysis into design. Design then becomes the process of adding implementation objects, adding implementation details, and making implementation decisions. Occasionally, an analysis object/class does not appear in the design but is distributed among other objects/classes for computational efficiency. Some redundant attributes or an object/class may be added for efficiency.

Thus, detailed design is primarily a process of refinement and adding implementation objects that are technology-dependent. These new objects and additional details should help better organize the application and augment the analysis model.

Class Design

During analysis, we focused on the logical structure of the information that is needed to build a business solution. During design, we need to look at the best way to implement the logical structure that helps optimize the application performance. Many of the effective implementation structures that we need are instances of container classes; examples are arrays, lists, queues, stacks, sets, bags, dictionaries, associations, and trees. Most object-oriented languages already have libraries that provide such classes.

Although we have defined business algorithms for building a business solution during analysis, we may need to optimize the algorithms for implementation. During optimization, we may add new classes to hold intermediate results and new low-level methods. These new classes are usually implementation classes not mentioned directly in the client's requirements document. They are usually service domain classes that support the building of the application classes. When new methods are added, some have obvious target objects as their owner. However, some methods may have several target objects for its owner. Assigning responsibility for the later kind of service can be very frustrating.[4] This is the fundamental problem when we invent implementation objects; they are somewhat arbitrary, and their boundaries are more a matter of convenience than of logical necessity.[5]

If we need to avoid recomputation to improve performance, we should define new objects/classes to hold these derived attributes (data). Remember that derived attributes must be updated when base values change. This can be done by

1. **Explicit Code**. Because each derived attribute is defined in terms of one or more attributes of base objects, one way to update the derived attribute is to insert code in the update attribute method of the base object(s). This additional code would explicitly update the derived attribute that is dependent on the attribute of the base object. This is synchronizing by *explicit code*.

2. **Periodic Recomputation**. When base values are changed in a bunch, it may be possible to recompute all the derived attributes periodically after all the base values are changed. This is called *periodic recomputation*.

3. **Triggers**. An active attribute has dependent attributes. Each dependent attribute must register itself with the active attribute. When the active attribute is being updated, a trigger is fired that informs all the objects containing the dependent attributes that the active attribute has a changed value. Then it is the responsibility of the derived object to update its derived attribute. This is called updating by *triggers*.

Sometimes the same service is defined across several classes and can be easily inherited from a common superclass. However, often the services in different classes are similar but not identical. By slightly modifying the prototype of the service, the services can be made to match so that they can be handled by a single inherited service. When this is done, not only must the name and the signature of the service match, but they should all have the same semantic meaning. The following adjustments are commonly made to increase inheritance:

1. When some services have fewer arguments than other services, the missing arguments are added but ignored in the method.

---

[4] These "implementation" services can also be easily overlooked as they are not inherently services of only one class.

[5] This becomes more difficult when we need to assign a service in an inheritance hierarchy. For implementation classes, the definitions of subclasses may be quite arbitrary and fluid. It is quite common to see services move up and down the hierarchy during the design step.

2. When a service has few arguments because it is a special case of a more general service, you can implement the special service by calling the general services with all the arguments.

3. When attributes in different classes have the same semantic meaning, choose one name for the attribute and move it to a common superclass.

4. When services in different classes have the same semantic meaning, choose one name for the service and apply 1 or 2 to take advantage of polymorphism.

5. When a service is defined on several different classes, but not in other classes that semantically should be in one group, define the service in the superclass and declare it as a no-op (a does nothing) method in the class that does not care about providing this service.

6. When common behavior has been recognized, a common superclass can be created to implement the shared behavior, leaving the specialized behavior in the subclasses. Usually, this new superclass is an abstract class.[6]

We strongly recommended that you do not use inheritance as purely an implementation technique. This happens when developers find an existing class that has implemented a large number of the services needed by a newly defined class, even though semantically the two classes are different. The developer may then want to use inheritance to achieve part implementation of the new class. This can lead to side effects because some of the inherited methods may provide unwanted behaviors. It can also lead to brittle inheritance hierarchies that are difficult to change as the analysis model evolves to reflect changing requirements. A better technique is to use delegation[7], which allows the newly formed class to delegate only the appropriate services.[8]

Association Design

In implementing associations, the designer must consider the access pattern and the relative frequencies of the different kinds of access. If the number of hits from query are low because only a fraction of the objects satisfy the criteria, an index should be used to improve the access to objects that are frequently retrieved. However, this is at a price as this will use more memory and updates are slower. Sometimes adding a

---

[6] Sometimes it is worthwhile to abstract out a superclass even if there is only one subclass in your application that inherits from it. If it has useful semantics, it will probably be needed in future extensions of the application or in other applications.

[7] In delegation, you create an association between the class and the newly formed class. Then the newly formed class can delegate the service from itself to the corresponding service of the existing class.

[8] Languages such as C++ let a subclass selectively make service public. When used properly, inheritance can do the equivalent of delegation for such languages.

new association that is derived from the base association provides direct access to the appropriate data.

If the association is only traversed in one direction, an association can be implemented as an attribute that contains an object reference. If the multiplicity is 1, it is simply a pointer to the other object. If the multiplicity is >1, then it is a pointer to a set of pointers to objects. If the many end is ordered, a list is used in place of a set. A qualified association can be implemented using a dictionary object.

A two-way association can be implemented as follows:

1. Add an attribute to the class on one side of the association and perform a search when a reverse traversal is required.
2. Add an attribute to both sides of the association. Use the same multiplicity techniques as for an association that is traversed in one direction.
3. Create an associate class, independent of either class. An associate class is a set of pairs of related objects stored in a single-variable size object. For efficiency, it is common to implement an associative object as two map objects.[9]

If the association has no services, but has attributes, attributes of an association can be implemented as follows:

1. If the association is one-to-one, the association attributes can be stored as attributes on either class.
2. If the association is many-to-one, the association attributes may be stored in the class on the many side.
3. If the association is many-to-many, it is best to create an associative class and assign the association attributes to the associative class.[10]

Generalization and Inheritance

Most object-oriented languages incorporate generalization into the language via class inheritance. Typically, a child class can inherit the attributes, services, behaviors, and relationships of the parent class(es).[11] By using this mechanism, the object-oriented paradigm gives analysts/developers a very powerful mechanism that not only helps organizes complex objects but also facilitates code sharing and code reuse in implementation. The properties of class inheritance are as follows[12]:

---

[9] Map objects are explained in Chapter 15.

[10] This approach can also be used for many-to-one associations because they can often evolve into many-to-many.

[11] The parent classes are called superclasses; we have also used ancestor class in this book.

[12] This is not as simple as a topic as we may lead you to believe. The assumption made on these properties are quite varied among the object-oriented languages. We have given you the properties that are consistent with C++ that implement generalization/specialization as defined in analysis.

1. Structural

   a. Attributes. Objects (instances) of the descendent class, which is a subclass of the parent class, has values for all the attributes of the ancestor class.
   b. Non-generalization relationships. Objects (instances) of the descendent class, which is a subclass of the parent class, have all the non-generalization relationships of the ancestor class.

2. Interface

   All the services that are provided by the ancestor class must also be provided by the descendent class. For an object that is instance of the descendent class is simultaneously an instance of its ancestor class.

3. Behavioral

   a. Inheritance without polymorphism (good child). In inheritance without polymorphism, *all* the methods that are supplied by the ancestor class for its services are also used by the descendent class to provide the corresponding services. This is code reuse and code sharing.
   b. Inheritance with polymorphism (bad child). In inheritance with polymorphism, some of the methods that are supplied by the ancestor class for its services are also used by the descendent class to provide the corresponding services. For the remaining services of the ancestor class, the descendent class supplies its own customized methods that replace the appropriate corresponding methods for use by instances of the descendent class.[13]

4. Mathematical

   a. Antisymmetry. If class A is a subclass of class B, then class B may not be a subclass of class A. In other words, if object A is a descendent of object B, then object B cannot also be a descendent of object A.
   b. Transitivity.[14] If class A is a subclass of class B and class B is a *subclass* of class C, then class A is a subclass of class B. An instance of class A is also an instance of class C and class B.

Delegation

The object-oriented model that we have built is based on the notion of class and not on the notion of an object. However, there are object-oriented computational models

---

[13] The ancestor class decides which services may be redefined using the keyword virtual. This must be planned for when defining the ancestor class.

[14] Transitivity makes it possible to organize the objects (classes) in an hierarchial manner. Because of this property, generalization is diagrammatically shown as an ancestral tree.

that are based on the object. These systems are usually called prototype systems. In a prototype system, there is no such mechanism as a class. Only objects exist, and a object may have a delegation relationship with any other object. When a service is requested from an object, it does the following:

1. If it has a method for the service, it will execute its own method,
2. If it has no method, it will delegate the execution of that service to an object that has a delegation relationship with it.
3. The delegation relationship is transitive. So if the delegated object does not have a method for the service, it will attempt to delegate the execution of the service to other objects with which it has a delegation relationship.

The reader should note that relationship is between objects, and that the delegation relationship is more generic than the is_a relationship as it can be used between any two objects.[15] Moreover, delegation can be established dynamically (at runtime), while class inheritance is fixed at creation time.

For a prototype system, analysis is done by thinking about a particular object and then drawing similarities and/or differences for other objects based on the particular object(s). Any object may be a prototype object during the analysis. The idea is to start with individual objects and then to specialize and generalize them as more complex cases are considered.[16] Lieberman has described this approach as compared to the object-oriented approach:

> Prototype systems allow creating concepts first, then generalizing them by saying what aspects of the concept are allowed to vary. Set-oriented (object-oriented) systems require creating the abstraction description of the set (class) before individual instances can be installed as members.

In a sense, this method of analysis is much closer to the way humans learn. We learn by either generalizing or specializing on instances. From this, one may be led to conclude that delegation is a better mechanism for implementing generalization/specialization. However, we will see in the next section that it is not quite that simple.

Orlando Treaty

Historically, there has been much debate over which mechanism (inheritance or delegation) is a more powerful concept for implementing generalization/specialization. Since 1987, we have seen that delegation can model inheritance, and, conversely, inheritance can model delegation. During OOPSLA 1987, which took place in

---

[15] Furthermore, in some languages not only the execution of services may be delegated but also the attributes can be inherited or shared.

[16] Our method is a modified prototype approach to building an object-oriented system.

Orlando, Florida, Lynn Stein, Henry Lieberman, and David Unger discussed their differences about delegation and inheritance and came up with a statement that reflected a need for both mechanisms. That resolution became known as the Orlando Treaty. In essence, the treaty recognizes two modes of code sharing: anticipatory sharing and unanticipatory sharing. Class inheritance-based systems are best for anticipatory code sharing and delegation-based systems are more suited for unanticipated code sharing.

The treaty characterized three dimensions for code sharing:

1. **Static versus dynamic**. Is the sharing determined when the object is created or can it be determined dynamically (at runtime)?
2. **Implicit versus explicit**. Are there explicit operations to indicate the code sharing?
3. **Per object versus per group**. Is sharing defined for whole groups of objects or could it be supported by individual objects?

Traditional object-oriented languages (i.e., C++, Smalltalk, and Simula) use static, implicit, per-group strategies in the design of their languages. By contrast, delegation-based languages use dynamic, explicit, and per-object strategies in the design of their languages.

There is a trade-off here between the two strategies. Delegation requires less space, but execution time is slower because of runtime binding. In contrast, class inheritance has faster execution but requires more space. If the class system is strongly typed,[17] there is an additional trade-off between safety versus flexibility. From the above discussion, one can conclude that delegation is great for building prototype systems; however, high performance and production quality systems would be better if they used a strong-typed class-based language, like C++.

Multiple Inheritance

We have intentionally given examples that use only single inheritance (each subclass has one and only one immediate superclass). However, there are real situations that are very effectively modeled by letting a subclass inherit from more than one immediate superclass. For instance, in our Person example, we assumed that all students are not employees. However, a better model may be that a person is both a student and an employee. With single inheritance, we would not be able to directly represent this multiple parent relationship. Other examples are German car manufacturer, BorderedTextWindow, and transformer toy. A German car manufacturer has

---

[17] C++ is a strongly typed language. One of the main features requested from development was this feature so that more testable and more reliable software can be delivered.

properties that are due to it being a German company and properties that are due to it being a car manufacturer. BorderedTextWindow has properties of a bordered window and properties of a text window. Finally, a transformer toy can act as a robot, car, plane, and boat. The mechanism that allow us to model these situations is called *multiple inheritance*.[18]

With multiple inheritance, we can combine several existing (parent) classes to form a new subclass of all the parent classes. It can access all the methods and contain all the attributes and relationships of all the parent classes. For example, let us use the inheritance tree from our original example that includes the Platypus. In this inheritance tree, the class **Platypus** inherits from both **Mammal** and **Endangered**. This is an example of multiple inheritance and is shown in Figure 11-4.

A more comprehensive example may be as follows. Let Carol, Frank, Mary, Susan, and Karen be employees of a company. Carol is in administration and her manager is Frank. Susan is in engineering and her manager is Mary. Karen works part-time and is also a student. Adam is also a student, but he does not work for the company. The inheritance tree for this example is shown in Figure 11-5.

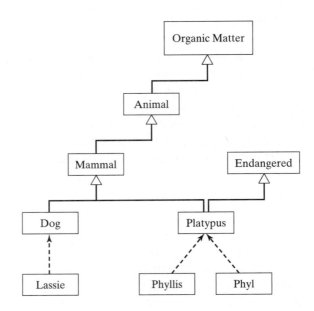

Figure 11-4   Multiple Inheritance for Platypus

---

[18] It should be noted that Java does not support multiple inheritance in classes. In the examples given here, those classes are better implemented as interfaces. The Java interface mechanism does support multiple inheritance.

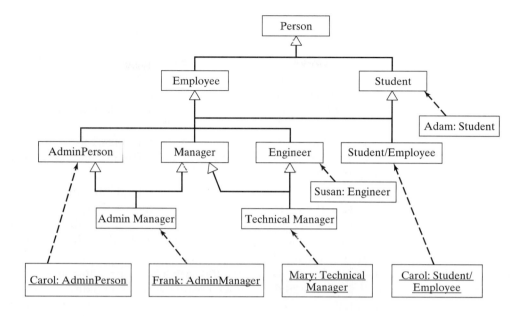

Figure 11-5   Multiple Inheritance for Student Employee Karen

Documenting Detailed Design

A detailed design is documented using many of the same diagrams that appear in the documentation of an analysis model. In particular, the detailed design employs a generalization/specialization class diagram, state diagrams, and collaboration diagrams. Diagrams that illustrate associations and aggregations do not appear in a design as those elements of the analysis model have been incorporated as new classes and/or as attributes of previously identified classes. In addition, a detailed design incorporates component diagrams. These component diagrams explicitly identify the classes realized by the components.

SUMMARY

In this chapter, we briefly discussed design. Despite the brevity on this topic, we have a few recommendations:

1. In system design, we believe that a subsystem must be a collection of objects (classes) in a single semantic domain.
2. In system design, we believe in using the client-server paradigm for establishing communication relationships between subsystems. We believe this produces more robust and more maintainable software.

3. For software control, we believe that both procedural-driven and event-driven are applicable, depending on the application/system to be built. In fact, we have used both simultaneously in one system.

4. We recommend using UML's deployment diagram to capture the physical topology on which the software application/system resides.

5. We recommend using the Utilities class of UML to capture underlying support functions of the operating system and non-object-oriented libraries.[19]

6. In detailed design of classes, it is best to take classes as found in analysis and keep them in the design. Then we should add implementation classes.[20]

7. In detailed design of association, we recommend implementing all associations with their attribute(s) as classes unless there are performance issues. A class implementation of association with attribute(s) accurately models the application/system. This helps make the software more maintainable and flexible for future features.

8. In detailed design, use delegation instead of inheritance if you expect to have the subclass and the superclass implemented on different processors.

9. In detailed design, multiple inheritance should be used only if all the parent classes resides on the same processor. If the parent class(es) reside on different processors, use delegation to implement multiple inheritance.

10. Consult with an object-oriented expert to find opportunities to use (1) templates, (2) patterns, (3) stereotypes, and (4) composite capabilities of UML. Also have the expert review all of your diagrams. Ensure that the expert reviews closely (1) multiple inheritance, (2) aggregation, (3) nonbinary associations, (4) category classes, (5) mapping of rules to constraints, and (6) exception handling. Adjust your diagrams to reflect the opportunities recommended by the expert.

11. We recommend using the component diagram of UML to capture your detailed physical design of components.

---

[19] A utilities class in UML is a class that is used to capture global variables and procedures. This is a modeling artifact rather than an implementation artifact. The global variables and procedures are not made accessible via an instance of this class.

[20] Adding implementation classes follows the same method as we described in the book, except now the domain is the appropriate technology.

12

Java Fundamentals

The previous chapters have focused on the development of a specification model, an analysis model, and a design model. In this and subsequent chapters, the emphasis is on translating the design model into on implemention. This chapter focuses on programming concepts.

INTRODUCTION TO THE JAVA LANGUAGE

In this section, we preview:

- Statement, the smallest executable unit within a Java program
- Unicode characters

Both of these constructs are important in understanding the construction of the language.

Example Statements

A statement is the smallest executable unit within a Java program. There are a large variety of statement types, but they are all *terminated by a semicolon*. The simplest statement is the empty or *null statement,* and it takes the following form:

```
;
```

A null statement is useful when the syntax of the language requires a statement, but the logic of the application does not. This statement behaves like a no-op (no operation).

One of the most commonly seen statements is the *assignment statement.* For example:

```
x = y + 1;
```

In this statement, x and y are variables; variables are storage locations that hold values. For example, we can store the value 7 in y, then y+1 is equal to 8. Thus, the assignment statement assigns the value 8 to x. More precisely, the right-hand side (y + 1) of this statement is evaluated and converted to a value compatible with the left-hand side variable (x).

Another commonly seen statement is the *if statement.* For example,

```
if (y < x) min = y;
```

If the value of y is less than the value of x, then the min is assigned the value of y.

We have given you of three statement types by examples. This is useful, but a more formal definition of statement is actually needed to write effective programs; we will give you a more formal definition later in this chapter. But first, we need to define the components that are allowed to be used to build a statement.

Unicode Character

While most programming languages use the standard ASCII character set, which can be stored in eight bits in a computer, Java uses the *Unicode character set,* which must be stored in 16 bits in a computer. The additional eight bits give Unicode an additional several million of characters for representing most international alphabets. This makes Java programs relatively easier to internationalize for non-English language users. The actual Unicode specification is a two volume set that lists thousands of characters, including both Japanese and Chinese characters. If this two volume specification set seems intimidating and confusing, do not fear. Unicode and ASCII are compatible. The first 256 characters (0x0000 to 0x00FF) are identical to the ISO8859-1 (Latin-1) characters which are the ASCII characters. If you are only using Latin-1 characters, you normally do not need to distinguish a Java Unicode character from the ASCII 8 bits character.

Though Unicode has defined approximately 34,000 characters, there are very few devices and platforms built to input or display these characters. Thus, Java programs that want to use the non-Latin-1 characters are written using a special Unicode escape sequences. To represent a Unicode character, the Unicode escape sequence \uxxxx may be used anywhere in a Java program. The xxxx is a sequence of one to four hexadecimal digits that is the Unicode encoded representation of the character.[1] Java also supports the use of escape sequences to represent certain special character values. The sequences are given in the Table 12-1.

Table 12-1 Escape Sequence Characters

Escape Sequence	Character Value
\uXXXX	XXXX is a sequence of one to four hexadecimal digits, which is the Unicode encoded representation of the character
\b	Backspace
\t	Horizontal tab
\n	Newline
\f	Form feed
\r	Carriage return
\"	Double quote
\'	Single quote
\\	Black slash
\XXX	XXX is the octal value of the encoded representation of the character; e.g. "\7" for the bell

These escape sequences *may only be used in char and String literals*.[2] They are usually used represent non-printable characters and to prevent the usual interpretation of these characters by the compiler; while the \u escape sequence is simply an alternative way to represent a character. Thus, Unicode \u escape sequences are processed before the other escape sequences. **CAUTION:** Java language is *case-sensitive*; i.e., uppercase letters are distinguished from lowercase letters.

PROGRAMMING ELEMENTS

A program is composed of elements called *tokens*, which are a collection of characters (alphabetic, numeric, and special) that constitute the basic vocabulary

---

[1] The encoded representation for each character is documented in the Unicode specification.

[2] char, String, and literal are defined in later sections in this chapter.

recognized by the compiler. The compiler translates these tokens into instructions that the computer understands. Tokens are separated by white space and/or comment text inserted for readability and documentation. There are five kinds of tokens in the language:

- Keywords
- Identifiers
- Literals
- Operators
- Punctuators

These are discussed in the sections that follow. The compiler translates these tokens into instructions that the computer understands. Tokens are separated by white space and/or comment text that are inserted for readability and documentation. We will take a short diversion and discuss comments before we discuss the different types of tokens.

Comments

In Java, three types of comments are supported:

1. A comment that begins with /* and continues until the next */. For example,

    ```
    /* line one of comment
       line two of comment
       ...
       last line of comment */
    ```

2. A comment that begins with // and continues until the end of line. For example,

    ```
    sum = x + y;      //add bonus to base pay
    ```

3. A comment that begins with /** and continues until the next */. For example,

    ```
    /** Author: Richard Lee
        Author: William Tepfenhart
        Program Name: Demo
        Version: 1.5
    */
    ```

The third type of comment is a special "doc comment." These comments are processed by the javadoc program to produce a simple on-line documentation for the Java source code.

CAUTION: The first style of comments *do NOT nest*. For example,

```
/* This outer comment will NOT encompass the inner comment below
...
/* Inner comment also using first style */
..
*/ // Intended end of outer comment, actual end is above
```

However, because the second comment type extends only until the end of the line, the first comment type may contain the comments of the second type. For example:

```
/*    begin of first comment form
      x = x+y;         // this is the second comment form
      end of first comment form  */
```

Reserved Words (Keywords)

Keywords are explicitly reserved words that have a predefined meaning in Java. They include words for data type declaration, statement formulation, and access control. The underlined keywords are reserved but not used. Table 12-2 lists the keywords.[3]

Table 12-2 Reserved Words (Keywords)

abstract	boolean	break	byte
case	catch	char	class
const	continue	do	double
else	extends	final	finally
float	for	*goto*	if
implements	import	instanceof	int
interface	long	native	new
null	package	private	protected
public	return	short	static
super	switch	synchronized	this
throw	throws	transient	try
void	volatile	while	*cast*
const	*future*	*generic*	*operator*
outer	*rest*	*var*	

---

[3] For details on each reserved word, consult www.javasoft.com.

Identifiers

An identifier is a sequence of alphanumeric characters along with the underscore character. The identifier must not start with a digit. Although legal, it is not advisable to use an underscore as the first character because compilers and hidden library code use the underscore as the first character. Uppercase letters and lowercase letters are treated as distinct characters. In theory, an identifier can be arbitrarily long, but due to limitations in some compilers, 31 characters is a good limit. Mixed uppercase and lowercase are used for functions and variable names.

Literals

Literals are constant values (e.g., 1 and 3.14159). Java provides some basic data types to capture integers, decimal numbers, characters, etc. These basic types are called *primitive* data types. The primitive data types[4] are *byte, short, int, long, char, float, double,* and *boolean*; they all may have literals. See the section primitive data types for full explanation of literals. Table 12-3 gives you all the literals.

Table 12-3 Literals

Literals	Examples	Comments
number	115, 25, 562345	Data type is int
number[l | L]	15L, 25l, 562345L	Data type is long
0xhex; 0Xhex	0x1A, 0XAF, 0x12	Hex integer[a]
0octal	0177, 0156476	Octal integer[b]
decimalNumber or decimalNumber[d | D]	23.34, 254.5677 23.34D, 254.5677d	Data type is double
decimalNumber[f | F]	23.45F, 254.5677f	Data type is float
[+ | −] number or [+ | −] decimalNumber	−115, +25l, −562345l −23.24f, +254.5677D, −10.	Signed number or Signed decimal number
decimalNumber [e | E] number	23.34E5, −2.5456e30	Exponent
'character'	'e', 'x', 'z'	Single character
"characters"	"example", "test"	Data type is String class
""	""	Empty string
\b		Backspace character
\t		Tab character
\n		Line feed character
\f		Form feed character
\r		Carriage return character

---

[4] Technically, String is not a primitive data type, but it is supported as an integral part of the language.

Table 12-3 Literals (*continued*)

Literals	Examples	Comments
\"		Double quote character
\'		Single quote character
\\		Backspace character
\uNNNN	\uAF12, \u12FF	Unicode escape
boolean values: true and false	true, false	Data type is boolean

[a] Reminder that hexadecimal is base-16 arithmetic; thus, the "digits" are 0–9 and A–F.
[b] Reminder that octal is base-8 arithmetic; thus, the "digits" are 0–7.

Operators

Operators are characters and/or character sequences with a special meaning. Most of the operators are used to perform arithmetic or logical operations on the primitive data types. An operator performs a function on either one, two, or three operands.

An operator that requires one operand is called a unary operator. The unary operators support either prefix or postfix notation. Prefix notation means that the operator appears before its operand:

```
operator operand
```

Postfix notation means that the operator appears after its operand:

```
operand operator
```

For example, ++ is a unary operator that increments the value of its operand by 1.

```
count++;
++count;
```

An operator that requires two operands is a binary operator. All of the binary operators use infix notation, which means that the operator appears between its operands:

```
operand1 operator operand2
```

For example, = is a binary operator that assigns the value from its right-hand operand to its left-hand operand.

```
cat = dog;
```

And finally a ternary operator is one that requires three operands. The Java programming language has one ternary operator, ?:, which is a short-hand if-else statement. The ternary operator is also infix; each component of the operator appears between operands:

```
operand1 ? operand2 : operand3
```

In addition to performing the operation, an operator also returns a value. The return value and its type depends on the operator and the type of its operands. For example, the arithmetic operators, which perform basic arithmetic operations such as addition and subtraction, return number—the result of the arithmetic operation. The data type returned by the arithmetic operators depends on the type of its operands: If you add two integers, you get an integer back. An operation is said to evaluate to its result.

We use the basic assignment operator, =, to assign one value to another. Java also provides several short cut assignment operators that allow us to perform an arithmetic, logical, or bitwise operation and an assignment operation all with one operator. We use this when we need to perform an operation on a variable and assign the result back into the variable.

Arithmetic Operators

The Java language supports various arithmetic operators for all floating-point and integer numbers. These include + (addition), − (subtraction), * (multiplication), / (division), and % (modulo). Table 12-4 lists the arithmetic and assignment operators. All operands in an arithmetic operation must be arithmetic; that is, they must be in the data type family of either integer or floating point. See section on primitive data types.[5]

Table 12-4 Arithmetic Operators

Operator	Function	Code Example
=	Assignment	var = 100; // var is assigned 100
%	Modulus (remainder)	var1 = 21 % 4; // var1 is assigned 1

+	Unary plus or addition	+10; // unary plus
		var 2 = var + 25; // var2 is assigned 126

++	Pre-increment (increment by 1 before using) or Post-increment (increment by 1 after using)	i = 5; j = 1;
		k = ++i + j; // i is now 6, k is assigned 7
		
		i = 5; j = 1;
		k = i++ + j; // i is now 6, k is assigned 6

---

[5] This is also called a *native* data type in some books.

Table 12-4 Arithmetic Operators (*continued*)

Operator	Function	Code Example

−	Unary minus or subtraction	−100; // unary minus
		var3 = −var1; // var3 is assigned − 1
		var3 = var1 − var; //var3 is now −127

− −	Pre-decrement (decrement by 1 before using) or Post-decrement (decrement by 1 after using)	i = 5; j = 1;
		k = − −i + j; // i is now 4, k is assigned 5
		
		i = 5; j = 1;
		k = i− − + j; // i is now 4, k is assigned 6

*	Multiplication	x = 10 * 25; // y is assigned 250
		y = var1 * var2; // y is assigned 126

/	Division	x = 20 / 5; // x is assigned 4
		zz = var2 / 2; // zz is assigned 63

+=, −=, %=, *=, /=	Operation plus assignment	x += y; // shorthand for x = x + y
		x −= y; // shorthand for x = x − y
		x %= y; // shorthand for x = x % y
		x *= y; // shorthand for x = x * y
		x /= y; // shorthand for x = x / y

Boolean Operators

The result of any boolean operation is a boolean value (i.e., true or false). The operands of the boolean operators are also always boolean. The boolean operators are given in Table 12-5.

Table 12-5 Boolean Operators

Operator	Function	Code Example

=	Assignment	b1 = true; // b1 is true
		b1 = b2; // b1 and b2 are true

!	Logical complement	b3 = !b1; // b3 is false
&	Boolean AND	b4 = b2 & b3; // b4 is false
|	Boolean Inclusive OR	b5 = b1 | b2; // b5 is true
^	Boolean Exclusive OR	b6 = b1 ^ b2; // b6 is false;
&=, |=, ^=	Operation plus assignment	b1 &= b2; // shorthand for b1 = b1 & b2

Note that to understand the code example, we need to assume that the code sample is one continuous block of statements.

Conditional and Relational Operators

Both conditional and relational operators are used in the test expression that is part of a control statement. Though the operands are not always boolean, the result of these operations *always results in boolean value.* The conditional and relational operators are given in Table 12-6.

Table 12-6 Conditional and Relational Operators

Operator	Function	Operands Type	Code Example

<	Less than	Integer or floating point	if (x 1 < 25) y1y2++;
			//If value of x1 is less than 25,
			// y1y2 is increased by 1;
			// else y1y2's value is unchanged.

<=	Less than or equal	Integer or floating point	if (24.5 < x2) x2 =5;
			// If value of x2 is less than or equal
			// to 25, x2 = 5;
			// else x2's value is unchanged.

>	Greater than	Integer or floating point	if (x3 > 32) x3 +=5;
			// If value of x3 is greater than 32,
			// x3's value is increased by 5;
			// else x3's value is unchanged.

>=	Greater than or equal	Integer or floating point	if (x3 >= 24) x2 = 5;
			// If value of x3 is greater than or equal
			// to 24, x2 = 5;
			// else x2's value is unchanged.

==	Equal	Primitive	if (xx == 15.5) b1 = true;
			// If xx's value is equal to 15.5,
			// b1 is assigned the value true;
			// else b1 is unchanged.

!=	Inequality (not equal)	Primitive	if (ch != 'c') b2 = false;
			// If the value of ch is not equal to c,
			// b2 is assigned the value false;
			// else b2 is unchanged.

==	Test if the same object is referenced	Object	// String is an object.
			String x = new String("same");
			String y = x;
			if (x == y) b1 = true; // x == y is true

!=	Test if different objects are referenced	Object	String x1 = new String("same"); String y1 = x1; if (x1 != y) b1 = true; // x1 != y is true

&&	Conditional AND	Boolean	if (x1 != y AND ch != 'c') b1 = false;
			// If x1 is not equal to y and
			// ch's value is not equal to c,
			// then b1 is assigned false;
			// else b1 is unchanged

Table 12-6 Conditional and Relational Operators (*continued*)

Operator	Function	Operands Type	Code Example

||	Conditional OR	Boolean	if (x1 != y OR ch != 'c') b1 = false;
			// If either x1 is not equal to y
			// or ch's value is not equal to c,
			// then b1 is assigned false;
			// else b1 is unchanged

?:	Conditional operator (shorthand for the if-then-else statement)	See if statement	x = (x1 > x2) ? x1: x2;
			// If x1 > x2, x is assigned the value of x1;
			// else x is assigned the value of x2

Note that the first eight operators are used to create boolean results by operating on non-boolean operands to provide a boolean result, while the \|\| and the && operators are used to operate on boolean operands. Thus, these two operators are normally used to combine the results of the other eight operators.

Bitwise Operators

Bitwise operations allow the programmer to manipulate individual bits on data types that are in the family of integers. This is useful for handling hardware interfaces for consumer electronic products. We do not encourage using these operators for Internet applications. The bitwise operators are given in Table 12-7.

Table 12-7 Bitwise Operators

Operator	Function	Comments
~	Bitwise complement	Unary operator; output bit is one if input bit is zero; else output bit is zero.
&	Bitwise AND	Binary operator; output bit is one if both input bits are one; else output bit is zero.
|	Bitwise Inclusive OR	Binary operator; output bit is a zero if both input bits are zero; else output bit is one.
^	Bitwise Exclusive OR	Binary operator; output bit is zero if both inputs are zero or both inputs are one; else output bit is one.
<<	Left shift	Binary operator; the first operand's bits are shifted left by the number of bits specified in the second operand. Zeros are inserted in the lower-order bits.
>>	Right shift with sign extension	Binary operator; the first operand's bits are shifted right by the number of bits specified in the second operand. If the original value is positive, zeros are inserted in the higher-order bits. Else the original value is negative, then ones are inserted in the higher-order bits.

Table 12-7 Bitwise Operators (*continued*)

Operator	Function	Comments
>>>	Right shift with zero extension	Binary operator; the first operand's bits are shifted right by the number of bits specified in the second operand. Zeros are inserted in the higher-order bits.
&=, |=, ^=, <<=, >>=, >>>=	Operation plus assignment	Behavior is same as above.

Class-Defined Operators

Finally, we have some class-defined operators. These are given in Table 12-8.

Table 12-8 Class Operators

Operator	Function	Operand Types	Comment
=	Assign the value of variable on right to the variable on left	Same types	This only allows two variables to reference the same object. A copy of the object is not created.
(type)	Cast	Any	This will cast an operand from its present type to the type specified.
new	Create an object of the class type	Class type, identifier	This is only used for class-defined types.
instanceof	Check if the object is an instance of the class	Object, class type	This check to see if the object is an instance of the class.
+	Concatenate two strings	String	This will form a new string by concatenation the two input strings.
object.service(args)	Invokes a method of the object	Arguments (args) may be primitive or class-defined type	These are usually programmer defined routines. This is covered in a later section.
class.service(args)	Invokes a static method of the class	Arguments (args) may be primitive or class-defined type	These are usually programmer defined routines. This is covered in a later section.

Punctuators

Punctuators include parentheses, braces, commas, dot, and colons. They are used to give structure to other tokens of the language.[6]

---

[6] Please consult an on-line Java tutorial for details.

PRIMITIVE DATA TYPES

Java provides a predefined set of primitive data types and the operators to manipulate these data types are provided. The following data type constructs are predefined:

- Primitive data types
- Constant values
- Symbolic variables
- Reference variables
- Constant variables
- Class "data type"
- Array "data type"
- String "data type"
- Exceptions

Each of these are described in the paragraphs that follow.

Primitive Data Types

In Java, there are two category of data types: primitive (basic) and class-defined.[7] Primitive data types are defined as part of the language, while the class-defined data types are defined by using the keyword class. A typical Java program uses many class-defined data types[8] that are provided in Java libraries. However, these class-defined data types are not an integral part of the language. In contrast, the primitive data types for integers, floating point number, characters, and boolean data are provided within the language.

The following primitive data types[9] are predefined:

1. For integers: *short* (number) (e.g., 15, 27, 32010)
2. For integers: *int* (number) (e.g., 1, 111, 1050, 105467)
3. For integers: *long* (number [1 | L]) (e.g., 1235, 125784321, 23L, 400l)[10]
4. For decimals: *float* (number [f | F]) (e.g., 1.1f, 123.34565443F)
5. For decimals: *double* ([number].number or number [d | D]) (e.g., 5.2345, 2.35467d, 567.86456D)

---

[7] These are data types defined by the programmer. These are the class constructs that we will define in Chapter 17.

[8] These are the class constructs defined by others that we will be using.

[9] The name is followed with the keywords in square brackets. The keywords are used in the language to identify them.

[10] A long constant may be distinguished from other integral constants by appending the letter l or L to it. Although a lower case 'l' is allowed, it is better programming style to use an upper case 'L' because the lower case can easily be mistaken for the digit one.

6. For character: *char* ('character') (e.g., 'a', 'd', '2')
7. For boolean values: *boolean* (true or false) (e.g., true, false)
8. For bits: *byte* (0xHexidecimal, 0XHexidecimal, 0Octal) (e.g., 0xA2. 0X12, 045)

For characters, the **String** class, which is a built-in class, is used. Because they are so commonly used, string literals ("characters") are tokens in Java language. Some examples of string literals are "the big black cat," "license plate x123," and "the sky is blue."

The *integral* types are byte, char, short, int, and long. All integral types, with the exception of char, may be signed. The single and double quotes are necessary in the character and string examples respectively.

Primitive data types are summarized in Table 12-9.

Table 12-9 Primitive Data Types

Type	Size	Instances	Default	Min Value	Max Value
Boolean	1 bit	True, false	False	N.A.	N.A.
Char	16 bits	Unicode character	False	\u0000	\uFFFF
Byte	8 bits	Signed or unsigned integer	\u0000	0x00 (−127)	0xFF (128)
Short	16 bits	Signed or unsigned integer	0	−32768	32767
Int	32 bits	Signed or unsigned integer	0	−2147483648	2147483647
Long	64 bits	Signed or unsigned integer	0	−9223372036854775808	9223372036854775807
Float	32 bits	IEEE 754 floating point	0.0	$\pm$3.40282347E+38	$\pm$1.40239846E−45
Double	64 bits	IEEE 754 floating point	0.0	$\pm$1.79769313486231570E+308	$\pm$4.9406564841246544E−324

N.A. = not applicable.

Constant Values

Every literal constant has an associated primitive data type and is non-addressable. The different kinds are

1. Literal integer constant (decimal, octal, hex) for integral data types (e.g., 1, 024, 0x1A, 0X1B2, 0)
2. Signed for integral data types except char (e.g., −8, +500, −27l, +2346l)

3. Long for long data type (e.g., 1L, –8l, –27l, +500L, +2346l)
4. Literal floating point constant (scientific, decimal) for float and double data types (e.g., 1.23e-3, 2.14E3, 3.14159)
5. Single precision (F/f) for the float data type (e.g., 1.23e-3F, 3.14159f)
6. Double precision (D/d) for the double data type (e.g., 1.23e-3D, 3.14159d)
7. Literal character constant for the char data type (e.g., 'a', 'd', '2', ' ')
8. Non-printable characters plus' and " (use a backslash) for the char data type (e.g., \n, \', \", \?, \\, \7 (bell))
9. Literal string constant for the string class (e.g., "", "a", "\a string?{}[]")

Symbolic Variables

In Java, a symbolic variable is identified by a user-supplied name. Each variable comprises a specific data type and is addressable. Two values are associated with a symbolic variable:

- rvalue: its data value
- lvalue: its location value (memory location)

To give a variable a type and a name, you write a variable declaration, which generally looks like this

```
type name
```

For example we declare a variable of int type and initialize it to 50 as follows:

```
int num;
num = 50;
```

The first line is a definition as storage is allocated. The second line assigns the rvalue of the constant "50" to the rvalue of the symbolic variable num. The lvalue of "50" is determined by the compiler and is not directly accessible to the programmer.

The following example also includes initializing the rvalue of the symbolic variables:

```
int y = 40;
char c ('d');
```

In the first line, the symbolic variable y is defined and its rvalue is initialized to 40. In the second line, the symbolic variable c is defined and is initialized to the character d.

Reference Variables

In Java, a reference variable holds an address as its value in memory. This provides for indirect reference, and because Java is a strong-typed language, each reference variable has an associated data type. Examples are:

```
Point ptr1;
String s;
Complex beginPoint, endPoint;
```

Constants

Constants[11] are useful for defining shared values that are not allowed to be changed. In Java, you may only create constants for instance and class variables. To declare a constant, use the *final* keyword before the variable declaration and include an initial value for that variable.

```
final int BUFSIZE = 1024;
static final float PI = 3.141592;
final boolean FLAG = false;
```

The static final variable declared within a class is equivalent to the C's #define constant. The complier computes the value at compiler time and uses it to pre-compute other compile-time constants that refer to this value.

Constants are useful for naming of various values that a variable may have and then to use it to test if the variable has that value.

Class "Data Type"

In addition to the primitive data types, the Java language has a construct that allows programmers to add their own data types. It is this construct that is used by the Java libraries and by application programmers to create the objects that are the building block of every object-oriented program. The mechanism for creating new programmer-defined data types is the *class* construct. The construct is an aggregation of named data elements, which may be of different types, and a set of methods that is designed to manipulate those data elements. From a programming perspective, a class is a way to introduce new data types into the program. Ideally, a well-defined class is as easy to use as the primitive data types.

From a language perspective, a class is a programmer's defined data type. A class definition is composed of two parts: class header and class body.

- The class header is composed of the keyword class followed by the class name.

---

[11] Neither the C or C++ constructs for *#define* nor *const* are available in Java. But *const* is reserved to help catch errors.

- The class body follows the class header and is embedded within curly braces {and}.
  The class body contains declarations for all instance variables and class variables (known collectively as member variables) for the class. In addition, the class body contains declarations and implementations for all instance services and class services (known collectively as member methods) for the class.

A form of class definition is as follows:

```
class myClassName     // Simple Class Header
{
    data elements (variables with their data types)
    and methods (services with their body)
}
```

For example, we declare the Point class as follows:

```
class Point {
// data elements (instance variables}
 int xord;
 int yord;
// methods (instance services)
 int getXCoordinate() {return this.xcord;}
 int getYCoordinate() {return this.ycord;}
 setCoordinate(int newX, int newY) {xord = newX; yord = newY;}
}
```

Once a class has been defined, we can use the class name every place where a data type can be used in the language. We will discuss class in depth in Chapter 14.

WHAT IS A STATEMENT?

A statement is the smallest executable unit within a Java program. It is terminated by a semicolon.

There are all kinds of statements in a Java program. We have categorized them as (1) simple, (2) compound, (3) execution control, and (4) branching. A simple statement is the smallest executable unit within a Java program. The compound statement is simply a collection of statements that are enclosed by the braces "{' and '}." An execution control statement is used for non-sequential execution. Finally, a branching statement is used to complement the execution control statements; it breaks the sequential execution of statements and causes the execution to go to the beginning of the iteration block and start a new iteration. In this section we will discuss the three simple statements: null statement, assignment statement, and service request statement. In addition, we will discuss the compound statement. The execution control statements and the branching statements will be covered in later sections. First, however, we will cover what an expression is.

Expressions

An expression is composed of one or more operations. Operations are captured in Java by operators. For example, the addition operation[12] is captured by the operator +. The arguments of the operation are referred to as operands. For example, the addition operation requires two operands.

Nearly all operations are unary (requiring only one operand) or binary (requiring two operands). Binary operators have a left and a right operand. Care must be taken as some operators represent both unary and binary operations. For example, the operator − is used to capture the negation of a number when it is used as a unary operator. However, as a binary operator it is used to capture the subtraction operation.

An expression evaluation performs all the operations captured in the expression and yields a result. Usually, the result is an rvalue of a data type that is determined by the data types of the operand(s). The order of the operator evaluation is determined by the precedence and associativity of the operators. Though ordering is very natural, the precedence is given in Table 12-10.

Table 12-10 Operator Precedence

Operators	Notes
. [] ()	The "." is used to access services (functions) and attributes (data variables) of an object.[a] The "()" group expressions and the "[]" is used for arrays.
++ −− ! ~ instanceof	The "++" is auto increment, while the "−−" is auto decrement. The "instance of" returns a boolean value based on whether the object is the named class that is argument to the service.
new (type) expression	The "new" operator is for the creating an instance of a class. The second operator is actually parenthesis "( )," which is being used to cast a value from one data type (including programmer defined data types) to another data type.
* / %	The "*" is multiply, while the "/" is divide. The "%" is modulus.
+ −	The "+" is add, while the "−" is subtract.
<< >> >>>	These are the bitwise shift operators.
< <= > >=	These are the relational comparison operators.
== !=	The relational quality or inequality operators.

---

[12] Note that "+" is an overloaded operator. For the String class, the "+" operator is used to concatenate two strings.

Table 12-10 Operator Precedence (*continued*)

Operators	Notes
&	The relational bitwise "and" operator.
^	The relational bitwise "exclusive or" operator.
|	The relational bitwise "or" operator.
&&	The relational "logical and" operator.
||	The relational "logical or" operator.
test ? trueOps : falseOps	Shorthand for if . . . then . . . else
= += -= *= /= %= ^= &= |= <<= >>= >>>=	The assignment operators.

[a] Note that when you access static members or constructors, you are really access members of an object where the "class" as the object.

Null Statement

The simplest statement is the empty or *null statement,* and it takes the following form:

```
;
```

A null statement is useful when the syntax of the language requires a state-ment, but the logic of the application does not. This statement behaves like a no-op (no operation).

Assignment Statement

One of the most commonly seen statement type is the *assignment statement.* It has the following form:

```
<variable> = <expression>;
```

The right-hand side of this statement is evaluated and converted to a value compatible with the left-hand side variable. A specific example is

```
x = y + 1;
```

In this statement, x and y are variables; $y + 1$ is the expression. Thus, the assign-ment statement assign the value of the expression $y + 1$ to x. More precisely, the right-hand side $(y + 1)$ of this statement is evaluated and converted to a value com-patible with the left-hand side variable (x).

Java also provides assignment operators that combine an assignment and some other operator. It has the following form:

```
<variable> <binary operator>= <expression>;
```

For example,

```
x += y; // this is same as x = x + y;
x *= y; // this is same as x = x * y;
```

Java provides for an unary operation statement. It has the following form:

```
<unary operator> <variable>;
```

For example,

```
++k; // this is same as k = k + 1;
```

This form is also an expression and may be used in an assignment statement. For example,

```
l = --k; // this is same as k = k - 1; l = k;
m = k++; // this is same as m = k; k = k + 1;
```

Service Request Statement

There is one more kind of statement that is used to execute services of class-defined data type. It has the following form:

```
<object identifier>.<service identifier>(<parameters>);
```

The object identifier is usually a reference to an instance of a class. The service identifier is the name of the service (method) and the parameters are the arguments that is being passed in the service call. A service request may also return a value and throw exceptions. This topic will be discussed extensively in Chapter 13 on class.

Block (Compound Statement)

A block (compound statement) is a series of statements surrounded by the braces "{' and'}" and is used principally to group statements into an executable unit. For example, a Java member method of a class is a compound statement. A compound statement is also used when the language syntax permits only a single statement to be specified and the application logic requires two or more statements to be executed.[13] Note that the compound statement does not end with a semi-colon.

```
{
    // a set of statements here
}
```

---

[13] Although it is possible to place a compound statement where you can place a statement, a compound statement is not terminated by a semicolon.

STATEMENT FLOW CONTROL

The default flow of control is sequential in Java, so every Java program begins with the first statement of main(). Each statement is executed in turn. When the final statement is executed, the program ends. However, sequential execution of statements is typically inadequate except for the simplest programs. In the following sections, we look at some of the control statements available in Java.[14]

If Statement

An if statement tests a particular condition. The form of an if statement is as follows:

```
if ( expression )  statement;
```

Whenever the expression evaluates to true, a statement (or a compound statement) is executed. Otherwise, the statement is skipped. In either event, the following statement is executed after the if statement has completed.

If-Else Statement

Closely related to the if statement is the if-else statement. It has the following form:

```
if ( expression )  statement-1;
else                    statement-2;
```

If the expression is true, then statement-1 is executed and statement-2 is skipped. However, if the expression is false, then statement-1 is skipped and statement-2 is executed. As with the if statement, after the if-else statement has completed, the following statement is executed.

Here is an example of using the if-else statement to get the minimum of two numbers:

```
if ( y < x  )
    min  = y;
else
    min  = x;
/* Below is the "following statement"   */
cout << "minimum is " << min;
```

If y < x evaluates to true, then the min is assigned the value of y; if y < x evaluates to false, then min is assigned the value of x. In either case, min is printed.

---

[14] Please consult Java language specification for a complete set of control statements.

For Statement

The for statement is an iterative statement typically used with a variable that is incremented or decremented. It is most commonly used to step through a fixed-length data structure, such as an array. The syntactic form of a for statement is:

```
for ( init-statement; expression-1; expression-2)
execution-statement;
```

The init-statement can either be a declaration or an expression. It is usually used to initialize a variable; however, it may be null. Expression-1 serves as the loop control. Iterations are performed as long as expression-1 evaluates to true. In each iteration, the statement is executed. The execution-statement may either be a single statement or a compound statement. If the first evaluation of expression-1 is false, the execution-statement is never executed. Expression-2 is evaluated after each iteration of the loop. It is usually used to modify the variable initialized in the init-statement. If the first evaluation of expression-1 is false, expression-2 is never evaluated.

The following is a simple example of using a for statement for initializing an array:

```
final int Max = 50;
float   float_array[Max];
for (int i =0; i <Max; i++)
{
    float_array[i] = (float) i;
}
```

In this example, each member of the array is initialized to its own index value as a floating point number. For instance, float_array[0] = 0.0, and float_array[15] = 15.0.

Switch Statement

A common programming practice is to test a variable against a set of values to find a match and perform a set of operations based on that match. The switch statement is a very effective way to implement multi-way execution control (i.e., using the switch to select one of many execution paths). For this to work the selector must be an integral value[15] such as char or int. Thus the switch statement selects from among sections of code based on the value of an integral expression. The form of the switch statement is as follows:

---

[15] This means that strings and floating point numbers may not be used as selectors. To handle these situations, you have to use a series of if-statements.

```
switch(integral expression) {
case integral value1: statement(s); break;
case integral value2: statement(s); break;
case integral value3: statement(s); break;
case integral value4: statement(s); break;
// other values
default: defaultStatement(s);
}
nextExecutableStatement;
```

First, the integral expression is evaluated and it produces an integral value. That integral value then compared against each integral value that follows the case token. If a match is found, the corresponding statement, which may also be a series of statements, is executed. If no match occurs, the default statement is executed. Note that in the above example that each case section ends with a break. This break causes the sequence of control to jump to the end of the switch body. This is the most commonly used form of the switch statement, but the break statement is actually optional. If the break statement is missing, the code for the following case statement(s) execute until a break or the end of the switch body is encountered.

The following is a simple example of initializing[16] an array using the switch statement:

```
const int Max = 50;
float float_array[Max];
for (int i =0; i <Max; i++) {
    switch(i%3) {
        case 0:float_array[i] = i/3; break;
        case 1:float_array[i] = i+2; break;
        case 2:float_array[i] = i+10; break;
        default::;//error logic
    }
}
```

In this example, each member of the array is initialized based on its remainder base 3. If the remainder is 0, the item is initialized to its own index value/3 as a floating point number. If the remainder is 1, the item is initialized to its own index value plus two as a floating point number. If the remainder is 2, the item is initialized to its own index value plus 10 as a floating point number. For instance, float_array[0] = 0.0, and float_array[15] = 5.0. Note that i is incremented after it is used.

Here are some guidelines to follow:

1. Use switch statements over if-then or if-then-else statements.

    • If-then clauses will not scale
    • If-then-else clauses are not easy to read and can lead to subtle bugs

---

[16] Notice that we begin initialization at index 0. All arrays in Java begin with an index of 0.

2. Always provide a default case when using switch statements.

3. Do not let one case clause run into another in the case statements (use break statements).

While Statement

A while statement will continually execute a block of statements while a condition remains true. This statement allows for control looping where a statement (or compound statement) is executed until the boolean expression is evaluated as false. The general form of the while statement is

```
while (boolean expression) {
    statement-1
}
statement-2
```

First, the boolean expression is evaluated. If the expression returns true, then statement-1, which can be a block of statements, is executed. After executing the statement-1, the expression is reevaluated, if it evaluates to true, statement-1 is executed, etc. until the expression evaluation returns a false. If a false is returned, the statement-1 is skipped and the statement-2 following the while statement is executed.

The following is a simple example of initializing an array using the while statement:

```
const int Max = 50;
float float_array[Max];
int i =0;
while(i <Max)
{ float_array[i] = i++; }
```

In this example, each member of the array is initialized to its own index value as a floating point number. For instance, float_array[0] = 0.0, and float_array[15] = 15.0. Note that i is incremented after it is used.

Do-While Statement

This statement allows for control looping where a statement (or compound statement) is executed until the boolean expression is evaluated as false. The syntactic form of the statement is

```
do statement
while (boolean expression);
```

The boolean expression is evaluated after every iteration of the statement (i.e., the statement is executed and then the expression is evaluated). Thus, the statement is always executed at least once.

The following is a simple example of initializing an array using the do-while statement:

```
const int Max = 50;
float float_array[Max];
int i =0;
do { float_array[i] = i++; }
while(i <Max);
```

In this example, each member of the array is initialized to its own index value as a floating point number. For instance, float_array[0] = 0.0, and float_array[15] = 15.0. Note that i is incremented after it is used. Caution, it is not always true that you can use the same boolean expression for both a while and do-while to do the same thing. In our example, this just happens to be true.

BRANCHING STATEMENTS

The Java programming language supports three branching statements:

- The break statement
- The continue statement
- The return statement

The break statement and the continue statement, which are discussed next, can be used with or without a label. A *label* is an identifier placed before a statement. The label is followed by a colon (:). The form is

```
statementName: statement ;
```

The Break Statement

The break statement is used with a block of statements that is used for iteration. Iteration (execution control statements) were discussed above. The break statement has two forms: unlabeled and labeled.

```
break;           //unlabeled form
break statementName;    // labeled form
```

We used the break statement within the switch statement earlier. As previously mentioned, the break statement terminates the enclosing switch statement and the flow of control transfers to the statement immediately following the switch statement. We can also use the unlabeled form of the break statement to terminate a for, while, or do-while loop. For example:

```java
public class BreakInFor {
    public static void main(String[] args) {
        int[] arrayOfInts = { 332, 112, 25, 436, 25, 212};
        int matchNo = 12;
        int i = 0;
        boolean found = false;
        for ( ; i < arrayOfInts.length; i++) {
            if (arrayOfInts[i] == matchNo) {
                found = true;
                break;          //This will break out of for loop
            }
        }
...//  Here you can test found flag and determine what to do
    }
}
```

The break statement terminates the for loop when the value is found. The flow of control transfers to the statement following the enclosing for.

While, the unlabeled form of the break statement is used to terminate the innermost switch, for, while, or do-while, the labeled form terminates an outer statement, which is identified by the label specified in the break statement. For example,

```java
public class BreakWithLabel {
    public static void main(String[] args) {
        int[][] arrayOfInts = { { 1, 2, 3, 4 },
                { 5, 6, 7, 8 },{ 9, 11, 12, 13 }};
        int match = 12;
        int i = 0;
        int j = 0;
        boolean found = false;
        search:
            for ( ; i < arrayOfInts.length; i++) {
                for (j = 0; j < arrayOfInts[i].length; j++) {
                    if (arrayOfInts[i][j] == match) {
                        found = true;
                        break search;
                    }
                }
            } //This is the closing brace for the search label
        ...   // This is the next statement
    }
}
```

The program is similar to the previous, but it searches for a value in a two-dimensional array. Two nested for loops traverse the array. When the value is found, a labeled break terminates the statement labeled search (the outermost loop). This syntax can be a little confusing. The break statement terminates the labeled statement; it does not transfer the flow of control to the label. The flow of control transfers to the statement immediately following the labeled (terminated) statement. Furthermore, if there was not a labeled break, it would have only terminated the innermost loop.

The Continue Statement

The continue statement is used with a block of statements that is used for iteration. Iteration statements (or execution control) were discussed above. Technically, the continue breaks the sequential execution of statements and causes the execution to go to the beginning of the iteration block and start a new iteration. We use the continue statement to skip the current iteration of a for, while, or do-while loop. We will look at both the unlabeled form and the labeled form.

```
continue;              // unlabeled form
continue statementName;       // labeled form
```

The unlabeled form skips to the end of the innermost loop's body and evaluates the boolean expression that controls the loop, basically skipping the remainder of this iteration of the loop. For example,

```
public class Count29 {
    public static void main(String[] args) {
        int[] arrayOfInts = { 332, 347, 29, 436, 25, 35, 29};
        int matchNo = 29;
        int count = 0;
        int i = 0;
        for ( ; i < arrayOfInts.length; ++) {
            if (arrayOfInts[i] != matchNc)  continue;
            // This skip to the end of fcr loop
            // count the "29"
            count++;
        }
        ...      //  The rest of the methcd
    }
}
```

The example[17] steps through a number array checking each number. If the current number is not 29, the continue statement skips the rest of the loop and proceeds to the next number. If it is 29, the program increments a counter Of course, we usually will be doing more things.

---

[17] This example is not good coding practice. It was used to show how continues work.

The labeled form of the continue statement skips the current iteration of an outer loop marked with the given label. For example,

```java
public class FindSubstring {
    public static void main(String[] args) {
        String searchMe= "The string that will be searched.";
        String subString = "se"; // We are looking for "se"
        boolean found = false;
        int max = searchMe.length() - subString.length();
        test:
            for (int i = 0; i <= max; i++) {
                int n = subString.length();
                int j = i;
                int k = 0;
                while (n-- != 0) {
                    if (searchMe.charAt(j++) !=
                        subString.charAt(k++)) {
                      continue test;
                    }
                }
                found = true;
                break test;
            }
        ...   //  statement after test
    }
}
```

The example[18] uses nested loops to search for a substring within another string. Two nested loops are required: one to iterate over the substring, and one to iterate over the string being searched. This example uses the labeled form of continue to skip an iteration in the outer loop, and it uses a labeled break to get out of the test loop.

The Return Statement

We use the return statement to exit from the current method and jump back to the statement within the calling method that follows the original method call. There are two forms:

```java
return;
return expression;
```

---

[18] Again, this is not an example of good programming practice. This example was intended only to demonstrate the labeled continue statement.

One that returns a value and one that does not. To return a value, simply put the value (or an expression that calculates the value after the return keyword: For example,

```
return count;
return ( a + b/c );
```

The value returned by return must match the type of method's declared return value.

When a method is declared void use the form of return that does not return a value.

```
return;
```

EXCEPTION HANDLING

Java provides a mechanism known as exceptions to help programs report and handle errors.

Throws and Try-Catch Block

Java requires that a method either catch or specify all checked exceptions that can be thrown within the scope of the method. This requirement has several components that need further explanation: "catch," "specify," "checked exceptions," and "exceptions that can be thrown within the scope of the method."

A method can *catch* an exception by providing an exception handler for that type of exception. *If a method chooses not to catch an exception*, the method must *specify* that it can throw that exception. Why did the Java designers make this requirement? Because any exception that can be thrown by a method is really part of the method's public programming interface: callers of a method must know about the exceptions that a method can throw to intelligently and consciously decide what to do about those exceptions. Thus, in the method signature you specify the exceptions that the method can throw.

Java has different types of exceptions, including I/O exceptions, runtime exceptions, and exceptions of your own creation, to name a few. For example, runtime exceptions are those exceptions that occur within the Java runtime system. This includes arithmetic exceptions (such as dividing by zero), pointer exceptions (such as trying to access an object through a null reference), and indexing exceptions (such as attempting to access an array element through an index that is too large or too small). Runtime exceptions can occur anywhere in a program and in a typical program can be very numerous.

The cost of checking for runtime exceptions often exceeds the benefit of catching or specifying them. Thus the compiler does not require that we catch or specify runtime exceptions, although we can. *Checked exceptions* are exceptions that are not runtime exceptions and are checked by the compiler; the compiler checks that these exceptions are caught or specified.

The statement "exceptions that can be thrown within the scope of the method" may seem obvious at first: just look for the throw statement. However, this statement includes more than just the exceptions that can be thrown directly by the method: the key is in the phrase within the scope of. This phrase includes any exception that can be thrown while the flow of control remains within the method. This statement includes both

- Exceptions that are thrown directly by the method with Java's throw statement
- Exceptions that are thrown indirectly by the method through calls to other methods

To indicate that an error has occurred within a program, use the throw statement. The form of the throw statement looks like this.

```
throw exception;
```

Exception is an object that inherits either directly or indirectly from the Exception class. The exception object's class indicates the type of error. The exception object contains a detailed message about the error, information about where the error occurred, and possibly other details about the error.

The throw statement interrupts the normal flow of the program and attempts to find an exception handler for the type of exception that was thrown. An exception handler is a block of code that can handle a particular type of error, either by recovering from it or by determining that the error is unrecoverable and attempting to provide a gentle exit from the program.

Java provides three statements that play a part in the handling exceptions:

- Try Statement. The try statement identifies a block of statements within which an exception might be thrown.
- Catch Statement. The catch statement must be associated with a try statement and identifies a block of statements that can handle a particular type of exception. The block of statements is executed if an exception of a particular type occurs within the try block.
- Finally Statement. The finally statement must be associated with try statement and identifies a block of statements that are executed regardless of whether or not an error occurs within the try block.

Here is the form for using these statements.

```
try {
    statements
} catch (exceptionType name) {
    statements
} catch (exceptionType name) {
```

```
        statements
} finally {
        statements
}
```

More than one catch statement can be associated with a try statement. Furthermore, a try statement must have at least one catch or finally statement associated with it.

Throwable Class

We can throw only objects that derive from the Throwable class. This includes direct descendants (that is, objects that derive directly from the Throwable class) as well as indirect descendants (objects that derive from children or grandchildren of the Throwable class).

Figure 12-1 illustrates the class hierarchy of the Throwable class and its most significant subclasses.

As we can see from Figure 12-1. Throwable has two direct descendants:

- Errors. When a dynamic linking failure or some other "hard" failure in the virtual machine occurs, the virtual machine throws an Error. Typically, Java programs should not catch Errors. In addition, it's unlikely that Java programs will ever throw Errors either.
- Exceptions. Most programs throw and catch objects that derive from the Exception class. Exceptions indicate that a problem occurred but that the problem is not a serious systemic problem. Most programs we write will throw and catch Exceptions.

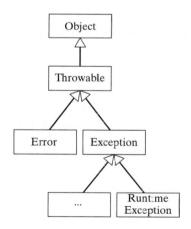

Figure 12-1   The Exception Hierarchy.

The Exception class has many descendants defined in the Java packages. These descendants indicate various types of exceptions that can occur. For example, IllegalAccessException signals that a particular method could not be found, and NegativeArraySizeException indicates that a program attempted to create an array with a negative size.

One Exception subclass has special meaning in the Java language: RuntimeException. The RuntimeException class represents exceptions[19] that occur within the Java virtual machine (during runtime). Because runtime exceptions[20] are so ubiquitous and attempting to catch or specify all of them all the time would be a useless exercise, the compiler allows runtime exceptions to go uncaught and unspecified.

When we design a package of Java classes that collaborate to provide some useful function to our users, we work hard to ensure that our classes interact well together and that their interfaces are easy to understand and use. We should spend just as much time thinking about and designing the exceptions that our classes throw.

Because many programmers will be using our class, we can be assured that many will misuse or abuse our class and its methods. Also, some legitimate calls to our methods may result in an undefined result. Regardless, we want our class to be as robust as possible, to do something reasonable about errors, and to communicate errors back to the calling program. However, we cannot anticipate how each user of our class will want the object to behave under adversity. So, often the best thing to do when an error occurs is to throw an exception. Each of the methods supported by our class might throw an exception under certain conditions, and each method might throw a different type of exception than the others.

When faced with choosing the type of exception to throw, we have two choices:

- Use one written by someone else. The Java development environment provides a lot of exception classes that we could use.
- Write one of our own.

We should go to the trouble of writing our own exception classes if we answer "yes" to any of the following questions. Otherwise, we can probably get away with using someone else's.

- Do we need an exception type that is not represented by those in the Java development environment?
- Would it help our users if they could differentiate our exceptions from those thrown by classes written by other vendors?

---

[19] An example of a runtime exception is NullPointerException. It occurs when a method tries to access a member of an object through a null reference. A NullPointerException can occur anywhere a program tries to dereference a reference to an object. The cost of checking for the exception often outweighs the benefit of catching it.

[20] The Java packages define several RuntimeException classes. We can catch these exceptions just like other exceptions. However, a method is not required to specify that it throws RuntimeExceptions. In addition, we can create our own RuntimeException subclasses.

- Does our code throw more than one related exception?
- If you use someone else's exceptions, will our users have access to those exceptions?
- Should our package be independent and self-contained?

If we plan to distribute our classes in a package, all related code should be packaged together. Thus, we should create our own exception class hierarchy. For the superclass, the java.lang package provides two Throwable subclasses that further divide the type of problems that can occur within a Java program: Errors and Exceptions.[21] Most of the applets and applications that you write will throw objects that are Exceptions.[22] It is good practice to append the word "Exception" to the end of all classes that inherit (directly or indirectly) from the Exception class. Similarly, classes that inherit from the Error class should end with the string "Error."

NAMESPACE

Java was designed to support the dynamic loading of modules over a distributed computing environment (e.g., the Internet); thus, it took a special effort to avoid name space conflicts. Thus, each name has a scope.

- Scope is the life-span of the variable, it determines what sections of code can use the variable. The location of the variable declaration, that is, where the declaration appears in relation to other code elements, determines its scope.

No Global Variables

In Java every data variable (attribute) and every method (service or function) is declared within a class. Thus, they are *members* (parts) of a class definition. *There are no stand-alone methods (functions).* Every class is also a part of a *package*. A package is a collection of classes. For a physical analogy, one can say that a package is a file that has a bunch of classes. Thus, one can reference any member of a class via its fully qualified name.

```
packageName.className.memberName
```

Note that packages may be packaged within a package so that the package name above may be multiple names separated by periods. Thus, an example of a fully qualified name may be

```
lee.rich.books.java.chapter.fifteen.code.point.x
```

---

[21] Because runtime exceptions do not have to be specified in the throws clause of a method, many packages developers ask: "Isn't it just easier if I make all of my exception inherit from RuntimeException?" For most of us, "No, your exceptions shouldn't inherit from RuntimeException."

[22] Theoretically, any Exception subclass could be used as the parent class.

Package and Imports

As the number of classes that you use grows, the need to use short and simple names for some classes increases. If you use classes from libraries, you also need to address class names that are in conflict. In this section, we will discuss "how Java assists you in handling these issues."

The basic construct to help organize the class is the package statement. The basic format is

```
package packageName;
```

If a package statement appears in a Java source file, it must be the first statement of the file. Of course comments and white space may precede the statement. Then you define a class as you normally would. That class and other classes that are defined within this package are grouped together. An example of a package is

```
package myTechpackage;
public  class MyFirstClass extends ItsSuperClass implements
        InterfaceOne, InterfaceTwo {
    ...  //Body of class definition here
    }
    /* The rest of this code is optional  */
public  class MySecondClass extends SecSuperClass implements
    InterfaceTwo, InterfaceFour {
        ...  //Body of class definition here
    }
    ...   // Additional class definitions
```

Packages can be further organized into a hierarchy analogous to the inheritance hierarchy where each level represents a different level of abstraction of the classes. The java library itself is organized using a package hierarchy. The top level[23] is called **java**. The next level include names such as **io**, **net**, **util**, and **awt**. Within the package **awt** is another package called **image**, and within that package is the class **ImageFilter**. Then you can reference this class anywhere in your java code via

```
java.awt.image.ImageFilter
```

However, all classes, such as PixelGrabber, that are in the same package may reference this class by using the class name only.

The *import* statement makes Java classes available to the current class under an abbreviated name. Any number of statements may appear in a Java program.

---

[23] By convention, the top-most level of the hierarchy is reserved for top-level domains on the Internet (EDU, COM, GOV, FR, US, etc.) Then it is followed by a reversed version of your domain name. This package naming convention guarantees a unique global identifier.

They must appear (1) after the optional *package* statement at the top of the file and (2) before the first class or interface definition in the file.

There are two forms of the *import* statement:

```
import package.class;
import package.*;
```

The first form allows the specified class in the specified package to be known by its class name alone. The second form of the import statement makes all classes in a package available by their class name.

For example, we can consider the two import statements:

```
import java.util.Hashtable;
import java.util.*;
```

The first import statement allows you to type "Hashtable" instead of "java.util.Hashtable." The second import statement makes all classes in the util package available by their class name. Thus, you can access not only Hashtable but also EventObject by their class name.

Packages of the Java API

The Java API consists of the classes and interfaces defined in the 23 packages: These are listed in Table 12-11.

Table 12-11   Java Packages

Package Name	Contents
java.applet	Applet classes
java.awt	Graphics, window, and GUI classes
java.awt.datatransfer	Data transfer classes
java.awt.event	Event processing classes and interfaces
java.awt.image	Image processing classes
java.awt.peer	GUI interfaces for platform independence
java.beans	JavaBeans component model API
java.io	Various types of input and output classes
java.lang	Core language classes
	Reflection API classes
java.math	Arbitrary precision arithmetic
java.net	Networking classes
java.rmi	Remote method invocation classes
java.security	Security classes

Table 12-11 Java Packages (*continued*)

Package Name	Contents
	Security access control
	Security interfaces
java.sql	JDBC SQL API for database access
java.text	Internationalization classes
java.util	Various useful data types
java.util.zip	Compression and decompression classes

Filenames and Directories

Because each java class is usually located in a separate source file, the grouping of classes by a package hierarchy is analogous to the grouping of files into a hierarchy of directories in your file system. The Java compiler reinforces this analogy by requiring you to create a directory hierarchy under your class directory that exactly matches the hierarchy of the packages you have created.

The Java interpreter knows where its standard system classes are installed, and it loads them from that location as needed. It looks up user-defined classes in or relative to the current directory. You can set the CLASSPATH by using the *setenv* command of your operating system.

Access to Members of a Class

In Java, a programmer can also control the access to the constructs that she/he create by controlling the visibility of the construct. When a protocol (service) or variable (attribute) is visible to another class, it means that the class's methods can call that protocol or modify that variable. To provide different granularity of protection of your constructs, Java provides the four "P's" of protection: package, public, protected, and private.

Here is an analogy that may help you remember these concepts. **Private** members are like secrets you never tell anybody. **Protected** members are like family secrets—you do not mind if the whole family knows, and even a few trusted friends, but you would not want any outsiders to know. **Public** members are known to the world; this means that there are no personal or family secrets here. **Package** members are only known by your closest friends but are not known even to your family.

Public

Because the fundamental building block of Java is a class or an interface. The first P, *public*, is used to build the distinction between the inside and the outside of a class.

First, all protocols and variables defined within the class are visible to the methods within the class. If you want to make any protocol or variable visible to all the classes outside of this class, you need to declare the protocol or variable with the modifier: *public*. This is an example of some *public* protocols.

```
public Interface newIntf {
    public int serviceOne( ... );
    public int serviceTwo( ... );
}
```

Note that we also placed a visibility modifier on the interface. When the *public* visibility modifier is applied to either a class or interface, it means the class or interface is visible to all the other classes.

Private

Since you are doing object-oriented programming, you know that public variables violates the encapsulation principle. How do you ensure that the methods of other classes do not modify your variables? Of course, there is a visibility modifier called *private* that gives you this protection and this is our second P. Below is a class with private variables.

```
public class myPrivateExample {
    private int myInteger;
    private float myNumber;
    public int serviceOne( ... );
    public  int serviceTwo( ... );
}
```

A private variable is only accessible to the methods defined within its class. Similarly, a private protocol is accessible only to methods within its class or interface. Private members (protocols and variables) are not inherited by its subclasses and, thus, are not accessible by methods within the subclasses.

Protected

The *protected* visibility modifier, our third P, is used to manage the accessibility of protocols and variables between a class and its subclasses. A protected member of a class is visible (1) within a class where it is defined, (2) with all of its subclasses (even if the subclass is defined in a different package), and (3) with all classes within the same package as the class. For example,

```
package First;
public class MyProtectedClass {
    ...
```

```
            protected float aProtectedMethod( ) { ... }
            ...
        }
        public class MySecondClass {
            ...
            public aMethod( ) {
                ...
                MyProtectedClass  mpc = new MyProtectedClass( );
                    // create an instance
                float x = mpc.aProtectedMethod( );
                    // use the protected service
                    ...
        }

        package MySecondPackage
        public class MySubclass extends MyProtectedClass {
            ...
            public aSubclassMethod( ) {
                ...
                float x = aProtectedMethod( );
                    // use the protected service
                ...
        }
```

Package

Finally, we get to the final P of visibility, which actually has no name. Historically, it has been called either "friendly" or "package." This is the default visibility when no visibility modifier has been specified. This default visibility states that only methods of classes within the same package have access to the default variables or default methods. So we will use *package* to refer to this visibility or access-specifier.

Summary

The previous discussion of class member accessibility is summarized in Table 12-12.

Table 12-12 Class Member Accessibility

Access to	Public	Private	Protected	Default
Same class	Yes	Yes	Yes	Yes
Class in same package	Yes	Yes	Yes	No
Subclass in different package	Yes	Yes	No	No
Non-subclass in different package	Yes	No	No	No

This may seem very confusing. However, if you are doing object-oriented programming, the following simple rules applies:

1. All variables must be declared private!
2. If you want others to use your service, declare the protocol (method) public.
3. If you want your service to be only used by your own methods, make the protocol private.
4. If you want subclass and thus classes within the same package to access the service, use protected. This should rarely be used.
5. Default should never be used.

TYPE CONVERSION

Java is a strongly typed programming language. This is good or bad depending upon your perspective. It is good in the sense that it enforces one to clearly identify type, prevents incorrect access to data, and assures that operations over values are semantically valid. On the other hand, strong typing makes it difficult to transition from treating a value at one level of abstraction (for example, as a shape object) in one part of the program and treating it at a different level of abstraction (for example, as a rectangle, circle, or line object) elsewhere.

To provide the programmer with the ability to change type, Java provides a casting mechanism. The casting mechanism converts the value of an object or primitive data type into another type. The result is a new reference or value, and the original object or value is not affected. Although the concept of casting is simple, the rules for what types in Java can be converted to what other types are complicated.

Casting Between Primitive Data Types

Casting between primitive data types enables you to "convert" the value of one primitive data type to another primitive data type. The following rules apply:

Rule 1. Boolean values cannot be cast to any other primitive type.

Rule 2. If the type to which you are casting is "larger"[24] than the type of the value you are converting, you do not have to use an explicit cast (i.e., the cast will be done for you by the compiler).

Rule 3. Casting integers to floating point values, or casting an int or a long or a float, or casting a long to a double may cause some loss of precision.

Rule 4. To convert from a value in a "larger type" to a "smaller" type, an explicit cast must be used.

---

[24] The primitive data types all have fixed size; thus, larger refers to the size of the data type. See the section primitive data types.

An explicit cast has the following form:

```
(primitiveDataType) expression
```

The primitiveDataType is the data type to which you are casting; while the expression is value that you want to convert. For example,

```
float x = 100.27;
int y = 7;
int z = (int) (x*y);
```

Here we see the use of the explicit casting of the expression (x*y) into an int. Note the parenthesis around x*y is necessary because of the precedence ordering and that the expression may be just a variable.

Casting Objects

Casting object types introduces two additional rules:

Rule 5. An instance of a class may only be casted to the subclasses or super-classes in its inheritance hierarchy. It may not be casted to other classes not in its inheritance hierarchy.

Rule 6. An instance of a class is also an instance of all its superclasses. Thus, you can use an instance of a class everywhere an instance of one of the super-classes is expected.

For example, if the data type expected is the class Object, you can use an instance of any class. As all classes are derived from the class Object. If the expected class in Number, you can use an instance of Integer, Boolean, etc.

When you cast an object to one of its superclasses, you lose access to all the subclass information (i.e., the services and the attributes). To perform the cast, the following form is used,

```
(className) object
```

where the className is the name of the class to which you want to cast the object. The object is the thing that you are casting.

Here is a simple example of a cast. Assume that you have the following classes: Human and Lawyer. We will assume that the class Lawyer is a subclass of the class Human. (Yes, we understand that this may be controversial.) Then the following code shows how we can cast an instance of Lawyer to an instance of Human:

```
Human h;
Lawyer l;
```

```
l = new Lawyer( ):    // This creates an instance of lawyer
h = (Human) l;        //  This casts the instance of lawyer to human
```

In addition to casting object to classes, you may also cast an object to an interface type.

Rule 7. You can cast an object to an interface only if that object's class or one of its superclasses actually implements that interface.

Casting an object to an interface allows you to access the services declared by that interface.

Converting Primitive Data Types to Objects

Rule 8. You may neither cast from a primitive data type to a class nor from a class to a primitive data type.

Instances of primitive data types and instances of classes are very different things in Java, and you cannot automatically convert between the two. However, the java.lang package includes several special classes that correspond to each of the primitive data types: Integer for int, Float for float, Boolean for boolean, etc.

In these classes, there are methods (service name new) to create an object-equivalent for all the primitive data types. For example, the following code creates an instance of the class Integer with the value 2001.

```
Integer theYear =  new Integer( 2001 );
    // make 2001 an instance of Integer
```

Once you have the object, you can treat the value as an object. When you want the primitive data type back, there is also a class service to do it. For example, to get theYear as an int,

```
int theYearAsInt = theYear.intValue( );
    // return year as an int
```

See the Java API for the other classes.

RECOMMENDED APPROACH

This chapter has covered some of the basic concepts of Java. For the reader unfamiliar with Java it is recommended that they

1. Go to the www.javasoft.com website and use their tutorials.
2. Search the World Wide Web for more material using the Java keyword.

Below are some recommendations on how to use statements covered in this unit

1. Use the while statement to loop over a block of statements while a boolean expression remains true. The expression is evaluated at the top of the loop.

```
while (boolean expression) {
    [statement | {statements}]
}
```

2. Use the do-while statement to loop over a block of statements while a boolean expression remains true. The expression is evaluated at the bottom of the loop.

```
do {
    [statement | {statements}]
} while (boolean expression);
```

3. Use the for statement to loop over a block of statements and include an initialization statement, a termination condition statement, and an increment statement.

```
for (initialization; termination; increment) {
    [statement | {statements}]
}
```

4. Use an if statement for simple decision making. A single statement block is executed if the boolean expression is true.

```
if (boolean expression) {
    statements
}
```

5. Use an if-then-else for decision making that requires different actions based on the decision. An if-then-else is an if statement with one boolean expression and two statement blocks. The first statement block is executed if the boolean expression is true, and the second is executed if the boolean expression is false.

```
if (boolean expression) {
    statements
} else {
    statements
}
```

6. Use an if statement with multiple expressions when you have a series of tests that narrows your scope of decision making.

```
if (boolean expression) {
    statements
} else if (boolean expression) {
    statements
}
```

7. Use the switch statement to branch on different values of a single variable or expression. The switch statement evaluates and integer expression and executes the appropriate case statement.

```
switch (integer expression) {
    case integer expression:
        statements
        break;
    ...
    default:
        statements
        break;
}
```

8. Throw an exception to indicate that an error occurred.

```
throw exception;
```

9. Use the try, catch, and finally statements to handle exceptions.

```
try {
    statements
} catch (exceptiontype name) {
    statements
} catch (exceptiontype name) {
    statements
} finally {
    statements
}
```

10. Use the unlabeled form of the break statement to terminate the innermost switch, for, while, or do statement.

```
break;
```

11. Use the labeled form of the break statement to terminate an outer switch, for, while, or do statement with the given label.

```
break label;
```

12. Use a continue statement to terminate the current iteration of the inner-most loop and to evaluate the boolean expression that controls the loop.

```
continue;
```

13. Use the labeled form of the continue statement to terminate the current iteration of the loop with the given label and to evaluate the boolean expression that controls the loop.

```
continue label;
```

14. Use return to terminate the current method.

```
return;
```

15. Use the form of return that takes a value to return a value to the method's caller.

```
return value;
```

SUMMARY

In this chapter, we learned about:

1. tokens
2. important keywords
3. primitive data types
4. statements
5. control statements (if, for, and switch)
6. name space
7. cast operators

Java has predefined data types that are well defined. The primitive data types given in Table 12-13 are predefined.

Table 12-13 Primitive Data Types

	Size	Comment	Family
Byte	8 bits	Signed	Integer
Short	16 bits	Signed	Integer
Int	32 bits	Signed	Integer
Long	64 bits	Signed	Integer

Table 12-13 Primitive Data Types (*continued*)

	Size	Comment	Family
Float	32 bits	IEEE 754-1985	Floating point
Double	64 bits	IEEE 754-1985	Floating point
Char	16 bits	Unicode 1.1 character	Character
Boolean	1 bit	True or false only	Boolean

CAUTION: The size of each primitive type is *defined by the language* and is not implementation dependent.

CAUTION: Java int types *may not be used* as a boolean type.

NOTE: Each Java primitive type has an equivalent class-defined type, e.g., Integer, Byte, Float, Double. These primitive types are provided in addition to class-defined types purely for efficiency. For example, an int is much more efficient than an Integer.

In addition, you learned the following programming constructs:

1. **Variable.** A variable is a container in your program that is used to hold data of a particular type.

   You must explicitly provide a name and a type for each variable you want to use in your program. The variable's name is its identifier. You use the variable name to refer to the data it contains. The variable's type determines what values it can hold and what operations can be performed on it. In addition to the name and type that you explicitly give a variable, a variable also has scope.

2. **Operator.** An operator performs a function on either one, two, or three operands. An operator that requires one operand is called a unary operator. An operator that requires two operands is a binary operator. And finally a ternary operator is one that requires three operands. In addition to performing the operation, an operator also returns a value. The return value and its type depends on the operator and the type of its operands.

3. **Expression.** An expression is a series of variables, operators, and method calls (constructed according to the syntax of the language) that evaluates to a single value. Expressions perform the work of a Java program. Among other things, expressions are used to compute and assign values to variables and to help control the execution flow of a program. The job of an expression is two-fold: perform the computation indicated by the elements of the expression and return some value that is the result of the computation.

4. **Statement.** Statements are roughly equivalent to sentences in natural languages. A statement forms a complete unit of execution. The following types of expressions can be made into a statement by terminating the expression with a semicolon (;).

```
assignment expressions
any use of ++ or --
method calls
object creation expressions
```

In addition to the expression statements described above, declaration statements and control flow statements also constitute a statement. A declaration statement is a statement that declares a local variable. The flow control statements include the branching statements and the exception handling statement.

5. Block. A block is a collection of statements between balanced curly braces.

6. Flow Control Statements

```
if statement
for statement
switch statement
while statement
```

7. Branching Statements

```
break statement
continue statement
return statement
```

8. Exception Handling

```
throws keyword
try-catch block
```

9. Class and Interface definition statements

10. Name Space statements

```
package statement
import statement
```

11. Access-specifier keywords: public, private, protected

12. Casting

13

Implementing Class and Interface

The class mechanism in Java allows developers to define their own data types in addition to the ones native to the language. At the initial implementation of the application/system, developers use this mechanism to implement the categories found in the model. Then in future releases of the application, developers will find class useful when (1) they need to add functionality to an existing data type (either native or user-defined), and (2) they need to introduce a new abstraction that cannot map onto one of the defined data types or be derived from it.

COMPONENTS OF A CLASS

A Java class is composed of six major parts:

1. **Collection of data variables declaration.** In object-oriented technology, this is the collection of attributes. There are two types of *member variables*: instance and class. *Instance variables* belong to an object, and *class*

variables belongs to "class" when it is treated as an object. There may be zero or more data members of any data type in this collection.

2. **Collection of member methods declaration and definition**. This is the set of service prototypes that can be applied to the objects of that class. In Java, these services are called methods. There are two types of *member methods*: instance and class. *Instance methods* belong to an object, and *class methods* belongs to "class" when it is treated as an object. In object-oriented technology, this corresponds to the services. There may be zero or more service prototypes in the collection.

3. **Level of visibility**. Each member (data or method) may be specified as having the following level of access (visibility): *private*, *protected*, or *public*.[1] In object-oriented technology, all the data variables should be private and all the methods that are accessible by other should be public. Protected should only be used when a subclass needs access to what would otherwise be a private member.

4. **Associated tag name**. This name serves as a type specifier for the user-defined class. Thus, the name may be used in the program where the primitive data type may appear.

5. **Constructors**. Constructors are neither methods nor are they members. They are used to initialize new objects.

6. **Attributes of the class**. These are the superclass and the interfaces that are used plus the visibility scope of the class.

The public member methods are referred to as the *class interface*; however, we prefer the term *class protocol*. A class with private data variables and public member methods is called an *abstract data type*. This is the enforcement of the information hiding and encapsulation principles in implementation. When used properly a class in Java supports the principle of information hiding and encapsulation. It also binds a collection of data members (i.e., the data variables) to a set of functions (i.e., the methods) and defines the characteristics of all instances created by that class. In brief, it provides one of the basic units of reusability.[2]

CLASS DEFINITION

A class definition is composed of two parts: class header and class body.

*   The class header is composed of the keyword class followed by the class tag name. The class header declares the name of the class along with other attributes. We will discuss those other attributes in a later chapter.

---

[1] Remember if there is no visibility modifier; it is the default or package modifier that is applied to the member.

[2] In Java, there are two basic constructs for reuse/abstraction: class and interface.

- The class body follows the class header and is embedded within curly braces { and }. The class body contains declarations for all instance variables and class variables (known collectively as member variables) for the class. In addition, the class body contains declarations and implementations for all instance services and class services for the class.

For example,

```
public class Person
{
    public String getName( ) { return ( name ); }
        ...
    private String name;
    private char sex;
    private int age;
        ...
}
public class Dog
{
    public String getName( ) { return ( name ); }
        ...
    private String name;
    private int age;
        ...
}
```

Note that the data variables are declared as private members, while the protocols (methods) are declared as public members of the class. The class is normally declared as public so that all other objects may access its instances.

CLASS BODY

The class body contains all of the code that provides for the life cycle of the objects created from it: constructors for initializing new objects, declarations for the member variables of the class and its objects, methods to implement the behavior of the class and its objects, and, in rare cases, a finalize method to provide for cleaning up an object after it has done its job.

Visibility

Each member of the class has a level of visibility. There are four levels of visibility (public, private, protected, and package) that a member may have. If a level of visibility is not explicitly stated for a member, the default visibility of package is used. The rules for using levels of visibility within the class body are

- All member declarations using the *public* keyword are accessible by other classes (objects).
- All member declarations using the *private* keyword are accessible only by the class itself.
- All member declarations using the *protected* keyword are accessible only by the class, its subclasses, and all classes in the same package as the class.
- All member declarations without a visibility keyword are accessible only by the class and all classes in the same package as the class.

The preferred order for organizing the member of the class is public, protected, (default), and private. When an object is instantiated, all members are accessible to its member methods. The level of visibility applies only to methods of another object, whether it is in the same class or in a different class. When a method has access to the private data of all objects of its class, it has *class scope*. Most member methods have access only to the private data of the object against which it was invoked; this is the *object scope*.

Data Variables

A data variable is a variable that may contain values for a specific data type. When the data type is a primitive data type, the variable is actually storing the value of the primitive data type. However, when the data type is a class-defined data type, the variable stores a "handle" (i.e., in C/C++ terminology, pointer) to an instance (object) of the class. For data variable initialization

1. If the variable is a class-defined data type, the default initialization is null. So the programmer normally has to initialize the variable in its constructor.
2. If the variable is a primitive data type, the programmer is allowed to initialize the variable directly at the point of definition in the class.
3. Java variable definitions may be initialized to any constant or nonconstant object.
4. Forward references to data members within the same class are not allowed because they will not yet have been initialized.

Instance Data Variables

The declaration of instance data variables is the same as variable declarations in most languages, with the exception that an explicit initializer is allowed. For example, the following code declares three instance data variables:

```
public class Person
{   ...
    int height =0;         /* Legal */
```

```
    int weight;
    String name;
}
```

Initialization is done in the constructor for the class. As with variable declarations, it is legal to combine the declaration of multiple data variables into one declaration. For example,

```
class Person
{   ...
    int height, weight;
        // multiple declaration data variables of type int
    String name;
    ...
}
```

When possible, declare instance data variables in increasing size of storage to optimize the alignment of storage on all machines. However, data members can also be of user-defined types. A class type can be declared as a data variable. For example, the following is a definition of Woman using a Man type as a data variable. That data variable contains a reference (handle) to the Man object.

```
class Woman
{   ...
    private String name;
    private Man husband;
        // pointer to Man object that is her husband
    ...
}
```

A class is not considered defined until the closing brace of the class body is seen by the complier; however, the class is considered to be declared after the opening brace. This allows a class to define pointers and references to itself as data members. Consider a link list of persons:

```
class LinkPerson
{   ...
    private Person me;
    private LinkPerson next;
    private LinkPerson prev;
    ...
}
```

Class Data Variables

The instance data variables are related to an instance of the class; however, the class itself may be considered an object as such it must have attributes (data variables)

and services (methods). How do we capture the characteristics of the class as an object? We use the keyword *static* to differentiate between instance members and "class" members of a class definition.[3] Thus, a class data variable is any data variable that has the keyword static as a modifier. Note that a class variable will not be "duplicated" when an instance of the class is created as it is not a variable that belongs to an instance but as a variable of the class as an object. Here is an example,

```
public class Employee {
    ...
    static public float avgSalary( )
        //callable via Employee::avgSalary()
            { ...code missing.. }
    public float getSalary( )
        //callable via instance.getSalary( )
            { ...code missing.. }
    static private float sumOfAllSalaries;
        // accessible only to static methods
    static public int noOfEmployees;
        // accessible via Employee::noOfEmployees
    private float mySalary;
        //accessible only via instance methods
    ...
}
```

In this example, we have three data variables: "sumOfAllSalaries," "noOfEmployees," and "mySalary." Two of them, "sumOfAllSalaries" and "noOfEmployees," are class data variables. These data variables will not be duplicated when an instance of Employee is created. Each instance does have its own copy (storage space) for the data variable "mySalary." However, all the instances share the same data variable for "sumOfAllSalaries." In fact, because the "noOfEmployees" is declared as public, it shares that single variable with other classes or instances of other classes.

Constants

Constants are useful for defining shared values within a class. In Java, constants may only be defined for instance or class variables and not for local variables. To declare a constant, you need to add the *final* keyword modifier to the variable declaration and include an initial value for that variable. Once initialized by the compiler, this value may not be changed at runtime. Here are some examples.

```
public class MixedBag {
    ...
```

---

[3] Yes, we are defining two kinds of objects all in one class definition!

```
        public final float pi = 3.141592;
            // Accessible to all class as MixedBag::pi
        private final boolean deBugOn = true;
            // Accessible to all methods within class
        final int max = 100;
            //Accessible to all classes in same package
        ...
    }
```

Initialization of Member Variables

We may use static initializers and instance initializers to provide initial values for class and instance members when you declare them in a class. For example,

```
class Room {
    static final int MAX_CAPACITY = 4;
    boolean full = false;
}
```

This works well for members of primitive data type. Sometimes, it even works when creating arrays and objects. But this form of initialization has limitations, as follows:

- Initializers can perform only initializations that can be expressed in an assignment statement.
- Initializers cannot call any method that can throw a checked exception.
- If the initializer calls a method that throws a runtime exception, then it cannot do error recovery.

If we have some initialization to perform that cannot be done in an initializer because of one of these limitations, we have to put the initialization code elsewhere.

1. To initialize class members, put the initialization code in a static initialization block. A class can have any number of static initialization blocks that appear anywhere in the class body. The runtime system guarantees that static initialization blocks and static initializers are called in the order (left-to-right, top-to-bottom) that they appear in the source code.

2. To initialize instance members, put the initialization code in a constructor. See Chapter 14 on constructors.

3. To initialize anonymous instance members of anonymous classes, use instance initialization blocks because these classes cannot declare constructors.

Other Attributes of a Class Member

We have shown relatively simple member-variable declarations, but declarations can be more complex. You can specify not only type, name, and access level but also other attributes, including whether the variable is a class or instance variable and whether it is a constant. Each component of a member variable declaration is more formally defined below.

1. **accessLevel**. Controls that other classes have access to the member variable by using one of four access levels: public, protected, package (no specifier), and private. Control of member methods can also be done in the same manner.

2. **static**. Declares this is a class variable rather than an instance variable. Use static also to declare class methods.

3. **final**. Indicates that the value of this member cannot change. It is a compile-time error if your program ever tries to change a final variable. By convention, the name of constant values are spelled in uppercase letters.

4. **transient**. The transient marker is not fully specified by The Java Language Specification but is used in object serialization to mark member variables that should not be serialized.

5. **volatile**. The volatile keyword is used to prevent the compiler from performing certain optimizations on a member (i.e., prevent usage of register to hold the variable). This is an advanced feature.

6. **type**. Like other variables, a member variable must have a type. You can use primitive type names such as int, float, or boolean. Or you can use reference types, such as array, object, or interface names.

7. **name**. A member variable's name can be any legal Java identifier and, by convention, begins with a lowercase letter. You cannot declare more than one member variable with the same name in the same class, but a subclass can hide a member variable of the same name in its superclass. Additionally, a member variable and a method can have the same name.

Member Methods

Whether we are using structured methods or object-oriented methods, there is a stepwise refinement process that involves decomposing a process (a service in object-oriented technology) into smaller subprocesses. Function constructs are used to capture the processes and subprocesses. In object-oriented technology and in Java, there is technically no such thing as a function. In place of the functions, we have *services* (term used in object-oriented analysis) and *methods* (term used in design and coding). Using the term *service* is important in analysis as it emphases "what we are providing"; while using the term *method* to describe the same thing in design and coding is also reasonable as we are focusing on "how to provide the service."[4] Because we are now in coding, we will use the term *method*.

A method (service), which is like a function, defines a way of doing something. However, a method differs from a function in that a method must belong to class or object. It may not stand-alone, while a function always stands alone. For example, the "main" program in Java program is defined as a method in a class, while the main program in a C program is a stand alone routine.

Member methods of a class are declared and defined inside the class body. A method definition consists of the service prototype and body. The service prototype (also called the header) is composed of a return type and a name, followed by a signature enclosed in parentheses, followed by optionally the keyword throws and a comma-separated list of exceptions. The signature consists of a comma-separated list of argument types. An argument type is any primitive type, or user-defined type. An argument name may follow each type specifier. The body(i.e., the code) follows the declaration and is enclosed in braces.[5] Thus, the basic form of a class is

```
return_type method_name (signature ) {
/* method body- i.e. the code */
statements
}
```

The return_type that precedes the method_name determines the data type[6] of the value that the method returns. The return mechanism will be explained below. The method_name is the name that a requestor uses to access the service. Finally, the signature is a list of parameters (arguments) that the method expects the requestor of the service to provide (i.e., it is the information that must be passed into the method before the service can be provided). It is a list of argument type and argument name[7] separated by commas.

For example:

```
class Person
{
 // member methods
    public String getName()
        // This is the service (method) declaration
            { return ( name ); }
            // This is the service definition or the method
        public char getGender() { return ( gender ); }
```

---

[4] In some textbooks, analysis is defined as just defining the interface (i.e., the prototype of the method), while design is the definition (body) of the method (i.e., the details on how to do it).

[5] The details on the definition will be covered in Chapter 14.

[6] For primitive data types, the return value is an actual value; however, for class-based data types, the return value is actually a pointer to an instance of the class. Return type may also be an array.

[7] Parameters are syntactically identifiers, and, as such, they can be used in the body of the method. Technically, these are formal parameters because they are placeholders for actual values that are passed to the method when it is called. On method invocation, the values of the argument corresponding to the formal parameter are used in the body of the method when it is executed.

```
    public int getAge() throws NotAllowed
        { if age > 40 then throw NotAllowed; else return ( age );}
    public void setName(String s) { name = s; return; }
    public void setSex(char s) throws NoSexChangeAllowed,
            IllegalGender {
        if (s != 'f' and s != 'm')
            then throw IllegalGender
        else if ( height > 6 and weight < 200 )
            then throw NoSexChangeAllowed;
        else gender = s;
        return;
    }
    public void setAge(int a) { age = a; return; }
        // data variables
    private String name;
    private char gender;
    private int age, height, weight;
}
```

The argument list is referred to as the signature of a service (method or function) because it distinguishes between two protocols with the same name. The name alone does not necessarily uniquely identify a method. However, the name and its signature *will* uniquely identify a method. For example,

```
class Person
{
// member methods
    public char getSex();
    private void setSex(char );
    private void setSex(int );
        ...
 // data members
    private char name[40];
    private char sex;
    private int age, height, weight;
}
```

We can use the setSex() service by using an integer as an argument as well as using char as an argument. This may be needed because in one application the gender may be captured as an integer (e.g., 1 for female, 0 for male) while in another application gender is captured as a character (e.g., f for female, m for male). The principle of encapsulation allows us to hide the details about how gender is represented internally; the methods will perform the appropriate conversions.

Below is a method definition for the minimum service.

```
class Math
{
```

```
int min(final int x, final int y) {
    if (y < x)
        return (y);
    else
        return (x);
    }
}
```

The return statement has two purposes. First, when a return statement is executed, control is passed immediately back to the requestor of the service. Second, if an expression follows the keyword return, the value of the expression is returned to the requestor. When an expression exists, it must be assignment-convertible to the return-type of the method definition header.

We need to take special note of the following conditions on the use of return:

1. When there is no expression, the return-type of the method must be void. This is used when the requestor does not expect a value to be returned.
2. Except for constructors, all methods must have a return type, even if it is void.
3. There are no default arguments and no inline methods. However, the Java compiler, javac, has an optimization option that will inline some methods.
4. Code blocks for Java methods are always specified within the class itself; there is no separate declaration and definition as there is in C++ code or as you might separate functions and their prototypes in C.
5. There are special Java methods called constructors that are used to create (instantiate) objects of the class. These special methods will be discussed in Chapter 14.

Member methods are distinguished from other methods by the following characteristics:

*   Member methods have full access privileges to the private, protected, package, and public members of the class.
*   Member methods of one class do not have access privileges to members of another class. However, when one class has a relationship with another class, it has access to the other class' public members.
*   Member functions are defined only within the scope of the class. This means that member service names are not visible outside the scope of the class. This requires that other classes have access to an instance of the class before it can use the class' services.
*   Member methods can overload only other member methods of its class.

Class Method

In an earlier section, we explained the differences between instance data variables and class data variables. In an analogous fashion, we have two type of methods:

instance methods and class methods. Again, we use the keyword *static* to differentiate class methods from instance methods. Class methods are available to any
instance of a class itself and can be made available to other classes. We now explain
the rest of the example from the class variable section. The code is repeated for the
reader.

```
public class Employee {
    ...
    static public float avgSalary( )
        //callable via Employee::avgSalary()
        {return ( sumOfAllSalaries / noOfEmployee ); }
    public float getSalary( )
        //callable via instance.getSalary( )
        { return mySalary; }
    static private float sumOfAllSalaries;
        // accessible only to static methods
    static public int noOfEmployees;
        // accessible via Employee::noOfEmployees
    private float mySalary;
        //accessible only via instance methods
    ...
}
```

There are two methods: avgSalary() and getSalary(). The avgSalary() service
is a class service (method) and can be accessed either with an instance of a class

```
...                  // code fragment
Employee rich = new Employee( );
    // Instantiate a new employee
float myComAvgSal = rich.avgSalary( );
    // Get avg salary-
```

or without an instance of the class via its class scope.

```
...                  // code fragment
float myComAvgSal = Employee::avgSalary( );
    // Get avg salary-
```

Details of Member Method Prototype

Though we have only shown some very simple prototypes, a method's header (service prototype) provides a lot of information about the method to the compiler, to
the runtime system, and to other classes and objects. Included is not only the name
of the service but also such information as the return type of the service, the number
and type of the arguments required by the method and which other classes and
objects can call the service.

To complete our knowledge of method header, each element of a method prototype is formally defined here.

1. **accessLevel**. As with member variables, this controls which other classes have access to a method using one of four access levels: public, protected, package(no specifier), and private.
2. **static**. Static declares this method as a class method rather than an instance method.
3. **abstract**. An abstract service has no implementation and must be a member of an abstract class.
4. **final**. A final service cannot be overridden by subclasses.
5. **native**. Methods implemented in a language other than Java are called native methods and are declared as such using the native keyword.
6. **synchronized**. Methods may be declared synchronized to ensure that the threads access information in a thread-safe manner.
7. **returnType**. Java requires that a method declare the data type of the value that it returns. If the method does not return a value, use the keyword void for the return type.
8. **methodName**. A method name (service name) can be any legal Java identifier.
9. **(paramlist)**. For passing information into a method through its arguments.
10. **[throws exceptions]**. To indicate the type of exceptions that the method throws.

The data type of the return value must match the method's return type. A compiler error results if you try to write a method in which the return value doesn't match the return type in the method header. Java supports method name overloading so that multiple methods can share the same name. Overloaded methods are differentiated by the number and type of the arguments passed into the method. Finally, Java supports a class overriding a method in its superclass. The overriding method must have the same name, return type, and parameter list as the method it overrides. This is used to implement generalization/specialization with polymorphism.

Abstract Class

An abstract class is a class with at least one method that is declared abstract, that is, it has no implementation. The form of an abstract class is

```
abstract class ClassName
{      // Methods
    ...   // Concrete methods
    abstract void myAbstractmethod( );
    ..   // Other abstract methods
    ...   // Attribtues
}
```

The key is that both the class and the method with no implementation must have the abstract keyword as a modifier.

NESTED, INNER, AND ANONYMOUS INNER CLASSES

In this section, we will discuss four constructs that are widely used in the Java libraries:

- Nested Classes. A nested class is a class that is a member of another class.
- Static Nested Classes. A static nested class is a nested class that is declared static.
- Inner Classes. An inner class is a nested class whose instance exists within an instance of its enclosing class and has direct access to the instance members of its enclosing instance.
- Anonymous Inner Classes. An anonymous inner class is an inner class with no name.

We may encounter nested classes of both kinds in the Java API and be required to use them. However, most nested classes that you write will be inner classes. Inner classes are used primarily to implement adapter classes. If you plan on handling events from the Abstract Window Toolkit (AWT), then you'll want to know about using adapter classes because the event-handling mechanism in the AWT makes extensive use of them.

Nested Classes

Java lets us define a class as a member of another class. Such a class is called a nested class and its form is

```
class EnclosingClass{
    . . .
    class ANestedClass {
        . . .
    }
}
```

A nested class is a class that is a member of another class. We use nested classes to reflect and enforce the relationship between two classes. We should define a class within another class when the nested class makes sense only in the context of its enclosing class or when it relies on the enclosing class for its function.

As a member of its enclosing class, a nested class has unlimited access to its enclosing class's members, even if they are declared private[8] because the nested class is inside of its enclosing class so that it has access to its enclosing class's members.

Like other classes, nested classes can be declared abstract or final. The meaning of these two modifiers for nested classes is the same as for other classes. Also, the visibility modifier (private, public, protected, and package) may be used to restrict access to nested classes just as they do to other class members. Any nested class can be declared in any block of code. A nested class declared within a method or other smaller block of code has access to any final, local variables in scope.

Like other members, a nested class can be declared static (or not). A nested class that is declared static is called a static nested class. This is shown in the following code:

```
class EnclosingClass{
    . . .
    static class AStaticNestedClass {
        . . .
}
```

As with static methods and variables (class methods and variables), a static nested class is associated with its enclosing class. And like class methods, a static nested class cannot refer directly to instance variables or methods defined in its enclosing class; it can only access them with an object reference.

Inner Class

A nonstatic nested class is called an inner class. These are shown in the following code:

```
class EnclosingClass{
    . . .
    static class AStaticNestedClass {
        . . .
    }
    class InnerClass {
        . . .
    }
}
```

An inner class is associated with an instance of its enclosing class and has direct access to that object's instance variables and methods. It cannot define any static members itself because an inner class is associated with an instance.

To help differentiate the terms *nested class* and *inner class*, we suggest you think about them in the following way. The term *nested class* reflects the syntactic relationship between two classes (i.e., the code for one class appears within the code

---

[8] This is fully consistent with the meaning of private and the other access specifiers. The access specifiers restrict access to members for classes outside of the enclosing class.

of another syntactically). In contrast, the term *inner class* reflects the relationship between instances of the two classes. Consider the following example:

```
class EnclosingClass {
    . . .
    class InnerClass {
        . . . // Can access instance variables and methods
              //of the EnclosingClass here
    }
}
```

The key feature about the relationship between these two classes is not that InnerClass is syntactically defined within EnclosingClass. Rather, it's that an instance of InnerClass can exist only within an instance of EnclosingClass and that it has direct access to instance variables and methods of its enclosing instance.

Anonymous Inner Classes

You can declare an inner class without naming it. For example:

```
public class Set {
    private Vector items;

    ...//code for Stack's methods and constructors not shown...

    public Enumeration enumerator() {
        return new Enumeration() {
            int currentItem = items.size() - 1;
            public boolean hasMoreElements() {
                return (currentItem >= 0);
            }
            public Object nextElement() {
                if (!hasMoreElements())
                  throw new NoSuchElementException();
                else
                  return items.elementAt(currentItem--);
            }
        }
    }
}
```

In this code the enumerator is an anonymous class. As this example shows, anonymous classes can make code difficult to read. You should limit their use to those classes that are very small (no more than a method or two) and whose use is well understood (like the AWT event-handling adapter classes).

PREDEFINED JAVA CLASSES

String Data Type

String is not a built-in or primitive data type; strings are instances of the String class. The String class is in the library java.lang.String. Thus, instances of String are objects of a class-defined data type. For example,

```
String nothing = ""; // an empty string
String greeting = "Hi, you all!";
```

Java string class is treated by the compiler almost as if it was a primitive data type.[9] In the following sections, we will discuss some of these unusual features and some commonly used services that are in the String class.

String Concatenation

The language overloads the "+" operator for string concatenation. For example,

```
String let3 = "abc";
String num3 = "123";
String coma = let3 + num3; // coma = "abc123"
String comb = num3 + let3; // comb = "123abc"
```

Note that the "+" operator joins two strings together in the order that they are received and exactly as they are given. There is no space character added between strings.

Conversion of an Object to a String Instance

The compiler automatically creates a String instance (object) when it encounters a double-quote constant in a program. When you concatenate a string with a non-string object, the non-string object is converted to a string.[10] For example,

```
String rating = "MA" + 17; // rating = "MA17"
System.out.println("Years of Service is " + yOfS );
```

In the first line, a String object is created for the double quoted constant MA and the integer 17 is converted to a string object "17"; then the concatenation is performed. In the second line, we assume that yOfS is an integer variable. For a variable,

---

[9] For example, JVM performs runtime bounds checking on accesses to String objects.

[10] The conversion of primitive data types to a String object is provided by the language. The conversion of class-defined data types is defined by the class designer.

the value of the variable is converted to a string. Thus, a String object is created for the double quoted constant and the value of the variable is converted to a string object; then the concatenation is perfomed.The string is then printed to the output device using the service println. Note that the "a" space character was provided to separate the word "is" from the value of yOfS.

Conversion from String to Integer and Vice Versa

To convert an int to a String, use

```
String s = String.valueOf(4);
```

To convert a String to an int, use

```
int a = Integer.parseInt("4");
```

Substrings

To extract a substring of a string, a substring service is provided by the class designers of the String class. An example that uses this service is

```
String ostr = "abcdefghijkl";
String subs = ostr.substring(3,5);// subs = "de"
```

Note that Java has a peculiar way to count the characters in a string. The first position in the string is counted as position 0; thus, the character "a" is at position 0. Thus, the substring function is requesting that it be formed from the characters from the position 3 to the position 5 *exclusive* (i.e., characters at positions 3 and 4). In addition, note that the string s.substring(a, b) always contains b − a characters. Thus, the length of the string subs is $5 - 3 = 2$.

Length of String

To find the length of a string, a length service is provided by the class designers of the String class. An example that uses this service is

```
String ostr = "abcdefghijkl";
int s_length = ostr.length();// s_length = 12
```

Individual Characters in a String

Just as char denotes a Unicode character, String denotes a sequence of Unicode characters. The class designer gave us a service to get an individual character in a string. The service charAt(n) returns the Unicode character that occupies position n in the string. Because the first position in a string is position 0, the n must be in the range of 0 and length() –1. For example,

```
String ostr = "abcdefghijkl";
char c5 = ostr.charAt(5);// c5 = 'f'
```

Immutable Property

An important feature of the String objects is that they are immutable. There are no services in the class that allows the programmer to change the contents of a String object. Thus, if we need to modify the content(s) of a String object, there are two ways that we can do it. First, we can use the substring service to get the parts of the string that we want to keep and then we can concatenate it with the new parts that we created (usually by using string literals). Secondly, we can use a mutable class StringBuffer. In this instance, we will have to create an object in the class String-Buffer from the String object. Since StringBuffer objects are modifiable, we would then modify the contents of the StringBuffer object and then create a new String object from the contents of the modified StringBuffer object.

Both String and StringBuffer are in the library java. lang. We will not list the complete set of services provided by these classes, but some of the more frequently used services are given in Table 13-1

Table 13-1 Frequently Used String Services

Signature	Comments
char charAt(int n)	Returns the character at position 'n'.
Int compareTo(String anotherString)	Compares the string to another string. The order is based on Unicode; it is alphabetical order for English with uppercase letters coming before lower case letters. It returns a positive number if the other string comes after the string. It returns 0, if the strings are identical. Finally, it returns negative number if the string comes after the other string.
Boolean endsWith(String suffix)	Determines whether the string ends with the characters (value) of suffix.
Boolean equals(Object anObject)	Determines whether the string is the same as another object. Note: = operator is not overloaded for objects of type String.
Boolean equalsIgnoreCase(String anotherString)	Determines whether the string and another string is the same, ignoring case differences.
Int length()	Returns the length of the string
String replace(char oldChar, char newChar)	Creates a new string where all the occurrences of oldChar have been replaced by the newChar.

Table 13-1 Frequently Used String Services (*continued*)

Signature	Comments
Boolean startsWith(String prefix)	Determines whether the string begins with the characters (value) of prefix.
String substring(int beginPosition, int endPosition)	Creates a new string using the characters between the beginPosition and the endPosition. It excludes the endPosition character from the new string.
String toLowerCase()	Creates a new string with all the upper case characters converted to lower case.
String toUpperCase()	Creates a new string with all the lower case characters converted to upper case.
String trim()	Creates a new string where all the leading and trailing spaces in the original string are eliminated.

StringBuffer Data Type

The java.lang package contains two string classes: String and StringBuffer.[11] We have already seen the String class. We should use the String class when we are working with strings that cannot change. StringBuffer, on the other hand, is used when we want to manipulate the contents of the string dynamically. For example,

```
public class ReverseAString {
    public static String reverseString(String source) {
        int len = source.length();
            //Create StringBuffer (the same size as source)
            //to append characters
        StringBuffer dest = new StringBuffer(len);
        for ( int i = (len - 1); i >= 0; i--)
        // Loop backwards over all the characters in source
        // and appends them to dest
        dest.append(source.charAt(i));
        return dest.toString();
    }
}
```

The Java compiler uses the String and StringBuffer classes behind the scenes to handle literal strings and concatenation. In Java, we specify literal strings between double quotes:

```
"Hello You All!"
```

---

[11] Note to C and C++ Programmers: Java strings are first-class objects, unlike C and C++ strings, which are simply null-terminated arrays of 8-bit characters.

Furthermore, we can use literal strings anywhere we would use a String object. For example, System.out.println accepts a String argument, so we could use a literal string in place of a String there. For example,

```
System.out.println("Put a literal in place of a string.");
```

We can also use String methods directly from a literal string. For example,

```
int lengthofLiteral = "Good Day Folks!".length();
```

Because the compiler automatically creates a new String object for every literal string it encounters, you can use a literal string to initialize a String. For example,

```
String myString = "This is exclusively mine";
```

The above construct is equivalent to, but more efficient than

```
String myString = new String("This is exclusively mine");
```

This will create two Strings instead of one. The compiler creates the first string when it encounters the literal string "This is exclusively mine," and the second one when it encounters new String.

We can use "+" operator to concatenate Strings together: For example,

```
String myDog = "Lassie";
System.out.println("My dog name is" + myDog + ".");
```

This is a little deceptive because Strings cannot be changed. However, behind the scenes the compiler uses StringBuffers to implement concatenation. The previous example compiles to

```
String myDog = "Lassie";
System.out.println(new StringBuffer().append("My dog name is").
append(myDog).append(".").toString());
```

We can also use the "+" operator to append values to a String that are not themselves Strings.

```
System.out.println("Java Number " + 5);
```

The compiler converts the non-String value (the integer 5 in the example) to a String object before performing the concatenation operation.

Number Data Types

The Number classes include

```
Byte
Double
```

```
Float
Integer
Long
Short
BigDecimal
BigInteger
```

There are two new classes (BigDecimal and BigInteger) that were added for performing high-precision arithmetic. BigInteger supports arbitrary-precision integers and BigDecimal support arbitrary-precision fixed-point numbers. Both classes have methods that provide for the analogues operations that we use on primitive data types.

The rest of the classes are wrapper classes for their corresponding primitive data types: byte, double, float, integer, long, and short. They can be used to create their corresponding primitive data type into objects. For example,

```
int i = 100;
// Make an object instance of i !
Integer integerObject = new Integer( i ):
```

In addition to its constructor for creating instances, it has a toString method that converts the object to a string. For example,

```
String stringForm = integerObject.toString();
```

Here are the wrappers for some other data types:

```
Boolean
Character
Void
```

Array Data Type

An array is an ordered collection of slots that are used to store elements. Each slot of the array holds an individual element. The size (number of slots) of the array is fixed at compile time.[12] An array can contain any type of elements (primitive types or class-defined types); however, all the elements in a specific array must all be of the same type. An array is a collection of data of a single data type; thus, an array that contains both strings and integers would be illegal.

To use arrays, we need to know three things: (1) how to declare a variable to hold an array, (2) how to create an array and initialize it with values, and (3) how to access/change the values in the array.

---

[12] If we want to store data of different types in a single structure, or if we need a structure whose size can change dynamically, use a Collection implementation, such as Vector, instead of an array.

Declaring a Variable to Hold an Array

There are two forms that we can use to declare a variable to hold an array. The first form is an array definition consisting of a type specifier, an identifier, and a set of square braces([ ]).

Here are the ways we can declare an array.

```
int [ ] myArray;
    // This declare myArray as an array of integers.
int myArray[ ];
    // This is the second form
```

For example,

```
float float_array[ 100 ];
String strangeWords[];
```

The dimension value is computed at compile time and must be a constant expression.

An alternative form for defining an array variable is to put the braces after the type instead of after the variable. For example,

```
float [] float_array;
String [] strangeWords;
```

The two forms are equivalent; however, the second form with the brackets after the variable name is often much more readable.

Initialization of an Array

There are also two ways to create an array and initialize it with values. The first way is to use the new operator. For example,

```
String [] strangeWords new String[20];
int[] intArray = new int[10];
```

The first line creates a new array of String with twenty slots for elements of type String, while the second line creates a new array of integers with ten slots for elements of type int. The number in braces is used to define the number of slots in the array. This is called the dimension value; it is computed at compile time and must be a constant expression. When you create an array using new, all its slots are initialized for you.

- The initial value of *0* is used for all slots in an numeric array.
- The initial value of *false* is used for all slots in a boolean array.

- The initial value of *null* is used for all slots in an object array.
- The initial value of '\0' is used for all slots in a character array.

For example, to initialize an array of non-primitive data types, we must use the new constructor to create the objects that are the elements referenced in the array. For example,

```
public class ClassArray {
    public static void main( String[ ] args ) {
            // Declaration of myArray of size 20
        Float [ ] myArray = new Float[ 20];
            // Assign values to the declared variable
        for( int i =0; i < myArray.length; i++ )
            myArray[i] = new Float ( i );
    }
}
```

To initialize an array of nonprimitive data types of variable dimension, we can use the following form:

```
public class VarArray {
    // This returns an array of references to objects.
    // In Java, we do not have to worry about garbage collection
    static void Object [ ] buildArray( Object[ ] theArray ){
        return theArray;
    }
    // Now we can use the buildArray method to create array
    // of different size
    // However, need to cast it to the proper data type
    public static void main( String[ ] args ) {
        // Create an array of Integers
        Integer [ ] myArray =
            (Integer) buildArray( new Object [ ] {
                new Integer( 21), new Integer( 33),
                new Integer (45), new Integer(65) );
        // Create an array of String
        String [ ] myStringArray =
            (String) buildArray( new Object [ ] {
                "abc", "cde", "de", "fgh", "aaaaa",
                "bbbbbbb", "zzzz", "fffff", "mmmmm" } );
        ... // Use the arrays!
        }
    }
```

The second way of creating the new array is to enclose the elements of the array inside braces, separated by commas. For example,

```
String [] chiles = { "red", "green", "jalapeno", "thai",
    "serrano", "mexican", "indian"};
int [ ] myArray = { 1, 2, 3, 4, 5, 6 };
```

By using this form, an array of the proper size is automatically created for you. For instance, in our example, chiles is an array of size 7. Note that each of the elements inside the braces must be of the same type as the variable that holds the array. That is, chiles is a String array, so all the elements must be of type String.

Access and Assignment by Position

Access and assignment are by position in the array. For example,

```
float   yy = float_array[10];
```

Elements of the array are numbered beginning with 0. Thus, in our example, yy is assigned the eleventh element in float_array. The language provides compile and/or runtime range checking on indexes.

To assign an element value to a particular slot, use the assignment operator. For example,

```
chiles[2] = "reddish green";
```

Note that String is a class and thus chiles is an array of objects. An array of objects is different from an array of primitive data types. An array of primitive data types, the value of the data type is stored in the array slot; while in an array of objects, a reference to the object is stored in the array slot. Thus, when you reassign a value in an object array, you are actually reassigning the reference that is stored in the slot. The object value is not copied as is done for primitive data types.

Here is a example,

```
public class LenArray {
    public static void main( String[ ] args ) {
            // Initialization
        int [ ] myArray = { 1, 2, 3, 4, 5, 6 };
            // Declaration of an array
        int [ ] myCopy;
            // Assign an array to the declared variable myCopy
        myCopy = myArray; // Two handles to the same array!
        for( int i =0; i < myCopy.length; i++ )
                // Increment values of the integers
            myCopy[i]++;
    }
}
```

Multidimensional Array

Multidimensional Java arrays are created by making arrays of arrays, just as in C/C++. For example,

```
MDA[ ][ ] mda = new MDA[100][4];
```

makes a four-element array of 100 arrays of references to objects of type MDA. This statement does not allocate memory for any MDA objects. There are two things one should keep in mind:

1. Accessing an undefined array element causes a runtime exception called ArrayIndexOutOfBoundsException.
2. Accessing a defined array element that has not yet been assigned to an object results in a runtime NullPointerException.

Interface

A Java interface defines a set of methods but does not implement them. A class that implements the interface agrees to implement all of the methods defined in the interface, thereby agreeing to certain behavior. Thus, an interface is a named collection of method headers (without implementations). An interface can also include constant declarations.

An interface definition has two components: the interface declaration and the interface body. The interface declaration declares various attributes about the interface such as its name and whether it extends another interface. The interface body contains the constant and method declarations within that interface. The form is

```
public interface InterfaceName
{
    // All methods are implicitly public and abstract
    returnType methodName1( parameters );
    ...
// More methods
    //// All constants are public static final
    datatype VARIABLE_NAME = expression;
    ...
// More constants
}
```

For example,

```
public interface MyInterface
        // This is the interface declaration
{       // This is the beginning of the interface body
```

```
        void myService1( );      // This is a method declaration
        int   myService2( );     // Another method declaration
        long myConst1 = 100000;  //My constant
        int myConst2 = 25;       // Second constant
}                                // This is end of body
```

The declaration for the interface uses the two required elements of an interface declaration: (1) the interface keyword and (2) the name of the interface. It also use the public access modifier, which is optional as all interfaces must be public.

Interface Declaration

An interface declaration can have one other component: the keyword extends and a list of superinterfaces. The full interface declaration looks like

```
public interface InterfaceName
    extends Interface1, Interface2, ..., InterfaceN
 // May extend unlimited number of interfaces
{
    // All methods are implicitly public and abstract
    returnType methodName1( parameters );
    ...
// More methods
    //// All constants are public static final
    datatype VARIABLE_NAME = expression;
    ...
// More constants
}
```

For example,

```
public interface MyInterface2
        // This is the interface declaration
    extends interface1, interface2
        // Extends 2 interfaces
{       // This is the beginning of the interface body
    void myService1( );       // This is a method declaration
    int   myService2( );      // Another method declaration
    ...
    long MY_CONST1 = 100000; //My constant
    int MY_CONST2 = 25;       // Second constant
}                             // This is end of body
```

The public access specifier indicates that the interface can be used by any class in any package. If you do not specify that your interface is public, then your interface will be accessible only to classes that are defined in the same package as the interface.

An interface can extend other interfaces just as a class can extend or subclass another class. However, while a class can extend only one other class, an interface can extend any number of interfaces. The list of superinterfaces is a comma-separated list of all of the interfaces extended by the new interface. An interface inherits all constants and methods from its superinterfaces, unless the interface hides a constant with another of the same name or redeclares a method with a new method declaration.

Interface Body

The interface body contains method declarations for all of the methods included in the interface. The method declaration is followed by a semicolon (;) because an interface does not provide implementations for the methods declared within it. All methods declared in an interface are implicitly public and abstract. The use of these modifiers on a method declaration in an interface is discouraged as a matter of style.

An interface can contain constant declarations in addition to method declarations. All constant values defined in an interface are implicitly public, static, and final. The use of these modifiers on a constant declaration in an interface is discouraged as a matter of style. Any class can use an interface's constants from the name of the interface, like this

```
InterfaceName.CONSTANTS_NAME
```

For example,

```
MyInterface.MY_CONST1
```

Classes that implement an interface can treat the constants as though they were inherited.

Member declarations in an interface disallow the use of some declaration modifiers; we may not use transient, volatile, or synchronized in a member declaration in an interface. Also, we may not use the private and protected specifiers when declaring members of an interface.

Using an Interface as a Data Type

When we define a new interface, we are in essence defining a new reference data type. We can use interface names anywhere we can use any other data type name. For example, to declare an array of MyInterface

```
private MyInterface[] myInterfaces = new MyInterface[200];
```

Implementing the Interface

An interface defines a protocol of services. A class that implements an interface adheres to the protocol defined by that interface. To declare a class that implements an interface, include an implements clause in the class declaration. Our class can implement more than one interface (the Java platform supports multiple interface inheritance), so the implements keyword is followed by a comma-separated list of the interfaces implemented by the class. The form is shown below.

```
public class ClassName extends ParentName
implements Interface1, Interface2, ..., InterfaceN
{
    ...          //body of class
}
```

The implements clause follows the extends clause, if it exists. When a class implements an interface, it is essentially signing a contract. The class must provide method implementations for all of the methods declared in the interface and its superinterfaces. Or, the class must be declared abstract. The method signature (the name and the number and type of arguments) for the method in the class must match the method signature as it appears in the interface.

EXAMPLE

Interfaces are best understood through examples, so let us look at a concrete example of an interface and two classes that use it to interact. This example is fairly simple, but it shows us how to create and use an interface. It also gives us some insight as to why we need them and how to decide when to use an interface versus when to use a class or an abstract class.

First, we are going to write a timer class, MyTimer, that allows objects to register to be notified after a certain amount of time has elapsed. The method is letMeSleep. It will have two arguments: the object that wants to sleep and the amount of time it wants to sleep.

Second, we will use a form of the publish subscribe pattern for objects to register with the timer. The timer will maintain a list of objects that want to "sleep" for a specific period of time. It will maintain the time and keep track of which needs to be notified.

Third, when the time has elapsed, the timer will call the object's wakeUp method.

To satisfy the first requirement, an object calls letMeSleep method, which is implemented like this

```
public synchronized boolean letMeSleep(SleepInterface caller,
    long time)
{
    int index = findNextSlot();
            // Get the next available slot in list
    if (index == NOROOM) {   // Is there room for another client
```

```
        return false;                           // OUT of Room
     else {
        sleepers[index] = caller;
        sleepFor[index] = time;
        new AlarmThread(index).start();
            // Create new thread for object
        return true;       // You are on the list
     }
  }
}
```

If it has space, then it registers the caller, starts a new AlarmThread for it, and returns true. After the specified amount of time has elapsed the timer will call the caller's wakeUp method. This satisfies the second requirement.

This leads to the third requirement. An object that wants to use the timer must implement the wakeUp method (so that the timer can call it to notify the object after the time has elapsed). But how is this enforced? It is enforced through the data type of the object being registered. The first argument to the letMeSleep method is the object that wants to be awakened. The data type of this argument is SleepInterface, which is the name of this interface.

```
public interface SleepInterface {
    public void wakeUp();          //This is an abstract method
    public long ONE_SECOND = 1000;   // in milliseconds
}
```

The interface defines the wakeUp method but does not implement it. It also defines a useful constant that represents the number of milliseconds in a second. Classes that implement this interface "inherit" the constants and must implement wakeUp.

Any object that is a SleepInterface instance (and can, therefore, be passed into letMeSleep) implements this interface (i.e., implements all of the methods defined by the interface). Thus, a SleepInterface object implements the wakeUp method, thereby satisfying timer's third requirement. For example, check out the following small class that implements the SleepInterface interface. The DisplayClock class is an applet that displays the current time and uses the Timer object to wake it up every second so that it can update its display.

```
class DisplayClock extends Applet implements SleepInterface {
    . . .                      // rest of the class body
   public void wakeUp() {
       repaint(); // This updates the screen
       timer.letMeSleep(this, ONE_SECOND);
       // Call timer to sleep for ONE_SECOND
   }
}
```

Why Can't I Just Use an Abstract Class?

At this point, many readers wonder how an interface differs from an abstract class. An interface is simply a list of unimplemented methods. By definition, these are abstract methods. Wouldn't the following Sleeper class do the same thing as the SleepInterface interface?

```
abstract class Sleeper {
    public abstract void wakeUp();
}
```

The short answer is no. The two are not equivalent. If Sleeper is an abstract class, then all objects that wish to use MyTimer must be instances of a class inherited from Sleeper. However, many objects that wish to use MyTimer may already have a superclass. For example, the DisplayClock is an Applet; it must be an applet to run inside a browser. But Java does not support multiple inheritance. So DisplayClock cannot be both a Sleeper and an Applet; hence, we use an interface instead. This is the practical explanation of the problem. The conceptual explanation is this: MyTimer should not force a class relationship on its users. It does not matter what their class is. It simply matters that they implement a specific method.

Do Interfaces Provide for Multiple Inheritance?

Often interfaces are touted as an alternative to multiple class inheritance. While interfaces may solve similar problems, interface and multiple class inheritance are quite different animals, in particular,

- A class inherits only constants from an interface.
- A class cannot inherit method implementations from an interface.
- The interface hierarchy is independent of the class hierarchy. Classes that implement the same interface may or may not be related through the class hierarchy. This is not true for multiple inheritance.

Yet, Java does allow multiple interface inheritance. That is, an interface can have multiple superinterfaces.

What Can I Use Interfaces For?

We use an interface to define a protocol of behavior that can be implemented by any class anywhere in the class hierarchy. Interfaces are useful for the following:

- Capturing similarities between unrelated classes without artificially forcing a class relationship
- Declaring methods that one or more classes are expected to implement

- Revealing an object's programming interface without revealing its class (Objects such as these are called anonymous objects and can be useful when shipping a package of classes to other developers.)

RECOMMENDED APPROACH

The fundamental building block of object-oriented technology is the class. One of the first things we have to do in coding is to translate the classes given in the model into class definitions. Here are some guidelines for the translation and coding.

1. Variables (attributes) are declared as **private** members. This is necessary for information hiding.
2. Methods (services) are declared as **public** members. This is necessary for other objects to have access to the public services of an object of this class.
3. Services that are only used by methods within the class are declared as **private** members.
4. Variables (attributes) and methods are declared as **protected** members if they need to be accessible to subclasses (derived classes) and not to the client classes of the derived classes.
5. Data members must be defined in the class declaration.
6. To separate the function declaration (interface definition) from the function definition (implementation definition), place the code for the member functions outside the class declaration, either in the same or different file.
7. Do not make a data member public unless (a) you make it read-only or (b) changing the data member has no impact on the behavior of the object.
8. Do not make implementation-related member functions public.
9. Each member function of a class should either modify or provide access to data members of that class. (Strong Cohesion)
10. A class should depend on as few other classes as possible. (Weak Coupling)
11. Classes should not communicate via global variables.
12. Minimize information exchanged between classes. Call by pointer or reference can help.
13. All application generalization relationships are implemented as public inheritance.
14. Use Abstract Base Classes as appropriate.
15. Capitalize the first letter of the class name.
16. The first letter of variables (fields) should be lowercase.
17. The first letter of services (methods) should be lowercase.
18. The first letter of references should be lowercase.
19. Capitalize all the letters of primitive identifiers that are static final.

20. When creating a class for general use, we should include definitions for

- equals( )
- hashCode( )
- toString( )

21. When creating a class for general use, we should consider implementing Cloneable and Serializable.
22. For each class, consider including our test in main( ).
23. Keep classes small and focused.
24. Use comments liberally.
25. Rethrowing exceptions is good practice.
26. Consider creating a cleanup method to clean up code. Finalize method is not guaranteed to be called.
27. When overriding finalize method, we should call super.finalize() in the method.
28. Keep our variables as private; use protected only in rare situations.
29. When we have a fixed-size collection of objects, use array as it is faster and more efficient than collections.
30. Try to use interfaces as the fundamental construct, not classes or abstract classes.
31. Remember that code is read more than written.
32. Consider documenting your class in a manner consistent with javadoc.

EXAMPLE

In Java, the class definition is placed in the .java file. Below is an example of a class definition for Window class.

```
    // package statement would be here if there was one
    // import statement(s) would be here if there were any
    // start class definition
class Window
{
    // public services (instance methods)
    public void add_box (Length x, Length y, Length width,
        Length height) {
        ...code here... }
    public void add_circle (Length x, Length y, Length radius) {
        ...code here... }
    public void move (Length deltax, Length deltay) {
        ...code here... }
    public int group_selection ( ) {
        ...code here... }
    public void ungroup_selection ( ) {
```

```
        ...code here... }
//private attributes (variables)
private Length xmin, ymin;
private Length xmax, ymax;
private LinkScreen next;
    / /private method(s)
private void add_to_selection (Shape* shape) {
    ...code here... }
}
```

SUMMARY

Class Definition

The components of a class definition in a .java file are as follows:

1. header (keyword **class** and tag-name) plus inheritance and interface implemented
2. opening brace; i.e., {
3. all the public method definitions [i.e., service prototypes (method header) and bodies]
4. all the attributes (as variables) and private method definitions
5. close brace; i.e.,}

When we declare a member variable such as aFloat in MyClass,

```
class MyClass {
    float aFloat;
}
```

we declare an instance variable. Every time we create an instance of a class, the runtime system creates one copy of each of the class's instance variables for the instance. We can access an object's instance variables from an object by using the object reference.

Instance variables are in contrast to class variables (which we declare using the static modifier). The runtime system allocates class variables once per class regardless of the number of instances created of that class. The system allocates memory for class variables the first time it encounters the class. All instances share the same copy of the class's class variables. We can access class variables through an instance or through the class itself.

Methods are similar: our classes can have instance methods and class methods. Instance methods not only operate on the current object's instance variables but also have access to the class variables. Class methods, on the other hand, cannot access the instance variables declared within the class (unless they create a new object and access them through the object). Also, class methods can be invoked on the class, we do not need an instance to call a class method.

By default, unless otherwise specified, a member declared within a class is an instance member. The class defined below has one instance variable: an integer named x. In addition, it has two instance methods: z( ) and setZ( ). These methods let other objects set and query the value of instance variable x.

```
class AnIntegerNamedZ {
    int x;
    public int z() {
        return x;
    }
    public void setZ(int newZ) {
        x = newZ;
    }
}
```

Every time we instantiate a new object from a class, we get a new copy of each of the class's instance variables. These copies are associated with the new object. So, every time we instantiate a new AnIntegerNamedZ object from the class, we get a new copy of x that is associated with the new AnIntegerNamedZ object.

All instances of a class share the same implementation of an instance method; all instances of AnIntegerNamedZ share the same implementation of z( ) and setZ( ). Note that both methods, z( ) and setZ( ), refer to the object's instance variable x by name. Question is "if all instances of AnIntegerNamedZ share the same implementation of z( ) and setZ( ), isn't this ambiguous?" The answer is "no." Within an instance method, the name of an instance variable refers to the current object's instance variable, assuming that the instance variable is not hidden by a method parameter. So, within z( ) and setZ( ), x is equivalent to this.x.

Objects that are not members of the class must access only the services of the instance or of the class. What services they are allowed to access is controlled by the access control keyword associated with the service prototype.

We can, when declaring a data variable, specify that the variable is a class variable rather than an instance variable. Similarly, we can specify that a method is a class method rather than an instance method. The system creates a single copy of a class variable the first time it encounters the class in which the variable is defined. All instances of that class share the same copy of the class variable. Class methods can only operate on class variables; they cannot access the instance variables defined in the class.

We use class variables for items that we need only one copy of and which must be accessible by all objects inheriting from the class in which the variable is declared. For example, class variables are often used with final to define constants; this is more memory efficient than final instance variables because constants cannot change, so we really only need one copy).

Similarly, when declaring a method, we can specify that method to be a class method rather than an instance method. Class methods can only operate on class variables and cannot access the instance variables defined in the class.

We also learned about an abstract class as a class with at least one method with no implementation.

Nested, Inner, and Anonymous Inner Classes

A nested class is a class that is a member of another class.

A static nested class is a nested class that is declared static.

An inner class is a nested class whose instance exists within an instance of its enclosing class and has direct access to the instance members of its enclosing instance.

An anonymous inner class is an inner class with no name.

String and StringBuffer

String and StringBuffer provide several other useful ways to manipulate string data, including concatenation, comparison, substitution, and conversion to upper and lower case. In the Java Development Kit (JDK) documentation, java.lang.String and java.lang.StringBuffer summarize and list all of the methods and variables supported by these two classes.

Numbers

Java provides a large number of wrapper classes.

- Byte
- Double
- Float
- Integer
- Long
- Short
- DigDecimal
- BigInteger
- Boolean
- Character

Array and Multidimension Array

Arrays are true class constructs in the Java language.

Multidimension arrays are defined as arrays of array.

Interface

An interface defines a protocol of behavior that can be implemented by any class anywhere in the class hierarchy. Interfaces are useful for the following:

- Capturing similarities between unrelated classes without artificially forcing a class relationship
- Declaring methods that one or more classes are expected to implement
- Revealing an object's programming interface without revealing its class.

14

Implementing Static Behavior

One of the major goals in our analysis was specifying the behavior of all the services associated with a class. In the previous chapter, we learned how to declare a service identification using a function prototype. In this chapter, we will see how to turn a service specification into executable code. In the previous chapter, we declared the functions by specifying their prototype within the body of the class definition. Capturing the definitions of the service (i.e., to capture the behaviors of the services) is discussed in this chapter.

WHAT IS A SERVICE?

Whether we are using structured methods or object-oriented methods, there is a stepwise refinement process that involves decomposing a process (a service in object-oriented technology) into smaller subprocesses. Service constructs are used to capture the processes and subprocesses. The "main" program in Java is a sequence of service calls that may call other services.

The Java language provides many service[1] mechanisms to perform some tasks, and the Java libraries provide additional service mechanisms. An important example of additional service mechanisms supplied by libraries is the input/output mechanisms that experienced Java programmers take for granted. In fact, input/output is not directly part of the language. The java.io package defines and declares a family of standard streams for the programmer to handle input and output to files.

A Java class is made up of one or more service calls; one of which may be main(). Every program[2] execution begins with main(). When a Java program[3] is executing and encounters a service name, the service is called[4] and control is passed to the corresponding server object that provide the service. The server object does its work, control is passed back to the calling environment, which can then continue its processing. A simple example of a program is as follows:

```
class HelloWorld {
    public static void main ( String args[ ]  {
        System.out.println( "Hello Everyone!" );
    }
}
```

This program that is composed of one line is part of the service *main* in the class *HelloWorld*. The class *HelloWorld* is made of only one service *main*. The *println* service is a predefined library function of the *out* class, which is part of the *System* package. This is the most minimal program that can be written in Java.

For the reader interested in running this program, do the following:

1. Use your favorite edit to create a source file named

   HelloWorld.java

2. Enter the above code into the file. Be careful that all the parenthesis, braces, and quotes are there.
3. Compile the source using your favorite Java compiler. If you are using JDK, the java compiler is called javac. The command line is

   javac HelloWorld.java

4. When you compile with no errors, the output is in the file

   HelloWorld.class

---

[1] This is called a method in Java; this is called a function in C++

[2] Note that with browsers, it may appear as if there is no main because the main is contained within the browser.

[3] More accurately, when a thread is executing. Java is a multi-threaded programming language.

[4] In many textbooks, this is called invocation (i.e., the function is invoked).

which is in the same directory as your source file. This is the Java bytecode file.

5. Run the bytecode file by using the Java interpreter. If you are using the Java Development Kit (JDK), the java interpreter is called java. The command line is

```
java HelloWorld
```

6. You should see the following string printed on your screen as a response:

```
Hello Everyone!
```

In the example, the main service of the class HelloWorld is the program and it calls the println service of the out object/class.

METHOD DEFINITION

Member methods of a class are declared and defined inside the class body. A declaration consists of the service prototype. The service prototype is composed of a return type and a name, followed by a signature (i.e., list of arguments) enclosed in parentheses, followed by the optional keyword throws and a comma-separated list of exceptions. The definition(i.e., the code) follows the declaration and is enclosed in braces.

In this section, we will look at the method declaration (prototype) and the method body.

Method (Service) Prototype

In Java, there are two type of constructs that helps programmers manage the usage of services (called *methods* in Java specification and *functions* in C++): *class* and *interface*. In an *interface*, a service is only declared and is not defined, while in a *class*, a service may be both declared and defined. These constructs give programmers the ability to separate the "interface" (i.e., the interface specification) from the implementation (i.e., the code). The declaration is called a prototype (method prototype in Java) and has the following forms[5]:

```
type name ( argument-declaration list ) ;
//Method Prototype for Interface
or
```

---

[5] There are actually two more fields: access-specifier and the "throws list-of-exceptions," which are both optional. The access-specifier has been discussed in Chapter 13 and the throw is a keyword that tells the compiler that this service may throw the following list of exceptions.

```
type name ( argument-declaration list )    // Method Prototype for Class
       ( class body  }                     // Class Body for class
```

Here, type is the return type of the service that may be either a primitive data type or a user-defined data type or void. The name is the service (method) name.

The signature (i.e., list of arguments) consists of a comma-separated list of argument type and argument name pairs. An argument type is any valid Java data type. This includes primitive data types such as doubles, floats and integers, and reference data types such as objects and arrays. This list defines the data types of the values that the caller must provide to the service. An argument name may follow each type specifier. When you declare an argument to a Java method, you may provide a name for that argument. This name is used within the method body to refer to the item.[6] In Java methods, arguments are passed by value.[7] When invoked, the method receives the value of the variable passed in. When the argument is of a primitive data type, pass-by-value means that the method cannot change its value. When the argument is of reference type (i.e., all non-primitive data types) pass-by-value means that the method cannot change the object reference but can invoke the object's methods and modify the accessible variables within the object.

For example, the method declaration and definition of a service that returns the greatest common denominator is

```
public int greatest_common_denominator( int arg1, int arg2 ) // method
declaration
/* This is the method definition  */
{    // return the greatest common denominator
    int temp;
    while ( arg2 )
    {
        temp = arg2;
        arg2 = arg1 % arg2;
        arg1 = temp;
    }
    return ( arg1 );
}   //End of method definition
```

Method Implementation

In Java, how a service does its work is called the *method definition*[8] or the *implementation*. For all services (methods) declared within a class, the implementation must

---

[6] A method argument name may be the same name as one of the class's member variables. If this is the case, then the argument is said to hide the member variable. To access the member variable, you must reference it through this—the current object:

[7] This is often the source of confusion—a programmer writes a method that attempts to modify the value of one its arguments and the method does not work as expected.

[8] We have been calling this the method in earlier chapters.

be included as a block of code enclosed in curly braces after the method prototype (declaration). The form is

```
type name ( argument-declaration list )    // Method Prototype for Class
{ class body  }                            // Class Body for class
```

The actions performed when a service is called are specified between the braces. The collection of statements or actions is sometimes called the *body* of the service and is also a *block* from a programming perspective. A method may cause another service to be executed by calling the other service within the body of itself.

A service call can cause one of the services to be invoked at runtime. A service invocation transfers control to the method being called and suspends execution of the calling method. When the called method has completed, the suspended calling method resumes execution at the point immediately following the call.

Below is an example of a service definition within a class construct.

```
public class MyIntegers {
        private int myNo = 25;
            /*The line below is the service prototype */
        public int getMin( int yourNo )
            /* The open brace starts the service implementation  */
        {   if ( yourNo < myNo )
            then return ( yourNo );
            else return ( myNo );      }
    /* The closed brace ends the service definition */
    }
```

The fourth line (third line of code) is the method prototype for the getMin service. The type that precedes the method name determines the data type of the value that the service returns; thus, the data type[9] of the return value is int. The return mechanism will be explained below. The method name is self-explanatory, and the signature is a list of parameters (arguments) that the method expects the caller of the service to provide. Parameters are syntactically identifiers, and as such they can be used in the implementation of the service.[10] In our example, there is one argument that has the data type of int.

The service implementation (definition) is everything after the method prototype starting with an open brace and ending with a close brace. In our example, it is the lines 6 through 8. Note that the syntactic identifier for the parameter is used in the implementation code.

---

[9] The access scope value of *public* will be explained in the next section.

[10] Technically, these are formal parameters because they are placeholders for actual values that are passed to the service when it is called. Upon service invocation, the values of the argument corresponding to the formal parameter are used in the implementation code when it is executed.

The return statement has two purposes. First, when a return statement is executed, control is passed immediately back to the caller. Second, if an expression follows the keyword return, the value of the expression is returned to the caller. When an expression exists, it must be evaluated to the type declared in the method prototype. Note that when there is no expression, the return data type of the service must be void. This is used when the caller does not expect a value to be returned.

Return Type

The return type plus the argument list defines the public interface of the service. The calling function needs to know only the prototype to call the service. As shown in the previous chapter, the prototype, which includes the public interface, is declared within the class definition.

The return type of a function may be either a primitive data type or a user-defined type or void.[11] For example, consider the following lines of code:

```
public class Dog {
    //  public  service (methods) only
    public int  getAge( ) { ... code is here...}
    public String getName( ) { ... code is here...}
    public Gender getSex( ){ ... code is here...}
    public void setAge( int newAge ){ ... code is here...}
    public Dog  getDog( ) { ... code is here...}
    ...
}
```

The getAge() service has a primitive return type, the getName() service has a String return type, the getSex() service has a user-defined return type, and the setAge() function has a void return type. The getDog() function has a user-defined return type and returns a reference (handle) to an instance of the class Dog.

Neither an array nor a prototype may be specified as a return type. However, when you return a reference to an object, there are some pitfalls of which you need to be aware (see "Passing Arguments"). A method without an explicit return value is assumed to have a return type of int; thus, a service that does not return a value must declare a return type of void.

Return Statement

The return statement is used to terminate a method that is currently executing and return control to the calling function. There are two forms for the return statement, *return* and *return expression*.

The first return statement is used when the return type is void and the second is used for the non-void return types. The expression may be arbitrarily complex and

---

[11] A service that does not return a value has a return type of *void*.

may involve a service call. However, for ease of maintenance, we recommend that the expression be only a variable of return type. An implicit conversion will be applied, if possible, in instances when the variable is not of the return type. A method can return only one value. If the application logic requires that multiple values be returned, the developer might do any of the following:

- Return an aggregate data type that contains multiple values. In this case, the developer creates a class to represent the aggregate and usually returns a reference to that class.
- Formal arguments of a class is passed by reference. This allows the method to have access to the lvalue of these arguments. Then the lvalue may be used to change the rvalue of these variables.
- A public static (i.e., quasi-global) variable may be defined and used as a second value that is returned by convention. We do not recommended this.

Only the first method is recommended for object-oriented technology when multiple values need to be returned. The second method is used when the service must access the member services of that variable (object). The third method should rarely be used for the following reasons:

1. The methods that utilize the public static variable(s) now depend on the existence and type of the static variable. This makes reuse more difficult.
2. There is a loss of encapsulation. Public static variable dependencies increase the likelihood of introducing bugs when programs are modified.
3. If a public static variable has an incorrect value, the entire program must be searched to find the error; there is no information hiding.
4. Public static variables violate the information hiding and encapsulation principles of object-oriented technology.
5. Recursion is more difficult to get correct.

BODY

All legal Java elements may be used in the body of a Java method. In addition, you can

- Use *this* in the method body to refer to members in the current object. The current object is the object whose method is being called.
- Use *super* to refer to members in the superclass that the current object has hidden or overridden.
- Use declarations for variables that are local to that method.

this

Typically, within an object's method body we can just refer directly to the object's member variables. However, sometimes we need to disambiguate the member variable name if one of the arguments to the method has the same name. For example,

```
public class Point {
    Point( x, y ) {
        this.x = x; //  "x" refers to the argument
        this.y = y;
    }
    private int x, y;
}
```

Some programmers prefer to always use *this* when referring to a member variable of the object whose method the reference appears. Doing so makes the intent of the code explicit and reduces errors based on name sharing. We can also use *this* to call one of the current object's methods. Again this is only necessary if there is some ambiguity in the method name and is often used to make the intent of the code clearer.

super

If our method hides one of its superclass's member variables by using the same name within our class, our method can refer to the hidden member variable through the use of *super*. Similarly, if our method overrides one of its superclass's methods, our method or any method within our class can invoke the overridden method through the use of super. For example,

```
class ClassA {
    protected boolean status;
    void myService() {
        status = true;
    }
}
```

and its subclass, which hides status and overrides myService,

```
class SubClass extends ClassA {
    boolean status;
    void myService() {
        status = false;                    // Update the local variable
        super.myService();     //  Access the superclass's myMethod
        boolean superStatus = super.status;  // Access the superclass's
        status
    }
}
```

The myService of the subclass does the following. First, it sets status (the one declared in SubClass that hides the one declared in ClassA) to false. Next, it invoked its superclass' overridden method. This sets the hidden version of the status (the one declared in ClassA) to true. Then it captures the superclass' status in a local variable.

Local Variables

Within the body of the method we can declare more variables for use within that method. These variables are local variables and live only while control remains within the method. For example,

```
findPoint(Point p , Point[] arrayOfPoints) {
    int i;        // local variable
    for (i = 0; i < arrayOfPoints.length; i++) {
        if (arrayOfPoints[i] == p)
            return p;
    }
    return null;
}
```

This method declares a local variable i that it uses to iterate over the elements of its array argument. After this method returns, i no longer exists.

Service Argument List

The argument list of a service may not be omitted. A service that does not take any arguments can be represented either with an empty argument list or the single keyword *void*. For example, the following two declarations of getAge are equivalent:

```
int    getAge()    { return age; }
int    getAge(void) { return age; }
```

The signature consists of a comma-separated list of argument types. An argument type is any primitive type or user-defined type. An argument name usually follows each type specifier. The argument name is used in the body of the service to access the argument as a variable of the defined type given in the signature.

Because it is used in the body as variables, each argument name appearing in a signature must be different from each other and different from the local variable names used in the body. The shorthand comma-separated type declaration syntax may not be used in the list of arguments.

Omitting an argument or using an argument of the wrong type would be caught at compile time because Java is a strongly typed language. Both the return type and the argument list of every service call are type checked during compilation. If there is a mismatch between an actual type and a type declared in the service prototype, an implicit conversion will be applied where possible. However, if an implicit conversion is not possible or if the number of arguments is incorrect, a compile time error is given.

We suggest that the argument list to any service be small. Some developers limit the number of arguments to seven; thus, less than seven. If one wants to adhere to this guideline, what does one do with services that require a long argument list? There are two ways to handle this:

1. The service may be trying to do too much; you may want to divide the service into two or more smaller specialized services.
2. Define a class type to do the validity checking. The validity checking can then be performed inside the class member service instead passing the data back to the caller. This provides better encapsulation and reduces the size of the code of the service.

It is sometimes impossible to list the type and number of all the arguments that might be passed to a service. In this case, you can suspend type checking by using ellipses (. . .) within the service signature. Ellipses tell the compiler that zero or more arguments may follow and that the types of the arguments are unknown. While Java supports this, a good analysis should prevent this from being a common practice.

PASSING ARGUMENTS

When a service is called, storage on a structure (referred to as the program's runtime stack) is allocated to the method. Furthermore, each formal argument is provided with storage space within the structure. The storage size is determined by the type specifier for the argument. That storage remains on the stack until the method is terminated. At that point, the storage is freed and is no longer accessible to the program.

The arguments found between the parentheses of the function call are referred to as the *actual arguments* of the call. Argument passing is the process of actual arguments initializing the storage of the formal arguments. We shall discuss argument passing mechanisms pass-by-value, pass-by-reference, and passing an array.

Pass-By-Value

The default process of argument passing in Java is to copy the rvalue of the actual argument into the storage allocated in the structure of the runtime stack for the formal argument. This is called *pass-by-value*.

In the process of pass-by-value, the contents of the actual arguments are not changed because the function access manipulates its local copies which is on the runtime stack. In general, changes made to these local copies are not reflected in the values of the actual arguments. Once the method terminates, these local values are not accessible to the program. This means that a programmer of the calling service does not need to save and restore argument values when making a service call.

Without a pass-by-value mechanism, each argument would have to be saved before a service call and restored after the service call by the programmer because they may be altered. Passing-by-value has the least potential for side effects and requires the least work by the programmer of the calling service.

```
In Java, all primitive data types are passed by value.
```

Unfortunately, as well-behaved as pass-by-value is, it is not suitable for every data type. When you need to pass a user-defined data type (i.e., either class or interface), we need to use pass-by-reference.

Pass-By-Reference (or Pointer)

The declaration of the formal argument as a user-defined data type overrides the default pass-by-value mechanism with the pass-by-reference mechanism.[12] The method receives the lvalue of the actual argument rather than a copy of the argument itself. This now gives the method access to the public services and public data of the object. This is very useful when the method needs to call services of the actual object.

EXAMPLES

Examples of the three "passing-by-value" mechanisms are shown below.

```
void Collision::calv(Ball ball1,  Length deltay)
{
    // this pass by reference; addresses to Ball and lside are sent to
    // the routine. The routine can call the services of Ball and Side.
}
```

In Java, the argument access syntax is shown below

```
void Collision::calv(Ball ball,  Side top)
{
    // here we use the operator "." to access the  methods of a
    //  class.
    ball.setYmin ( ball.getYmin() + top.getDeltay() );
    //assuming there are member functions called setYmin
    // getYmin for class Ball and getDeltay for class Side.
}
```

---

[12] Note for C++ programmer, an Array is just a user-defined data type. It behaves just like any other object.

IDENTIFIER'S SCOPE

Recall that an identifier is a name for a data item or object. The identifier must be unique when used, because the program usually uses the identifier to access the data (rvalue). This does not mean, however, that a name can be used only once in a program. A name can be reused if there is some context to distinguish between different instances of the name. A good example of using context is overloading a service name, as in the following:

```
void    setSex(char );
void    setSex(int );
```

This example shows the signature of a protocol being used as a context. The two services have the same name (setSex) so the name is overloaded. However, each service has a unique signature.

A second and more general context is *scope*. Java supports three kinds of scope: *file scope, local scope,* and *class scope.* A name may be reused in a distinct scope; each variable has an associated scope, which, together with the name, uniquely identifies that variable. A variable is visible (accessible) only to the code within its scope. For example, a local variable declared within a compound statement is accessible only by the statements within the compound statement.

Local scope is that portion of the program contained within the definition of a service, that is, the method block. Each method represents a distinct local scope. Furthermore, within a method, each compound statement (or block) containing one or more declaration statements represents an associated local scope. Local block scopes may be nested. The argument list is treated as being within the local scope of the method.

Class scope is where every class maintains its own associated scope. Within class scope are the names of all its class members.[13]

File scope is the outermost scope of a program; it encloses both local and class scope. It is that portion of the program that is not contained within a class or a function definition. In Java, we normally associate a package with the file scope.

The *scope operator* ("::") supports the ability of a line of code to access the static public methods or static public variables in another scope. An example of an object-oriented use of the scope operator is provided in Chapter 17 when static members are discussed.

POLYMORPHISM

All animals eat (that is part of the definition of an animal), but different animals eat in different fashions. This is an example of polymorphism. Here we examine the implementation of polymorphic methods in greater detail.

---

[13] Both data variables and member methods are within the class scope.

Overriding Methods

When a service of an object is called, the Java interpreter looks for the method definition (i.e., the code) in the class that created the object. If it does not find the method, it passes the call up the class hierarchy until a method definition is found. Thus, the class inheritance mechanism allows you to define and use methods repeatedly in subclasses without having to duplicate the code itself.

However, there are times when you want an object to respond to the same service call as defined in some class, but you want it to behave in a different manner. In this case, you can override that method. Overriding a method involves defining a method in a subclass that has the same prototype (name, arguments, return type, etc.) as the method in the superclass. Now, when the service is called, it will find the method in the subclass first and it will be executed instead of the one in the superclass. For example,

```java
//This is the two dimension class
public class TwoDimension {
    public void printMyCord( )// This print my coordinates
        { System.out.println( "X coordinate is " + x +
        ", Y coordinate is " + y + "."); }
    private int x = 5;
    private int y = 75;
}


//This is the three dimension class
public class ThreeDimension extends TwoDimension {
    public void printMyCord( )// This print my coordinates
        { System.out.println( "X coordinate is " + x +
        ", Y coordinate is " + y +
            ", Z coordinate is " + z +  "."); }
    private int z = 55;
}


//This is the object that will instantiate the objects and use the
service
public class Test {
    public static void main( String args[] ) {
        TwoDimension printMe;
        printMe = new TwoDimension( ); // instantiate a TwoD object
        printMe.printMyCord( );        // print coordinates
        printMe = new ThreeDimension( );
        // instantiate a ThreeD object
        printMe.printMyCord( );        // print coordinates
    }
}
```

The results are as follows: the first statement should output the following text:

```
X coordinate is 5, Y coordinate is 75.
```

and the second statement should output the following text:

```
X coordinate is 5, Y coordinate is 75, Z coordinate is 55.
```

Calling the Original Method

There may be two different purposes to override a method of a superclass:

1. To replace the definition of the original method completely.
2. To augment the original method with additional behavior.

We have just shown you how to do the first; override a method in a subclass by giving that method a new definition. However, if you want to augment the method, you must be able to call the original method in the body of the overriding method. To call the original method from inside a method definition, use the *super* keyword to pass the method call up the hierarchy. For example,

```
// Superclass
public class MyParentClass {
    public theService( String a, String b, int c )
        {  .... a lot of code here...}
    ... // more code
}

// Subclass
public class MyChildClass {
    public theService( String a, String b, int c )
        // child's theService method
        {    // some code here
            super.theService( a, b, c );    // call the parent's
            //theService method
            // some more code here
        }
        // end of child's theService method
    ...    // more code
}
```

The super keyword is a placeholder for this class's superclass; this is similar to this keyword being a placeholder for the class.

CREATING OBJECTS AND DESTROYING OBJECTS

We have learned how to implement classes and their associated methods. However, actions and tasks that we expect an application/system to perform are usually on specific objects. In fact, we explained the object-oriented communication and control mechanisms as a message passing paradigm between objects. We should expect that the execution of the program does not operate on classes but on a specific object(s). For a program to be able to operate on a specific object, it must be able to create and destroy it. In this section, we will learn how objects are created and managed by the program.

Introduction

An object needs memory and some initial values when it is used by the program. For most of the primitive data types supplied by the language, the language provides for this through declarations that are also definitions. For example,

```
public class Example {
    public void funx( )
        {
            int n = 300;
            short z[100];
            String a = "this is a string";
            . . .
        }
        ...
}
```

All the objects (i.e., n, z[100], and a) are created at function (block) entry when the function funx() is called. Typically, memory space is taken from a runtime system stack. The int object n would be allocated four bytes off the stack, the array of short object z would be allocated 200 bytes off the stack, and the a would be allocated 32 bytes off the stack. In each case, the compiler generates the code for the construction and initialization of these objects. Furthermore, because these are local variables the compiler will generate the code to deallocate these objects upon exit from the function.

In creating user-defined data types (classes), the user of these data types (classes) can expect similar management of the class-defined objects. A class needs a mechanism to specify object creation and object destruction behavior, so that other functions can use objects of this class in a manner similar to the primitive data types.

Constructor Methods

In addition to the services that you define, you also need to declare and define some constructor methods in your class definition. A *constructor method* is a special method that defines how an object is initialized when it is created. It allows[14] the client programmer to initialize data values of data members of the object, change values of static variables of a class, and create aggregate objects.[15] A constructor may be overloaded and can take on arguments. Overloading is commonly used as a vehicle to provide a set of alternative initializations.

Constructors look a lot like a method with the following differences:

- Constructors must have the same name as the class name.
- Constructors may not have a return type.
- Constructors may not throw exceptions.
- Keywords of *final* and *static* are not meaningful for constructors and should not be used.

For example, we will add two constructors to Person example:

```
class Person
{
    //constructors
    Person( )   {  ; }  //Normally there would be code in the
      //definition
    Person( String pName, char pGender, int pAge )
        { name = pName; gender = pGender; age = pAge; }
    // member methods
    ...      //instance and class methods are not shown here
    // data variables
    private String  name;
    private char gender;
    private int age, height, weight;
}
```

In the first constructor, we show the default constructor: Person(). If you provide no implementation for the default constructor (as we have shown here), you do not need to explicitly declare and define it. The compiler does this for you for every class that you define. In the second constructor, we show three arguments that are used to initialize the values of three of our instance variables.

These constructor methods are normally called when a program uses the "new" to create a new instance of a class. For example,

```
Person peter = new Person( );  // Use the default constructor
Person paul  = new Person ( "Paul Jones", 'm', 25 );  //Use a
  //user-defined constructor
```

When this occurs, Java

1. Allocates memory for the object by getting storage from the heap.

---

[14] We can also use static initializers and instance initializers to provide initial values for class and instance members when you declare them in a class.

[15] A constructor is called only at instantiation (i.e., when object is created).

2. Initalizes the object's instance data variables to either their initial values (as specified by the code) or to a default value (if not specified in the code). The default value for number is 0, objects is null, booleans is false, and character is "0."

3. Calls the class constructor method (as specified by the signature in the call). You may have many constructors, but each must have a unique signature.

Thus, in the first new statement, Peter's instance variable values are: name is a null string, gender is "0", age is 0, height is 0, and weight is 0. Paul, which is instantiated using the user-defined constructor, has the following instance variable values: name is Paul Jones, gender is "m," age is 25, height is 0, and weight is 0.

Note that the constructor has no return-type and cannot use a return-expression statement. Because initialization is usually linear code, the return statement is usually not written. Moreover, there is usually nothing complicated about the constructor code.

A constructor (and any prototype) may specify a default value for one or more of its arguments using the initialization syntax within the signature. For example, consider the following prototype for a constructor of Person that initializes only the name, sex, and age of a Person object:

```
Person(String n, char s='U',  int a= -1);
```

This constructor provides a default argument initializers that can be invoked with or without a corresponding actual argument. If an argument is provided, it overrides the default value; otherwise, the default value is used. For example,

```
main()
{
   Person baby1 = new Person("Undecided");
   // This is a baby in infancy
   Person baby2 = new Person("Susan", 'F');
   //  This is a baby girl in infancy
   Person bill = new Person("Bill Gates", 'M', 35);
   // This is Bill Gates in middle age
   Person rich = new Person ("Rich", , 50);
   // This is an illegal use of default values
   Person p50 = new Person(, , 50);
   // This is an illegal use of default values
};
```

Note that the arguments to the call are resolved positionally. A programmer must then do the following:

• Specify the default initializer for all or only a subset of its arguments.

- Supply the rightmost uninitalized argument with default initializer before any arguments to its left may be supplied.
- Specify the default initializer(s) in the service declaration.
- Arrange the arguments so that those most likely to take user-specified values occur first.[16]

Calling Another Constructor

Some constructors that you define may have the same behavior as a previous constructor plus a little bit more. To avoid duplicating identical behavior in multiple constructor methods in a class, it makes sense to be able to just call the common constructor from within the body of the other constructors. Java provides a special syntax for doing this. The prototype is

```
this( arguments );
```

The arguments to the this (keyword) are the appropriate arguments to the constructor being called. Note that this calls a constructor within the same class and that the call may only be made within a constructor method.

Overloading Constructors

Like all other methods, constructors may also take a varying numbers and types of parameters, enabling you to declare and define as many constructors as necessary to create objects with any combination of initialized values. There is a significant restriction that must be observed when creating many constructors. In particular, the argument lists of constructors must be type distinguishable. This is illustrated in the example below

```
class Point {
    Point(int x, int y) { ; }
    Point(int y, int x) { ; } // This is not type distinguishable from
    //the above
    ...
}
```

This example would give a compiler error, as we cannot distinguish which of the two definitions should be used in the following example:

```
p = new Point(3,4); // is 3 supposed to be x or y?
```

---

[16] This is done because once a default is used for an argument, all arguments to the right of it must also be defaulted.

Calling Sequence of Constructors

Constructors can not be technically overridden as they must be the same name as the current class. Thus, you do not inherit constructors and you must create new constructors for each class in the inheritance hierarchy. Much of the time this works as the Java interpreter in the creation of an object first calls the class's constructor, then it calls the constructors with the same signature for all of its superclasses. So the initialization moves up the hierarchy tree as each superclass constructor is called.

However, if you want to change how your object is initialized (i.e., not only initializing the new variables that has been added but also to change values for the variables inherited from the superclasses), you must explicitly call the superclass's constructors and then change whatever you need to change.

To call the constructor of the superclass, you use the following prototype:

```
super( arguments );
```

Similar to using the this constructor, the super constructor calls the constructor of the immediate superclass (which will in turn call the constructor of its immediate superclass and so on). For example,

```
// Superclass
public class MyParentClass {
    public MyParentClass( String a )
        {   myString = a + "special";}
    ...     // more code
    protected String myString;
}


// Subclass
public class MyChildClass {
    public MyChildClass( String a, String b, int c )
        {
            super( a );     // call the parent's constructor
            myString = myString + b + "tail = " + c;
            ...         // some more code here
        }
            ...     // more code
}
```

In this example, you see that the child method modifies the parent's variable myString after it has been initialized by the parent's constructor. Note that the parent's constructor must be called before the code of the child's constructor can modify the variable of the parent.

Visibility of Constructor

We can specify what other objects can instantiate an object of your class by using an access specifier in the constructors' declaration.

- Private. No other class can instantiate the class. The class may contain public class services (sometimes called factory methods), and those methods (code of the services) can construct an object and return it, but no other classes can.
- Protected. Only subclasses of your class and classes within the same package as the class can create instances of it.
- Public. Any class can create an instance of your class.
- No specifier. Only classes within the same package as the class can construct an instance of it.

Finalizer Method

The intent of the finalizer method is to be the equivalence of the destructor in C++ without worrying about garbage collection. The finalizer method is called just before the object is garbage collected and its memory reclaimed. The finalizer method is simply finalize( ). The Object class (mother of all classes) defines a default finalizer method that does nothing. When a useful finalizer method is needed, you need to override the finalizer method by using the following prototype:

```
protected void finalize( )
```

Inside the body of the finalize method, include any clean up you want to do. Typically, it is used to destroy complex or aggregate objects, or change values of the static variables of a class. You should also call super.finalize( ) to allow your super-classes to finalize also.

Because garbage collection in most Java Virtual Machines (JVM) are very poor, most large development projects try to avoid garbage collection and you may need to have the clean up done (for example, breaking of relationships) well before garbage collection anyway. We strongly recommend that you call the finalizer method everywhere you would have called a destructor in C++; thus, for most applications, having automatic garbage collection is of limited value to the programmer.

CONSTRUCTOR AND FINALIZER CODING GUIDELINES

This section summarizes coding guidelines on constructors and the finalizer method.

Constructor Coding Guidelines

- Constructors create instances from a class definition.

- The instance space is allocated before any user-defined constructor is called.
- Constructors can be defined with values to initialize data members or to be passed to setup methods.
- Constructors implicitly return an instance of a class.
- In coding the constructor, do not define a return type or make an explicit return.
- A class can have many constructors, each of which accepts different arguments.
- Each class should define a default constructor (no args), a copy constructor (arg = a reference to the same class), and an assignment operator.
- Constructors should be used for data member initialization.

Finalizer Coding Guidelines

- There is only one finalizer method per class.
- If you do not write one, the compiler will provide a standard one, but it may not be what is needed.
- Finalizer does not take any arguments.
- A finalizer method should perform any necessary cleanup before an object is destroyed.
- Any type of operation can be performed within the finalize() method. Usually, they are used to destroy complex or aggregate objects or change the values of the static variables of a class.

RECOMMENDED APPROACH

In writing the code for the class definition in .java file, the data variables are declared and may be defined, but the functions are both declared and defined.

To help us code the method body, the following coding rules for instance member functions are given:

1. A member method has access to:

   - All members (data and services/methods) of the object
   - All arguments passed to it via the calling object
   - All local variables within its (method) scope
   - Global variables (i.e static public variables) within its class scope
   - *this*, which is a pseudo data member of any object (contains the address of the object)

2. When you need to declare local variables, keep variables at the smallest possible scope.
3. When you need to access a function of a superclass, place the superclass name and scope operator before the service name.

To close this section, we show the usage of the coding rules to our example as follows:

```
public class Person
{
// member functiors
    public String     getName( )  const { return name; }
    public char       getSex( )   const { return sex; }
    public int        getAge( )  const { return age; }
    public void       setSex( char s ) { this.sex = s; }
    public void       setAge( int a )
        { if a > Person::defaultAge then age = Person::defaultAge; else
        age = a; }
// data members
    public static final int defaultAge = 39;
    private String name;
    private char sex;
    private int  age, height, weight;
}
```

SUMMARY

To implement the service specification, we can place the code in .java file. Coding the service specification is more restrictive than coding a procedural function. The rules for coding a method are

1. A member method has access to:

   - All members (data and functions) of the object
   - All arguments passed to it via the calling object
   - All local variables within its (method) scope
   - Class global (static) variables within its class scope
   - *this*, which is a pseudo data member of any object (contains the address of the object)

2. When you need to declare local variables, keep variables at the smallest possible scope.
3. When you need to access a service of a superclass, place the superclass name and scope operator before the service name.

We use constructors and finalizer to create and delete objects in our application. Here is a review of this topic.

- To create an instance of a class, a special constructor operation must be used.
- Multiple constructors for a single class can be defined, distinguished by the number and types of their arguments.

- A constructor is executed whenever a new instance of a class is requested.
- Each class has one finalizer method.
- Finalizer method do not take any arguments.
- A finalizer method should perform any necessary cleanup before an object is destroyed.
- Any type of operation can be performed within a constructor or destructor.
- Within the finalizer method, the superclass's finalizer method should be called.

15

Implementing Dynamic Behavior

One of the major goals in our analysis was specifying the behavior of all the services associated with a class. In the previous chapter, we learned how to turn a static behavioral specification into executable code. We captured the definition of static functions. In this chapter, we will see how to turn a dynamic behavioral specification into executable code. We will discuss capturing the definitions of the functions (i.e., to capture the dynamic behaviors of the services that are best modeled with a state machine).

In writing the code for a dynamic class, it is best to use a state machine that is part of a library supplied by a third party. If such a library is available, then use it. This book does not cover the implementation of dynamic behavior using such libraries, as the exact mechanism depends on the particular product used. Instead, we will show you a simplified way of writing code for a state model for instructional purposes. In the code we do not address the issue of atomic action that may not be interrupted as this is beyond the scope of this book.

ELEMENTS OF DYNAMIC BEHAVIOR

In this chapter, we capture dynamic behavior in the form of code. This is perhaps one of the most complicated aspects of object-oriented programming, as we are talking about coding methods that implement multiple kinds of behavior. Our task is straight-forward.

1.   We must capture information about states.

   • code identifying all of the allowed states
   • track the current state

2.   We must implement the actions performed.

   • the actions themselves are state independent

3.   We must implement the transition semantics.

   • transition guard conditions
   • exit action
   • transition actions
   • entry actions
   • do actions

4.   We may also need to implement continuous activity while an object is in a state.

We begin by examining the transformation of a simple state model into code. We then extend that to include nested substates and concurrent state machines.

SIMPLE STATE DIAGRAMS

To help illustrate implementing dynamic behavior we use the microwave oven example[1] developed in Chapter 8 and illustrated in Figure 15-1. The approach taken here consists of the following activities:

1.   Implement the actions performed by the object.
2.   Add state.

   • Introduce a set of constants for capturing state.
   • Add a state variable to the class.

3.   Introduce helper methods for managing state entry and exit actions.
4.   Implement the event handlers (methods) for responding to events.

Implement the Actions Performed by the Object

Implementing dynamic behavior is a matter of selecting the appropriate set of static behaviors to execute. As a result, we must first implement the actions identified in

---

[1] For instructional purposes on state model coding, we will assume that the microwave oven is the object; that is, there is no refinement of the oven class.

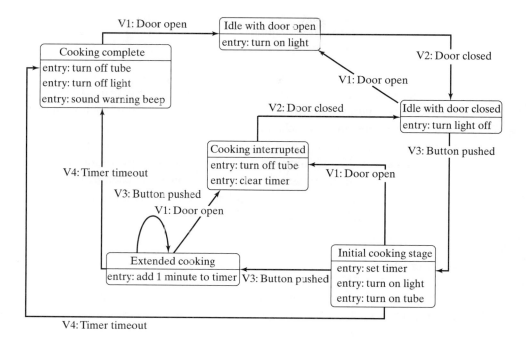

Figure 15-1   State Diagram for Microwave Oven from Chapter 8.

the state diagram. Each action is actually independent of state with which it may be associated[2] and is implemented using the mechanics described in Chapter 19. There is one method for each action that an object can perform.

From Figure 15-1 we can see that we have methods for turning on and off the light turning on and off the tube, adding a minute to the timer; clearing the timer; setting the timer; and sounding a beep. These methods are declared and defined as follows:

```
public class Microwave {
        protected void turnOnLight()      { light.turnOn( ); return; }
        protected void turnOffLight()     { light.turnOff( ); return; }
        protected void turnOnTube()     { tube.turnOn( ); return; }
        protected void turnOffTube();      { tube.turnOff( ); return; }
        protected void addMinuteToTimer() { timer.addT( 1 ); return; }
        protected void clearTimer()      { timer.clear( ); return; }
        protected void setTimer()      { timer.setT( ); return; }
        protected void soundBeep();       { beeper.beep( 1 ); return; }
        ...
        private Light light;
```

---

[2] That is, an action may be associated with many states and with transitions.

```
        private Tube tube;
        private Timer timer;
        private Beeper beeper;
    }
```

The methods are declared protected[3] because they are associated with state actions performed within the object and other objects that are not an instance of a subclass or an instance of a class in the same package should not be able to invoke them directly. This is one aspect of information hiding — we keep the basic primitive actions localized to the appropriate objects and require others to request more abstract services of the object. We also gave you some pseudocode in the body to show how these services may be implemented. We assume that the appropriate objects are instantiated when the oven object is created and that they have all the services requested.

Adding State

We capture the various states accessible to the object by defining a set of constants that represents a value for each distinct state. An object uses a data variable to track the current state. Some guidelines to follow are:

1. Create a state variable.

    - The number of theoretical states are too large.
    - When you add attributes that are state independent, it has no effect.
    - States are easier to create than repartioning of the variables.

2. Name the constant to capture accurately the condition of the class.

    - People make assumptions based on the name of that constant.

Future designers/programmers will make extensions based on their interpretation of the named constant. Example code for the microwave oven follows:

```
public class Microwave {
    // These are the constants for the states
    // The compiler will not enforce its usage; the programmer must do
    //this her/himself
    public static final  int InitialCooking = 1;
    public static final  int Complete = 2;
    public static final  int IdleDoorOpen = 3;
    public static final  int  IdleDoorClosed = 4;
```

---

[3] Because state machines usually have quite complex behavior that may require performance tuning, private is probably too restrictive.

```
            public static final  int Interrupted = 5;
            public static final  int Extended = 6;

            // This is the state variable
            protected int  myState =  IdleDoorClosed;  // Set value upon
            //instantiation
            //  Note that "protected int myState =  4;"  will compile; very
            //bad practice.
            ...
        };
```

We defined six symbolic constants: InitialCooking, Complete, IdleDoorOpen, IdleDoorClosed, Interrupted, and Extended. They have class scope, and they are made accessible to everyone. The myState data variable holds the current or active state. Because Java does not support enumerated data types, it is the responsibility of the programmer to use the symbolic constants instead of the direct values.

Introduce Helper Methods for Managing State Entry and Exit Actions

Two additional helper methods are defined to capture the behaviors associated with entering and exiting states. These methods are declared as private. All actions to be performed on state entry (or exit) are now localized to one method.[4] This frees us from having to repeat the same set of code in multiple places within our program. The code for this follows.

```
    private void onEntry() {
        switch (myState) {
        case InitialCooking:
            setTimer();
            turnOnLight();
            turnOnTube();
            break;
        case Complete:
            turnOffTube();
            turnOffLight();
            soundBeep();
            break;
```

---

[4] Capturing all of the entry or exit behaviors for all of our states in one method might be viewed by some as increasing coupling, but we are actually decreasing coupling by introducing a new abstraction. Code for capturing entry into a particular state is localized in this one method as opposed to coding a duplicate within every method that produces a transition. The alternative, for objects with complex behaviors, would be to introduce a single method entry or exit for every state. This has the effect of significantly increasing the overall complexity of our object. In this example, it is the difference between adding one method and six methods.

```
        case IdleDoorOpen:
            turnOnLight();
            break;
        case IdleDoorClosed:
            turnOffLight();
            break;
        case Interrupted:
            turnOffLight();
            clearTimer();
            break;
        case Extended:
            addMinuteToTimer();
            break;
        default:
            // should signal an error here
        }
    }
```

This code utilizes the switch statement of Java to select the appropriate actions to perform based on the current value of the myState data variable.

Two key points should be made; every case should end with a break statement and there should always be a default condition in the switch statement. Even though some states do not have actions to perform on entry and on exit, it is reasonable to include those states in the helper methods as it makes maintenance of the code easier.

Similar code can be written for an onExit() method and onTransition() method.[5]

The class definition is modified to declare these helper methods.

```
public class Microwave {
    // These are the constants for the states
    // The compiler will not enforce its usage; the programmer must do
    //this her/himself
    public static final  int InitialCooking = 1;
    public static final  int Complete = 2;
    public static final  int IdleDoorOpen = 3;
    public static final  int  IdleDoorClosed = 4;
    public static final  int Interrupted = 5;
    public static final  int Extended = 6;

    // This is the state variable
    protected int myState =  IdleDoorClosed;  // Set value upon
    //instantiation
```

---

[5] In this example, both onExit() method and onTransition() are not required as we do not have any states that require processing on exit nor do we have any transition actions.

```
// Helper methods for managing state
private void onEntry( )
    { ... the body of the onEntry given above ...  }
private void onExit( )
    {   ...the body is left as exercise for reader... }
...
}
```

This has implemented the logic to invoke the entry and exit actions to the various states.

Implement the Event Handlers (Methods) for Responding to Events

It is now necessary to introduce a method for each event to which the object must respond. There are four messages to which the microwave oven must respond: door open, door close, push button, and timer time-out. Capturing these messages introduces four new methods, doorOpen(), doorClose(), buttonPush(), and timerTimout().[6] There are no arguments in the methods because the corresponding messages do not have any arguments. In the case in which arguments had been present in a message, the method implementing it would include arguments. Thus, we have to add these services.

```
public class Microwave {
    ...             // This is the old stuff above
    // The PUBLIC SERVICES (I.e. the services that you advertise!)
    public void doorOpen( )    { ...see below for code ... }
    public void doorClose( )     { ...left as exercise for reader ... }
    public void buttonPush( )     { ...left as exercise for reader ... }
    public void timerTimeout( )  { ...left as exercise for reader ... }
    ...
}
```

These methods are declared as public because they are the interfaces by which other objects invoke dynamic behavior.

The state specific code for handling an event can be rather complex: it must perform the checks for the guard conditions, and if the guard conditions are met then it performs the sequence of actions required for the transition. In the case of the microwave oven, our task is simplified by the fact that we do not have guard conditions on the transitions. In this case, we implement the switch condition to select the appropriate code for the current state. This is similar to what was done for the helper methods. The cases key off the current state to select the state specific handler for the event. The logic is captured in code in the following fashion:

---

[6] We assume that these events are external to the "Oven" object.

```
void doorOpen() {
    switch (myState) {
    case InitialCooking:
        myState = Interrupted;
        onEntry();
        break;
    case Complete:
        myState = idle;
        onEntry();
        break;
    case IdleDoorOpen:
        // Shouldn't get here, the door is already opened!
        break;
    case IdleDoorClosed:
        myState = IdleDoorOpen;
        onEntry();
        break;
    case Interrupted:
        // Shouldn't get here, the door is already opened!
        break;
    case Extended:
        myState = Interrupted;
        onEntry();
    default:
        // signal an error condition here!
    }
}
```

All states should be represented in this case statement as a state is an internal property of an object and event generators send the event to the object without knowing the internal state. As a result, every state should handle the event in some fashion, even if it just means that the object ignores the event.

In some cases, an event can result in any one of several transitions based on the guard condition. To capture the logic of guarded transitions, we construct an if-else condition statement inside the case statement for each particular state. The if-else set of conditionals is structured from the most restrictive condition to the least restrictive condition. This assures that the appropriate transitions are performed for a given set of circumstance. An example is given below.

```
if (cond1) {          // most restrictive condition
    onExit();         // must do the exit action
    action1();        // must do the transition action
    state = state2;   // set the new state
    onEntry();        // perform the entry action for new state
}
else if (cond2) {     // less restrictive condition
    onExit();         // must do the exit action
```

```
            action2();        // must do the transition action
            state = state3;   // set the new state
            onEntry();        // perform the entry action
    }
    else                      // least restrictive condition
    {
        // must handle the default case
    }
```

This code performs the exit action for the past state, the action associated with the transition, and the entry action for the new state for each possible transition out of the past state for a given event. The final else condition handles the case where the state has a default action that it performs for that event.

The "do action" needs to be handled differently as it is not part of the atomic action and is a long, continuous action that can be interrupted. Internal transitions are also not handled. Both are beyond the scope of this book. One should probably use multithreading for the do action and perform an internal transition just by performing the exit and entry conditions.

NESTED STATE DIAGRAMS

Implementing nested state diagrams is only slightly more sophisticated than implementing simple state diagrams. The basic principles are identical. In the same way that we implemented state as a state variable, we use a substate data variable with a set of symbolic constants for identifying the substates.[7] In this section, we will use a modified version of the microwave oven that incorporates nested states within a cooking state as illustrated in Figure 15-2. Note that we have created two substates, Initial and Extended, to the state Cooking. All the changed code will be in **bold**.

Implement the Actions Performed by the Object

In exactly the same manner as was done for the simple state diagram, we first code all actions that can be performed by our microwave oven. The results are shown below.

```
public class Microwave {
        protected void turnOnLight()    { light.turnOn( ); return; }
        protected void turnOffLight()   { light.turnOff( ); return; }
        protected void turnOnTube()    { tube.turnOn( ); return; }
        protected void turnOffTube();   { tube.turnOff( ); return; }
        protected void addMinuteToTimer() { timer.addT( 1 ); return; }
```

---

[7] Note that the constants will probably be either private or protected. It is not advised to make substates public. Also there are other ways to implement substates that are beyond the scope of the book.

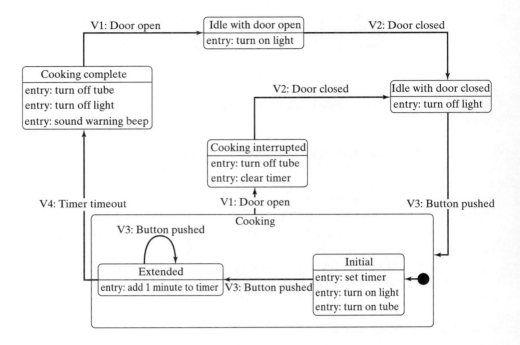

Figure 15-2   Microwave Example Utilizing Nested State Diagrams.

```
protected void clearTimer()      { timer.clear( ); return; }
protected void setTimer()        { timer.setT( ); return; }
protected void soundBeep();      { beeper.beep( 1 ); return; }
...
private Light light;
private Tube tube;
private Timer timer;
private Beeper beeper;
}
```

The code for this case is identical with the previous example.

Adding State

In this example, we now have five primary states with one of them having two sub-states. We shall introduce two sets of constants to capture this information. One set captures the primary states while the other captures the substates associated with cooking.

```
public class Microwave {
    ...              //The code above
    // These are the constants for the states
```

```
// The compiler will not enforce its usage; the programmer must do
//this her/himself
public static final int Cooking = 1;    //This has been created to
hold the substates
public static final  int Complete = 2;
public static final  int IdleDoorOpen = 3;
public static final  int  IdleDoorClosed = 4;
public static final  int Interrupted = 5;
public static final  int NotInState = 0;    //This is a substate,
used when substate is created
public static final  int Initial = 1;     //This is a substate
public static final  int Extended = 2;    // This is a substate
//These are the two state variables
private int myState = IdleDoorClosed;         //  This is the
  //primary state variable
private myCookingState = NotInState;    // This is the substate
  //variable for the Cooking state
...
}
```

As this example illustrates, the cooking state has a third state not illustrated in the diagram. This is necessary as when an instance of Oven is created, the "cooking" substate does not exist; the substate exits when the cooking state is entered. Thus, the "NotInState" is used to capture an implied semantics concerning the situation where the microwave oven is not in the cooking state.

Introduce Helper Methods for Managing State Entry and Exit Actions

As was done previously, we declare the same set of helper functions—onEntry() and onExit(). However, there are differences in their implementation to account for the substates for the cooking state. In addition, we add helper methods for the cooking substates.

```
public class Microwave {
    ...      //See above for all the code
    private void onEntry()         { ...code here... }
    // helper method for managing state
    private void onExit()          { ...code here... }
    // must have this now
    private void onCookingEntry() { ...code here... }
    // new helper method
    private void onCookingExit()  { ...code here... }
    // new helper method
    ...
}
```

The revised code for the onEntry() method appears below.

```
void onEntry() {
    switch (myState) {
    case Cooking:
        // This now lets us take care of managing entry into cooking
        //separately.
        onCookingEntry();
        break;
    case Complete:
        turnOffTube(); // this is the onEntry code
        turnOffLight(); // this is the onEntry code
        soundBeep(); // this is the onEntry code
        break;
    case IdleDoorOpen:
        turnOnLight(); // this is the onEntry code
        break;
    case IdleDoorClosed:
        turnOffLight(); // this is the onEntry code
        break;
    case Interrupted:
        turnOffLight(); // this is the onEntry code
        clearTimer(); // this is the onEntry code
        break;
    default:
        // should signal an error here
    }
}
```

The major difference from the previous example is that we now call a helper method for entry into the cooking state.[8] The code for the onCookingEntry() is responsible for setting the substate information and performing the entry actions required for the specific substate. In our case, this is simple because there is only a single entry point and no history.

```
void onCookingEntry() {
    switch (myCookingState) {
    case NotInState:
        myCookingState = Initial;
        onCookingEntry();
        break;
    case Initial:
```

---

[8] This example is rather trivial in the sense that cooking only has two substates. However, when a state has multiple substates and re-entry conditions based on past history these methods can become quite complex. The separation of managing substates into separate methods allows us to manage that complexity, by focusing on smaller portions of the problem at any given time.

```
        setTimer(); // this is the onEntry code
        TurnOnLight(); // this is the onEntry code
        TurnOnTube(); // this is the onEntry code
        break;
    case Extended:
        addMinuteToTimer(); // this is the onEntry code
        break;
    default:
        // shouldn't get here!
        break;
    }
}
```

If our microwave oven had more complex behavior while cooking, we might have to establish the appropriate entry substate and then use a switch statement to handle the variety of behaviors expected based on the specific entry substate.

We modify the onExit() method so that it calls the onCookingExit() method, which captures the exit conditions for substates.[9]

```
    void onExit() {
    switch (myState) {
    case Cooking:
        onCookingExit();
        break;
    case Complete:
        break;
    case IdleDoorOpen:
        break;
    case IdleDoorClosed:
        break;
    case Interrupted:
        break;
    default:
        // should signal an error here
    }
}
```

This allows us to capture more complex behaviors in the cooking state should they exist (or get added in the future). The implementation for this microwave oven sets the myCookingState data member to the NotInState value.

---

[9] The onExit() method was unnecessary in the simple state diagram because none of the states incorporated exit conditions. The version of the microwave presented here does not have explicit onExit actions but an implicit one associated with substate management.

Implement the Event Handlers (Methods) for Responding to Events

Finally, we have to implement the handler code for the events. This is similar to what was done before, but we now have to take into account the substates. This can be done in one of two manners:[10]

1. Incorporate additional switch statement within the primary event handler code.
2. Provide a helper method that captures handling events within a state.

If there are not many substates then the first approach may be preferable. In general, however, the second approach is the better approach. We will demonstrate the second approach here for the button pushed event. First we declare the appropriate substate handler methods.

```
public class Microwave {
    ...      //Assume all the code that we have discussed
    // These are the public services for the events
    public void buttonPushed() { ... code goes here... }
    public void doorOpen()     { ... code goes here... }
    public void doorClose()    { ... code goes here... }
    public void timerTimeout() { ... code goes here... }
    // These are internal services
    private void buttonDownInCooking()  { ... code goes here... }
    private void doorOpenInCooking()    { ... code goes here... }
    private void timerTimeoutInCooking() { ... code goes here... }
    ...
};
```

The button Pushed() method call invokes the appropriate state specific behavior. In the case of the cooking state, it invokes the buttonPushedInCooking() method. This is demonstrated in the code fragment below.

```
void buttonPushed() {
    switch (myState) {
    case Cooking:
        buttonPushedInCooking();      //All the details are handled by
         //the service; see below
        break;
    case Complete:
        break;
    case IdleDoorOpen:
        break;
```

---

[10] There are other ways of doing this; but the more sophisticated ways are beyond the scope of this book.

```
        case IdleDoorClosed:
            // If there were action on transition, it goes here
            myState = Cooking; // Change state to cooking
            onEntry( );  // Need to enter state of cooking
            break;
        case Interrupted:
            break;
        default:
            // should signal an error here
        }
    }
```

The buttonPushedInCooking() method implements the handling associated with the substates. This is shown below.

```
    void buttonPushedInCooking() {
        switch (myCookingState) {
        case NotInState:
            // This should not happen
            break;
        case Initial:
            onCookingExit();// In case we have exit condition
            myCookingState = Extended;
            onCookingEnter();
            break;
        case Extended:
            onCookingExit();// transition to same state.
            onCookingEnter();
            break;
        default:
            break;
        }
    }
```

The case for the Extended substate illustrates how transitions to self are implemented. First we execute the exit method for leaving the state and then execute the entry method for returning to the state.[11]

CONCURRENT STATE DIAGRAMS

Implementing concurrent state diagrams is only slightly more sophisticated than implementing nested state diagrams. We need to extend the thread class to

---

[11] In the unified modeling language (UML), you are also allowed to have events that only have actions and stay in the same state that is, without executing the exit and entry actions. The implementation of this capability is left as an exercise for the reader.

get parallelism. In the same way that we implemented state as a state variable, we use a state data variable with a set of symbolic constants for identifying the states of the parallel machines. In this section, we will use a modified version of the Microwave oven that incorporates both nested states and parallel state machines within a cooking state as illustrated in Figure 15-3.

Note that we have added a parallel state machine to the original nested sub-states. We also added two external events: a light-on and a light-off. These events allow the user of the microwave to turn on and off the light only when the microwave is in the cooking state.

Introduction

We use essentially the same code from the previous example. We only show you the changes that need to be made to the code, so please be aware of this as we go through the example.

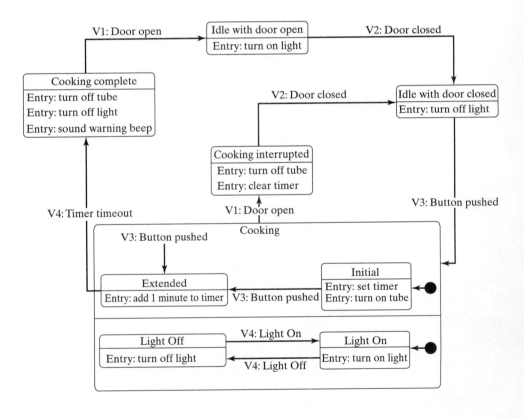

Figure 15-3   Microwave Example Utilizing Nested State Diagrams.

Changes to the Microwave Class

For understanding, we will discuss each of the elements of the state machine and discuss where the changes are.

1. **Actions Performed by the Object.** There is no changes as there is no new action.
2. **Adding States.** We take the substate data variable out of this class. We will put them in their own state machine.
3. **Helper Methods.** We will modify the code for two helper methods: onCookingEntry() and onCookingExit(). We will only modify the code for the case where the state value matches "Cooking."(Details will be given below.)
4. **Event Handlers.** We have to add two new event handlers. lightOnPushed() and lightOffPushed().

We start with the adding of two Thread objects to the represent the parallel state machines. The changes will be in **bold**.

```
public class Microwave {
        ...              //The code above
    // These are the constants for the states
    // The compiler will not enforce its usage; the programmer must do
      //this her/himself
    public static final  int Cooking = 1;       //This is the enclosing
      //state
    public static final  int Complete = 2;
    public static final  int IdleDoorOpen = 3;
    public static final  int  IdleDoorClosed = 4;
    public static final  int Interrupted = 5;
    //These are the one state variable and two threads for the parallel
      //state machines
    private int myState = IdleDoorClosed;       //  This is the primary
      //state variable
    private SubMach1 thread1;      // This is a parallel state machine
      //for "cooking tube"
    private SubMach2 thread2;    // This is a parallel state machine for
      //"light"
    ...
}
```

Now, we make the changes on the onCookingEntry() method.

```
void onCookingEntry() {
    // On entry to state cooking, neither thread will be active
    if thread1 == null
```

```
            then { thread1 = new SubMach1();   thread1.start(); }
         if thread2 == null
            then { thread2 = new SubMach2();   thread2.start(); }
         thread1.onEntry();   // Get state machine one to process
           //onEntry
         thread2.onEntry(); //    Get state machine two to process
           //onEntry
         default:
             // shouldn't get here!
             break;
         }
    }
```

Corresponding, we make the following changes to onCookingExit() method.

```
    void onCookingExit() {
        // On exit to state cooking, kill the substate state machines
        if thread1 != null
            then {  thread1.stop(); }
        if thread2 != null
            then { thread2.stop(); }
        default:
            // shouldn't get here!
            break;
        }
    }
```

In the above code, we have seen how the parallel state machines are created and destroyed. Now we need to see how they are used to process events. We do not show all the changes for each event handler.[12] All the changes are very similar. We show the buttonPushed(), and we add the two new event handlers: lightOnPushed() and lightOffPushed().

First, the buttonPushed() method is not changed. We change the helper method buttonPushedInCooking(). The changes are shown below.

```
    void buttonPushedInCooking() {
        thread1.buttonPushed();  // notify first state machine!
        thread2.buttonPushed();  // notify second state machine!
    }
```

We now add the one of the two new event handlers with its corresponding helper method. The second one is left as an exercise for the reader.

---

[12] Note that you can build a more flexible version by having an event handler as part of the state machine. We decided against adding this additional complexity in this book.

```
void lightOnPushed() {
    switch (myState) {
    case Cooking:
        lightOnInCooking();      //All the details are handled by the
          //service; see below
        break;
    case Complete:
        break;
    case IdleDoorOpen:
        break;
    case IdleDoorClosed:
        break;
    case Interrupted:
        break;
    default:
        // should signal an error here
    }
}


void lightOnInCooking() {
    thread1.lightOnPushed();  // notify first state machine!
    thread2.lightOnPushed();  // notify second state machine!
}
```

Creating a Parallel State Machine

We declared two new data variables: thread1 and thread2, which are of the class SubMach1 and SubMach2. We show how to write the necessary class SubMach1[13] for the parallel state machine that formerly was the nested substates in the following sections.

Extending Thread Class

To make the class SubMach1 run in a separate thread, we must have the class inherit from the Thread class.

```
public class SubMach1 extends Thread {
    // NOTE that we will go ahead and use the do nothing run method of
    thread
    // NOTE that the run method is not used. We just needed the thread!
    ... //  This is the body of the class. See below!
}
```

---

[13] The other state machine is left as an exercise for the reader.

Implement the Actions Performed by the Object

In exactly the same manner as was done for the simple state diagram, we first code all actions that can be performed by our specific state machine. The results are shown below.

```java
public class SubMach1 extends Thread {
    //Note that we only added the necessary actions!
    protected void turnOnLight()      { light.turnOn( ); return; }
    protected void turnOffLight()     { light.turnOff( ); return; }
    protected void addMinuteToTimer() { timer.addT( 1 ); return; }
    protected void setTimer()         { timer.setT( ); return; }
    ...
    private Light light;
    private Timer timer;
}
```

We only added the actions that were needed to support the present model. This makes the class smaller but less flexible.

Creating States

In this machine, we now have two states. We introduce two constants to capture this information.

```java
public class SubMach1 extends Thread {
    ...              //The code above
    // These are the constants for the state
    // The compiler will not enforce its usage; the programmer must do
      //this her/himself
    public static final  int NotInState = 0;  //This is state, used
      //when machine is created
    public static final  int Initial = 1;      //This is a state
    public static final  int Extended = 2;     // This is a state
    //These are the two state variables
    private int myState = NotInState;   // This is the state variable
    ...
}
```

The states are identical to the substates of the nested state diagram.

Introduce Helper Methods for Managing State Entry and Exit Actions

As was done in the simple state diagram, we declare the same set of helper functions[14]—onEntry() and onExit(). The onExit() method contains no action, so we make it a void method

```
public class SubMach1 extends Thread {
    ...      //See above for all the code
    private void onEntry()     { ...code below... }// helper method
    for entry actions
    private void onExit()        { ; }// helper method for exit actions
        ...
}
```

The code for the onEntry() method appears below.

```
void onEntry() {
    switch (myState) {
        case NotInState:
            myCookingState = Initial;
            onEntry();
            break;
        case Initial:
            setTimer(); // this is the onEntry code
            TurnOnLight(); // this is the onEntry code
            TurnOnTube(); // this is the onEntry code
            break;
        case Extended:
            addMinuteToTimer(); // this is the onEntry code
            break;
        default:
            // shouldn't get here!
            break;
        }
    }
        // should signal an error here
    }
}
```

Implement the Event Handlers (Methods) for Responding to Events

Finally, we have to implement the handler code for the events. This is similar to what was done before.

```
public class SubMach1 extends Thread {
    ...      //Assume all the code that we have discussed
    // These are the public services for the events
    public void buttonPushed()  { ... code goes here... }
```

---

[14] Note that you can also have nested states within this machine. This is again left as an exercise for the reader.

```
    public void doorOpen()     { ... code goes here... }
    public void doorClose()    { ... code goes here... }
    public void timerTimeout() { ... code goes here... }
    public void lightOnPushed() { ... code goes here... }
    public void lightOffPushed() { ... code goes here... }
    ...
};
```

The button Pushed() method is shown below.

```
void buttonPushed() {
    switch (myState) {
        case NotInState:
            // This should not happen
            break;
        case Initial:
            onExit();            // In case we have an exit condition
            myCookingState = Extended;
            onEnter();
            break;
        case Extended:
            onExit();// transition to same state.
            onEnter();
            break;
        default:
            break;
    }
}
```

Finally, we close by showing the code for the lightOnPushed() method:

```
void lightOnPushed( ) { ; } // In this case, we do not care!.
```

SUMMARY

To implement the state model for a class, we can use a third party state machine template or we can write our own state machine using the reference model above.

Coding the state machine is more restrictive than coding a static method. The rules for coding a state model are:

1. Create a state variable.
2. Name the state to capture accurately the condition of the class.
3. Use constants so that you can symbolically represent state values.
4. Use switch statements over if-then or if-then-else statements.
5. Always provide a default case.

6. Use break at the end of a clause.
7. Create private methods (subroutines) for common logic shared across clauses.

16

Implementing Generalization/ Specialization

In the previous chapters, we saw how an object is created (instantiated) and how static and dynamic behaviors are defined. To create objects properly, however, we also need to establish the proper relationships between objects. Now we will begin to look at implementing relationships. This chapter is devoted to the generalization/ specialization relationship.

INTRODUCTION

From a maintenance and development perspective, inheritance is the one mechanism that helps manage code sharing, code reuse, and code extensions. Through inheritance, developers can build new classes on top of an existing hierarchy of classes. This avoids redesigning and recoding every time from scratch. The new classes inherit both the methods and data variables from existing classes. Inheriting methods enable code sharing and thus reuse, while inheriting data variables enables structure sharing among objects. The combination of these two aspects of inheritance provides a very powerful software modeling and coding mechanism.

Java Inheritance Hierarchy

In Java, the extends clause declares that your class is a subclass of another; therefore, by definition, a *subclass* is a class that extends another class. A subclass inherits all of the members in its superclass that are accessible to that subclass unless the subclass explicitly hides a member variable or overrides a method. Note two things: (1) an override method may be accessed by using the super keyword, and (2) constructors are not members and are not inherited by subclasses. The term *superclass* refers to a class's direct ancestor as well as to all of its ascendant classes. We can specify only one direct ancestor for our class. Java does not support multiple class inheritance. However, even when we omit the extends clause from our class declaration, our class has a superclass. So, every class in Java has one and only one immediate superclass. Then we should ask: "Where does it all begin?"

The top-most class, the class from which all other classes are derived, is the *Object* class, which is defined in java.lang. The Object class defines and implements behaviors that every class in the Java system needs. It is the most general of all classes. Its immediate subclasses, and other classes near top of the hierarchy, implement general behavior; classes near the bottom of the hierarchy provide for more specialized behavior.

Generalization/Specialization Mapping to Inheritance

In object-oriented analysis and design, generalization/specialization is the mechanism of deriving a new category from an old one. That is, an existing category can be added to and the addition altered to create a specialized category. Because a category becomes a user-defined type in object-oriented programming, generalization/specialization in Java is implemented through inheritance via the mechanism of class derivation. In Java, generalization/specialization is implemented as a hierarchy of related types that share code and external interfaces (method prototypes).

When there is multiple generalization/specialization, there are two mechanisms that we can use:

- interface(s)
- aggregation with delegation

The rest of this chapter covers these topics.

INHERITANCE

Derived Class and Base Class

In Java, a derived class is used to define a subclass of a *base class* (superclass). A base class is any predefined class definition. A derived class inherits variables and methods from its *base class* (superclass) and all of its ancestors. The derived class can use these members as is, or it can hide the member variables or override the methods. All methods may be redefined unless a method is declared as final.[1] It then can be extended by adding both new data members and new member methods.When a class hierarchy is translated into a set of related derived classes, a base-class pointer may be used to address any object of the derived classes. The form for the subclass is as follows:

```
modifiers class class-tag-name extends parent's class-tag-name
```

Specifying a Derived Class

A class **Derived** can be derived from another class **Base** using the following form in the class header for **Derived**:

```
public class Derived extends Base
{
    // member declarations
};
```

An example of a standard class definition and a derived definition is given below:

```
public class Person
{
    public Person(String n, char s, int a)  { ... code is here... }
    public String    getName()             { ... code is here... }
    public char      getSex()              { ... code is here... }
    public int       getAge()              { ... code is here... }
    public void      setName(String n)     { ... code is here... }
    public void      setAge(int a)         { ... code is here... }
    // Variables
    private   String      name;
    private   char        sex;
    private   int         age, height, weight;
}
public class Employee extends Person
{
    public Employee(String  n, char s, int a, int n = 0)   { ... code
    is here... }
    public int       getSalary() {return salary;}
    public void      setSalary(int a) {salary = a; }
    // Additional Variable
    private   int     salary;
};
```

---

[1] This differs from C++, where the method must be declared as virtual.

In this example, **Employee** is a derived class and **Person** is the base class. Private members of **Person** are not accessible to the class **Employee**. For example, the class **Employee** has no way of accessing the weight data member, but it can access the age via the two functions getAge() and setAge(). "Class Employee" is a subtype of the type "class Person." An instance of **Employee** is also an instance of **Person**, but an instance of **Person** may not necessarily be an instance of **Employee**.

Frequently a derived class extends the base class by adding new members. In this example, **Employee** has added one new data member (salary) and three new functions (constructor, getSalary(), setSalary()). The results may be summarized as in Table 16-1.

Table 16-1 Relationships Along Lines of Inheritance for Services and Attributes

Class	Employee Services	Employee Attributes
Person	getName	String name;
	getSex	char sex;
	getAge	int age;
	setName	int height;
	setAge	int weight;
Employee	getSalary	int salary;
	setSalary	

This chart shows that every instance of **Employee** has its own data fields for name, sex, age, height, weight, and salary, and only the salary attribute is truly an "employee" semantic domain attribute. The other attributes of employee are in the "person" semantic domain. Similar reasoning should be applied to the services. For good cohesion and low coupling, applications dealing with an instance of **Employee** as an "employee" should never need to access the attributes associated with an employee being a person.[2] However, the services (methods) are shared and available to all the instances. In fact, the common services of **Person** are shared with other instances who are either instances of **Person** or from another derived class of **Person**.

Inheriting from a Derived Class and Implementing Association

A class can be derived from another derived class. For example, let us add **Manager** to the hierarchy of **Person** and **Employee** as follows:

```
public class Manager extends Employee
{     final static int Max = 20;
```

---

[2] The object-oriented paradigm and language allow an application access only to the services of Person when an instance of Employee is viewed as a Person object.

```
public Manager(String n, char s, int a, int n = 0) { ...
initialization code goes here ...}
    public Employee   getEmployee(int n) {return group[n];}
    public void setEmployee(Employee e, int a) {group[a] = e;}
    protected void finalize() {... free employees here ...  }
    //This is clean up code
    // Variables
    public Employee    group[Max];
}
```

In this example, **Manager** is the derived class and **Employee** is the base class. Private members of **Person** and **Employee** are not accessible to the class **Manager**. For example, the class **Manager** has no way of accessing the weight data member nor can it access the salary data member directly.

"Class Manager" is a subclass of the class "class Employee," which is a subclass of "class Person." An instance of **Manager** is also an instance of both **Person** and **Employee**. But an instance of **Person** may not necessarily be an instance of **Manager** nor an instance of **Employee**.

Manager has added one new data member (group) and four new services (constructor, finalize, getEmployee(), setEmployee()). The group variable is an array of the references to the instances of Employee. This is a very common way of capturing an association. The results may be summarized in Table 16-2.

Table 16-2 Manager Inheritance

Class	Manager Services	Manager Attributes
Person	getName	String name;
	getSex	char sex;
	getAge	int age;
	setName	int height;
	setAge	int weight;
Employee	getSalary	int salary;
	setSalary	
Manager	getEmployee	Employee group[Max];
	setEmployee	

Every instance of **Manager** has its own data fields for name, sex, age, height, weight, salary, and group. Once again, the only attribute that is uniquely "managerial" is the group that the manager supervises. The attribute of salary is still tied to the concept of employee, while the rest of the attributes are tied to the concept of person. Conceptually, a manager is also an employee and a person. We realize that many developers may not agree with the above statement; however, this is what the model says.

Below is a program that uses the above three classes.

```
public class test {
    public static void main( String args[ ] )
    {   //    created as an instance of Employee
        Employee ed = new Employee("Edward", m, 21, 70000);
        //    Edward gets a raise!!
        ed.setSalary(250000);
        //    Time for a boss
        Manager jane = new Manager("Jane", f, 25);
        //    Managers get paid a lot!!
        jane.setSalary(1000000);
          //    Put Ed in Jane's group
        jane.setEmployee( ed, 0)
         //    Lower Edward's salary
        ed.setSalary(150000);
    }
```

Adding Polymorphism

A method defined in the base class may be overridden unless keyword *final* is specified in the prototype declaration of the service in the base-class definition. If a derived class wants to *override* this method, it must declare and define a derived method that matches the original method's prototype. This is called *polymorphism* in the object-oriented world. The selection of which method definition is invoked is dynamic. For example, it is very common in object-oriented programming to have a collection of pointers to base objects. These pointers normally point to objects of the base class and objects in a derived class(es).

Because the service is defined in both classes, there must be a rule by which one of the methods is invoked. The rule is that the method selected is based on the class of the object to which it is being pointed and not on the type of pointer type.

If the object being pointed to is an object of the derived class, the method invoked would be the method of the derived class. If a derived class does not have this method declared in its class definition, then the default is to try and find it in the base class. If it cannot find it in its base class, it would search the "base class" of the base class ad infinitum until it is found. Remember, the method must be defined in the original base class.

There is a difference between selection of an appropriate overridden method and the selection of an overloaded member methods (services). Overloaded member methods can be determined at compile-time because they must have a unique signature. It can also have different return-types, although we have not seen an example of this. An overridden method has an identical prototype. It cannot be resolved at compile-time. In the example below, polymorphism is added to setSalary() for **Employee** so that the company can give bonuses to the managers.

In this example, the **Employee** class code is

```
public class Employee extends Person
{
    public Employee(String n, char s, int a,int n=0)
    final public int   getSalary() { return salary; }
    public void   setSalary(int a) { salary = a; }
    // Variable
    private int    salary;
}
```

Note that the only change to **Employee** is to declare getSalary() final. This prevents the subclass from overriding this method.[3] Based on the above code for **Employee**, the **Manager** class code is

```
public class Manager extends Employee
{   final static int Max = 20;
    public Manager(String n, char s, int a, int n = 0)
    { ... initialization code goes here ...}
        public Employee   getEmployee(int n) {return group[n];}
        public void setEmployee(Employee e, int a) {group[a] = e;}
        protected void finalize() {... free employees here ...  }
        //This is clean up code
        //  This is the where we override setSalary
        public void setSalary( int s) {super.setSalary( s + bonus() ); }
        private int bonus () { return 2500000; } // big bonuses here
        // Variables
        public Employee    group[Max];
}
```

Note that in class **Manager**, setSalary() is both redeclared and redefined. This means that the implementation of setSalary() is different from that of **Employee**. When all the new salaries are set, all the managers increase their salary by an additional bonus of $2,500,000, while the salaries of the non-management employees will increase only by the set amount. The results are shown in Table 16-3.

Table 16-3 Manager Salary Example

Class	Manager Services	Manager Attributes
Person	getName	String name;
	getSex	char sex;
	getAge	int age;
	setName	int height;
	setAge	int weight;

---

[3] If you want to prevent any subclassing of your class, use final as a class modifier.

Table 16-3 Manager Salary Example (*continued*)

Class	Manager Services	Manager Attributes
Employee	getSalary ~~set Salary~~	int salary;
Manager	getEmployee setEmployee setSalary	Employee group[Max];

The strikethru on the setSalary() function in **Employee** means that an object of type **Manager** will not use the method definition given in the class **Employee**. Instead, it will use the setSalary() method definition given in its own class.

The use of polymorphism hides behavior from the user of the services. For example, because of the way we have defined setSalary(), the following program using the latest definition of setSalary() yields the same results as the earlier main program that used only the employee's setSalary() service.

```
public class test {
    public static void main( String args[ ] )
    {   //    created as an instance of Employee
        Employee ed = new Employee("Edward", m, 21, 70000);
        //    Edward gets a raise!
        ed.setSalary(250000);
        //    Time for a boss
        Manager jane = new Manager("Jane", f, 25, 25000);
        //    Managers get paid very little with big bonuses!
        jane.setSalary(50000);
        / /    Put Ed in Jane's group
        jane.setEmployee( ed, 0)
        //    Lower Edward's salary
        ed.setSalary(150000);
    }
```

In the previous program where the manager inherited without polymorphism, Jane's salary was exactly $1,000,000 as shown in the main program code where the coder of the main program knows her salary. In this program, however, the coder would have assumed that her salary is $50,000, but, in fact, it is $2,550,000 because when her salary is set, a bonus is added to the base salary. Now, we understand the real reason why managers are so excited about object-oriented technology!

Abstract Class

Sometimes, a class that we define represents an abstract concept and should not be instantiated. An example is food in the real world. You do not see an instance of Food! What you see are instances of carrot, apple, and banana. Food represents the abstract concept of things that we all can eat. It does not make sense for an instance of food to exist.

Similarly in object-oriented design, you may want to model an abstract concept without being able to create an instance of it. For example, the Number class in the java.lang package represents the abstract concept of numbers. It makes sense to model numbers in a program, but it does not make sense to create a generic number object. Instead, the Number class makes sense only as a superclass to classes like Integer and Float, both of which implement specific kinds of numbers. A class such as Number, which represents an abstract concept and should not be instantiated, is called an abstract class. An abstract class is a class that can only be subclassed; it cannot be instantiated.

To declare that our class is an *abstract class*, use the keyword abstract before the class keyword in your class declaration:

```
abstract class Number {
    . . .
}
```

If we attempt to instantiate an abstract class, the compiler displays an error and refuses to compile your program. Note that an abstract class is not required to have an abstract method in it. But any class that has an abstract method in it or that does not provide an implementation for any abstract methods declared in its superclasses must be declared as an abstract class.

Abstract Service (Method)

An abstract class may contain abstract services, that is, service prototypes with no implementation. In this way, an abstract class can define a complete programming interface, thereby providing its subclasses with the service declarations for all of the methods necessary to implement that programming interface. However, the abstract class can leave some or all of the implementation details of those services up to its subclasses. As a result the body of the service is undefined in the abstract class. Notationally, it is declared in the abstract class as follows:

```
public abstract class BaseClass
{
    public:
        abstract   int   foo( );   // This is an abstract service!
}
```

A class with at least one abstract service is an *abstract class*. For example, consider the following:

```
public abstract class Item
{
    // Abstract Services
```

```
        public abstract void        cut();
        public abstract void        move(int dx, int dy) ;
        public abstract Boolean      pick(int px, int py);
        public abstract void        ungroup() ;
}
public abstract class Shape extends Item
{
    // Services
    public abstract  void       cut();
    public            void       draw() { write(Color_Foreground);}
    public            void       erase() { write(Color_Background);}
    public abstract  void       move(int dx, int dy);
    public abstract  Boolean    pick(int px, int py) ;
    public            void       ungroup() {}
    public abstract  void       write(Color color);
    // Variables
    private int x, y;
}
public  class Box: public Shape
{
        public        Boolean     pick(Length px, Length py)
        { ... code is here ... }
        public        void        move(Length dx, Length dy)
        { ... code is here ... }
        public        void        cut()
        { ... code is here ... }
    protected  int width, height;
}
class Circle extends  Shape
{
        Boolean     pick(int px, int py) { ... code is here ... }
        void        move(int dx, int dy) { ... code is here ... }
        void        write(Color color)   { ... code is here ... }
        void        cut()                { ... code is here ... }
    protected int radius;
}
```

Here, there are two abstract base classes: **Item** and **Shape**. All the services of **Item** are abstract. **Shape** defines only one of these services: ungroup(). In addition, it added a new abstract service: write(). **Box** and **Circle** do not have any abstract services, so they are sometimes called *concrete classes*. The reason is that the program can instantiate an instance of a concrete class, but it may not instantiate an instance of an abstract class. From the above discussion this must be so, as an abstract class has undefined services.

IMPLEMENTING GENERALIZATION/SPECIALIZATION

In earlier chapters, we have defined a class and captured the attributes and services from our design. In addition to capturing the attributes and the service prototypes, the relationships must also be captured. In this section, we look at ways to implement the generalization/specialization relationship.

Because we have just learned inheritance. This is the most direct mechanism for implementing generalization/specialization. We will look at the code necessary to represent the generalization/specialization for Platypus. Below are the abbreviated class definitions.

```
public class Endangered
{  // class definition for Endangered  }
public class OrganicMatter
{  // class definition for Organic Matter  }
public class Animal extends OrganicMatter
{  // class definition for Animal  }
public class Mammal extends Animal
{  // class definition for Mammal  }
public class Platypus extends Mammal
{  // class definition for Platypus  without being endangered}
   // Note: "public class Platypus extend Mammal, Endangered" is
   //illegal
```

In this example, "class Animal extends OrganicMatter" tells the compiler that OrganicMatter is the superclass of Animal. The extends keyword means that an instance of Animal is also an instance of OrganicMatter. The line "class Platypus extends Animal" tells the compiler that the platypus has one superclass as parent; however, we would also like for Platypus to have Endangered also as a superclass. This is not allowed because Java implements only single inheritance.

In other programming languages, such as C++, a class may have more than one superclass and they inherit the combined variables and methods from the all those superclasses. This is called multiple inheritance. In those languages, we can implement multiple generalization/specialization using multiple inheritance. To avoid the complexity of multiple inheritance, however, Java supports only single inheritance. So we must employ other mechanisms for implementing multiple generalization/specialization. There are two mechanisms that can help us do this:

- interfaces
- aggregation with delegation

Interfaces

Java has created a new construct that is on the equivalent level of class; this construct is called an *interface*.

Let us review what an interface is. When we define a new interface, we are in essence defining a new reference data type. We can use interface names anywhere we can use any other data type name. An interface is a collection of service prototypes without actual definitions. The simple form of an interface definition is as follows:

```
visibility-modifier interface interfaceName {
    // Methods Prototypes which will be public and abstract
    // Variables which will all public static and final ; i.e.
      //constants only
}
```

An interface definition has two components: the interface declaration and the interface body. The interface declaration declares attributes about the interface such as its name and its visibility. The visibility-modifier is nearly always public. The public visibility specifier indicates that the interface can be used by any class in any package. If you do not specify that your interface is public, then your interface will be accessible only to classes that are defined in the same package as the interface. The interfaceName is any legal Java identifier. An interface can contain only constant declarations and service (method) declarations.

An interface can extend other interfaces just as a class can extend or subclass another class. However, while a class can extend only one other class, an interface can extend any number of interfaces. The list of superinterfaces is a comma-separated list of all of the interfaces extended by the new interface. An interface inherits all constants and methods from its superinterfaces, unless the interface hides a constant with another of the same name or redeclares a method with a new method declaration. The second form of an interface definition is

```
visibility-modifier interface interfaceName extends
anotherInterfaceName {
    // Methods Prototypes which will be public and abstract
    // Variables which will all public static and final ; i.e.
      //constants only
}
```

All methods declared in an interface are implicitly public and abstract. The use of these modifiers on a method declaration in an interface is discouraged as a matter of style. All constant values defined in an interface are implicitly public, static, and final. The use of these modifiers on a constant declaration in an interface is discouraged as a matter of style. Any class can use an interface's constants from the name of the interface, like this

```
interfaceName.constantName
```

Classes that implement an interface can treat the constants as though they were inherited.

Member declarations in an interface disallow the use of some declaration modifiers; we may not use transient, volatile, or synchronized in a member declaration in an interface. Also, we may not use the private and protected specifiers when declaring members of an interface. Previous releases of the Java platform allowed us to use the abstract modifier on interface declarations and on method declarations within interfaces. However, this is unnecessary because interfaces and their methods are implicitly abstract. We should no longer be using abstract in our interface declarations or in our method declarations within interfaces.

An example of two interfaces is shown below:

```
//  The Athlete interface is a "base interface"
public interface Athlete {
    public void run( );   //This becomes abstract also
    void throw( );        // This becomes public and abstract
    public void catch( ); //This becomes abstract also
    float speed = 4.5;    // This becomes public final static
}
// The BaseballPlayer interface extends the Athlete interface
public interface BaseballPlayer extends Athlete {
    void hitBall( );      // Recommended form for method declaration
    void runBase( );
    // Can access Athlete's constant speed via Athlete.speed
}
```

In this example, we defined two new interfaces: Athlete and BaseballPlayer. As we can see, the BaseballPlayer extends the Athlete. It means that inheritance also exists between interfaces, but a derived interface only inherits the service prototypes and the constants of their "base" interfaces. We showed also the various legal forms for declaring constant variables and interface methods.

Now interfaces may be an interesting abstract construct. But how do we put such a construct to use? In Java, a class may only extend one other class, but it can implement as many interfaces as it likes. We now have to revisit the definition of a class and use the long form of its header. The form for class is as follows:

```
modifiers class className extends superClass implements
list-of-interfaces {
    class body
}
```

The list of modifiers is extensive. This was covered in Chapter 13. The className is any legal identifier, and the superClass is the name of the base class. The list of interfaces is a command-separated list of interface names.

Now we can revisit our example and fully implement the multiple generalization specialization model for the Platypus.

```
        public interface Endangered
        {  // interface definition for Endangered  }
```

```
public class OrganicMatter
{  // class definition for Organic Matter  }
public class Animal extends OrganicMatter
{  // class definition for Animal  }
public class Mammal extends Animal
{  // class definition for Mammal  }
public class Platypus extends Mammal implements Endangered
{  // class definition for Platypus }
```

Aggregation with Delegation

Though the use of interfaces is very powerful, it has a restriction that each class that implements the interface must provide its own implementation. This makes code reuse less manageable in situations where we have multiple classes that want to use the same code. There is another less-known form for implementing generalization/specialization that can be used when code reuse is desirable: aggregation with delegation. It is this mechanism, aggregation with delegation, that is covered in this section.

The implementation of aggregation with delegation is done with concepts and mechanisms that we already know. First, we create an interface hierarchy of all the categories.

```
public interface RootInterface { all its service prototypes}
public interface PlusOne extends RootInterface
{ all PlusOne service prototypes }
...
public interface PlusN extends PlusNminusOne
{ all PlusN service prototypes }
```

Now we have created the hierarchy for the one instance of a "sub-interface" to be an instance of an "interface." But this does not manage the code. To manage the code portion, we need to create a corresponding class for each of the interfaces that can reuse code when appropriate. The form is shown below.

```
modifiers class childClass extends superClass implements
parentInterface {
    childClass( )      { instanceOfParent = new parentClass( ); }
    [public prototype of first public method in parentInterface]
    { ... delegation code ...}
    [public prototype of second public method in parentInterface]
    { ... delegation code ...}
        ...      // The remaining prototypes of public methods in
        parentClass
    protected void finalize() { instanceOfParent.finalize(); }
    //This is clean up code
    ...      // The normal stuff in a class body
    // New Attribute for the aggregation
```

```
        parentClass instanceOfParent;
    }
```

Here is how it works. In the class definition, you add all the public services[4] of the parent interface. Then in the body of the service, we delegate the work to the parent's method for the same service. Note that an instance of a childClass is also an instance of the interface and all of the interface ancestors.

For example, consider the following situation, we have two classes:

```
public class Font
{
    Font ( int w, int h)   { width =w; height = h; }
    public void write(Color color) { this.color = color; }
    private int width, height;
    private Color color;
}
public class MyString
{
    MyString( char c)   { String a = new String( "\"" + c + "\"" );  }
    public String  getString()   { return a; } //  return the string
    public void    print()       {System.out.println( a ): }
    //  to stdout
    private String a;
}
```

Now we want to add a class Text that needs to inherit the font capabilities from Font and the character capabilities from String. In addition, class text needs to extend class superText. Because Java is single inheritance, we cannot do this unless we also use aggregation and delegation. Below is all the interfaces and classes that are needed.

```
public interface Font        //Redefine Font as a pure abstract class
 //or concept
{
    public void write(Color color);
}
public interface MyString    //Redefine MyString as a pure abstract
 //class or concept
{
    public String getString();     // return the string
    public void    print();        // to stdout
}
public class FontImpl implements Font     // A realization of Font
```

---

[4] We cannot have protected members in the parent class unless the child class is in the same package as the parent class. Thus, protected methods must be made public and protected variable should be made private with public getters and setters.

```
    {
        FontImpl ( int w, int h)    { width =w; height = h; }
        public void write(Color color) { this.color = color; }
        private int width, height;
        private Color color;
    }
    public class MyStringImpl implements MyString    // A realization of
    MyString
    {
        MyStringImpl( char c)
        { String a = new String( "\"" + c + "\"" );   }
        public String  getString()    { return a; } //  return the string
        public void      print()      {System.out.println( a ): }
        //  to stdout
        private String a;
    }
    public class Text extends SuperText implements Font,  MyString
    {
            Text ( int width, int  height, char c) :
                {
                    //Create the aggregates
                    font = new FontImpl( width, height );
                    //create instance of parent
                    myString = new MyStringImpl( c );
                    // create instance of other parent
                    .... //  other initialization code
                }
        // This is the implementation of Font interface
        public void write(Color color) { font.write( color); return; }
        // delegation here
        // This is the implementation of MyString interface
        public String  getString()  { return myString.getString(); }
        // delegation here
        public void      print()
            { font.print(); System.out.println( "from Text" ); return; }
            // polymorphic method
        ...      //  new member functions
        private FontImpl font;            // font class!
        private MyStringImpl myString;   // myString  class
        ...      //  new data members
    }
```

First, we converted both Font and MyString to interfaces.[5] Then we made two
new classes, FontImpl and MyStringImpl, which implement each of the respective

---

[5] There is a school of thinkers (we are among them) who believe that all method calls should be to
instances of interface, that is, we should separate the abstraction from its implementation.

interfaces. Then we made the class definition of Text that uses single inheritance plus aggregation and delegation to use all the previous mentioned constructs. Text implements both interfaces and that delegation is used in the implementation of the services in these interfaces. We showed polymorphism in the print() service as we first called the parent method and then added code of our own.

THE OBJECT CLASS

The Object class sits at the top of the class hierarchy tree in the Java platform. Every class in the Java system is a descendent, direct or indirect, of the Object class. This class defines the basic state and behavior that all objects must have the ability

- to compare oneself to another object
- to convert to a string, to wait on a condition variable
- to notify other objects that a condition variable has changed
- to return the class of the object

In our class design, we may want to override the following Object methods. [6]

```
clone
equals/hashCode
finalize
toString
```

We cannot override these Object methods (they are final):

```
getClass
notify
notifyAll
wait
```

Clone Method

We use the clone method to create an object from an existing object. To create a clone, we write:

```
aCloneableObject.clone();
```

Object's implementation of this method checks to see if the object on which clone was invoked implements the Cloneable interface, and throws a CloneNotSupportedException if it does not. For some classes the default behavior of Object's clone method works just fine. Other classes need to override clone to get correct behavior.

---

[6] The equals/hashCode are listed together as they must be overridden together.

Object does not implement Cloneable, so subclasses of Object that do not explicitly implement the interface are not cloneable. If the object on which clone was invoked does implement the Cloneable interface, Object's implementation of the clone method creates an object of the same type as the original object and initializes the new object's member variables to have the same values as the original object's corresponding member variables.

The simplest way to make your class cloneable then, is to add implements Cloneable to your class's declaration. For example:

```
public class CloneClass implements Cloneable
{
    ... // code for CloneClass methods and constructors
    protected Object clone() {
        try {
            CloneClass c = (CloneClass)super.clone();// clone itself
              partially
            ....       // clone vector instances, array instances,
            etc.
            return c;// return the clone
          } catch (CloneNotSupportedException e)
          {
        // this shouldn't happen because CloneClass is Cloneable
        ... // error logic
            }
    }
}
```

Clone should never use new to create the clone and should not call constructors. Instead, the method should call super.clone, which creates an object of the correct type and allows the hierarchy of superclasses to perform the copying necessary to get a proper clone.

Equals and HashCode Methods

We must override the equals and hashCode methods together. The equals method compares two objects for equality and returns true if they are equal. The equals method provided in the Object class uses the identity method to determine if objects are equal (if the objects compared are the exact same object the method returns true).

For some classes, however, two distinct objects of the same type might be considered equal if they contain the same value(s). An example of this situation is the Integer class,

```
Integer one = new Integer(1);
Integer two = new Integer(1);
```

```
if (one.equals(two))    // This will compare values, not object
  //identifiers
    System.out.println("Object One is equal to Object Two");
```

This program displays objects that are equal even though object "one" and object "two" reference two distinct objects. They are considered equal because the objects compared contain the same integer value. Our classes should only override the equals method if the identity function is not appropriate for our class. If we override equals, then we should override hashCode as well.

The value returned by hashCode is an int that maps an object into a bucket in a hash table. An object must always produce the same hash code, but the hash code is not necessarily unique. Writing a "correct" hashing function is easy; just ensure that it always returns the same hash code for the same object. Writing an "efficient" hashing function, one that provides a sufficient distribution of objects over the buckets, is difficult and is beyond the scope of this book. Even so, the hashing function for some classes may be obvious.

Finalize Method

Java allows us to create as many objects as you want (limited, of course, by what your system can handle), and we never have to worry about destroying them. The Java runtime environment deletes objects when it determines that they are no longer being used. This process is called garbage collection.

An object is eligible for garbage collection when there are no more references to that object. References that are held in a variable are naturally dropped when the variable goes out of scope. Or you can explicitly drop an object reference by setting the variable to null.

The Java platform has a garbage collector that periodically frees the memory used by objects that are no longer needed. The Java garbage collector is a mark-sweep garbage collector. A mark-sweep garbage collector scans dynamic memory areas for objects and marks those that are referenced. After all possible paths to objects are investigated, unmarked objects (unreferenced objects) are known to be garbage and are collected.[7] The garbage collector runs in a low-priority thread and runs either synchronously or asynchronously depending on the situation and the system on which Java is running. It runs synchronously when the system runs out of memory or in response to a request from a Java program.

The Java garbage collector runs asynchronously when the system is idle, but it does so only on systems, such as Windows 95/NT, that allow the Java runtime environment to note when a thread has begun and to interrupt another thread. As soon as another thread becomes active, the garbage collector is asked to get to a consistent state and terminate.

---

[7] A more complete description of Java's garbage collection algorithm might be "a compacting, mark-sweep collector with some conservative scanning."

Before an object gets garbage-collected, the garbage collector gives the object an opportunity to clean up after itself through a call to the object's finalize method. This process is known as finalization. This is needed when the programmer might have to release resources, such as native peers, that are not under the control of the garbage collector.

ToString Method

Object's toString method returns a String representation of the object. You can use toString along with System.out.println to display a text representation of an object, such as the current thread: For example,

```
System.out.println(Thread.currentThread().toString());
```

The String representation for an object depends entirely on the object. The String representation of an Integer object is the integer value displayed as text. The String representation of a Thread object contains various attributes about the thread, such as its name and priority. The toString method is very useful for debugging. It is advisable for us to override this method in all our classes.

GetClass Method

The getClass method is a final method that returns a runtime representation of the class of an object. This method returns a Class object. Once you have a Class object you can query it for various information about the class, such as its name, its superclass, and the names of the interfaces that it implements.

One handy use of a Class object is to create a new instance of a class without knowing what the class is at compile time. The following sample method creates a new instance of the same class as obj, which can be any class that inherits from Object (which means that it could be any class):

```
Object createNewInstanceOf(Object obj) {
    return obj.getClass().newInstance();
}
```

If you already know the name of the class, you can also get a Class object from a class name. The two lines shown here are equivalent ways to get a Class object for the String class .

```
String.class          // First way
Class.forName("String")   //Second way
```

The first is more efficient than the second.

Notify, NotifyAll, and Wait Methods

We cannot override Object's notify and notifyAll methods and its three versions of wait. This is because they are critical for ensuring that threads are synchronized.

When the active thread has a lock that prevents other threads from running, the notifyAll method releases the lock and wakes up all threads waiting on the object in question. The awakened threads compete for the lock. One thread gets it, and the others go back to waiting.

The Object class also defines the notify method. This method arbitrarily wakes up one of the threads waiting on this object.

The Object class contains three wait methods[8]:

1. wait( ) waits for notification indefinitely.
2. wait(long timeout) waits for notification or until the timeout period has elapsed. Timeout is measured in milliseconds.
3. wait(long timeout, int nanos) waits for notification or until timeout milliseconds plus nanos nanoseconds have elapsed.

SUMMARY

In Java programming, we have three mechanisms to implement the generalization/specialization hierarchy of the object-oriented model:

- inheritance
- interfaces
- aggregation with delegation

For inheritance, a subclass (derived class) inherits variables and methods from its superclass (base class) and all of its ancestors. The following list specifies the rules of inheritance:

1. Subclasses inherit those superclass members declared as public or protected.
2. Subclasses inherit those superclass members declared with no access specifier as long as the subclass is in the same package as the superclass.
3. Subclasses do not inherit a superclass's member if the subclass declares a member with the same name. In the case of member variables, the member variable in the subclass hides the one in the superclass. In the case of methods, the method in the subclass overrides the one in the superclass.

---

[8] Besides using these timed wait methods to synchronize threads, you also can use them in place of sleep. Both wait and sleep delay for the requested amount of time, but you can easily wake up wait with a notify, but a sleeping thread cannot be awakened prematurely.

4. Creating a subclass can be as simple as including the extends clause in your class declaration. However, you usually have to make other provisions in your code when subclassing a class, such as overriding methods or providing implementations for abstract methods.

5. When a class hierarchy is translated into a set of related derived classes, a base-class pointer may be used to address any object of the derived classes.

The subclass can use these members as is, or it can hide the member variables or override the methods. The following guidelines and rules are provided:

1. Member variables defined in the subclass hide member variables that have the same name in the superclass.

2. While this feature of the Java language is powerful and convenient, it can be a fruitful source of errors. When naming your member variables, be careful to hide only those member variables that you actually wish to hide.

3. All methods may be redefined unless a method is declared as final.

4. Super is a Java language keyword that allows a method to refer to hidden variables and overridden methods of the superclass

5. A subclass cannot override methods that are declared static in the superclass. In other words, a subclass cannot override a class method.

6. A subclass can hide a static method in the superclass by declaring a static method in the subclass with the same signature as the static method in the superclass.

7. A subclass must override methods that are declared abstract in the superclass, or the subclass itself must be abstract.

In addition, we learned about abstract classes and abstract method. The following rules apply:

1. An abstract class is a class that can only be subclassed; it cannot be instantiated.

2. An abstract class is not required to have an abstract method.

3. Any class that has an abstract method in it or that does not provide an implementation for any abstract methods declared in its superclasses must be declared as an abstract class.

For interfaces, the following rules apply:

1. An interface can contain only constant declarations and service declarations.

2. An interface may extend any number of other interfaces.

3. A class may implement as many interfaces as it wishes.

4. All services declared in an interface are implicitly public and abstract. The use of these modifiers on a service declaration in an interface is discouraged as a matter of style.

5. All constant values defined in an interface are implicitly public, static, and final.
The use of these modifiers on a constant declaration in an interface is discouraged as a matter of style.

6. Classes that implement an interface can treat the constants as though they were inherited.

7. Member declarations in an interface disallow the use of some declaration modifiers; you may not use transient, volatile, or synchronized in a member declaration in an interface.

8. Also, you may not use the private and protected specifiers when declaring members of an interface.

For aggregation and delegation, the following rules apply:

1. To use aggregation and delegation for implementation of multiple generalization/specialization, you must separate concepts from implementation of the concepts. This requires setup of two parallel and corresponding hierarchy of classes and interfaces.

2. A class that uses aggregation and delegation for implementation of a generalization/specialization hierarchy must implement the appropriate interface and delegate the work of the appropriate services to the instance of an appropriate class.

3. Polymorphism can be easily done as the class control its own implementation of the interface services.

Here is a summary of some Java coding reminders.

- Variables (attributes) declared in the base class are inherited by its derived classes and need not be repeated in the derived classes.
- However, the derived classes can only directly access variables that are *public* or *protected*.
- Service prototypes declared in a base class are also inherited in the derived classes.
- Methods defined in a base class are also inherited in the derived classes.
- Constructors are not inherited.
- If a service cannot be overridden by a derived class, then it must be declared *final* in its first appearance in a base class.
- Services that override inherited methods must be declared and redefined in the derived class.
- A service and its overridden versions must have the same prototype.
- All member services except constructors and overloaded **new** can be overridden.
- In an abstract service (method), only the service prototype is provided by the base class. In other words, implementation must be provided by a derived class.

- It is good practice to always do clean up in finalize() method. If there is inheritance, it is good practice to call the finalize() method in the parent class.
- Use the keyword *this* as a reference to the current object.
- Use the keyword *super* as a reference to the current object's superclass.
- All services declared in an interface are implicitly public and abstract.
- The use of these modifiers on a service declaration in an interface is discouraged as a matter of style.
- All constant values defined in an interface are implicitly public, static, and final.
- The use of these modifiers on a constant declaration in an interface is discouraged as a matter of style.
- Classes that implement an interface can treat the constants as though they were inherited.
- Member declarations in an interface disallow the use of some declaration modifiers; you may not use transient, volatile, or synchronized in a member declaration in an interface.
- Also, you may not use the private and protected specifiers when declaring members of an interface.

17

Implementing More Relationships

In the previous chapter, we discussed the implementation of generalization/specialization. As we built the analysis model, however, we used two additional types of relationships, aggregation and association. Although aggregation and association are not explicitly supported in many object-oriented languages including Java, we believe that they should be implemented in a standard way. In this chapter, we look at some accepted mechanisms for implementing these two relationships.

INTRODUCTION

Some of the issues involved in implementing association and aggregation were presented in Chapter 11. They are repeated here for reference as these issues are usually revisited during implementation.

Implementing Association

There are three approaches to implementing associations: inner classes, maps, and vectors. Because Java (like most languages) does not support association objects directly, the most common approach uses the Collection classes to store references.

A binary (one-to-one) association is usually implemented as an attribute in each of the classes participating in the association. Each attribute contains a reference to the other object. We can also implement a binary association as two Map objects, with each Map object giving access in one direction across the relation. A many-to-one association requires either a set of objects or an array of objects (if the association is ordered). In this case, we suggest using the vector class.

In implementing associations, the implementor must consider the access pattern and the relative frequencies of the different kinds of access. If the number of hits from a query is low because only a fraction of the objects satisfy the criteria, an index should be used to improve the access to objects that are frequently retrieved. However, this is at a price as it will use more memory and updates will be slower. Sometimes, adding a new association that is derived from the base association provides for direct access to the appropriate data.

The simplest association to implement is one that is only traversed in one direction. In this case, it can be implemented as an attribute that contains an object reference. If the multiplicity is 1, it is simply a reference to the other object. If the multiplicity is more than 1, it is a reference to a collection. In most cases, an appropriate collection is a set or a vector. If the many end is ordered, a vector is used. A qualified association can be implemented using a map object.

There are three ways to implement a two-way association:

1. Add an attribute to the class on one side of the association and perform a search when a reverse traversal is required.
2. Add an attribute to both sides of the association. Use the same multiplicity techniques as for an association that is traversed in one direction.
3. Create an associate class, independent of either class. An associate class is a set of pairs of related objects stored in a single variable-sized object. For efficiency, it is common to implement an associative object as two map objects.

If most of the traversal is from the "many" side to the "one" side and new members are added frequently to the links, then number 1 is recommended. When updates are infrequent and speed of access in both directions is critical to your application, number 2 is recommended. An associative class is recommended when maximum flexibility is needed for future enhancements and performance is not an issue.

Implementing Attributes of an Association

If the association has attributes but no services, then the attributes of an association can be implemented as follows:

1. If the association is one-to-one, the association attributes can be stored as attributes of either class.
2. If the association is many-to-one, the association attributes may be stored in the class on the "many" side.
3. If the association is many-to-many, it is best to create an associative class and assign the association attributes to the associative class.

Implementing Aggregation

Since aggregation is also not supported in most object-oriented languages, including Java, it is implemented using similar rules as for association. There are two approaches: buried array of references and embedded objects.

1. An aggregation can be implemented as an array of pointers (references) to objects. This is done when we have either replaceable components or directly accessible components in the aggregate.
2. An aggregation can also be implemented as a distinct contained object. This is done when we want the components of the aggregation to be changed only through methods of the container object.
   This can justify a use of inner class.

REFERENCES

Since the foundation of implementing association and aggregation is a reference to an instance of a class and a collection of references to instances of a class, collection and iterator will be reviewed.

The Collection interface is the root of the collection hierarchy; it is the least common denominator that all collection constructs. A *Collection* represents a group of objects, known as its *elements*. A collection is used to pass collections around and manipulate them when maximum generality is desired. Some implementations allow duplicate elements and others do not; while some are ordered and others unordered. (See below.)

The Collection interface is shown below:

```
public interface Collection {
   // Basic Operations
   int size();
   boolean isEmpty();
   boolean contains(Object element);
```

```
    boolean add(Object element);    // Optional
    boolean remove(Object element); // Optional
    Iterator iterator();

    // Bulk Operations
    boolean containsAll(Collection c);
    boolean addAll(Collection c);    // Optional
    boolean removeAll(Collection c); // Optional
    boolean retainAll(Collection c); // Optional
    void clear();                    // Optional

    // Array Operations
    Object[] toArray();
    Object[] toArray(Object a[]);
}
```

The interface does about what we expect, given that a Collection represents a group of objects. It has services to tell us how many elements are in the collection (size, isEmpty), to check if a given object is in the collection (contains), to add and remove an element from the collection (add, remove), and to provide an iterator over the collection (iterator).

The add service is defined generally enough so that it makes sense for collections that allow duplicates as well as those that do not. It guarantees that the Collection will contain the specified element after the call completes, and returns true if the Collection changes as a result of the call. Similarly, the remove service is defined to remove a single instance of the specified element from the Collection, assuming the Collection contains the element, and to return true if the Collection was modified as a result.

The object returned by the iterator service deserves special mention. It is an Iterator, which is very similar to an Enumeration, but differs in two respects:

- Iterator allows the caller to remove elements from the underlying collection during the iteration with well-defined semantics.[1]
- Method names have been improved.

The Iterator interface is shown below:

```
public interface Iterator {
    boolean hasNext();
    Object next();
    void remove();    // Optional
}
```

---

[1] There was no safe way to remove elements from a collection while traversing it with an Enumeration. The semantics of this operation were ill-defined, and differed from implementation to implementation.

The hasNext service is identical in function to Enumeration.hasMoreElements, and the next service is identical in function to Enumeration.nextElement. The remove service removes from the underlying Collection the last element that was returned by next; but it may be called only once per call to next. If this condition is violated, it will throw an exception. Note that Iterator.remove is the only safe way to modify a collection during iteration; the behavior is unspecified if the underlying collection is modified in any other way while the iteration is in progress.

The following code snippet shows us how to use an Iterator to filter a Collection, that is, to traverse the collection, removing every element that does not satisfy some condition:

```
static void filter(Collection collection) {
    for (Iterator iterator = collection.iterator( ); )
    iterator.hasNext( ); )
        if ( !cond( iterator.next( )  )  )
            iterator.remove( );
}
```

The following rules will help you deal with references:

- References to different classes (interfaces) may not be equated without casting.
- The exception is that a public inherited subclass (derived class) reference can be assigned to a superclass (base class) reference.
- A base class reference must always be cast to a legal derived class reference.
- An object reference may always be assigned the void reference. However, a void reference must be cast to a legal object reference.

STATIC MEMBERS

It is sometimes necessary that all objects of a particular class access the same variable. This may be some condition flag or counter related to the class that changes dynamically in program execution. Examples are averages and running totals. Sometimes it is more efficient to provide one variable for all objects in one class than to have each object maintain its own copy. Examples of this are error handling routines common to the class and reference to free storage[2] for the class. For these situations, a static class member is an effective mechanism to use.

A static data member acts as a global variable for its class. For object-oriented programming, there are three advantages to using a static data member over a global variable:

---

[2] This is used in real-time programming in which we manage our own storage to avoid the garbage collector giving us unpredictable behaviors.

1. Information hiding can still be enforced. A static member can be made nonpublic; if there were a global variable, it cannot.
2. A static member is not entered into the program's global name space. This reduces the possibility of an accidental conflict of names.
3. Even if the static member is public, a weak form of encapsulation is preserved. Nonmembers require the use of a scope operator (e.g., X::PublicStaticMember) to access the static member.

There is only one instance of a static data member of a class, a single shared variable that is accessible to all objects in the class. Static members obey the public/private/protected/package access rules in the same manner as nonstatic members. Static data members may also be constant, class objects, or collections.

A static member method is used to access static data members of the class. It is not allowed to access any nonstatic data member. A static member method does not contain a *this* pointer, therefore, any explicit or implicit reference to *this* pointer results in a compile-time error. An attempt to access a nonstatic class member is an implicit reference to a *this* pointer and results in a compile-time error.

The definition of a static method is the same as a nonstatic member method; however, a static member method may not be declared *volatile*. A static member method may be invoked through a class object or a reference to a class object in the same manner that a nonstatic member method is invoked. However, a static member method can be invoked directly even if no class object is ever declared.[3]

IMPLEMENTING ASSOCIATION

Binary Association

The most direct mechanism is to implement a binary association as an attribute of each class.[4] Below is an example of using references to capture the spouse relationships between two people.

```
public class Person
{
    //Services
    publicPerson(String n, char s, int a) { ... code here ... }
    publicPerson getSpouse() { return spouse; }
    publicvoid setSpouse(Person p) { spouse = p; return; }
            ...
    private String name;
        private char sex;
```

---

[3] This is done by use the class scope operator.
[4] This allows traversal in both directions.

```
                    private int age;  . . .
                    private Person  spouse;
          }
```

In the previous example, we have added the spousal relationship that is a "from-Person-to-Person" relationship. By adding an attribute that is a reference to the Person class, this relationship is captured. The setSpouse() function establishes one side of the relationship, while the getSpouse() function navigates the relationship.

The reader should note that it is the programmer's responsibility to establish and update both sides of the relationship. This is often rather tricky. For example, managing the spouse relationship can be accomplished within the setSpouse method as follows:

```
void Person::setSpouse(Person p)
{
    if (spouse != p)                        // if this is not the current
    spouse
    {
        if (spouse == 0)                    // not currently married (p isn't
        //nil because of first if)
        {
            spouse = p;                     // set the spouse
            spouse.setSpouse(this);         // let the new spouse know
            about marriage
            return;                         // nothing else to do
        }
        if (spouse.getSpouse() == this)    // the old spouse doesn't know
          //about the divorce
        {
            Person old = spouse;            // use a local variable to hold
            old spouse
            spouse = null;                  // handle the divorce on this
            side of relation
            old.setSpouse(null);            // inform the other person of
              //the divorce
        }
        spouse = p;                         // now set the new spouse even
        if it is no spouse (nil)
        if (spouse != 0)                    // if this wasn't a divorce
        {
            spouse.setSpouse(this);         // let the new spouse know
              //about the marriage
        }
    }
    return;
}
```

This implementation of setSpouse() first checks to make sure that the spouse is a change in value and must be handled. There are two basic cases that it must handle: (1) this is a new marriage and (2) it is already married. In the first case, it sets the spouse attribute and informs the other spouse of the marriage. This gives the spouse a chance to establish its side of the association. In the second case, it must first allow the previous spouse to update its role in the marriage. If the previous spouse believes the marriage still exists, then it must first be divorced. To divorce the spouse, it sets its spouse attribute to null and informs the other person of the divorce by invoking the setSpouse() method with a null argument. It then sets the spouse attribute to the new spouse specified in the argument of the method. If the new value for the spouse attribute is an actual instance of **Person** (not null), then it informs the new spouse of the association. Otherwise, this was a divorce and the spouse attribute holds a null value.

If there are attributes of the association, each attribute should be added to only one of the classes. The frequency of accessing the attribute within the functions of each class should be used as the criteria for assigning the attribute.

Many-to-One Association

One way to implement a many-to-one association is to have references to the singleton object as an attribute of the objects on the "many" side. Then the program can navigate the relationship from the "many" side to the "one" side. The program can navigate the relationship directly from the "many" side to the "one" side. However, navigating from the "one" side to the "many" side requires a search of all of the objects on the "many" side using the association attribute. The following is an example of how to implement many-to-one association using references to the singleton object:

```
public class Person
{
    // Services
    publicPerson(String n, char s, int a, Person pop, Person mom)
    {...code here.. }
    publicPerson getFather() { return father; }
    publicPerson getMother() { return mother; }
    publicVector   getChildren( ) {... need to search for all
    references to yourself.. }
    privatevoid setFather(Person p) { father = p; return; }
    private void setMother(Person p) { mother = p;  return; }
    // Variables
    privateString  name;
    privatechar sex;
    privateint   age;   . . .
    privatePerson  father;
```

```
        privatePerson   mother;
    }
```

   In this example, two many-to-one relationships have been implemented: children-to-father and children-to-mother. The data member "Person father" is the implementation of the buried reference on the "many" side for the children-to-father relationship. The setFather() function is used to establish the relationship from the child to the father; setFather() is declared as a private function as it should be restricted to creation time. In fact, the best way to implement this is to have a father and a mother as required arguments in the constructor of the Person class. Then, a Person object may not be created without a father or a mother. If this is done, the two private functions, setFather() and setMother(), would not be needed. The getFather() function is used by the child to get to the father.

   The getChildren() function is the function on the "one" side of the relationship and allows a father or mother to navigate either the children-to-father or the children-to-mother relationship to get all of its children. The code for this is not given. If this is implemented in a relational database, a (SQL) call that searches the appropriate column for a match is appropriate; while in an object-oriented database, a set may need to be traversed. In either case, a collection of references to the Person objects is returned.

   If the relationship is between two classes, this function would be in the class on the "one" side and all the other functions and attributes are in the class on the "many" side. There is no set functions on the "one" side because there is no attribute added to the class on the "one" side. The traversal from the "one" side to the "many" side can be very expensive.

   If fast traversal is critical, then it would be better to add attributes to both sides of the association. In this case, the attribute added to the class on the "one" side is not a buried reference, but a vector of references to a class object on the other side. This has the disadvantage of making updates of the relationship fairly complex. In the example below, father is on the "one" side of the association while child is on the "many" side of the association.

```
    public class Person
    {
        // Services
        publicPerson(String   n, char s, int a, Person mom, Person dad)
        {...    code here ... }
        publicPerson getFather() { return father; }
        publicPerson getMother() { return mother; }
        publicVector   getChildren( ) {return children; }
        public boolean removeChild(Person p) { boolean x   =
        children.remove(p); return x; }
        publicboolean   addChild(Person p) { boolean x = children.add(p);
        return x; }
        privatevoid setFather(Person p)
```

```
                { father = p; if ( p.addChild(this) ) then return; else
                "error" }
        privatevoid setMother(Person p)
                { mother = p; if ( p.addChild(this) ) then return; else
                "error"; }
        // Variables
        privateString name;
        privatechar sex;
        privateint    age;
        privatePerson  father;
        privatePerson  mother;
        private Vector children;
    }
```

The implementation of the setFather(), setMother(), addChild(), and remove-Child() will be complex if we incorporate into the model the ability to adopt children. These methods must manage the integrity of the relationship. If there are attributes of the association (such as the date of birth), then they should be kept in the class on the "one" side of the relationship (the child).

Many-to-Many Association

A many-to-many association can be implemented in either of the following ways:

1. Add an attribute to both sides as a Vector of references to class objects of the other side. This is good for traversal but has update complexity.
2. Implement a distinct association object that is independent of either class in the association. An association object is a set of pairs stored in a single variable-size object. The set would consist of two pointers, one to each of the classes in the association.

The first technique is similar to the approach used in implementing a many-to-one association using buried references on both sides.

To better understand the second technique, let us add the class Company and the relationship "works-for" between Person and Company. Initially, you might decide that this is a many-to-one relationship. However, an individual may work for more than one company, and a company usually has more than one employee. This is a many-to-many relationship. Using the association object, we can create an object that has a set of pairs of pointers. In each pair, the first pointer points to a Person object and the second pointer points to a Company object. This is illustrated in Figure 17-1.

The first pair captures that person1 works for company1, and the second pair captures that person1 works for company2. The rest of the pairs should be self-explanatory. A very maintainable way of implementing an association object is to use multi-map objects.

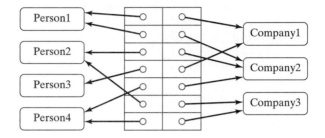

Figure 17-1   Association Object: Works-For.

IMPLEMENTING AGGREGATION

In (UML), there are two forms of the "aggregation" concepts that are captured in its notation: aggregation (unfilled diamond) and composition (filled diamond). The decision to choose these two forms were driven much more by implementation than by the formal analysis concepts discussed in Chapter 9. Thus, corresponding in implementation there are two ways to implement an aggregation: buried reference and inner class.

Buried Reference

Buried references are implemented in a similar manner to what was done in implementing an association. To understand this, let us add two more classes to our Person example. The two classes are Hand and Body. Because a person should have a body and two hands, we use this example to show how to implement composition (aggregation).

The following code is for the buried reference implementation:

```
public class Person
{
    public Person(String n, char s, int a) { ... code here ... }
    ...
    private String    name;
    ...
    privatePerson  spouse;  //binary relationship
    privateBody    body;    //reference to body
    privateHand    l_hand;  //reference to left hand
    privateHand    r_hand;  //reference to right hand
}
```

The constructors for initializing the references are the same as for an association. Similarly, because each object (body, l_hand, and r_hand) of the composition exists by itself, other functions may access the other objects directly. This is also true with the spouse object in the association.

Inner Classes

Using the same example, here is the implementation using embedded objects for composition.

```
public class Person
{
    publicPerson(String n, char s, int a)
        { ...;
    body = new Body();
    l_hand = new Hand();
    r_hand = new Hand(); ... }
...
    private  String  name;
        ...
    privatePerson  spouse;  //binary relationship
    class Body { ... class definition ... }
    privateBody  body;  //object within object
    class Hand ( ... class definition ... }
    privateHand  l_hand; //object within object
    privateHand  r_hand; //object within object
}
```

In the constructor, you would just instantiate the body, l_hand, and r_hand using the new keyword.

IMPLEMENTING STATIC MEMBERS

It is the unique property of a static data member that its variable (a single instance) exists independently of any objects in the class. This allows it to be used in ways that are illegal for nonstatic data members. For example, static members are accessible anywhere the class is in scope, and static data members act as global variables for the class. Normally, a static data member holds data that needs to be shared among all instances of the class. It is declared with the keyword static and is accessible in the form "className::identifier" when the variable has public visibility. For example,

```
public class Person
{
publicstatic int    pubdata = 12;  //initialize static variable
privatestatic int   pridata;
}
```

```
public class Test
   main( )
   {
       int tmp1 = Person::pubdata; // legal
       int tmp2 = Person::pridata;  // illegal
   }
}
```

Pridata does not have public visibility, so it is not accessible to any method, including the Main() method. However, pubdata has public visibility and is accessible to all methods that use the proper form for accessing it.

The initialization of static data members is same as that of nonstatic data members. Static member methods are services that are provided by the class and do not require an instance of the class in order to be accessed. A static member method can be called without an instance prefix and is accessible by the form "className::functionName" (signature). For example,

```
public class Person
{
publicstatic int getTotal()  // get the number of person instances
    { ... code for service is here ... }
    ...
private static int no_of_people;  // this is incremented by the
 //constructor
                               // and decremented by the destructor
}

public class Test {
   main()
   {
       int total = 0;
       total = Person::getTotal()
       Person p = new Person ( "Joe", m, 25);
       int ptotal = 0;
       ptotal = p.getTotal();
   }
}
```

The static method getTotal() is accessed directly by using its class name and the scoping operator in the second statement of Main(). In the fifth statement of Main(), it is accessed as a service of an object of the class Person. Both means of access are legal; however, a static member method may only use static variables and arguments of its signature in its service definition. Below is an example that illustrates what is legal and illegal in a static member method.

```
class Person
{
```

```
       public static int   pubdata;
       public static int   clsfcn1() { ... code below... }
       public          int   instdata1;
       public          int   instfcn1() { ...access to all instance and
       //class members ... }
       private static int   pridata;
       private static int   clsfcn2() {... rules are same as
       clsfcn2 ... }
       private          int   instdata2;
     private          int   instfcn2() { ...access to all instance and
     //class members ... }
   }

   Person::clsfcn1()
   {
   int tmp1 = Person::pubdata; // legal
   int tmp2 = Person::pridata; // legal
   int tmp3 = Person::instdata1; // illegal
   int tmp4 = Person::instdata2; // illegal
   int tmp5 = Person::instfcn1(); // illegal
   int tmp6 = Person::instfcn2(); // illegal
   int tmp7 = Person::clsfcn2(); // legal
   };
```

Thus, a static function may access any static data members or any other static method of the class within its function definition. However, it has no access to the nonstatic members.

RECOMMENDED APPROACH

Because many database layer software for object-oriented systems use references and collections of references, we recommend using the buried references approach to implement both association and aggregation. Static functions are to be used as a mechanism to access shared data among objects of the same class.

SUMMARY

In this chapter, we learned about implementing association, aggregation, and static members. Furthermore, we learned how to use static data and static functions to handle the "global data" shared by objects in the same class.

The following summarizes the key points of this chapter:

- References and the collection classes are used to implement association and aggregation.

- The following are some rules regarding references that you should keep in mind:

    1. References to different classes (interfaces) may not be equated without casting. The exception is that a public inherited subclass (derived class) reference can be assigned to a superclass (base-class) reference.
    2. A base-class reference must always be cast to a legal derived class reference.
    3. An object reference may always be assigned the void reference; however, a void reference must be cast to a legal object reference.

- An vector is used to implement the "many" side of a relationship.
- Aggregation may be implemented either by inner classes or by referenced objects.

Unified Modeling Language

Unified modeling language (UML) is a modeling language for documenting and visualizing the artifacts that we have specified and constructed in the analysis and design of a system. This appendix gives a broad understanding of what UML is and what UML is not.

INTRODUCTION

UML is a generic syntax for creating a logical model of a system. It is normally used to describe a computer system as it is understood at various points during analysis and design. The syntax was defined originally by Jim Rumbaugh and Grady Booch to contain all the constructs available in each of their own methods but with a common graphical representation. Later they were joined by Ivar Jacobson who added syntax for defining requirements with Use Cases, and the language was finalized by a committee of object-orientation experts.

The syntax has been designed to be independent of any particular target language, software process, or tool, but it is sufficiently generic and flexible that it can be used customized, using user-defined extensions, to accommodate almost all language, tool, or process requirement. Though the syntax itself is well defined and reasonably easy to understand, to apply it to a particular project is much less easy to define. This requires the definition of a set of semantics that are appropriate for a particular architecture and software process. This is left to the users.

What Is the Unified Modeling Language?

UML is a language that unifies the best engineering practices for modeling systems.

- It is a language for capturing knowledge (partial semantics) and for expressing that knowledge (syntax).
- Its purpose is for modeling of systems.
- It provides a visual illustration of that model.
- It is a collection of best practices.
- It is used to produce a set of artifacts that can be delivered.
- It has world-wide support.

What UML Is Not

UML is **not**

- a visual programming language
- a tool or repository specification
- a process

What Are the Goals of UML?

The stated goals of UML are to

- be an expressive visual modeling language that is relatively simple and extensible.
- have extensibility and specialization mechanisms for extending, rather than modifying the core concepts.
- be independent of any programming language.
- be process independent.
- support high-level concepts (framework, patterns, and components).
- address recurring architectural complex issues using the high-level concepts.
- be scalable and widely applicable (over many domains).

Why Use UML?

We produce products and services that address customer needs and requirements. Requirements may be considered the *problem,* and the products and/or services may be considered the *solution.* The problem and solution occur within some domain (space or context). For a good solution to be produced, first, the problem must be understood. The solution must also be understood for it to be constructed and used. Furthermore, the solution must be organized (architecture) to facilitate its realization and adhere to the constraints of the domain. Thus, to solve problems, the appropriate knowledge of the problem and solution must be captured (modeled), organized (architecture), and depicted (diagrams) using some mechanism that enables communication and leverage of our knowledge. UML is the mechanism of choice of industry.

What Are the Diagrams of UML?

UML has the following diagram types:

- Use-case diagrams
- Static-structure diagrams

  - Object diagrams
  - Class diagrams

- Interaction diagrams

  - Sequence diagrams
  - Collaboration diagrams

- Statechart diagrams
- Activity diagrams
- Implementation diagrams

  - Component diagrams
  - Deployment diagrams

Each of these diagrams are defined in the following sections.

What Are the Most Important UML Diagrams?

The most important models in the UML syntax are

- Use Case Diagrams. Use cases are used to capture the way in which the users want to use the system and form an outside-in definition of the requirements for the computer system in a way that can be understood by users and developers.
- Class Diagrams. Class diagrams are used to define the static structure model of the system. The static structure model identifies the objects, classes, and relationships among them.
- Interaction Diagrams (usually Sequence Diagrams). Interaction diagrams are used to capture the functional requirements. They are used as a tool to

help in deciding how the functionality required to support the use cases is to be distributed across the classes (Objects). They can also be used as a mechanism for mapping the required system functionality onto the objects in a way that produces functionally coherent, maintainable, reusable, and extensible classes.

- Statechart (Dynamic) Diagrams. Statechart diagrams are used to capture the dynamic view of the system. The state diagrams that make up the model show the dependence of the functionality on the state of the system. They also show the system functionality from an object-centric point of view (rather than the use-case-centric point of view). This helps in detailed design to ensure the correct coding of the conditionally of the operations. It also allows a maintainable, coherent, and robust coding of a class that encapsulates the dynamics. To ignore this view totally is to miss an in-depth understanding of the functionality of each individual class.

UML DIAGRAMS

UML defines nine types of diagrams: class, object, use case, sequence, collaboration, state chart, activity, component, and deployment diagrams. In all the diagrams, concepts are depicted as symbols and relationships among concepts are depicted as paths (lines) connecting symbols. Each of these elements may also have a name.

Use-Case Diagram

A use-case diagram describes the functionality and users (actors) of the system. It is used to show the relationships between the actors that use the system and the use cases they use (and also the relationship between use cases). A single use case can also be thought as a procedure by which an external actor can use the system. Taken together, the use cases define the full functionality of the system from an outside-in perspective and can be used as a basis from which to develop system tests.

The two concepts in a use-case diagram are:

- Actor. Represents users of the system, including human and other systems.
- Use Case. Represents services or functionality provided by the system to the users.

A use case is represented by an oval. The name of the use case can appear within or below the oval.[1] A description of the use case is attached to the use case as an attribute. It describes in prose (or sequence diagram) the sequence of interactions across the system boundary that make up the procedure by which the system is used.

---

[1] The majority of UML tools place the name of the use case below the oval.

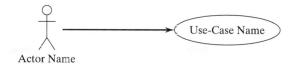

Figure A-1   Use-Case Diagram.

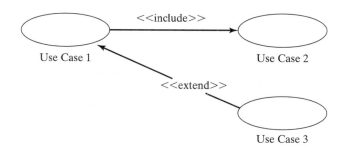

Figure A-2   The Extend and Include Relationships Among Use Cases.

The use case is attached to at least one actor, represented by a stick man, by a line called a "communicates" relationship. It shows which actor or actors outside the system are involved in the use case. A basic use-case diagram is illustrated in Figure A-1.

A use case can be related to another use case by either an "include" or an "extend" relationship. An "include" relationship indicates that the procedure of the used use case is part of the procedure of the using use case. The arrow is, in effect, an unconditional call to the procedure in the used use case. An example of the include relationship is illustrated in Figure A-2 in which use case 1 includes use case 2.

If the procedure of the use case is an alternative or partial alternative course to a defined in another use case, then an "extend" relationship is used from the "extending" use case to the "extended" use case. The procedure in the "extending" use case then replaces all or part of the procedure in the "extended" use case under conditions specified in the "extending" use case. This is illustrated in Figure A-2 in which use case 3 extends use case 2.

Include and extend relationships allow all possible procedures to be specified without duplication.

The boundaries of the system are illustrated in a use-case diagram as a boundary rectangle including the use cases with the actors outside of it. The name of the system appears at the top of the rectangle. A typical use-case diagram incorporating the boundary rectangle appears in Figure A-3.[2]

---

[2] Many books on UML and UML tools do not incorporate the boundary rectangle in use-case diagrams. The assumption is that the boundaries are well known and the rectangle is redundant.

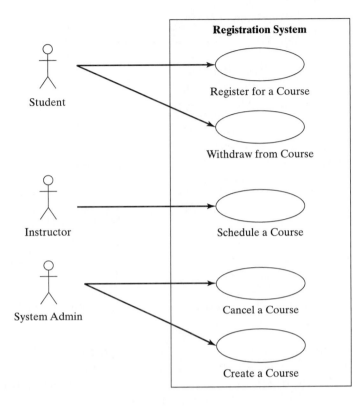

Figure A-3   Use-Case Diagram for a Registration System.

Associated with a use-case diagram is usually the corresponding use-case details. The details may be captured as either a sequence diagram or in a textual description. Use cases are discussed in Chapter 3.

Class Diagram

A static structure diagram describes the static structure[3] of a system. In other words, it describes how the system is structured instead of how it behaves. It describes "what things are" and their static relationships with other things. To describe all the objects in a system would be rather tedious as many of them have similar characteristics, and, in any case, some of them are created and destroyed as a program

---

[3] Object diagrams describe actual objects and their relationships; class diagrams describe types of objects and their relationships.

proceeds. Class diagrams are, therefore, used more often than object diagrams to show this view.[4]

Classes define the types of objects that exist within the system. Classes can have attributes that are usually primitive data members of objects and operations that define methods that can be performed on the object. The visibility of attributes and operations to other objects can be defined as can their signatures including types, default values, parameters, parameter types, and return types.

Object relationships between classes show what links can exist between objects and define constraints on those links including the relative quantity of instances linked by an association. Class diagrams can also show packages that group classes, dependencies between classes, and dependencies between the packages that contain them. Generalization/specialization relationships that relate classes in a supertype/subtype relationship can also be included.

A typical static model usually consists of many class diagrams that, taken together, define the static structure of the system. How they are organized depends largely on the architecture of the system.

The concepts and paths in this diagram are

- Class

  - Object
  - Class
  - Parameterized class
  - Constraints
  - Packages

- Relationship

  - Association
  - Associative object (association class)
  - Aggregation
  - Composition
  - Generalization
  - Dependency
  - Interfaces

Some key diagrammatic elements are common across all UML diagrams. These are illustrated in Figure A-4. The note with the dashed line connecting to another UML element is a mechanism for attaching textual comments in the diagram. Constraints are illustrated as comments within curly braces. The comment can contain anything. Stereotypes are used to create a new type of UML element (this is how one extends UML).

---

[4] Actual objects become important when they interact with other objects so it is more useful to view them in interaction diagrams.

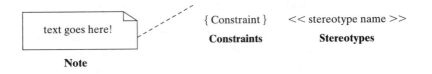

Figure A-4   Common Representational Elements Across UML Diagrams.

Class.   A class represents entities with common characteristics and behaviors (i.e., attributes, services, rules, and relationships). The following paragraphs describe how objects, class, and parameterized classes are documented in UML.

Figure A-5 illustrates how objects are represented in UML. An object is illustrated as a rectangle with the name underlined. The full name of an object is the object name and the class name separated by a colon. In some cases, either the object name or class name is not present. In all cases (and diagrams illustrating objects), the name of the object is underlined to distinguish it from a class.

In UML a class may appear in multiple diagrams. One result of this possibility is that different diagrams may suppress all or some attributes or operations. If a single attribute or operation is given, the rectangle for the class is partitioned into three sections. An empty section does not mean that there are no attributes or operations associated with the class, only that they have not been shown in that diagram. Figure A-6 illustrates two ways in which classes (as opposed to templated classes) are represented in UML diagrams. The first example illustrates how a class is represented when the attributes and operations associated with the class are suppressed. The second example illustrates a class with the attributes and operations represented. In the second example, the name of the class appears in the top section, the attributes in the middle section, and the operations in the bottom section.

Figure A-5   UML Notation for Objects.

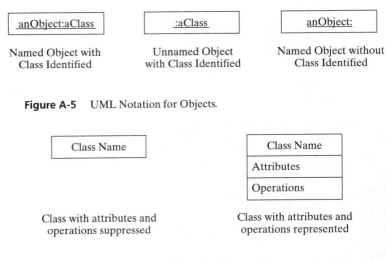

Figure A-6   UML Representations for Classes.

Attributes are specified according to the following notation:

```
visibility name: type = default-value
```

where

- *visibility* is public (+), protected (#), or private (–)[5]
- *name* is a string by which the attribute is identified
- *type* is the attribute type
- *default-value* is a value assigned to the attribute unless specified otherwise.

At a minimum, the name of the attribute must be specified. The other fields are optional.[6] A derived attribute, one that is computed rather than stored, is indicated by a "/" before the attribute declaration.

Operations are specified according to the following notation:

```
visibility name (parameter-list) : return-type [property-string]
```

where

- *visibility* is public (+), protected (#), or private (–)
- *name* is a string by which the operation is identified
- *parameter-list* contains comma-separated parameters whose syntax is given by direction name: type = default-value

  - *direction* indicates if the parameter is for input (in), output (out), or both (in out)
  - *name* is the name of the parameter
  - *type* is the type of the parameter
  - *default-value* identifies the default value of the parameter

- *return-type* is a comma-separated list of return types
- *property-string* indicated property values that apply to the operation

As was the case with attributes, only the name of the operation must be specified; the other fields are optional.

---

[5] The visibility parameter does not have rigorous semantics in UML. In fact, the interpretation of this parameter is usually locally defined based on the semantics of visibility employed by the programming language used in implementation. Hence, a C++-oriented development organization and a Smalltalk-oriented development organization may use the same visibility for an attribute, but mean different things by it.

[6] We should not be concerned with identifying the type associated with an attribute during analysis as that is a design decision. Because class diagrams are used during analysis and design, UML must support documenting our model with the appropriate levels of detail.

Figure A-7 illustrates the notation for a parameterized class. A parameterized class (templated class) is a class in which the type specified for one or more attributes (or parameters and/or return-values in operations) is specified as a formal argument of the class specification. In this example, the formal parameter is "T" and serves as placeholder for type information within the class specification.

A use of a parameterized class is called a bound element. It creates a new class with the formal parameters bound to the argument. There are two forms for illustrating a bound element, which appear in Figure A-8. The first form uses what can be considered C++ semantics for specifying a bound element in a template. In this case, the class name is the parameterized class name with the name of the bound class within angle brackets. The second form uses a dependency arrow (the dashed arrow) with a dependency prototype of bind shown in doubled angle brackets and the binding for the parameter shown in single angle brackets.

Figure A-9 illustrates how a constraint can be attached to a class. Anything may appear within the braces identifying the constraint. Most practitioners use a textual description of the constraint. However, UML does provide a formal language, Object Constraint Language, that can be used to document constraints.

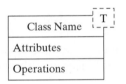

Figure A-7   A Parameterized Class.

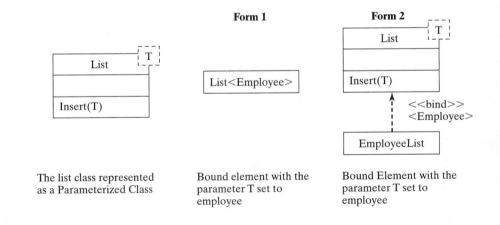

Figure A-8   Two forms of bound elements.

Figure A-9   Attaching a Constraint to a Class.

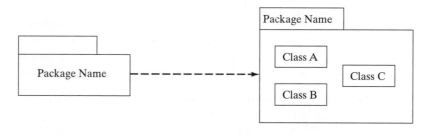

Figure A-10   Package Diagram.

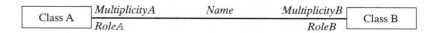

Figure A-11   Associations In UML.

Figure A-10 shows a package diagram. According to the UML specification, a package is illustrated using a folder-style icon. When the classes contained within the package are suppressed, the name of the package goes in the center of the folder. When the classes are present, the name of the package goes in the tab portion of the folder. Dependencies between packages are illustrated as a dashed arrow pointing in the direction of the dependency.

Relationships.   Relationships can exist between instances of classes or between classes. Associations and aggregations are relationships that relate two or more other instances of classes (association and aggregation). Generalization and special- ization are relationships between two classes.

Figure A-11 illustrates the basic representation of an association in UML. An association is drawn as a line connecting two classes. The line is labeled with the name of the association, the multiplicities of the two classes (number of objects of the given class) participating in the association, and the roles that an instance of each class takes within the association. All of these labels are optional.

The multiplicity associated with one end of an association can be given in any of the forms identified in Table A-1.

Table A-1 Multiplicity Keys and Their Interpretation

Key	Interpretation
*	Any number of objects (including none)
1	Exactly one object
n	Exactly n objects (n is an integer)
0...1	Zero or one (indicates the assocation is optional)
$n...m$	Range from n as minimum to m as maximum (n and m are integers)
2, 4	Discrete combinations (as in two doors or four doors)

The default assumption about an association is that it can be traversed by an object at either end of the association. In many cases, this assumption is not valid. To indicate unidirectional traversal the line connecting the two classes is replaced by an arrow pointing in the direction of traversal. This is illustrated in Figure A-12.

Figure A-13 illustrates how an association class is expressed. The association class is connected to the link between the two classes participating in the association by a dashed line. The association class can have attributes and operations associated with it.

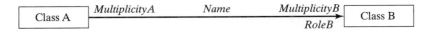

Figure A-12   Unidirectional Traversal Across an Association Is Indicated by an Arrow.

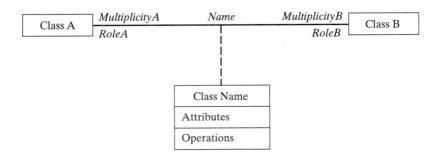

Figure A-13   Association Class.

Figure A-14 shows an association class that has been promoted to a full class. A derived association has been introduced to capture the fact that there is an association between Class A and Class B. The derived association is denoted through the use of a "/" in front of the association name.

Figure A-15 illustrates the diagram for a qualified association. Qualifiers can be used to denote key lookup in a map.

Figure A-16 illustrates the use of constraints on relationships. There are two cases, one in which the constraint is on the association itself and one in which the constraint is across two relationships. The constraint is expressed in the same fashion as constraints on classes (as a condition within curly braces).

Figure A-14   Promoting an Association Class to a Full Class and Introducing a Derived Association.

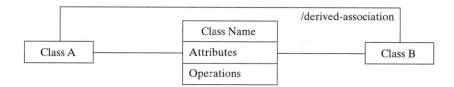

Figure A-15   Qualified Association.

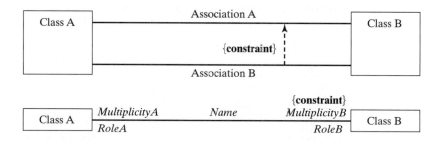

Figure A-16   Use of Constraints on Relationships.

Figure A-17 illustrates how aggregation and composition are documented. Unidirectional navigation across the aggregation or composition is illustrated using an arrow in the same manner as for associations. Constraints can be anything and must appear in curly braces. Multiplicity is denoted in the same fashion as done for associations.

Figure A-18 shows generalization and specialization. The generalization is indicated as the class with the point of the triangle pointing at it. Subclass 1 illustrates single generalization, while Subclass 2 illustrates multiple generalization. Generalization can have a discriminator that distinguishes between different kinds of generalizations.[7]

Figure A-19 illustrates how dependencies between classes are documented. Dependencies are typically associations that are created dynamically.

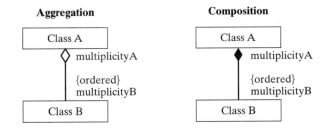

Figure A-17   Aggregation and Composition.

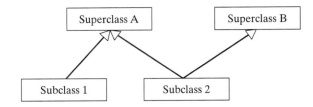

Figure A-18   Generalization and Specialization.

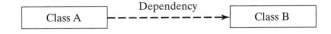

Figure A-19   Dependency.

---

[7] This diagram can be used to express multiple and dynamic classification. For this diagram, one employs a discriminator to establish which combinations are legal. Classification is different than inheritance, in the sense that multiple classification allows multiple types for an object without defining a specific type for that purpose.

Figure A-20 illustrates how an interface can be specified using classes. The dashed line with the triangle at the end is used to indicate that the implementation class realizes the interface. An alternative way of documenting interfaces uses a lollipop style icon to represent the interface as shown in Figure A-21.

Typical class diagrams illustrating the static structure of the Breakout Game are illustrated in Figures A-22 through A-24.

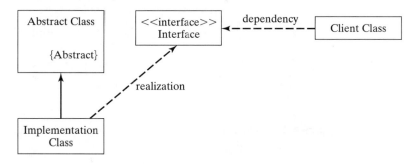

Figure A-20   Interface Diagram Using Classes.

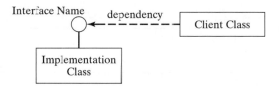

Figure A-21   Alternative Form for Representing Interfaces.

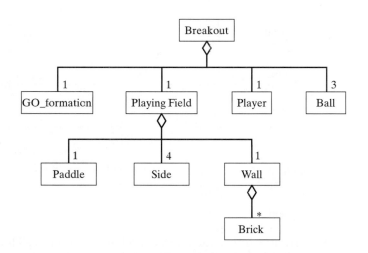

Figure A-22   Class Aggregation for Simplified Version of Breakout Game.

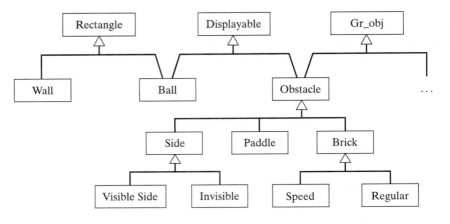

Figure A-23   Inheritance Diagram from Simplified Breakout Game.

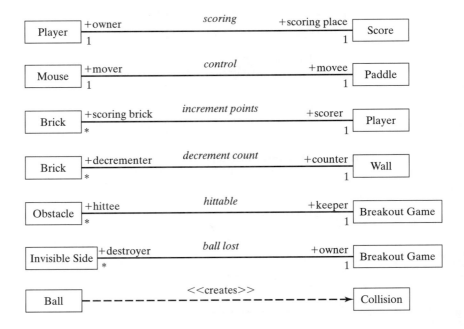

Figure A-24   Association Diagram from Breakout Game.

Sequence Diagram

Sequence diagrams capture the interaction between objects. These interactions are modeled as exchanges of messages. These message exchanges result in some desired behavior. It can show the interactions that take place, both across the system boundary and between objects inside the system, to fulfill the requirements defined for one or more paths through a use case.

The concepts and paths in this diagram are

- Object of a particular type (class or interface), which represents the role that the object plays in the interaction.
- Lifeline, which represents the existence of the object over a period of time.
- Activation, which represents the time when an object is performing some method.
- Message. Represents communication between objects.

A sequence diagram, such as shown in Figure A-25, is a diagram that shows actual objects and interactions between objects in the horizontal direction and sequence in the vertical direction. The vertical dotted lines represent the lifetime of the object and horizontal arrows the interactions or messages between objects. These messages can represent any kind of message (specifically a call to an operation on the target object). Messages can include sequence numbers, operation names, and actual parameters. Narrow elongated boxes on the object lifelines represent the "activation" of the object when interactions are sequential and represent calls to operations. The operation remains active until all the sequential operations, which it calls, have completed and returned, thus, allowing it to return control to its caller.

Figure A-26 shows a typical sequence diagram taken from the microwave oven example in Chapter 7.

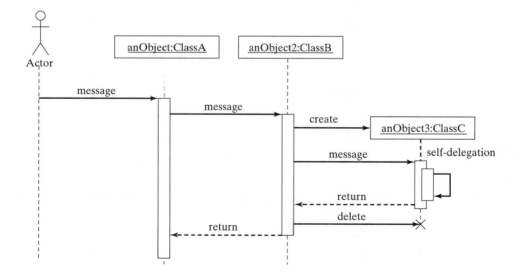

Figure A-25   Sequence Diagram.

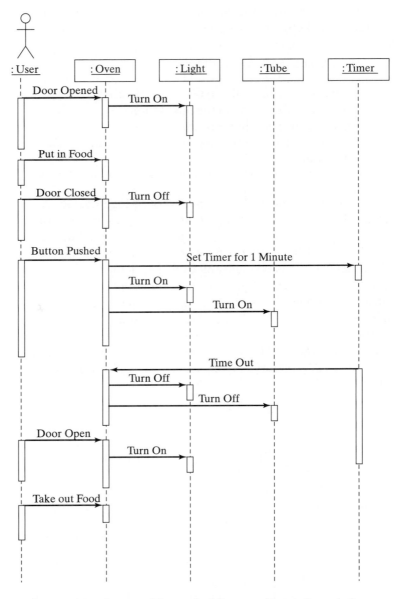

Figure A-26   Sequence Diagram for Microwave Oven in Scenario 2.

Collaboration Diagram

A collaboration diagram captures the interactions among objects. These interactions are modeled as exchanges of messages. These message exchanges result in some desired behavior.

A collaboration diagram is functionally equivalent to a sequence diagram with two exceptions:

- It shows links between objects along which messages can flow whereas only the messages are shown in a sequence diagram.
- The order of the messages can only be seen in their numbering as the vertical dimension is used to show static relationships along with the horizontal dimension.[8]

A collaboration diagram is used to show how groups of objects work together to perform a piece of functionality required for one path through a use case.[9]

The concepts and paths in this diagram are

- Object of a particular type (class or interface), represents the role that the object plays in the interaction.
- Relationship rule, represents role that the link may play within the interaction.
- Message, represents communication between objects.

Figure A-27 illustrates a collaboration diagram. The service request is of the form

```
sequence-number : [condition] : message ( arglist )
```

where

- *sequence-number* identifies the order in which the service request was dispatched

  - * is used to indicate iteration (for example, 2* indicates that the second service request repeats)
  - sequence numbers can be sequential integers or based on a decimal scheme

- *condition* is an optional condition that is to be evaluated to determine if the request is sent
- *message* is a string identifying the service request
- *arglist* is a list of arguments formatted in the same fashion as the arglist for an operation

Figure A-28 is a collaboration diagram from Chapter 5.

---

[8] This makes the collaboration diagram effectively an object diagram with messages on the links.

[9] Sequence diagrams are better for fully specifying a use case as they can include conditional functionality in various ways without confusing the order of the messages.

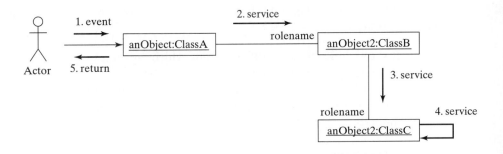

Figure A-27   Collaboration Diagram.

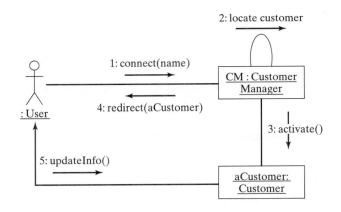

Figure A-28   UML Notation for a Collaboration Diagram.

Statechart Diagram

A statechart diagram describes how the functionality of an object depends on its state and how its state changes as a result of the events that it receives. It is used to show the dependency of operations on the order of their calling (i.e., on the state of the object when a call to an operation arrives at the boundary of an object).[10]

The concepts and paths in this diagram are

- State, which represents an abstraction of the attribute values of an object. It represents a period between events during which the object is stable. If an object has many internal states, the state model can be simplified by using "nested states" within a simpler state model.

---
[10] Those familiar with structured methods may recognize them as "Entity Life Histories."

- Event, which represents a condition that can be detected by the object. Events can cause a transition to another state and/or they can cause one or more actions to be triggered. An incoming event, normally a call to one of the object's public operations, causes a different response by the object depending on its current state. Operations are coded such that their response is conditional on the state of the object.
- Transition, which represents a response by an object to an event received by it. The response produces a change in the object, which can constitute a change in state. The mechanism for identifying if a change in state occurs is a *guard condition*. A guard condition is a Boolean expression in terms of event parameters and the state variables and functions of the object to which the state diagram belongs. When an event triggers the transition, the value of the guard condition is evaluated. If the value evaluates to true, the transition occurs; otherwise, the transition does not occur. Not all transitions have an associated guard condition.
- Action, which represents a set of operation that is done inside of a state or on a transition.

In UML, three additional constructs are added: *history state*, *activity*, and *timing mark*. A *history state* is used to capture the concept that a state must "remember" its substate when it is exited and be able to enter the same substate on subsequent reentry into the state. An *activity* is an operation or set of operations within a state that takes time to complete; thus, it is not instantaneous and can be interrupted. Some activities continue until they are terminated by an external event (usually a state change) and others terminate on their own accord. A *timing mark* construct is used to capture real-time constraints on transition. The most common use of a timing mark is to capture the maximum limits on the elapsed time between events.

Figure A-29 illustrates a simple state diagram. States are represented by rounded boxes. Transitions are represented by arrows between states. An event/action block on the transition defines the event, which causes the transition, any conditions that qualify the event, and any actions that take place. Event/action blocks can also be contained within states. These can be used to define what actions take place on entry into or exit from the state or when the object receives an event while in that state that does not require it to change state.

More complex state models incorporate nested states (i.e., substates). The UML diagram for illustrating a nested state diagram is illustrated in Figure A-30. The transition from the nested solid circle identifies the entry substate. Actions are associated with the nested states rather than the encompassing state.

Figure A-31 is from Chapter 7. This example illustrates the how nested concurrent states are represented.

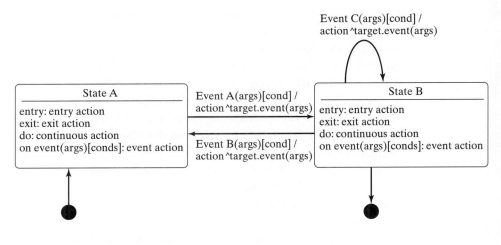

Figure A-29   Simple State Diagram.

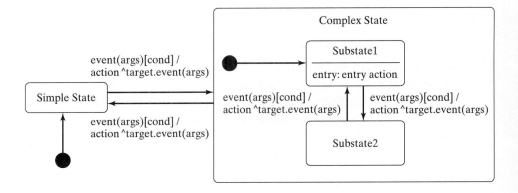

Figure A-30   Nested State Diagram.

Activity Diagram

An activity diagram can be used anywhere in the model to show a flow of activity; however, it is usually reserved for defining the flow of business level events outside the scope of the system.[11]

---

[11] It was introduced to provide some syntax for business process modeling that is separate from the model of the system requirements, the use cases, and the model of the internal system architecture defined by all the other diagram types.

Course registration request

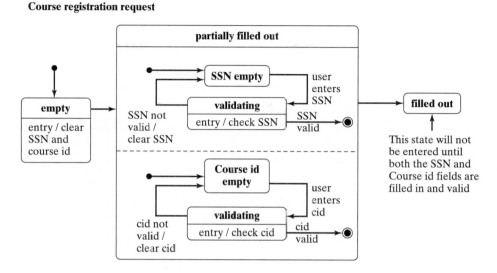

Figure A-31   Concurrent State Chart Diagram for a Course Registration Request.

In some methods, an activity diagram is used to describe activities either

- within an object (i.e., capturing state and its relationship with an interaction), or
- between objects (i.e., capture state dependencies across objects).

The concepts and paths in this diagram are

- Swimlane, which represents responsibilities of one or more objects for actions within an overall interaction.
- Action state, which represents atomic, or non interruptible, actions of an entity.
- Action flow, which represents relationship between different action states of an entity.
- Object flow, which represents the utilization of objects by action states and the influence of these states on the object.

An activity diagram is similar to a state diagram in that they represent sequences of activity but are closer in semantics to flowcharts in allowing action states. Swimlanes allow activities associated with action states to be assigned to business level actors.

Figure A-32 shows a basic activity diagram. The solid circle at the top indicates the start point. The rounded rectangles (sausages) identify activities. The arrows

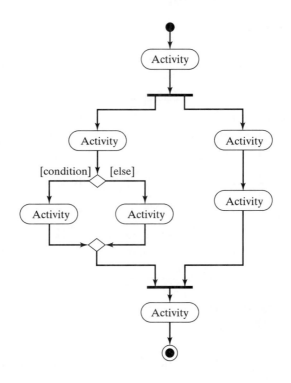

Figure A-32   Activity Diagram.

represent a transition. Conditional behavior is identified by branches and merges. A diamond represents a branch point if one arrow enters and multiple arrows exit or a merge if several arrows enter and one arrow exits. Concurrent behavior is identified by forks and joins. A dark bar represents a fork if one arrow enters and multiple arrows exit or a join if multiple arrows enter and a single arrow exits.

Figure A-33 is an activity diagram from Chapter 6 that illustrates the use of swimlanes.

Component Diagram

A component diagram describes the organization and dependencies among software implementation components. It shows the structure of software components that are used to implement the system. These components can include source files, re-locatable code, and executables.

Figure A-34 illustrates a component diagram. The concepts and paths in this diagram are

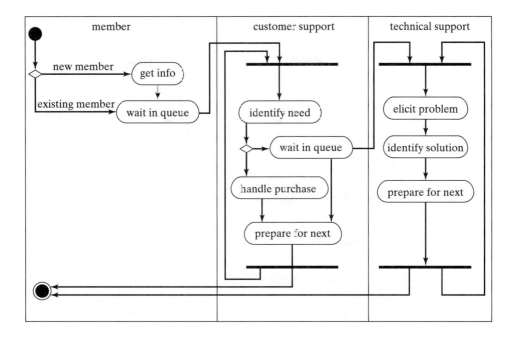

Figure A-33 An Activity Diagram for a Customer Support System.

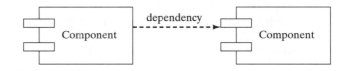

Figure A-34 Component Diagram.

- Component, which represents distributable physical units such as source code, object code, or executable code.
- Dependency, which represents the dependency between components.

If a group of classes forms a component, we may define another way in which other components use it by applying a special UML construct: an interface. The interface allows components to be designed for use by other components without any knowledge of the internal structure of the used component. Thus, the using component depends on the interface to the used component, not on its implementation. This makes it possible to design components that are polymorphic (i.e., substitutable for one another).

Figure A-35 is a component diagram from Chapter 11.

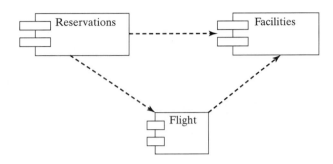

Figure A-35   Component Diagram for a Flight Reservations System.

Deployment Diagram

A deployment diagram describes the configuration of processing elements and the mapping of the software implementation components to the processing elements. It shows instances of processor nodes, their interconnection, instances of the components that run on them, and the dependence between the instances. The concepts and paths in this diagram are

- Component, which represents distributable physical units such as source code, object code, or executable code.
- Node, which represents a processing or computation resource.

Figure A-36 illustrates a deployment diagram. It consists of two processors with a single component on each. The processors are connected by (TCP/IP). There is a dependency between the Graphical User Interface (GUI) component on central processing unit (CPU) 2 with the myComponent on CPU 1.

Figure A-37 is an example of deployment diagram taken from Chapter 11 that shows a physical device (TicketPrinter) connected to a CPU (the AgentTerminal).

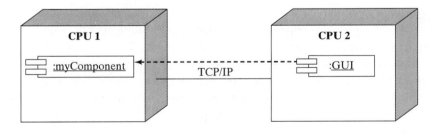

Figure A-36   Deployment Diagram.

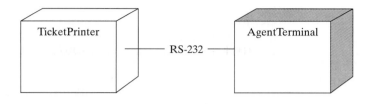

Figure A-37 Deployment Diagram.

UML GLOSSARY

Table A-2 is a glossary of UML terms used in this book.

Table A-2 Glossary of UML Terms

Term	Definition
Activity diagram	A diagram of state behavior in which individual states are sequential steps representing the operations of an interaction. The interaction is typically the service of a given class, and the activity diagrams describes the serial events that take place within it.
Actor	An entity outside of a system that interacts with it. An actors activities are described by a use case.
Action	An operation or a set of operation that is done inside of a state or on a transition. It cannot be interrupted.
Action flow	It represents the relationship between different action states of an entity.
Action state	It represents atomic, or non-interruptible, actions of an entity.
Activation	The time when an object is performing some method.
Activity	An operation or set of operations within a state that takes time to complete. Thus, it is not instantaneous and can be interrupted.
Adornment	A graphical element used to denote some particular property or state.
Aggregation	A hierarchy containment relationship in which the part(s) can be exist without the container.
Association	A peer-to-peer relationship between objects.
Associative object	Special case of an object relationship in which the attributes (information) of the relationship needs to be kept.
Attribute	An inherent property of a class. It has a name and a type.
Class	A descriptor for a set of objects with identical attributes, behaviors, rules, and relationships.
Class diagram	It describes the static structure of a system.

Table A-2 Glossary of UML Terms (*continued*)

Term	Definition
Collaboration diagram	It captures the interaction between objects.
Compartment	A visual display area that can take part of or all of a UML elements. For example, a UML class shows the class name, services, and attributes in separate compartments.
Component	A distributable physical unit, usually of software.
Component diagram	It describes the organization and dependencies among software implementation components.
Composition	A hierarchy containment relationship in which the part(s) can NOT exist without the container.
Constraint	A semantic relationship between the model elements that describes conditions that must be maintained as true. If the constraint is violated then the model is considered semantically invalid.
Dependency	A semantic relationship between two or more model elements. It shows that one element would be affected by the change or absence of another element.
Deployment diagram	It describes the configuration of processing elements and the mapping of the software implementation components to the processing elements.
Element	Any UML concept.
Event	A noteworthy occurrence that, in a state diagram, may trigger the transition from one state to the next.
Export	In the context of packages, it makes an element accessible outside its enclosing namespace by adjusting its visibility.
Generalization /specialization	A hierarchical relationship between classes in which the subclass (child class) inherits all the attributes, operations, rules, and object relationships (association and aggregation) of its superclasses.
History state	Remember its substate when it is exited and be able to enter the same substate on subsequent reentry into the state.
Inheritance	A mechanism for implementing generalization/specialization in some programming languages. Also used in UML as equivalence of generalization/specialization.
Interaction diagram	A UML diagram that describes how a group of objects collaborate in some behavior, typically by exchanging messages. Sequence diagrams and collaboration diagrams are different kinds of interaction diagrams.
Interface	Makes the using component depends on the interface to the used component, not on its implementation.
Lifeline	In a sequence diagram, it shows the lifetime of the object in the given interaction.
Message	Represents an interaction between objects.
Multiplicity	It shows the allowable numeric range of values that a given UML element has with another element.

Table A-2 Glossary of UML Terms (*continued*)

Term	Definition
Node	It represents a processing or computation resource.
Note	It shows textual information with regards to a UML model element
Object constraint language (OCL)	A text language for specifying constraints and queries using expressions, guard conditions, actions, preconditions, postconditions, assertions etc.
Object diagram	It describes actual objects and their relationships. Rarely used.
Object relationship	Association or aggregation or composition.
Operation	A service or function of an instance of a class that can be requested to perform. An operation consists of a name and a list of parameters.
Package	A mechanism for organizing model elements into groups. Packages may be nested. Inner packages can see elements in enclosing packages without imports.
Package diagram	It is a class diagram that shows the packages within a system, their interfaces plus the dependency between packages and either other packages or their interfaces.
Relationship	Relates two or more other instances of classes (association and aggregation) or relates two classes (generalization and specialization).
Realize	To provide the implementation for a specification element. This is shown using a dotted generalization relationship.
Refinement	Specifies that a model element is a more refined version of a generalized element. (i.e., generalization/specialization).
Statechart diagram	It describes how the functionality of an object depends on its state and how its state changes as a result of the events that it receives.
Static structure diagram	Either a class diagram or an object diagram.
Stereotype	Used to create a new type of UML element. This is how one extends UML.
Sequence diagram	It captures the interaction between objects. These interactions are modeled as exchanges of messages.
State	A condition or interaction that satisfies a condition during the lifetime of an object. This is depicted in UML state and activity diagrams as a rectangle with rounded corners.
Sub-system	A package with one or more interfaces and is designed to representation a component that is the implementation of the sub-system.
Swimlane	It represents responsibilities of one or more objects for actions within an overall interaction.
Timing mark	It is used to capture real-time constraints on transition. The most common use of a timing mark is to capture the maximum limits on the elapsed time between events.

Table A-2 Glossary of UML Terms (*continued*)

Term	Definition
Transition	A relationship between two states that indicates that an object will progress from the first state to the second when a specified event takes place.
Use case	A meaningful unit of functionality provided by a system or class instance that is visible to one or more actors.
Use-case diagram	It describes the functionality and users of the system.
Visibility	A designation that describes the scope of access for a particular attribute or operation. In UML, this is public (+), private (−), and protected (#).

B

Java Language Summary

This appendix provides a summary or quick reference for the Java language.

Language keywords are shown in bold. Arguments and values that are provided by the developers are shown in italics. Optional constructs are indicated by square brackets (except in the array section). If there are several options that are mutually exclusive, they are shown separated by pipes. For example,

```
[ public | private | protected ]
```

This appendix is divided into the following sections:

- Reserved Words. Words reserved for use by the language itself.
- Comments. How to add comments to the program.
- Literals. There are constants or values in a program.
- Variable Declaration. They are the slots that hold values.
- Variable Assignment. How do we assign values to variables?
- Operators. Methods or services predefined. These are usually for the primitive data types.
- Loop and Conditions.

- Class and Interface Definitions.
- Objects. How to create and use objects.
- Arrays.
- Method and Constructor Definitions.
- Packages and Importing. How to organize your classes.
- Exceptions and Synchronization. How to handle exceptions.

RESERVED WORDS

Table B-1 contains the reserved words. Some of the words are reserved, but presently not used. We cannot use these words to refer to classes, methods, or variable names. Table B-1 lists the keywords.[1]

Table B-1   Reserved Words (Keywords)

abstract	boolean	break	byte
case	catch	char	class
const	continue	do	double
else	extends	final	finally
float	for	goto	if
implements	import	instanceOf	int
interface	long	native	new
null	package	private	protected
public	return	short	static
super	switch	synchronized	this
throw	throws	transient	try
void	volatile	while	

COMMENTS

There are three forms for comments (same as C++):

```
/* This is a multiline comment that must end
   with an asterick and a forward slash
   with no space.
   Here is the final line.   */

// This is a single line comment

/** Java document comment */
```

---

[1] For details on each reserved word, consult www.javasoft.com.

LITERALS

Table B-2 describes the literals supported by Java.

Table B-2 Literals

Literals	Examples	Comments
number	115, 25, 562345	Data type is int
number[l | L]	15L, 25l, 562345L	Data type is long
0x*hex*; 0X*hex*	0x1A, 0XAF, 0x12	Hex integer[a]
0*octal*	0177, 0156476	Octal integer[b]
decimalNumber or *decimalNumber*[d | D]	23.34, 254.5677 23.34D, 254.5677d	Data type is double
decimalNumber[f | F]	23.45F, 254.5677f	Data type is float
[+ | −] *number* or [+ | −] *decimalNumber*	−115, +25l, −5623451 −23.24f, +254.5677D, −10.	Signed number or Signed decimal number
decimalNumber [e | E] *number*	23.34E5, −2.5456e30	Exponent
'*character*'	'e', 'x', 'z'	Single character
"*characters*"	"example", "test"	Data type is String class
""	""	Empty string
\b		Backspace character
\t		Tab character
\n		Line feed character
\f		Form feed character
\r		Carriage return character
\"		Double quote character
\'		Single quote character
\\		Backspace character
\u*NNNN*	\uAF12, \u12FF	Unicode escape
boolean values: true and false	true, false	Data type is boolean

[a] Reminder that hexadecimal is base-16 arithmetic; thus, the "digits" are 0–9 and A–F.
[b] Reminder that octal is base-8 arithmetic; thus, the "digits" are 0–7.

VARIABLE DECLARATION

Table B-3 gives the basic variable declarations.

Table B-3 Variable Declarations

Language Construct	Data Type(s)
[**byte** | **short** | **int** | **long**] *varname;*	Integers (pick a data type)

Table B-3   Variable Declarations (*continued*)

Language Construct	Data Type(s)
[**float** | **double**] *varname;*	Floats (pick a data type)
char *varname;*	Character
boolean *varname;*	Boolean
className varname;	"Class name" type
interfaceName varname;	"Interface name" type
myType varname, varname, varname;	Multiple variables of myType where myType can be any primitive data type or a class or an interface

The options shown in Table B-4 are available for class and instance variables. The options can be used with a variable declaration.

Table B-4   Options for Variable Declarations

Language Construct	Explanation
[**static**] *variableDeclaration*	Class variables by using static keyword
[**final**] *variableDeclaration*	Constants by using final keyword
[**public** | **private** | **protected**] *variableDeclaration*	Access control (pick one)
[**volatile**] *varname;*	Modified asynchronously by using volatile keyword
[**transient**] *varname;*	Not persistent by using transient keyword

VARIABLE ASSIGNMENT

Table B-5 gives the various forms of variable assignment.

Table B-5   Variable Assignments

Language Construct	Explanation
variable = [*value* | *value expression*];	Assignment statement
variable += [*value* | *value expression*];	Add and then assign
variable −= [*value* | *value expression*];	Subtract and then assign
variable *= [*value* | *value expression*];	Multiply and then assign
variable /= [*value* | *value expression*];	Divide and then assign
variable %= [*value* | *value expression*];	Modulus and then assign
variable &= [*value* | *value expression*];	Logical "and" and then assign

Table B-5   Variable Assignments (*continued*)

Language Construct	Explanation
variable |– [*value*	*value expression*];	Logical "or" and then assign
variable ^= [*value*	*value expression*];	Logical "xor" and then assign
variable++	Postfix increment
++*variable*	Prefix increment
variable—	Postfix decrement
—*variable*	Prefix decrement
variable <<= [*value*	*value expression*];	Left shift by value and then assign
variable >>= [*value*	*value expression*];	Right shift by value and then assign
variable >>>– [*value*	*value expression*];	Zero-fill right shift by value and then assign

OPERATORS

All operators take arguments. An argument may be a variable, a value, or an expression that evaluates to a value of the correct type. The defined operators are given in Table B-6.

Table B-6   Operators

Language Construct	Explanation
argumentOne + argumentTwo	Addition
argumentOne - argumentTwo	Subtraction
*argumentOne * argumentTwo*	Multiply
argumentOne / argumentTwo	Division
argumentOne % argumentTwo	Modulus
argumentOne < argumentTwo	Less than (Boolean value as result)
argumentOne <= argumentTwo	Less than or equal to (Boolean value as result)
argumentOne > argumentTwo	Greater than (Boolean value as result)
argumentOne >= argumentTwo	Greater than or equal to (Boolean value as result)
argumentOne == argumentTwo	Equal (Boolean value as result)
argumentOne != argumentTwo	Not equal (Boolean value as result)
argumentOne && argumentTwo	Logical and (Boolean value as result)
argumentOne || *argumentTwo*	Logical or (Boolean value as result)
! *argument*	Logical not (Boolean value as result)
argumentOne & argumentTwo	AND for bit operations
argumentOne	*argumentTwo*	OR for bit operations

Table B-6 Operators (*continued*)

Language Construct	Explanation
argumentOne ^ *argumentTwo*	XOR for bit operations
argumentOne << *argumentTwo*	Left shift for bit operations
argumentOne >> *argumentTwo*	Right shift for bit operations
argumentOne >>> *argumentTwo*	Zero-fill right shift for bit operations
~ *argument*	Complement for bit operations
(*type*) *objectName*	Casting; type must be a data type
objectName **instanceOf** *className*	Instance of
boolean expression ? *trueOp* : *falseOp*	Ternary (if) operator

LOOPS AND CONDITIONS

The loops, shown in Table B-7, are controlled by a boolean expression that can be evaluated to be true or false. A block is a set of statements enclosed in a set of curly braces or a single statement with no curly braces. Statements is a set of statements with no blocking.

Table B-7 Loops and Conditionals

Language Construct	Explanation
if (*boolean expression*) *block*	Conditional
if (*boolean expression*) *blockOne* **else** *blockTwo*	Conditional with else clause

switch ([**integer** | **char**] **expression**) {
    case *value* : *statements*
    case *value* : *statements*
    ...
    default : *statements*
}
	Switch statement
	(can only be used with integer or char
	 data types.)

for (*initializer*; *boolean expression*; *change*) *block*	For loop
while (*boolean expression*) *block*	While loop
do *block* **while** (*boolean expression*)	Do loop
break [*label*] ;	Break from a loop or switch
continue [*label*] ;	Continue loop
label: *statement*	Labeled statement—used for loop control

CLASS AND INTERFACE DEFINITIONS

In this section, the body is the code that defines the class or the code that defines the interface. It is enclosed in curly braces. The basic class definition is as follows:

```
class className body
```

Any of the optional modifiers shown in Table B-8 can be added to the basic class definition.

Table B-8   Options for Class Definitions

Language Construct	Explanation
[**abstract**] **class** *className body*	Cannot be used to instantiate an object
[**final**] **class** *className body*	Cannot be subclassed
[**public**] **class** *className body*	Accessible outside the package
class *className* [**extends** *Superclass*] *body*	Inherits from the superclass
class *className* [**implements** *Interfaces*] *body*	Implements one or more interfaces

The basic interface definition is as follows:

```
interface interfaceName [ extends anotherInterface ] body
```

Any of the optional modifiers shown in Table B-9 can be added to the basic interface definition.

Table B-9   Options for Class Definitions

Language Construct	Explanation
[**abstract**] **interface** *interfaceName body*	Redundant
[**public**] **interface** *interfaceName body*	Redundant

OBJECTS

Within an object, there are two types of variables and methods: class or instance. Class variables are shared by all the instances of the class, while instance variables are not shared by each instance (i.e., each instance has its own storage space for the instance variable, while there is only one storage location for a class variable). Class variables and methods are distinguished from the instance variable by the keyword static. In this section, instanceVar will be used to represent instanceVariable and classVar to represent class variables. We will also use service to represent calling an instance method and classService to represent calling a class method. Table B-10 shows how instances can be created and how services are requested.

Table B-10   Objects

Language Construct	Explanation
object = **new** *className*( );	Create a new instance
object = **new** *className*(*arg1, arg2, ...*);	Create a new instance using parameters
object.instanceVar	Instance variable
object.service( )	Instance method with no parameters
object.service(*arg1, arg2, ...*)	Instance method with parameters
object.classVar	Class variable
object.classService( )	Class method with no parameters
object.classService(*arg1, arg2, ...*)	Class method with parameters
className.classVar	Class variable via class as the object
className.classService( )	Class method with no parameters via class as the object
className.classService(*arg1, arg2, ...*)	Class method with parameters via class as the object

ARRAYS

The brackets in this section are used as part of the array definition. We use *type* to represent that we need to use a data type name (either primitive data type or a class name or an interface name). *Index* and *numberOfElements* must evaluate to an integer. Features of using arrays are shown in Table B-11.

Table B-11   Arrays

Language Construct	Explanation
type varName[ ]	Array variable
type [ ]*varName*	Alternative form of array variable
new *type varName*[*numberOfElements*]	Create a new array of objects
varName[*index*]	Element access
varName.length	Length of the array

METHOD AND CONSTRUCTOR DEFINITIONS

The basic method definition is as follows:

```
returnType methodName( ) body
returnType methodName( parameter1, parameter2, ... ) body
```

where the returnType is a primitive data type, a class name, an interface name, or void. The body is the method definition that is a block of code enclosed in curly braces. The method parameters look like this

```
type parameterName
```

where type is a primitive data type, a class name, or an interface name. The keywords in Table B-12 can be used for method variations.

Table B-12 Options for Method Definitions

Language Construct	Explanation
[**abstract**] *returnType methodName( ) body*	Abstract method
[**final**] *returnType methodName( ) body*	Final method—cannot be overridden
[**public** | **private** | **protected**] *returnType methodName( ) body*	Access control
[**static**] *returnType methodName( ) body*	Class method
[**native**] *returnType methodName( ) body*	Native method
[**synchronized**] *returnType methodName( ) body*	Thread locking before executing

Constructors are shown in Table B-13.

Table B-13 Constructor Definitions

Language Construct	Explanation
className( ) block	Basic constructor
className(parameter1, parameter2, ...) block	Constructor with parameters
[**public** | **private** | **protected**] *className( ) block*	Access control

In either the method or the constructor body, you can use the language constructs shown in Table B-14.

Table B-14 Options for Method Definitions

Language Construct	Explanation
this	Reference to current object
super	Reference to object's immediate superclass
super.*methodName( )*	Calls a superclass method

Table B-14   Options for Method Definitions (*continued*)

Language Construct	Explanation
this(...)	Calls the specific class constructor
super(...)	Calls the specific superclass constructor
return [*value*]	Returns or returns a value

PACKAGES AND IMPORTING

The following construct defines a package:

```
package packageName;
```

in which the classes following this statement are included in the same file.
To import classes from another package

```
import packageName.*
```

to get all the public classes in the package. Or use

```
import packageName.className
```

to get a specific class from a specific package.

EXCEPTIONS AND SYNCHRONIZATION

Table B-15 presents the key constructs for exception handling and synchronization.

Table B-15   Exceptions and Synchronization

Language Construct	Explanation
try *block1*	Guarded statements
catch (*exception*) *block2*	Executed if exception is thrown
[**finally** *block3*]	Clean-up code
synchronized (*object*) *block*	Waits for lock on the object

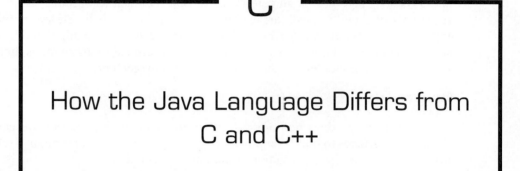

C

How the Java Language Differs from C and C++

This appendix discusses the differences between the Java language and C and C++. The following major differences are described in this appendix.

- C data types that are not supported. Three data types (struct, union, and pointer) that are part of the C and C++ languages are not supported.
- Fixed-size primitive data types.
- Operators that are different. There are differences in how certain operators work as compared to both C and C++.
- Arguments are different. The command line arguments passed are different in number and in type from those passed to a C or C++ program. Variable-length arguments lists are not supported.
- Java Arrays are first-class objects.
- Java Strings are first-class objects. In C and C++, strings are simply a null-terminated array of characters. In Java, strings are instances of the String class provided in the java.lang package.
- Memory management. There is automatic garbage collection in Java.

435

- Miscellaneous differences. There are several other minor differences between the C and C++ language and the Java language.

C DATA TYPES NOT SUPPORTED

The Java language does not support pointers, struct, or union.

Pointers

The Java language passes all references to objects (such as variable assignment, arguments of a method call, array elements) by using implicit references (not an explicit pointer type). A reference is a pointer that cannot be manipulated by using pointer arithmetic. Thus, we cannot construct a reference to anonymous memory. This prevents common errors due to pointer mismanagement.

Struct and Union

The Java language does not support either struct or union. Instead, we can use classes or interfaces to build composite types. For example, in C, we might declare a structure that contains information about employees like this.

```
struct employee {
    char name[SizeOfName];
    char address[SizeOfAddr];
    long empId;
    double baseSalary;
    double (*computePay)(double, double);
};
```

The last line of this structure is a reference (pointer) to a function. When we allocate and initialize an employee structure, we must supply the structure with a pointer to a function, and that function must be defined as indicated in the struct declaration. The computePay function must accept two doubles as arguments, and it returns a double. Here is the code for the function.

```
double computePay(double salary, double percent)
{
    return (salary + salary * percent);
}
```

Note that even though baseSalary is part of the structure, we still need to supply that value to the function. Here is a main program that creates and initializes an employee structure and then computes the salary with a 10% bonus for that person.[1]

---

[1] The main program has access to information (the employee's salary) that ideally should be kept private.

```
main()
{
 struct employee James = {
    "James",
    "Somewhere in the World",
    007,
    80000.00,
    computePay
 };
 printf( "my Pay for this month = %f\n", James.computePay(James.salary,
 0.10) );
}
```

In the Java language, instead of the struct[2] declared above, you declare a class
to maintain information about employees:

```
class Employee {
    String name;
    String address;
    long empId;
    private double baseSalary;
    double computePay(double percent) {
      return (salary + percent * salary);
    }
    Employee(String name, String address, long id, double salary){
      this.name = name;       // "this" is needed to access the instance
      variable
      this.address = address;
      empId  = id;
      baseSalary = salary;
    };
}
```

The baseSalary instance variable is declared private. This means that only an
instance of this class has access to the salary information, thereby keeping the information protected from prying eyes. (This cannot be done with a C struct.) A constructor is included for completeness.

```
class MainClass {
  public static void main(String arcs[]) {
    Employee james = new Employee("James", "SomeWhere", 007, 80000.0);
    System.out.println("James' pay  = " + james.computePay(0.10));
  }
}
```

---

[2] In the Java language, the need for structures is made completely obsolete by classes. Classes provide for
a cleaner way to bundle data and methods together and a way to keep the data private to the class.

This application can compute James's pay without ever obtaining the salary information directly.

Enumerated Data Types

C++ incorporates an enumerated data type that allows one to specify a range of values allowed for variables. For example, in C++ one would capture the allowed values for color of a traffic light using

```
enum traffic_light_value {red, yellow, green};
```

One would use this to set the value of current color of a traffic light as

```
traffic_light_value current_color = red;
```

This provides a nice abstraction for capturing attributes that have limited allowed values (such as state variables).

Java does not provide this mechanism, so one has to adopt one of two approaches:

1. Introduce a set of constants.
2. Introduce a class representing the enumeration.

Either approach works.

PRIMITIVE DATA TYPES

- All Java primitive data types have consistent sizes and behavior across platforms and operating systems. (In C and C++, size is platform-dependent.)
- There are no unsigned data types (as in C or C++). *Note:* "Char" is an exception as it is a 16-bit, unsigned integer, but it should rarely be manipulated as an integer.
- The boolean primitive data type can have two values: true or false. Booleans are not integers and may not be treated as integers. (In C or C++, booleans may be treated as integers.) *Note:* We are allowed to cast a "0" or "1" to a boolean type.
- Casting between data types is more controlled in Java; automatic casting occurs only when there will be no loss of information. All other casts must be explicit.
- The primitive data types cannot be cast to objects, or vice versa. There are wrapper classes to convert values between objects and primitive data types.

OPERATORS

- Operator precedence and association behaves as it does in C.
- The "new" keyword binds tighter than the dot notation. (This is different in C++.) Thus, the following two expressions are equivalent:

```
new myClass().myMethod();  // Assume myClass returns an object
(new myClass() ).myMethod();
```

- Operator overloading as defined in C++ is not allowed in Java.
- The "," operator of C has been deleted.
- The ">>" operator produces an unsigned logical right shift.
- Although the syntax of the if, while, for, and do statements are syntactically the same as in C or C++, there is one significant difference. The test expression construct must return an actual boolean value. (In C and C++, the expression can return an integer.)
- *Note:* the "+" operator can be used to concatenate strings.

ARGUMENTS

Command Line

The command line arguments passed to a Java application are different in the following two ways:

- in number
- in type

from those passed to a C or C++ program.

For the number of parameters

- In C and C++, when we invoke a program, the system passes two parameters to it:

  - argc—the number of arguments on the command line
  - argv—a pointer to an array of strings that contain the arguments

- When we invoke a Java application, the system passes only one parameter to it:

  - args—an array of Strings (just an array—not a pointer to an array) that contain the arguments

    We can derive the number of command line arguments with the array's length() method.

For the first command line argument:

- In C and C++, the system passes the entire command line to the program as arguments, including the name used to invoke it. For example, if we invoked a C program like this

```
diff file1 file2
```

then the first argument in the argv parameter is diff.
- In the Java language, we always know the name of the application because it is the name of the class where the main method is defined. So, the Java runtime system does not pass the class name we invoke to the main method. Rather, the system passes only the items on the command line that appear after the class name. For example, if you invoked a Java application like this

```
java diff file1 file2
```

then the first command line argument is file1.

Method Arguments

Java does not support mechanisms for variable-length arguments lists to methods (as in C or C++). All method definitions must have a specific number of arguments.

ARRAYS

Arrays are first-class objects in Java.

- All references to arrays and their contents are done by implicit references. There is no use of pointer arithmetic.
- Array boundaries are strictly enforced. An attempt to read or write beyond an array boundary is a compiler and runtime error.
- Passing an array to a method passes the reference to the original array.
- Arrays of objects are arrays of references that are initialized an array of null pointers.
- Java does not support multidimensional array (as in C or C++). In Java, we must create arrays that contain other arrays.

JAVA STRINGS

- By convention, C and C++ strings are null-terminated arrays of characters. To operate on and to manage the strings, we treat them as we would any other array. That is, with all the issues of tracking the pointer arithmetic so that we do not stray off the end of the array. There is no real entity in C and C++ that is a string.

- Java strings are first-class objects. Strings as objects provide several advantages to the programmer:

  - The manner in which we obtain strings and elements of strings is consistent across all strings and all systems.
  - Because the programming interface for the String and StringBuffer classes is well defined, Java Strings function predictably every time.

- The String and StringBuffer class does extensive runtime checking for boundary conditions and catches errors for you.

To illustrate why this is an important feature of the Java language, let's look at a small example.

This C function copies the contents of string1 into string2.

```
int myStringCopy(char *string1, char *string2)
{
  for ( ; *string1 != '\0'; string1++, string2++)
    *string2 = *string1;
}
```

This uses pointer arithmetic to step through both strings copying one into the other. While pointers are powerful tools, this power can be the source of many errors. One common source of errors is pointers that stray off the end of an array. The myStringCopy function above has such an error: the for loop in the function does not check the length of string2; thus, if string1 is longer than string2, the string copy writes right over the end of string2. This corrupts whatever was stored in memory after string2; thus, the behavior of the program is unpredictable.

Java strings, however, are first-class objects deriving either from the String class or the StringBuffer class. This makes finding and fixing an entire class of common and frustrating programming errors such as the one illustrated above trivial. Here is the program above (including the error) rewritten in the Java language.

```
class StringCopy {
    public static void main(String args[]) {
      String s = "This is a test string that must be longer than the
      other string!";
      StringBuffer t = new StringBuffer("This is second string!");

      System.out.println(s + ", " + t);
      myStringCopy(s, t);
      System.out.println(s + ", " + t);
    }
```

```
static void myStringCopy(String string1, StringBuffer string2) {
    int i, len = string1.length();

    for (i = 0; i < len; i++)
        string2.setCharAt(i, string1.charAt(i));
}
}
```

Notice that this translation uses the String class, the StringBuffer class, and the methods appropriate for obtaining specific characters instead of character arrays and pointers.

Like the C version, the Java language version of the myStringCopy method loops over the length of string1 and never checks the length of string2. Thus, when string1 is longer than string2, the method tries to obtain characters beyond the end of string2. However, when we run the Java language version, we see the following runtime error message.

```
Exception in thread "main" java.lang.StringIndexOutOfRangeException
String index out of range: 13
    at java.lang.Exception.< init >(Exception.java)
    at java.lang.StringIndexOutOfRangeException.
    < init >(StringIndexOutOfRangeException.java)
    at java.lang.StringBuffer.setCharAt(StringBuffer.java)
    at strcpy.myStrCopy(strcpy.java:23)
    at strcpy.main(strcpy.java:15)
```

The primary difference between the Java language version of this program and the C version is that the Java program will reliably and obviously crash, whereas the C program will do something unpredictable.

MEMORY MANAGEMENT

All memory management in Java is automatic. All Java objects are created by using the "new" keyword and the memory is allocated from the heap, and a runtime garbage collector (the "gc") frees that memory when the object is no longer in use. Thus, in Java, the C's malloc() and free() functions do not exit. To free an object for automatic garbage collection, remove all references to that object (i.e., assign all variables and array elements pointing to it to null).

MISCELLANEOUS

There are several other minor differences between the C and C++ language and the Java language.

- Through a mechanism known as varargs, C and C++ allow us to provide a variable number of arguments to a function. This is not supported by the Java language.
- While goto is a reserved word in the Java language, it is not implemented or supported by the Java language.[3] We can use the labeled break and continue statements to break out of and continue executing complex switch or loop constructs.
- The Java language provides a *finally* statement for use with Java exceptions. The finally statement delimits a block of code used to release system resources and perform various other cleanup operations after the try statement.
- Java does not have a preprocessor (i.e., cannot use #define or macros). Constants can be created by using the final modifier when declaring class or instance variables.
- Java does not support template classes as in C++. Please note that the "generic" keyword has been reserved for this.
- Java does not include C's "const" keyword or the ability to pass by const reference explicitly.
- Java classes are single-inheritance. Not multiple-inheritance as in C++. Java provides some aspects of multiple inheritance via interfaces. Multiple generalization/specialization can always be implemented by using the aggregation and delegation mechanism.
- All functions must be tied to a class (i.e., stand-alone functions are not allowed).

---

[3] One of these days, the dreaded goto will disappear. Of course, at that time some smart guy is going to reintroduce it.

Bibliography

These are some of the references used in creating the material of the course. Unfortunately, this is a rapidly evolving field and there is no one book that will give you in-depth coverage of all the topics that we introduced to you in the course. The references are given in alphabetical order by authors and do not represent the importance of the respective books.

Banks, J, J. Carson, II, B. Nelson, and D. Nicol, *Discrete-Event Systems Simulation Third Edition*, Prentice Hall, Upper Saddle River, N.J., 2001.

Blaha, Michael and William Premerlani, *Object-Oriented Modeling and Design for Database Applications*, Prentice Hall, Upper Saddle River, N.J., 1998.

Booch, G., *Software Engineering with Ada*, Benjamin Cummings, Menlo Park, Calif., 1983.

Booch, G., "Object-oriented Development," *IEEE Trans. on Software Engineering*, vol. SE-12, no. 2, pp. 211–21, February 1986.

Booch, Grady, *Object Oriented Design with Applications*. Benjamin Cummings, Publishing Co., Menlo Park, Calif., 1991.

Booch, Grady, James Rumbaugh, and Ivar Jacobson, *The Unified Modeling Language User Guide*, Addison-Wesley, 1998.

Brooks, F.P., *The Mythical Man-month: Essay on Software Engineering*, Addison-Wesley, Reading, Mass., 1982.

Brooks, F.P., "The Silver Bullet, Essence and Accidents of Software Engineering," *Information Processing 1986*, (ed.) H.J. Kugler, Elsevier Science Publishers B.B. (North-Holland), 1986.

Chen, Peter, "The entity-relationship model—Toward a unified view of data," *ACM Trans. on Database Systems*, 1(1) March 1976.

Coad, Peter and Edward Yourdon, *Object-Oriented Analysis*. Yourdon Press, Englewood Cliffs, N.J., 1991.

Coad, Peter and Edward Yourdon, *Object-Oriented Design*. Yourdon Press, Englewood Cliffs, N.J., 1991.

Cockburn, A., Writing Effective Use Cases (Draft 3), Addison Wesley Longman, Reading, Mass., 2000.

Codd, E., "Extending the database relational model to capture more meaning," *ACM. Trans. on Database Systems*, 4(4), December 1979.

Eckstein, R., M. Loy, and D. Wood, *Java Swing*, O'Reilly & Associates, 1998.

Embley, David W., Barry D. Kurtz, Scott N. Woodfield, *Object-Oriented System Analysis: A Model-Driven Approach*. Yourdon Press, Englewood Cliffs, N.J., 1992.

Englander, R. and M. Loukides, *Developing Java Beans*, O'Reilly & Associates, 1997.

Entsminger, Gary, *The Tao of Objects: A Beginner's Guide to Object-Oriented Programming*, Yourdon Press, Englewood Cliffs, N.J., 1992.

Flanagan, D., *Java In A Nutshell: A Desktop Quick Reference (3rd Edition)*, O'Reilly & Associates, 1999.

Fowler, M. and K. Scott, *UML Distilled A Brief Guide To The Standard Object Modeling Guide (2nd Edition)*, Addison Wesley Longman, Reading, Mass., 1999.

Goldsein, N. and J. Alger, *Developing Object-Oriented Software for the Macintosh Analysis, Design, and Programming*, Addison-Wesley, Reading, Mass., 1992.

Graham, Ian. *Object-oriented Methods*. Addison-Wesley, Reading, Mass., 1991.

Halter, S. and S. Munroe, *Enterprise Java Performance*, Prentice Hall, Upper Saddle River, N.J., 2001.

Harold, E. and M. Loukides, *Java I/O*, O'Reilly & Associates, 1999.

Horstmann, C. and G. Cornell, *Core Java 2, Volume 1: Fundamentals (Fifth Edition)*, Prentice Hall, Upper Saddle River, N.J., 2000.

Horstmann, C. and G. Cornell, *Core Java 2, Volume 2: Advanced Features (Fourth Edition)*, Prentice Hall, Upper Saddle River, N.J., 1999.

Jacobson, I., M. Christerson, P. Jonsson, and F. Overgaard, *Object-Oriented Software Engineering—A Use Case Approach*, Addison-Wesley, Wokingham, England, 1992.

Jacobson, I., Booch. G, and J. Rumbaugh, *The Unified Software Development Process*, Addison-Wesley, Reading, Mass., 1999.

Kernighan, B.W. and D.M. Ritchie, *The C Programming Language*, Prentice-Hall, Englewood Cliffs, N.J., 1978.

Khoshafian, Setrig and Razmik Abnous, *Object Orientation: Concepts, Languages, Databases, User Interfaces*. John Wiley, New York, 1990.

Knudsen, J., *Java 2d Graphics*, O'Reilly & Associates, 1999.

Kuhn, T., *The Structure of Scientific Revolution (2nd edition)*, University of Chicago Press, Chicago, 1970.

Lewis, J. and W. Loftus, *Java Software Solutions, Foundations Of Program Design, Second Edition*, Addison Wesley, Reading, Mass., 2000.

Martin, James and James Odell, *Object-Oriented Analysis and Design*. Prentice Hall, Englewood Cliffs, N.J., 1992.

McMenamin, S.M. and J.F. Palmer, *Essential System Analysis*, Yourdon Press, Englewood Cliffs, N.J., 1984.

Meyer, B., *Object-Oriented Software Construction*, Prentice-Hall International (UK) Ltd., Cambridge, UK, 1988.

Oaks, S., *Java Security (2nd Edition)*, O'Reilly & Associates, 2001.

Oaks, S., H. Wong, and M. Loukides, *Java Threads*, O'Reilly & Associates, 1999.

Page-Jones, Meilir, *Fundamentals of Object-Oriented Design in UML*, Addison-Wesley, Reading, Mass., 2000.

Quillian, M. Ross. "Semantic Memory," In Marvin Minsky (Ed.), *Semantic Information Processing* (216–269). Cambridge, Mass., 1968.

Ross, D., "Applications and extensions of SADT," *IEEE Computer*, April 1985.

Rumbaugh, J., M. Blaha, W. Premerlani, F. Eddy, and W. Lorensen, *Object-Oriented Modeling and Design*, Prentice-Hall, Englewood Cliffs, N.J., 1992.

Rumbaugh, J., "Getting Started: Using Use Cases To Capture Requirements," *J. Object-Oriented Programming*, Sept. 1994.

Rumbaugh, J., I. Jacobson, and G. Booch. *The Unified Modeling Language Reference Manual*, Addison-Wesley, Reading, Mass., 1999.

Sally Shlaer and Stephen Mellor, *Object-Oriented Systems Analysis: Modeling the World in Data*. Yourdon Press, Englewood Cliffs, N.J., 1988.

Shlaer, Sally and Stephen Mellor, *Object Lifecycles: Modeling the World in States*. Yourdon Press, Englewood Cliffs, N.J., 1992.

Stevens, Perdita and Rob Pooley, *Using UML Software Engineering with Objects and Components*, 2000.

Stein, L.A., H. Lieberman, and D. Ungar, "A shared view of sharing: The Treaty of Orlando," *Object-Oriented Concepts, Databases, and Applications*, (eds.) W. Kim and F.H. Lechosky, ACM Press, New York, 1989.

Stroustrup, Bjarne, *The C++ Programming Language*. Addison-Wesley, Reading, Mass., 1991.

Walden, Kim and Jean-Marc Nerson, *Seamless Object-Oriented Software Architecture Analysis and Design of Reliable Systems*, Prentice Hall, Englewood Cliffs, N.J., 1995.

Winston, M.E., R. Chaffin, and D. Herrmann, "A taxonomy of part-whole relations," *Cognitive Science*, 11:417–44, 1987.

Wirfs-Brock, Rebecca, *Designing Object-Oriented Software* Prentice-Hall, Englewood Cliffs, N.J., 1990.

Yourdon, E.N. and L.L. Constatine, *Structured Design: Fundamentals of a Discipline of Computer Program and Systems Design*, Prentice-Hall, Englewood Cliffs, N.J., 1979.

Zukowski, J., *Java AWT Reference (Java Series)*, O'Reilly & Associates, 1996.

Index

Note: The letter *f* following a page number refers to a footnote.